Leadville: Colorado's Magic City

For all those charming ladies who every summer make Healy House live again. And for Kay, who made it all possible . . . and worthwhile.

LEADVILLE:
Colorado's Magic City

By Edward Blair

PRUETT **P** PUBLISHING COMPANY
Boulder, Colorado

First Edition
  2 3 4 5 6 7 8 9

Printed in the United States of America

Library of Congress Cataloging in Publication Data

Blair, Edward.
    Leadville, Colorado's magic city.

    Bibliography: p.
    1. Leadville, Colo.—History.   2.   Mines and mining—Colorado—Leadville—History.   I.   Title.
F784.L4B54   978.8′46   79-26349
ISBN 87108-665-4

Author photo taken by Robert Bomier

Acknowledgments

No work of this type can be accomplished without the help and support of a number of institutions and individuals. It is for a decade of favors and services that I thank the staff of the Colorado Historical Society's library in Denver. And with equal gratitude for an equal number of years of considerate and knowledgeable assistance I thank the staff of the Western History Collection of the Denver Public Library, with special thanks to Kay Wilcox and Hazel Lundberg. I always received quick and thorough service in the libraries and research centers in Colorado Springs; the Penrose Library, the Tutt Library, and the Pioneers' Museum. I was welcomed at college and university libraries in Greeley, Gunnison, Golden, Denver, and the Norlin Library in Boulder where John A. Brennan and his staff were especially effective at digging out forgotten, but not lost, materials on the Magic City.

Out of state I visited, with varying degrees of success, success based on their holdings, not their skill or willingness, the libraries at the University of New Mexico, University of Arizona, University of Wyoming, University of California at Berkeley where I found a treasure trove, Stanford University, and the Henry E. Huntington Library where one needs at least a week to admire the setting and his good fortune in being able to do research in such exquisite surroundings. Historical societies and archival holdings in Kansas, Missouri, Maine, Arizona, Wyoming, Nevada, and Wisconsin were helpful, especially in tracking down biographical information on the early citizens of Leadville. A special note of thanks to Mr. Howerton, Mr. Leary, Mr. McCluggage, and Elaine Everly in the National Archives. They do an excellent job in the worst facility I visited, and I visited over a hundred libraries, museums, and repositories. The National Archives is a national disgrace, but the staff is outstanding. I spent much less time in the files of the Library of Congress, but was pleased with the help I received, and was impressed with the reception for a somewhat lost country boy from Colorado.

A number of individuals made significant contributions ranging from asking, "How's the book coming?" to unearthing some lost or forgotten source that proved invaluable. Such was Annie Meyer, who was my first contact with the heirs of August R. Meyer, all of whom were more than willing to help. Special thanks to Gina Woods for alerting me to the excellent dissertation on the Colorado smelting industry by Dr. James Edward Fell, Jr., and Duane Smith for his interest in Leadville, baseball, Horace Tabor, and my project.

The Leadville people I've saved for last because my debt to them is greatest. I know I'll not be able to mention everyone, but some special favors must be recognized. Bobbi Marshall has been a constant source of help and sound criticism; as have Nancy Manly and Sherrie Warford. A special thanks to Karen Dunn, who was there to help when help was needed. My debt to Bob Rinker goes on, day in and day out. He's been a constant help and companion in so many projects that a simple thanks is ridiculously inadequate, but it is all I have. David Parry and, before him, Roger McClurg, curators of the Colorado Mountain History Collection in the Lake County Public Library, have been friends and helpers. A lot of memories and thanks are tied to those who follow. They helped me put the early pieces of the Leadville puzzle together: My uncle, Harold "Burky" Burkhardt, who had a special love for Leadville; Leona Albertson, who gave me a peek at the treasures in the public library; Alan Hafer and Andy Fishburn, who are good teachers, good companions, and good researchers, to say nothing of good friends. James Andrews, Fran Bochatey, Nelson Fugate, Rose Green, John Pitts, Leroy Wingenbach, John Richards, Norma Wilson, Mike Donovan, Eddie and Bill Kerrigan, and Bob and Sally Elder all had a hand in the works, and if there is good in the final product some of the credit is theirs. I have warm memories of the late Terrance "Ted" Connors and his staff in the Clerk and Recorder's Office, and the late Emmett Irwin, Lake County Treasurer for many years, both enthusiastic Leadvillites all their lives.

My debt to Don and Jean Griswold for the fine work they have done in a quarter century of digging into the past of the area is incalculable. And for the numerous personal assists and their friendship, thanks. And, finally, thanks to the people, past and present, of the Magic City. It is their story. I hope they enjoy it.

"There has been but one Leadville. Never will there be another."

Carlyle Channing Davis in
Olden Times in Colorado,
1916.

Preface

A preface is something that comes before, which does little to explain why it is generally written last. I suppose it's actually the author's attempt to explain, not why the reader should read the book, but why the author went to all the time and trouble to write it. I have no desire to break with tradition over such a cornerstone of literary history as the preface, so I, too, will try to explain, as much to myself as to the reader, why, and maybe how, I found myself writing a history of Leadville.

I was fascinated by Leadville, the used look of the town and the rough hewn, harsh lined faces of its older citizens, as far back as I can remember, and since I was born in Leadville's old St. Vincent's hospital, that "far back" goes to first memories. Memories of Mary Moberg pulling her wagon up Seventh Street and Sue Bonnie in her fringed leather jacket spinning stories of Indians, miners, and "Baby Doe" Tabor. It is little wonder that my first attempt at serious writing was a novel about Leadville. I never finished it, much to the chagrin of some of my fellow citizens in eighth grade penmanship, but more pressing matters interceded and puberty overwhelmed creativity. It wasn't a very good novel anyway.

After puberty and college took their toll, I returned to Leadville as a junior high school history teacher and began in my second or third year teaching a seventh grade elective called "Leadville History." The rest was easy. It was clear to the teacher that a readable, accurate history of Leadville spanning the final quarter of the nineteenth century and the first quarter of the twentieth was needed. I decided rather immodestly that I was the one to do the job. That was over ten years ago.

Looking back on the project, I'm reminded, as I was so often during the project, of Winston Churchill's famous quote about writing a book. "To begin with it was a toy, and amusement; then it became a mistress, and then a master, and then a tyrant." This book — this mistress, master, and tyrant — which has kept me off the streets and out of trouble when I might well have used a bit of trouble, hopefully will serve two purposes. First, it was and is an attempt to set the record straight, to give Leadville a fair and accurate portrayal. Second, I hoped to present the Leadville picture in a readable fashion, escaping the rigors of hard fact, except when nothing but hard fact would do. I have tried to reproduce the text of all quotes as accurately as possible as to spelling and word usage, and rather than follow each deviation from the norm with a scholarly "sic," I have relied upon the reader's good sense in these matters.

This is a social history. I hope it is also sociable history. I dreamed most of creating a palatable, factual record of historic events, and maybe do my part in seeing Leadville receive some of the acclaim it is due. After all, it was one of the biggest, wildest, richest, and longest running mining camps in the American West, and it put its stamp on a generation of mining men, their women, and their bank accounts. And that, my friend, is magic, or at least potent reality.

Edward Blair at Healy House.
Leadville, Colorado

Contents

Prologue

Pike's Peak or Bust

The spring of 1849 saw the greatest western migration in American history. California gold lured men from all over the world. Colorado in 1849 did not exist, even in men's imaginations. It was merely a mountainous barrier that lay between the cities and farms of the East and the waiting wealth of California.

The eastern part of Colorado, along a line south from Denver, was Kansas Territory. The northeastern corner of the Centennial State belonged to Nebraska; the rest, except a narrow slice along the present southern border that in 1850 became New Mexico Territory, was part of Utah Territory.

After the California excitement died down, a few men remembered stories they had heard about gold in the Rocky Mountains and returned to try their luck. One such man was William Green Russell, a Georgia cracker, who, with his two brothers, Levi and Oliver, organized a small party of Georgians in 1858 and set out for the unknown. He was related, through marriage, to some Oklahoma Cherokees, and when crossing the Indian Territory he recruited a party of about one hundred Indian gold seekers, many of whom were related to him. The Indians and Georgians, happy with the protection the other afforded, headed west in search of the rainbow's end. Once north of the Arkansas River they began prospecting, working their way north along the face of the Front Range. By the time they reached Cherry Creek, near the present site of Denver, a large number had become discouraged. This, plus their fear of an attack by local Arapahoes, convinced most that home was where they belonged. Only about a dozen Georgians and Cherokees stayed on. A couple of months later, in July of 1858, those who remained struck a pocket of gold in Dry Creek in what is now south Denver.

Not long after the strike was made, a group of mountain traders wandered by while the prospectors were working the gulch. The prospectors' labor only netted about $800 worth of gold, but the traders carried the word and inflated the value. In Kansas City they told of a rich find at the base of the mountains in the western end of Kansas Territory. The rush was on!

Those who had missed their chance in '49, either because they did not go, or because they did not locate a bonanza when they got to California, seemed determined to be Johnny-on-the-spot in '59. Also, the national situation had a lot to do with the enthusiasm the word "gold" carried. The country was suffering from the effects of the Panic of 1857, while the threat of sectional violence hung heavy in the air. Kansas was rapidly becoming the practice field for the Civil War, and many settlers there and in the "States" were more than willing to pull up stakes and cast their lot with the gold seekers.

A few stalwarts crossed the open, windswept prairie during the winter of 1858-59. The main army of seekers waited for spring. As soon as grass began to look as if it could support their teams the tide swept west. They "wested" in ox-carts and in wagons, on foot and on horseback. There were those who pushed wheelbarrows or hand carts, and some even tried the fabled wind-wagons, great sailing ships on wheels that were becalmed in the first gully west of Independence. Many died of hunger; more of thirst and Indian raids.

It is estimated that over 100,000 people headed west in the Pike's Peak gold rush, and at least half of these turned around before they got to the gold fields. Another 25,000 turned homeward soon after they found that it was not as easy as expected. And it was expected to be very easy.

One Iowa newspaper reported that Pike's Peak was "solid gold" and was mined by toboggan. The miners slid off the mountain and the runners scraped the gold off as they went. It was a lot of fun and very profitable. The story of the young fellow heading west with a wheelbarrow filled with flour sacks to shovel his gold into seems to illustrate the notion of the uninformed, but optimistic, Fifty-Niner.

Fortunately for those who perpetrated the myth, major strikes were made early in 1859 that saved the promoters' bacon, for there were men, broke and hungry, who were ready to cry "hoax" and hang a few promoters.

George A. Jackson, a knowledgeable miner who got his training in the gold fields of California, located a rich find on Chicago Creek in January of 1859 near the present town of Idaho Springs. A short time later, John H. Gregory, a muleskinner by trade, found paydirt a few miles from Jackson's claim on Clear Creek. He was grubstaked by an Indiana group, who helped him develop the first lode mine in the area. William Green Russell, still busy, got his second, larger reward in a gulch in the same general area. He located a good placer about three miles below Gregory Gulch in what is now known as Russell Gulch.

By fall 1859, prospectors had penetrated the mountains and crossed the Continental Divide. Towns were growing, not only at the foot of the mountains, but in the mountains. Such one-street communities as Denver, Boulder, Colorado City, Black Hawk, Mountain City, and Golden claimed greatness far in excess of their size.

I

The First Magicians

It was 1859 and autumn. A. G. Kelley bent over his pan and watched the bright gold flecks in the early morning sun, and he knew that this time he had found more than "just colors." He also knew that winter came early and with sudden fury in the high mountains of Colorado, and all the gold in the world could not build a fire with wet tinder or bring down game when there was none. He gathered his gear, carefully noted his location so he could find it the following spring, and set out for winter quarters.

Kelley spent the winter in Auraria, a small town opposite fledgling Denver on the west bank of Cherry Creek, where he devoted his time to talking about his find and gathering a party to return with him in the spring. Kelley, unlike the Hollywood prospector, was not as concerned about having it all to himself as he was concerned about getting his share. Without help he knew he was fair game for accidents, Indians, or bandits. There was the very real need for help in ditching, felling trees, ripping lumber, building cabins and long toms, and setting up sluicing operations. Also it was nice to have someone to borrow a chew from or to enjoy a pipe and conversation with in the evening.

Kelley was eager to get back to his diggings before some other prospector "preempted" them, so on February 15, 1860, he and twenty-five gold seekers left Auraria for the valley of the upper Arkansas. Winter was still very much with them as they waded through waist deep snow. Horses were not used on winter excursions of this type, because it was almost impossible to find feed for them.

They fought their way from what is now Colorado Springs into South Park, originally called Bayou Salado by French furtrappers. Going was easier through "the Park," since the snow seldom

lays deep in the flat, windswept meadows. Finally, the winter wastes of South Park behind them, they located what must have been Trout Creek Pass, the only good all-weather pass through the Mosquito Range. They hurried down the easy slope to the Arkansas River. From there it was about twenty miles of relatively easy going as they followed the ice-filled river up to the site of Kelley's discovery.

They arrived on Friday, March 9, and immediately set to work organizing a mining district. They named it "Kelley's Mining District" in honor of their benefactor, but it was popularly called "Kelley's Bar" or "Kelleysburg." Today the small town of Granite straddles the river just above Kelley's site.

Kelley was not the only prospector to go deep into the Colorado Rockies during the summer and fall of 1859. James McNulty and John Gibbs are said to have made a rich find someplace in the Upper Arkansas River Basin that same summer. It may have been either of these men, or an unknown third party, who wandered into the Gregory Gulch diggings one day late in the fall of 1859 and told a tale of a rich placer he had found in the mountains. Whoever he was, his story was quickly grabbed up by S. S. Slater, a disappointed gold seeker.

Slater sought the old fellow out and asked him when he was going back. The old prospector replied that he had had enough of mountain hardships and was going back to the States. He was generous enough, though, and told Slater the location of his find.

Slater, like his counterpart Kelley, gathered a group of friends during the winter, and on March 19, 1860, set out from Mountain City, now the eastern section of Central City. In Slater's party were Abe Lee, George W. Stevens, Dick Wilson,

Tom Williams, Isaac N. Rafferty, and John Currier. Some sources claim Rafferty's younger brother accompanied them.

The winter of 1859-1860 was a severe one, as Kelley and his followers had already determined, and the going was slow for the Slater group. They followed Bear Creek to the South Platte and then went up into South Park. They failed to locate Trout Creek Pass and crossed Mosquito Range someplace east of the present town of Granite, reaching the Arkansas River to find it littered with the machinery of the placer miner. Kelley's Bar by this time was a thriving, but crowded, community. Still Slater and his followers were not discouraged. According to Slater's information their find still waited for them up river. They pushed on, visiting with the miners as they went.

Above Kelley's Bar they ran into a small group who were diligently working the short, narrow gulch called Cache Creek, named for a party of prospectors who in 1854 were forced to cache their supplies and flee a band of Utes. Good color

was discovered in '54, and in '60 the diggings still proved rich. But Cache Creek, like all the good river property and tributaries in the area, was taken up. Rufus Alvord and James Miller had tried both Kelley's Bar and Cache Creek, were dissatisfied with the prospecting, and cast their lot with Slater's Mountain City men.

Between the present towns of Buena Vista and Leadville, the Arkansas River runs through a narrow gorge about ten miles long with the town of Granite about halfway from either end. North of the gorge are the broad meadows of Hayden Flats, named for the Hayden family who first settled in the valley, and not for Dr. F. V. Hayden and his party of Army surveyors and engineers who passed through the area naming landmarks and mapping the area in 1873. The Slater party, moving north through the snow covered meadows, encountered another small group in the upper end of Hayden Flats and stopped to parlay.

Surely the winter silence was happily broken with gay greetings since both groups were from

Hayden Flats, where the boys from Ountain City met the Jones party from Iowa in April of 1860. At left is Mount Elbert, 14,433, Colorado's highest peak. At right is 14,421 foot Mount Massive, the second highest in the state. *Photo Source: Geological Survey in the National Archives.*

Winter, then as now, is harsh, cold, and long in the open meadows of the upper Arkansas Valley. *Photo Source: Author's Collection.*

Mountain City. Slater was not the only prospector in the Gregory diggings who had heard about gold in the Arkansas Valley. W. P. Jones had also got the word, and like Slater, had organized a party. Four of them, "E. Johnson, Old man Boon, Sailor Jones, and myself," recalled Jones, "set out from Mountain City in March. One had a little money, one had provisions, one had pack and mule and one was a great hunter and trapper." They had all they needed but lady luck, and they hoped to find her somewhere along the way.

They got caught in a blizzard in South Park, lost their way, and simply stumbled west until they struck the Arkansas River about six miles south of Granite. They avoided the Kelley diggings and worked their way north into Hayden Flats.

It was early April by then and still no sign of spring. Snow lay two feet deep and the river was frozen over in most places, making it necessary to build fires to thaw the sand and gravel banks before panning could begin. The small party of prospectors explained to Slater and his boys that for all their work, after fighting the wind and water and bone-chilling cold, they had found nothing worth noting and were more than willing to move on. After some discussion the enlarged party

divided into three groups. They agreed that the first party, made up of Iowans and led by Jones, would prospect the first likely gulch. The second party, Slater's bunch from Mountain City, would prospect the second likely gulch, and the third party, a group that appears to have been made up of odd lots and led by a stranger named Johnson, would prospect the western side of the valley along the base of Mount Massive.

For some unexplained reason the Slater group is now known to history as the Stevens party, and George W. Stevens took over as leader of the party. Why the change? A plausible explanation might be that none of these groups had a fixed leader and were simply identified by writers of the period by the name of a prominent member. Whatever the cause, it was "Stevens' group," along with Jones and his boys, who started up the east bank of the Arkansas in early April of 1860. The Johnson party crossed the Arkansas and moved westerly across the snow covered meadows toward the stark, gray and white face of Mount Massive.

The Jones party, according to plan, turned east at the first likely gulch. It has been Iowa Gulch ever since, honoring the home state of its first white citizens. Stevens and his group skirted a few small hills and dry gulches. About a mile

5

and one-half north of Iowa Gulch they encountered a small stream running into the Arkansas from the east, and they set to work immediately. Their first pans showed some color, but it was not rich enough to backslap about. They continued to pan and work their way up the gulch. Winter hung on and they had to take time out from their panning to thaw the stream bed and hunt game. As they moved upstream the colors got better. Near the site of present-day Leadville, where the gulch is crowded between Carbonate Hill and the west flank of Rock Hill, Abe Lee came up with a pan that promised to make rich men of them all.

The three groups that organized in Hayden Meadows had made an agreement that if any made a good strike they would build signal fires and fire four shots to let the other two groups know about their good fortune. True to their word, Stevens' men built signal fires on the surrounding hills and four shots were fired. Jones, out gathering wood, heard the shots. He recalled years later, "There was no one around to hear, but I just lifted my hat and gave three cheers." Back in camp he told "the boys," and immediately they headed north across the ridge that separated them from California Gulch. On top of

the ridge they could see the fires of their California Gulch compatriots. They traveled the better part of the night, tramping most of the time through deep, crusted snow, arriving early on the morning following Lee's discovery. Most sources give April 26 as the discovery date, but since the news had reached Kelley's diggings by the twenty-fifth, and the gulch record book has Abe Lee recording his and other claims on April 24, it seems likely that the discovery was made some days earlier. Possibly on April 16 as reported by S. B. Kellogg, but more probably around April 20, since it is unlikely that the men in California Gulch would have waited a week to organize a mining district, especially when such a district would give them title to their find.

Jones and his Iowans listened eagerly as Lee and the others told them how it happened. They dug deeper than usual and filling a pan "Abe Lee was called, as being the oldest prospector to pan the stuff." While Lee squatted before an open spring, the rest went back to the fire to get warm. They noticed Lee looking intently into the pan and one fellow shouted, "What have you got, Abe?"

"Oh, boys," yelled the delighted forty-niner,

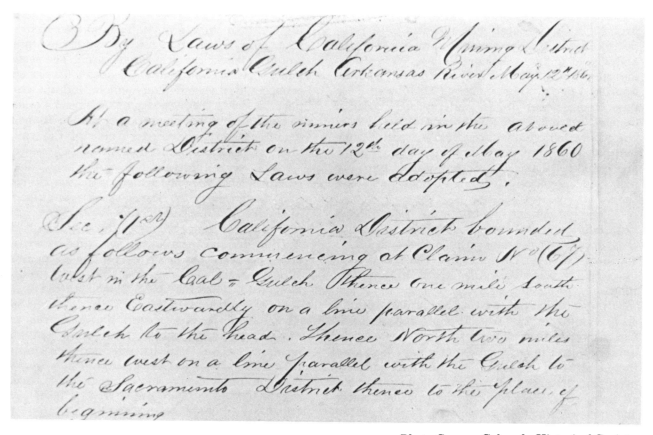

Photo Source: Colorado Historical Society.

"I've just got California in this here pan." The gulch had a name, a hero, and a legend. W. P. Jones' story of Abe Lee's discovery is only one of many, but because of his presence at the first telling, it promises more accuracy than most.

That same afternoon representatives of the group from the base of Mount Massive arrived to inspect the diggings. They were impressed, but they too had found some likely ground and decided to stick with Colorado Gulch, as it was later called. On or about April 26, a group from Kelley's Bar arrived to find the gulch already staked by the small band who had made the discovery. According to Lewis Dow, who accompanied the miners from Kelley's diggings, the first arrivals had set up "California Mining District" and staked discovery claims of 100-foot lengths. Then they did themselves a favor by staking "speculative claims" on all the rest. There was no limit on speculative claims. A man could have as many as he had the energy to stake. Consequently the fourteen miners in the district had everything worthwhile sewed up when the men from Kelleysburg arrived. The new arrivals demanded and got a miners' meeting. As a result of that meeting the district rules were rewritten.

The official "Bylaws of California Mining District, California Gulch, Arkansas River" were adopted on May 12, 1860. They first outlined the extent of the district. "California District bounded as follows commencing at Claim No. (67) west in the Cal. Gulch thence one mile South thence Eastwardly on a line parallel with the Gulch to the head. Thence North two miles thence west on a line parallel with the Gulch to the Sacramento District [lower half of California Gulch] then to the place of beginning."

Another section insured the growth of the area. "All men are entitled to one Gulch claim, one Lode claim, one Hill claim and one Dry gulch claim by preemption." The provision outlawed all speculation claims, but to allow some latitude, they added a following section, "All men are entitled to hold one" of each of the four types of claims by purchase in addition to their preemption claims. The restriction on purchases was repealed in April of the following year to make it possible for men to form companies and work larger areas with more elaborate equipment.

The size of the various claims was every bit as important as the number. Claims were "100 feet up or down the gulch and shall hold the gulch pay streak let it run which way it may." Lode, hill, and dry gulch claims were one hundred feet square.

Other provisions noted that claims not worked would be up for grabs. The miners' code provided for the selection of juries and listed "a Justice of the Peace, a Sheriff, a Recorder and a Stake Driver" as the district's officers. The recorder, Abe Lee, was secretary at all miners' meetings, while the justice of the peace presided. No description of the sheriff's duties was included, it being assumed that everyone knew what a sheriff did. The stake driver measured and officially staked all claims.

Those early lawgivers quickly realized that water was a major source of trouble and listed several restrictions pertaining to ditching, water rights, and the disposal of used water. They also sought to protect transportation by providing that the "wagon road up this gulch shall be respected." It was necessary lest some zealous gold seeker sluice the road, which was not unheard of. They addressed themselves to the pollution problem in Section (27) stating that "Any persons killing Beef Cattle in this district shall do so at a distance of three hundred yards from the main gulch, and shall also burn up or bury offal within three days thereafter or be subject to a fine of ten dollars for each beef." They included in this provision as in others that the fines would be paid to the informant, which made policemen of the whole camp and surely had something to do with the relative peace that prevailed.

Another provision stipulated that the recorder use a notebook for his records and not allow them to be "kept on loose sheets of paper," which suggests that Abe Lee had possibly been a little slipshod in his duties during the first weeks of the district's existence.

The gulch's population, like that of any other mining district, ebbed and flowed with every change of wind and weather. A new find would bring men running. Oldtimers said seventy people arrived the day after the discovery. The amazing thing about that statement is not the numbers, but the speed with which the word traveled. By mid-summer it was estimated that five thousand souls called California Gulch home, though they were in fact scattered throughout the surrounding area in every draw and gulch and along every stream and river bank.

One of the first arrivals after discovery was Horace Austin Warner Tabor and his wife, Augusta, the first woman in California Gulch. With them was their son Maxcy, named after Tabor's good friend and companion, Nathaniel Maxcy. Another good friend, S. P. Kellogg, had arrived a week or two before.

Tabor, a native of Vermont, married his boss's daughter, Louisa Augusta Pierce, in Augusta, Maine, January 31, 1857. Instead of staying home and working in his father-in-law's business, he took his new wife and infant son to Kansas, where he had homesteaded some two years earlier. Life in Kansas was rough. The land was untamed and gave no quarter. In addition, the sectional differences that led to the Civil War were making a battlefield of Kansas. Tabor, who always found himself involved with the affairs of any community he resided in, was selected to travel as a representative to the Kansas Territorial Legislature in Topeka. He left his wife and son in the care of friends and went to the capitol. It was clear to all who cared to see that the nation was on the road to civil war, and Tabor was bound to be right in the middle of it unless something unexpected occurred. Gold in the western end of Kansas Territory was the unexpected ingredient in Tabor's destiny. Tabor was ambitious and dreamed of wealth and influence, and the gold at the end of the Kansas rainbow provided him with a solution to his dreams. Forsaking his farm and a possible political career, he loaded his wife, son,

and belongings into the wagon, hitched up his oxen, and set out for Denver.

It was a long and arduous journey to the land of his dreams, and it appeared that the rainbow had faded shortly before he reached the gold fields. He arrived in Denver in mid-June 1859, and after a short stay went with his wife, child, yoke of oxen, wagon, and two friends to Payne's Bar. Mrs. Tabor was the first woman there and started the first of her many "stores." She sold pastries and bread, did mending, and nursed the sick while Horace prospected. He located a promising claim, but was cheated out of it by a man who told him he better leave before winter set in because the snowslides in the area were something fierce. Tabor took the advice, yoked his oxen, and headed back to Denver. When he told his story to the boys in town he got the old horse laugh. They explained that the area was not subject to snowslides, and the winters were not exceptionally severe. He immediately went back up Clear Creek Canyon and found the old codger industriously working his claim. A more forceful man would have put up a fight, but Horace was a genial man, not given to violence. Confident that

Horace Austin Warner Tabor, born near Holland, Vermont, November 26, 1830. *Photo Source: Colorado Historical Society.*

Louisa Augusta Pierce Tabor, born in August, Maine, March 29, 1833. *Photo Source: Colorado Historical Society.*

his destiny lay elsewhere, he let the man have the diggings and returned to Denver.

Horace and his family wintered in Auraria, and there he heard Kelley talk about his find in the mountains and vowed to go with him. When it came time to leave his wife was ill. After waiting four days Tabor determined to go. Augusta later recalled, "The 19th of February, 1860, I was lifted from a bed of sickness to a wagon, and we started for the new mining excitement." The Tabors and their Kansas friends traveled south from Auraria to Colorado City, an enterprising little community near the site of Colorado Springs, then turned west. They camped at Manitou, and Tabor, Kellogg, and Maxcy went ahead and tried to clear a road. No wagons had been over the route before and it consisted of nothing but a narrow footpath. They cut their way up what became Ute and Wilkerson passes and struggled into South Park, where they encountered some Utes. They were friendly, but Mrs. Tabor saw little to recommend them. "They were a thieving people and it was unpleasant to have them around us," she said.

While in the Park they lost their way and after a few false attempts at locating themselves they left it up to God and luck. They stood a stick on end, then let it fall, determined to travel in the direction it indicated. The stick fell, they followed, and in a short time they located Trout Creek Pass, which led them down out of South Park to the Arkansas River near the present town of Buena Vista. From there they made the short journey upriver to Kelley's diggings where Horace immediately staked a claim and set to work. He found gold in Cache Creek, whip-sawed lumber to make sluice boxes, and set to work building his fortune. "We found plenty of gold," Augusta recalled, "but there was so much black sand and we did not know how to separate it."

One day after they had been in Cache Creek about a month, a man wandered into camp and told about the gold in California Gulch. Augusta recalled the man "told us to move up, telling us to go up until we came to the first large bald mountain on the road, then turn up that gulch around the bald mountain." The man explained that it would take them all day, but they could "probably see the smoke of their [miners in California Gulch] campfire."

They reached California Gulch, according to Augusta, on May 8, 1860, and started up the gulch, first going through the Sacramento District and eventually to the California District near the point where the gulch narrows. A crisis

was pending in the gulch and the Tabors arrival relieved the situation. Food was running out, game was becoming harder to find, and starvation was becoming a very real threat. The Tabors slaughtered their faithful oxen, the meat was dried over fires Indian fashion, and the camp was saved. As soon as the meat was dried, a young volunteer set out for Denver to purchase supplies while another went south into the San Luis Valley to the Mexican settlements. Both were successful, and supplies arrived before the dried meat ran out.

California Gulch is about seven miles long and runs east and west. Before the gold seekers interrupted the quiet flow of nature, the small stream of clear cold water was a favorite watering place for mule deer. Its banks were lined with rough grass and scattered clumps of sage brush. Pine trees, lodgepole for the most part, crowded the water course, covered the ridges on either side and, along with alpine fir and spruce, blanketed the surrounding hills up to timberline. Some aspen groves broke the dark pine green on south slopes and near the base of Mount Massive on the west, but these were small, hard-put trees. The gulch, toward its mouth, is broad, one-quarter of a mile or so, and its pitch is slight. About four miles above the point where it joins the Arkansas River it begins to narrow and the pitch increases. It was immediately above and below the narrows that the major placer claims were located.

Below the gulch is the infant Arkansas, already showing signs of greatness. The river north and south of California Gulch flows through broad meadows for about twelve miles, courtesy of a great glacier that slowly carved the neighboring hills and broadened the valleys. West, across the valley of the Arkansas from California Gulch, is Mount Massive, one of the most impressive mountains in all America. It is as its name implies, a massive pile of ancient granite, broad shouldered, brutish, and unyielding; a perfect sentinel for a high, wild, and limitless landscape.

In the shadow of Mount Massive on one of the many streams at its feet, the Colorado Mining District was located by the Johnson party during the same period that saw the discovery of gold in California Gulch. It was a prosperous area, but lacked the size and wealth of the more famous gulch to the east. In the broad valley between the two gulch districts was the Arkansas Independent District. No large fortunes were made due to the fine character of the gold, though one expert claimed, "The Arkansas River for seventy miles from its source . . . is gold bearing." In spite of this and the prediction that "when placer mining shall come to be conducted on a larger scale and with more appropriate means, it may and probably will become ... a business of considerable importance," placer mining on the Arkansas River never produced notable amounts of gold except at Kelley's Mining District.

Just south of California Gulch is Iowa Gulch. After the excitement in California Gulch subsided, prospectors worked all the gulches in the area and several returned to Iowa Gulch, where some good colors and low pay claims were located during the summer of 1860. A mining district was organized called the Adams District. Iowa Gulch is narrower than California Gulch, several miles longer and carries more water. It is a beautiful glacial valley, filled with aspen, spruce, lodgepole pine, and large meadows of lush grass and columbines. For a time it did not suffer the assault on its beauty as did its northern neighbor. Extensive mining operations in recent years, however, have destroyed most of its original charm.

Oro City, as it was finally dubbed, became the social and economic hub of the area. It had one long main street that ran the length of California Gulch. On either side of the street were scattered cabins, tents, bough huts, wagons with people living in and under them, and saloons that ran the gamut from two whiskey barrels supporting a rough board bar to log structures with real dancehall girls and sounds that served as music.

Once the rush was on the numbers in the camp swelled daily. Prospectors were a migrant group, and even if they had a good claim they were not averse to taking a few days off to go over the hill to a new find and check the prospects. They seldom stayed long, though, since they were required by miners' law to work their claim "one day in every seven" or the claim would be declared "vacant" and was then up for grabs. Many formed partnerships with their neighbors. Maybe four men would hold four adjacent claims, do all their work together, and share the profits. In these cases a couple could leave for a week or two and the others would remain and work the claim.

There were those, of course, who stayed with their claim, worked hard, saved their gold and retired rich men in the fall. George Stevens, it was said, left the camp in the fall of 1860 with 239 pounds of gold, plus five hundred dollars cash "in hand" for his claim, and was never seen or heard of again by the gulch fraternity. Others ran from strike to strike and never hit it, while some had to

serve a long apprenticeship before they realized their dreams. Still others saw the business opportunity. Augusta Tabor was one. She quickly set up her baking business and in addition served meals. She found that some men "did not like men's cooking and would insist upon boarding where there was a woman." And no wonder! The regular fare for men was beans and bacon, corn meal mush, and venison, duck or bear meat when they could get it, but wild meat was an infrequent delicacy. Sourdough bread was common and the ever ready, always present, coffee pot heard a lot of stories and dreams as its owners sat around sipping its licorice-colored contents.

The average miner was anything but well dressed. Most were bearded. They wore heavy woolen shirts, or on hot days stripped to the tops of their faded red longjohns. The lower half was covered with canvas trousers tucked into their boot tops. A good many wore a hat, the worse for wear the better, apparently, since all seemed to be sweat-rimmed and broken-brimmed and a shade of several colors, none of them original. Still the dress and meals were suited to the work.

The population of California Gulch was over ninety percent men, and most of them were under thirty. Respectable women, and there were some, were treated like queens. Augusta recalled how, when she arrived, the men all stopped work and built her a cabin. Even the women of questionable virtue, and those for whom there were no questions, received the exaggerated kindnesses of the miners. The women, from whatever segment of the social strata, were thankful and helped the men in return.

During the second summer when restrictions on purchased holdings were repealed, the major claims in the gulch became concentrated in fewer and fewer hands. Gradually many of the original claim holders became employees of their former friends and partners. There were no hard feelings or social stigmas. It was simply the economics of mining. Those who struck it bought out those who did not. The sale price ran anywhere from a pair of mules, or a year's grubstake, to several thousand dollars in gold. It was legal to hold as many claims as you could through purchase, and many held dozens. They organized mining companies, ditched-in water, hired large crews and set to work with long toms, several sluices in a series, working large amounts of gravel every day. Those who were employed were sure of a wage. With careful management they could build a stake for themselves, so that when news of the next big strike in the San Juans or in the Gunnison country roared into camp, they would be ready to roar out with it.

Meanwhile the days were long and the work hard, and when the call "Oh, Joe" started at the bottom of the gulch announcing that it was quitting time, the men were more than ready for some relaxation. Many gathered with friends near their tents, around the fire, or at a neighbor's cabin for an evening pipe and conversation. Others went looking for excitement in one of the many saloons and make-shift bars that lined the road up the gulch. One saloon is said to have been made entirely of pine boughs and was the largest establishment of its type in Oro City. Gambling was the biggest attraction, and three-card monte was apparently the most popular game in the gulch, especially with those who made their living gambling. "Monte," as it was affectionately called, was easy to learn and was "chiefly used for separating fools from their money." The dealer laid out three cards, showing one, and shuffled them around in shell game fashion. The victim's task was to point out the correct card. The odds were two to one against him in an honest game, and there were very few of those.

Shooting craps was also popular in the gulch, and of course those two old pauper makers, stud and draw poker, emptied many dust pouches. Another diversion of a similar nature was racing. The miners of the gulch, or any gulch for that matter, would stage foot races, horse races, wagon races, and later on when towns began to develop they added fire company races, drilling races, and mucking races.

Problems that concerned the camp were handled with forthright, democratic dispatch. Those convicted of crimes were quickly dealt with; justice was swift and uncomplicated. California Gulch, like others, provided the possibility of four punishments: fines, beatings, banishment, or hanging. Usually a small fine, the displeasure of the miners' meeting, and a few words of advice were all that were necessary to put a wrongdoer on the straight and narrow. Newcomers to the gulch were put straight in short order. One day a greenhorn came galloping up the gulch's one road, splashing mud on everyone and everything as he went. Suddenly he was halted by a bearded miner holding a menacing revolver at the greenhorn's chest. "Hold on there, stranger," the miner smiled sourly. "When ye go through this yere town, go slow, so folks kin take a look at ye." The greenhorn took the hint and walked his horse the rest of the way up the gulch.

Most men in California Gulch carried either side arms, a rifle, or a shotgun. By far the most popular weapon was the Sharps rifle, or "Beecher Bible" as it was affectionately called. It earned its famous nickname in 1854 when Hartford, Connecticut's fire eating abolitionist, Henry Ward Beecher, entreated God-fearing New Englanders to help stop the spread of slavery in the territories. He suggested every man grasp a Bible in one hand and a Sharps rifle in the other and head for Kansas. There's evidence that only a few took up his call for the sake of Kansas, but many going west filled at least one hand as he suggested.

The Sharps rifle could be fired faster than other guns of the period, especially the clumsy muzzleloaders. And it was more accurate and had a longer range. It was popular in mining camps and among homesteaders. Buffalo hunters used it, especially the later .50 caliber weapon, and it was popular on both sides during the Civil War. The carbine Model '59 was quite effective under five hundred yards, but the "long gun" was, in good hands, an effective weapon up to eight hundred yards! Miners arrived with a variety of weapons ranging from bowie knives and shotguns to small "stingy guns" also made by Sharps. Some, of course, carried their old squirrel rifles, and a few got along with a sharp tongue and fast feet.

Still, with all the weapons, the rough environment, and the lure of gold, there were relatively few acts of violence, especially among the miners. The gambling fraternity periodically eliminated one of their own, or occasionally shot a distraught pilgrim, who, dreaming of greater riches, lost all he had worked for to a man with clean boots and a new deck of cards.

Occasionally, peaceful God-fearing men and greedy gold seeking men drew a bead on one another. Two newcomers, Mathews and Bryant, bought a claim from a man by the name of Kennedy for $1,000 and half of what they took out of the diggings. Shortly after the discussion Kennedy sent word to Mathews and Bryant to come by and finalize the deal. They instead requested that he come over. Neither showed up and on Tuesday, May 29, 1860, Mathews and Bryant went to work on the property. Kennedy had apparently changed his mind, though, and decided to hold the claim for his son-in-law. Seeing the boys working the claim, Kennedy grabbed his shotgun and told them to leave. Words were exchanged and he attempted to shoot Bryant, "but his gun snapped [misfired]." Bryant and Mathews returned to their cabin for their

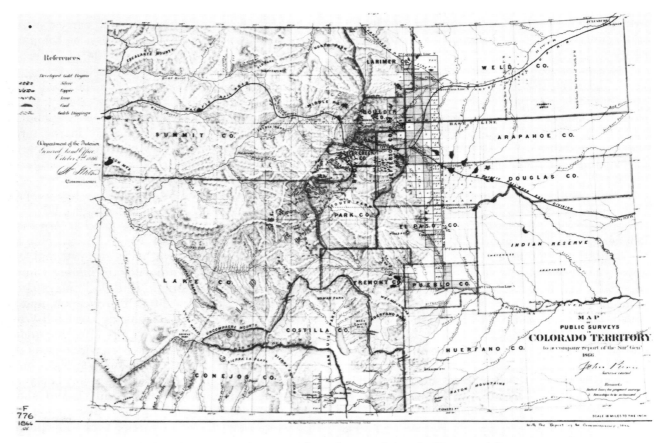

Colorado Territory in 1866. *Photo Source: Colorado Historical Society.*

weapons. In the meantime Abe Lee, recorder, dropped by Kennedy's cabin on his way up the gulch. He found Kennedy "fixing up his shot gun" when he arrived. Kennedy asked Lee to sell him a "box of good caps." Lee declined, knowing Kennedy was up to no good, and left. Mathews and Bryant returned with their placer tools, a shotgun and a rifle, and went back to work. Kennedy soon appeared with a double-barreled shotgun and a rifle. He told them to leave and again pulled up to fire. His first barrel snapped and the second one fired, but missed. Bryant fired back with his rifle. Kennedy dropped the shotgun and grabbed the rifle. As he pulled down on Mathews, Mathews grabbed the shotgun and fired first. The blast killed Kennedy where he stood.

Mathews was tried by a miners' court held in Kennedy's cabin. J. W. Carter defended him, while a Mr. Burkhardt acted for the prosecution. The verdict was innocent. The defendant's major argument was self-defense, but he also had a strong argument under the miners' code, which stated that claims could not be held for persons not in the gulch. Mathews, according to Abe Lee,

continued business as usual, "worked the claim, and when he had made his stake floated away on the outgoing tide."

Religion was a sometime thing in the camp, with many of the miners gathering without benefit of clergy for Sunday prayer meetings. Probably the first officially sanctioned man of the cloth to visit the gulch was Father Machebeuf, Catholic missionary of French descent from the San Luis Valley. He later became head of the Denver diocese. He did not establish a permanent church or mission in the area, but visited on several occasions and ministered to Catholic needs.

Probably the first clergyman to reside in the camp was one F. W. Gray, a twenty-seven-year-old preacher from Missouri. He possibly was the preacher who Edward Lewis mentioned in his diary, May 27, 1860. It was Sunday and Lewis noted, "Universalist preaching at Recorder's office in P.M.; did not go." Whether Gray preached or mined, history does not record, and he was easily overshadowed by that colorful and durable roving Methodist missionary, "Father" John Dyer. Dyer arrived in South Park in July of 1861 and, after ministering to the needs of the Park's several communities, journeyed over Mosquito Pass to California Gulch. Earlier a Reverend William Howbert held Dyer's territory, but he was removed from that post by the presiding elder, John M. Chivington, who later gained fame at La Glorietta Pass and infamy at Sand Creek. Little is known of Howbert, but Dyer does say "he left in disgrace."

Dyer claims many firsts. First to cross Mosquito Range in midwinter, first mail carrier over Mosquito Range, first Protestant preacher in many areas, and surely Colorado's first skier. His skis were wider than modern skis and nearly ten feet long. He guided and propelled himself with a long pole. On the flat he poled himself along like Huck Finn on his raft. On downhill grades he forced the pole down into the snow and braked his descent. Many of his trips are hair-raising tales of daring and raw courage.

In the gulch's first year Fairplay was the closest mail stop; from there it was delivered by whoever was going that way. Finally, to the relief of the gulch fraternity, the U. S. Postal Service established a post office in Oro City, Kansas Territory, on February 16, 1861, with William L. McMath, postmaster. When Colorado became a territory later in the month, the postal service began revising its structure to accommodate the change, and the Oro City post office was recommissioned in Colorado Territory on May 8, 1861, with J. Leroy Lewis as postmaster. That fall, on September 25, 1861, Lewis left and Wolfe Londoner's brother, Julius, became postmaster. Postmasters changed almost every year thereafter until 1868 when Tabor took the job and added the service to a general merchandise establishment he had just initiated.

The postal service authorized the postmaster at Oro City, Kansas Territory, to "engage a suitable person" to supply Oro City with mail delivery once a week from Tarryall, some thirty miles east on the other side of Mosquito Range. The man selected for the job was Pony Duncan, described as being "that prince of 'good fellows,'" who delivered the mail with clockwork regularity every Tuesday.

Wolfe Londoner, the town's first real merchant, arrived shortly after the Tabors in 1860, following Horace's own hand-wrought trail. He brought with him a large load of supplies and whiskey-a-plenty. Whiskey usually was mixed with gulch water and tobacco juice to make it go further, which might explain why some oldtimers could stand up to the bar and belt shot after shot

of straight whiskey without falling through the floor. Another reason was training. They did it, many of them, day after day.

Not long after Londoner set himself up in business he had company. Chief Colorow, the massive, renegade Ute, who terrorized a good many mining men and camps, arrived in the gulch with his squaws. The chief made it a habit of dropping by the gulch from time to time to do a bit of trading, and on these buying sprees he made Londoner's office his headquarters. "It was my duty to ask him to dine with me and keep on the right side of him," Londoner recalled.

On this particular occasion he invited the chief to dinner, not realizing that all of his squaws were with him. When the dinner guests arrived Mrs. Londoner was short of food, so they went without so the Utes would have plenty and not be insulted by their lack of hospitality. The menu called for soup. The chief and his five wives dug in. After each mouthful Colorow "would spit alongside the table." Londoner was upset, no doubt for his wife's sake more than his own. "It was the most villainous thing I ever encountered, but durst not say a word."

Revenge was in the offing, though not actively sought.

An hour or so later Londoner was in his store when his business partner, Dr. Fouts, who was a sometime physician and the store's bookkeeper, dropped by to inform Londoner that he was going up the gulch to collect some bills. No more than ten minutes passed before the 270-pound-plus hulk of Colorow darkened the doorway.

"There was the old fellow with his hands over his stomach and looking very pale, for an Indian."

Colorow asked where Dr. Fouts was, and Londoner informed him of the doctor's visit a few minutes before and his leaving for the upper gulch.

"Injun heap sick."

"What is the matter?" Londoner asked. "What have you been doing, drinking whiskey?"

"No, no, eat too much."

"What do you want?"

"Want Fouts."

"Fouts gone."

"You give me medsin."

Londoner admits to being scared, especially since he was the one who fed the chief. He felt he better do something, so he fetched a tin cup, filled it with Epsom salts, and gave it to the chief with liberal amounts of water. The chief had trouble, but got it down and left.

The next morning Londoner opened up the store and went to the gulch to get a bucket of water. There he met his patient, who was much the worse for wear. "While he had weighed probably 275 pounds the day before, he looked now like an umbrella cover."

Londoner inquired about the Ute's health.

"No good, white man heap bad."

"What's the matter, Colorow?"

"Oh, heap sick, pretty near die, no more medsin, see your partner."

Londoner helped him up to the store, and then rousted his associate out and explained the problem.

"How much did you give him, for God's sake?"

"I gave him a tin cup full," Londoner explained.

"Why, that was enough to kill an elephant."

And so the summer wore on and toward the end of August the more perceptive began to notice ice along the stream banks in the morning and a sharper chill in the air. The sky took on an even deeper blue and the stars hung large and bright and near. The aspens rustled, dry in the cold, first-light breezes, and danced gold in the late afternoon sun. The days were clear and warm, but the chill at sundown hinted of winter. Many miners washed a last few pans and loaded up, never to return. Others boarded up their cabins, stored their equipment for the coming season, and headed for winter quarters in Denver and points east. When the miners loaded up, the gamblers, bunco artists, ladies of easy virtue, and other forms of social lice followed. A few prepared to wait out the winter in California Gulch.

One of the ladies of easy virtue appears to have been a real lady with no small amount of virtue, if we accept a rather loose definition of both lady and virtue. Her name remains a mystery, but to the gulch fraternity she was known as Red Stockings, because of her habit of wearing red silk stockings. According to Charles H. Dow, who was one of the early journalists to visit and write

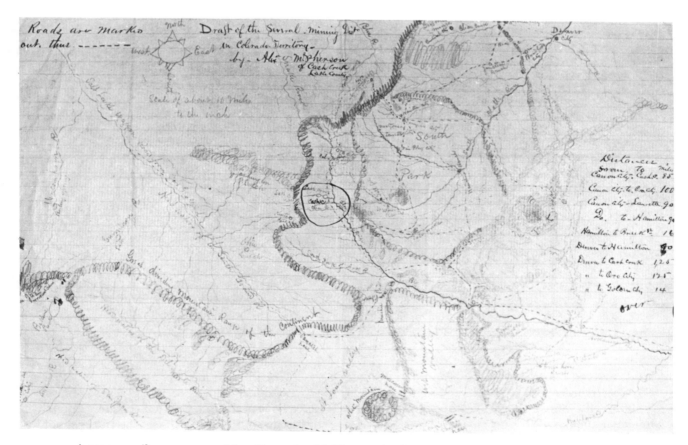

A rare pencil map prepared by Alexander McPherson in the early 1860s. Note the misspelling of Cache (Cash) Creek. *Photo Source: Author's Collection.*

about the area, Red Stockings was the daughter of a wealthy Boston merchant. She had been well educated and was a cultured, refined lady. While traveling in Europe she met and became the "temporary wife" of a French nobleman. She later reenacted the scene with a successful New York gambler. He dissolved the union and she decided to give the West a try. She settled on Oro City.

She spent the summer of 1860 in the gulch, and accounts of the period describe her riding up the community's only street on a fine mare, both costumed to fit their positions as queens of California Gulch. At the end of the summer she gave an extravagant party for those who remained. A party, Dow says, "which for savage splendor was never surpassed in Colorado." And then she left and was never seen again. Some say she settled down and became respectable. Others, well they just did not know, but they enjoyed speculating.

Those hardy souls who decided to winter in the gulch planned to do some trapping and a little gold washing during the occasional thaws. Those who remained finally found a use for that heavy black mud that clogged their sluices and filled their pans. They used it for caulking their cabins against the cold winter wind, which by late September was beginning to blow up the gulch from the already snow-covered slopes of Mount Massive.

The old hotel in Oro City long after the boom had passed them by. *Photo Source: CMHC, Lake County Public Library.*

II

Waiting

On February 28, 1861, Colorado became a territory. As early as 1859 there was a territorial push, and in fact a quasi-territorial government was established with jurisdiction over an area roughly one third again the size of present-day Colorado. Still it had no powers, other than those it assumed, and in the high mountains men were not inclined to follow any government but the one they had organized and the one back in Washington, D. C., which was a long way from Colorado. So when the official territorial government went into effect in February 1861, there was no law in Colorado worthy of the name except miners' law.

The new government set up counties and ordered elections of county officials. Lake County was organized with Oro City as temporary county seat. The county was enormous, second largest in Colorado and larger than many states. It was bounded on the east by Park and Fremont counties, on the south by Conejos County, on the west by Utah Territory, and on the north by Summit County. Elections were held and the county commissioners were Captain S. D. Breece, Alexander McPherson, and William Snyder. Eli Blair was elected sheriff and Colonel Austin became probate judge.

The new county government remained inactive for fifteen years, while the miners continued to solve their problems with miners' meetings and community action. The miners' first task in the spring of 1861 was to get more water. The previous year water had been a problem and with plans for more sophisticated gold washing methods it was necessary to find more water for the gulch. The result of their deliberations was the construction of a ditch to nearby Evans Gulch.

The big news in the spring of 1861 was not in Evans Gulch, however, but was two thousand miles east on a small island in the harbor of Charleston, South Carolina. There, on April 12, the first shots were fired in a four-year conflict that would change the character of the nation, indeed the world. While remote, Colorado was torn by economic problems as a result of the conflict and was decimated by the warring armies' appetites for strong young men.

Colorado was from the outset strongly Union in sentiment, but there were large numbers of Southerners in the various camps. Virginia McConnel estimates in *Bayou Salado* that "about one third of the people of the new territory of Colorado were southern sympathizers in 1861." Many headed home when news of the war reached the gold fields. Others, Union sympathizers, banded together in small groups and headed for the nearest recruiting stations.

Denver actually had reason to believe there was a southern insurrection in the works, and the governor called for troops. California Gulchers sent word that they had 2,000 men who were ready to march when the word was issued. In a neighboring gulch a Confederate flag was hoisted on one occasion and almost precipitated a civil war in the meadows and woods of the upper Arkansas Valley, but fortunately the Seccessionists were persuaded that it would be a lot wiser and a good deal more healthful to take the flag down. There were some arguments, some fights, and some threats of violence in the upper Arkansas Valley, but for the most part those who stayed signed a "separate peace" and continued to work their placers.

Over five million dollars worth of gold had been extracted from roughly three miles of gulch by the war's end. Figures on production in California Gulch run in excess of one hundred million dollars the first year. The above figure represents a reasonable guess based upon several of the more reliable sources such as Hollister, Henderson and Emmons. But by 1865 the placer gold had petered out and California Gulch was all but deserted. In 1866 the county seat was moved to Dayton (Twin Lakes), then in 1868 to Granite. From 1865 to 1868 no deaths were reported, no violence erupted, no births recorded. The land began to heal, even though a couple hundred hopefuls still worked the area. The gulch ran clear again, the game returned, and the excitement that was California Gulch gave all indications of being a thing of the past; but the wealth already gained was no more than an hors d'oeuvre compared to the feast that lay beneath the surrounding hills.

In 1868 there was a short flaming of the old fire when some old-timers located one of the sources of the gulch's gold. Their's was not a new idea. Several had tried to locate the mother lode, but had not been successful. Two knowledgeable miners, Cooper Smith and Charles J. Mullen, were credited with the discovery of a gold-bearing lode called the Printer Boy. They seem to have been employed by a moneyed man from Philadelphia, J. Marshall Paul. Management of the enterprise was under the able direction of Charles L. Hill.

Hill developed the mine and built the first stamp mill in the county. The ore was of remarkable quality, but the water, without proper pumping equipment, finally closed the mine. Still the two years of its highest production, 1868 and 1869, made its owners a tidy sum and the Printer Boy became known across the land through its displays of gold bearing quartz.

A number of other lode mines were developed at the same time as the Printer Boy. The Pilot Tunnel, located just east of the Printer Boy, was a sporadic gold producer for a number of years. The Five-Twenty on the other side of the Printer Boy was more successful. By 1872 it, like the Printer Boy, had a stamp mill eagerly pounding gold ore to a refinable pulp. Other operations such as the New Brunswick, Berry Tunnel, and American Flag seem to have promised more than they were able to deliver.

The mines that developed in the wake of the Printer Boy, though lesser in all but their beholder's eyes, were subject to the same handicaps faced by J. Marshall Paul's prize, namely, water, labor, transportation, and smelters. Water in many of the mines in the district required a major pumping effort. California Gulch in the first decade after the Civil War had neither the means nor the skills required to pump large quantities of water. Labor was in short supply and transportation almost nonexistent. And smelters? That was the greatest need. Only the highest grade ore went to the mill and a sizable portion, due to inefficient milling, went over the side and into the tailing pond as waste. They were a decade too soon.

Horace Tabor, like so many others, left the gulch in the early sixties when the gold began to grow lean. He went over to Buckskin during the fall of 1862, built himself a cabin, and hauled his family over Mosquito Range in September of that year. Once in the camp he busied himself with the community's affairs, was elected to the school board, ran a successful grocery store, was appointed postmaster, and dreamed his dreams while Augusta tended to the details of store and post office. When Tabor returned to California Gulch in 1868 he brought his store with him, and on November 30, 1868, was appointed postmaster for Oro City.

Oro City was one of the few communities that really served the needs of its citizens. It never required people to move to town, rather it followed the people. In its early years it was scattered up and down California Gulch, as the population diminished and those remaining clustered in the upper end of the gulch, that became Oro City. Then in 1868 the Printer Boy drew miners up the gulch and Oro City followed. In fact, in amoebic fashion, the town split into Upper and Lower Oro. The official site of Oro City was wherever the post office was located, and in 1868 that was Upper Oro, or Oro Number Two as it was occasionally called.

About a mile and a quarter above Upper Oro a small water wheel turned a saw that provided the building materials for growth and progress. Doc Brut kept the only lodging in the gulch during the summer of 1872, and it was "a first-class, substantial, workingmans eating house" that was "crowded day and night." Four years later the town proudly announced "we have a first class hotel, Joseph Pearce, proprietor; a general store, where every want and luxury can be supplied, owned by H. A. W. Tabor; an elegant billiard hall, Wm McDermith, proprietor;" and a "well conducted saloon." It was without a house of "doubtful fame," which was noted as assurance of the citizens' noble character. The gulch had a school run by Miss McLaughlin that got underway July 15, 1872. An observer noted, "There are only ten or twelve families in the gulch, one can hardly imagine where her fifteen or twenty pupils come from." The Odd Fellows

Lodge had come to town in 1872 and by 1876 had fifty members. The community claimed to have a thriving social and cultural life.

Winter slowed the mining activity, and probably should have stopped it, but some hardy souls persisted. It was said that Tom Starr, owner of placer holdings in the vicinity of Lower Oro, worked year round, winter and summer. One old-timer, Joseph H. Wells, was convinced that the winter of 1866-1867 was the worst. The first snowfall began on September 16 and it did not stop for four days. When it did forty inches of snow lay on the ground, and that was just the beginning. He claimed stock were not wintered in the gulch until 1871 when he boarded "three head." For those who decided to wait out the winter, the practice was to lay in enough food in the fall to hold everyone until spring. Beef was especially important. "It would freeze and we would lay it on the snow and use it as we needed it." It would be years before science caught up, but Wells knew then that "It was just as good when six months old, kept in this manner, as at any time."

Other communities, like Oro City, continued to work and wait and hope that civilization would finally find them. Granite, the county seat, was slowly dying. In 1872 a traveler noted, "Granite looks a little rusty, and most of the houses are to let." The town consisted of two hotels, a store, post office, the usual saloon, blacksmith shop, a brewery, and about thirty or forty shacks "inhabited by swallows." Cache Creek was all but deserted. The Twin Lakes area, popular with tourists even then, was quiet. The great tourist influx in early July of 1872 consisted of "Two young Englishmen, a doctor, and Mr. Kline," a man of some wealth from Philadelphia. Other communities in the area included a small settlement at the point where California Gulch meets the Arkansas River. By late 1875 the location was identified as Malta, though it was generally known as Swilltown, a misnomer for Schwilltown, after Ferdinand A. Schwill, the town's first postmaster. In spite of the Oro Citys' efforts to be all things to all people, a small settlement began to emerge about one-half mile below Lower Oro. It was first identified in 1873 or 1874 and was called

Upper Oro as William H. Jackson found it in August of 1873. *Photo Source: Geological Survey in the National Archives.*

Slabtown, according to H. A. W. Tabor. It was this Slabtown, a common, illbred renegade, that would give birth to the magic city of Leadville.

In 1867, in response to changes in mining laws in Washington, the miners in the gulch were obliged to rewrite their own laws. "At a meeting of the miners at the house of John Leahey in Oro City January 1, 1867, S. H. Fouts was chosen chairman and A. S. Weston Sect." A. S. Weston, C. W. Floyd, S. D. Breece, J. W. Tisdale, and John Leahey were appointed to "draft laws for the district and to define the boundaries of the same."

Since only a few miners remained in the gulch and the gold was harder to come by, the miners increased the legal size of their holdings and put all abandoned claims up for preemption. The old district was increased in size. It was bounded "on the North by the divide [later named Prospect Mountain] between Evan's Gulch and Birdseye Gulch. On the East by the top of the range East of the Arkansas River. On the South by the divide between Iowa Gulch and Empire Gulch. And on the West by the Arkansas River."

In 1873 the U. S. Geological Survey teams headed by Dr. F. V. Hayden entered the area, first camping at Twin Lakes. With the survey was a photography team headed by William H. Jackson, who became one of the West's most famous photographers. According to Jackson they camped at Twin Lakes for around two weeks

The lower, larger of the Twin Lakes where the Hayden Survey Team camped in August, 1873. *Photo Source: Geological Survey in the National Archives.*

and sent parties out from their camp into the surrounding area to collect data and take pictures. While in camp he kept busy developing negatives, repairing his equipment, and fishing. "Made arrangements with the old man [Derry] to keep his boat while here at $2. per day." When he arrived, July 20, 1873, he went fishing, but only caught two. The next day a number of them tried their luck and did much better. "Had all we wanted for supper and gave some to Dr. to take to camp with him."

From the Twin Lakes site Jackson and his assistants tried to climb Mount Elbert, but had trouble with their mules and had to settle for photos of Twin Lakes taken from an open spot below timberline. After several short trips around the lakes and up Clear Creek Canyon, Jackson again stopped at Derry's where they "treated us to a neat little lunch which made us forget some of their other unpleasant traits." Then, on Sunday, August 3, they set out for the Gunnison country. On the seventeenth they were back. The next day he stopped at Derry's, had some milk, raisins and gingerbread, then "Took cut-off over hills and about 11 rejoined camp at Weston's ranch on the Arkansas." On the nineteenth he stopped to photograph Mount Massive, then with his crew headed over Tennessee Pass to Mount of the Holy Cross where on Sunday, August 24, 1873, he took his famous Holy Cross photo. After the photo was taken Jackson and his men returned to the Arkansas Valley and on August 27 arrived in Oro City, where they stayed the night and the next day left for Denver and home.

Another young leader of a party under Dr. Hayden was Henry Gannett. Gannett and a crew of seven had the task of surveying the area. It apparently was Gannett who named, or at least officially baptised, Mount Massive. Over the years a variety of new names, Mount McKinley, Mount Eisenhower, and Mount Churchill to name a few, have been suggested as worthy replacements for Gannett's original.

William H. Stevens first visited the area in 1865. He was a mining man of some skill and searched for signs of "blossom rock." He inspected the area, noted its possibilities, even sampled some rock outcroppings on Rock Hill, then left. He returned in 1873 to pursue an idea. From Ann Arbor, Michigan, came Alvinus B. Wood, said to have been "one of the keenest observers and finest 'prospectors' in the United States." He and Stevens formed a partnership in 1874 and immediately began planning an extensive placer mining operation that would successfully and systematically wash the California

Gulch gravels and the banks on either side. Both men were convinced that plenty of gold remained in the gulch gravels, either missed by the placer miner's haphazard methods, or returned to the gulch as a result of the poor methods of recovery employed by the placer miner.

The few miners remaining in the gulch had already arrived at the same conclusion as Wood and Stevens and had decided that the real need was great quantities of water. They began the construction of a ditch that would travel eleven miles and tap the headwaters of the Arkansas, but they lacked the resources to complete the project. The newcomers jumped in. Stevens provided the resources while Wood furnished the engineering knowhow. The gulch provided the initial labor, but soon additional workers arrived in hopes of making a bit of money to finance their prospecting. Stevens and Wood organized the Oro Mining Ditch and Fluming Company, then claimed several sites and purchased many others. It is reported that Stevens spent $50,000 on the ditch, which was completed in 1875. It was an immediate success, except that Wood and Stevens were plagued with that same heavy black sand that had confounded placer operations in the gulch since those halcyon days of 1860.

There is a general disagreement as to who discovered the true nature of the bothersome stuff, but Wood seems likely. Stevens was knowledgeable as far as mining matters go, but his real skill was that of a promoter. Wood on the other hand was a mining engineer and trained metallurgist. Development and production were his strong suits. The pair gathered samples of the "black mud" and Wood took them across Mosquito Pass to a friend, Hermann Beeger, in Alma where they were assayed. Beeger's assay showed the ore ran twenty-seven percent lead and fifteen ounces of silver to the ton.

Wood and Stevens quietly prospected the upper slopes of the gulch until they located an outcropping in the area that Stevens had surveyed in 1865. They took samples and found it contained a high percentage of lead and twenty to forty ounces of silver. They located a number of lode claims in the area, but kept quiet and continued to wash gold from the gulch below. Several placer claims they wanted were in the hands of others. Some they quietly purchased, others they waited on. Finally they were deemed abandoned and open to anyone who cared to preempt them, and preempt them they did. By the fall of 1875 they controlled a considerable portion of California Gulch.

California Gulch just above Old Oro. On the right is Rock Hill, site of Wood and Stevens' Rock Mine. *Photo Source: CMHC, Lake County Public Library.*

During the winter of 1875-1876 Wood and Stevens put men to work lode mining on a hill south of the gulch on a claim they named the Rock. The miners became curious. They could see nothing worth digging for and finally were convinced that they were working for a pair of fools. Finally one of the employees, a Mr. Walls, approached Stevens. "It's a great curiousity I have to know what ye are doin' this diggin' here for, Mr. Stevens. I've wurruked for yez mony a day and attinded to by buzziness, but I can't for the life of me see what ye are afther."

"You can't, eh?"

"No, sir, there is not a culler [gold] in all this stuff we are takin' out."

"Have you examined it closely?"

"Yes, sir, and I'm sure there is not a culler in it—not a culler, sir; it is nothing but a lot of black, dirty rocks."

"Well, Walls, it is not gold that I have been working for. This is carbonate of lead. I think there is some silver in it and enough lead to make it pay to mine it."

Walls left shortly and he and his brother-in-law, a man named Powell, went into business for themselves. They discovered the highly productive Adelaide mine on the north end of Iron Hill. Others continued to work and wonder.

While Wood and Stevens are given credit for the discovery of the Leadville carbonates that led directly to the silver boom in the late seventies, there is ample evidence that the presence of silver had been known for years. In August of 1860 the Washoe District was organized in McNulty's Gulch just north of Fremont Pass. It was a silver mining district built mainly around H. C. Justice's silver lode. The Homestake Mine, a silver producer, opened in 1871 and as early as the fall of 1873 the Territorial Assay Office in Oro City was daily recording silver samples from what became the Leadville District. One source claimed that as early as 1871 it was not only known that lead existed on the site of Steven's Rock mine, but that the ore was put to a practical use. "It so happened that the supply of bullets for the guns of the pioneers extablished here had become exhausted." The camp was out of lead and ingenuity had to find a substitute. "Rich lumps of carbonate of lead ore were selected," and placed in a hollowed out bowl in a large tree trunk. A hole was bored in the stump at the base of the bowl, the top of the bowl was heaped with wood, and the whole mass ignited. The hot, liquid lead ran out of the hole and into waiting bullet molds. "True," it was recalled, "the lead was impure and hard, but it served its purpose."

On October 15, 1873, L. F. Bradshaw, Frank to those who knew him, Jake Lightfoot, and John Durham located the Oro La Plata. John C. Hume recalled in a paper for the Society of Leadville Pioneers that Bradshaw told him several times about his silver mine, and even offered to deed him one-quarter interest in it if he would help him work it. Others suggest it was Maurice Hayes, the territorial assayer, who confirmed the discovery of silver-bearing lead carbonates in the Leadville District. He surely ran the assays on the Oro La Plata samples and probably assayed other silver-lead ore from the same general area and during the same period.

The conclusion is unavoidable. Lead carbonates were detected and mined in several locations prior to Wood and Stevens' discovery. And, rather than discovery, they were responsible for locating the first paying silver lode in California Gulch and having the financial resources and technical knowhow to develop their find.

Wood and Stevens staked their parent claims, the Rock and the Lime, claims that faced each other across California Gulch, in June of 1874. The following spring they picked up the Stone. All three claims were in Wood's name and were separate from the holdings of the Oro Mining Ditch and Fluming Company. The pair staked the Bull's Eye and the Iron, plus a number of lesser claims in 1876, which gave them virtual control of Rock and Iron Hills, both named after their claims. In the spring of 1876 they announced their findings. Its effect on mining was negligible at first. Few knew the value of the carbonates, and most were inclined to take a wait and see attitude. Fred Conant, a news reporter from the *Colorado Springs Gazette*, visited the area and failed to see anything to recommend. He reported to his readers that it was "desolate in the extreme." It was not destined to remain that way for long.

August R. Meyer was a native of St. Louis and, unlike many, did not fall into mining and smelting as the result of a lucky strike or the mysterious workings of fate. Meyer went to Switzerland at fourteen to study chemistry and geology. From Switzerland he went to the school of mines at Freiberg, Saxony. He then worked and traveled, exploring the mining industry in Europe and finally finished his education at the University of Berlin. He returned to St. Louis for a short stay, and in 1874 left for Colorado. His success in Colorado was quick and complete. He left the state in 1881, a wealthy, respected, and successful man.

August R. Meyer at about the time of the Leadville boom. *Photo Source: Author's Collection.*

Meyer stopped first in Fairplay where he was appointed territorial assayer for the district. While there he appears to have led the way in constructing a sampling works at Alma, which, in 1879 was owned by Meyer, though the original construction was probably done under the auspices of the St. Louis Smelting and Refining Company. He then scouted the area for ore that could be processed in the Alma plant. The ore at the Rock attracted him, no doubt as a result of the Beeger assay, and, though it was too complex for the works at Alma, he took a chance on three hundred tons and shipped it all the way to St. Louis.

Freighting the ore was a monumental task. Ox teams were imported from New Mexico to pull the wagons, and the ore was hauled over Tabor's old route to Colorado Springs, where it was transferred to rail and shipped to St. Louis. It failed to even pay the haulage, much less make either Meyer, or Wood and Stevens, a profit. But they were not discouraged. The following spring Meyer shipped another fifty tons of higher grade material. Lead at that time was six cents a pound, silver at about $1.16 per fine ounce, and the ore ran sixty percent lead and carried twenty to forty ounces of silver per ton.

Uncle Billy Stevens, as he was called, was not as popular as the nickname suggests, and a number of old hands detested him. Why is not clear, but much of it was no doubt due to his money and power and his highhanded manner. Physically he was short and stocky, tightly built, red faced, sandy haired, one eyed, and he gave the general impression of being "metalic."

Meyer's ore shipment made one thing clear to Uncle Billy: if the Stevens-Wood enterprise was to flourish, help would have to be imported. There were simply too few men in the area willing to work for wages. Stevens' quest for workers is a confused story at best. One source, a Mr. Munger, who was one of a group from Detroit who answered Stevens' call, claimed he advertised for five thousand workers. Others put the figure someplace between one hundred and two hundred men, which seems more likely. The number of Detroit men who accepted Stevens' promise of free transportation to Oro City and jobs when they got there was ninety-eight.

The men apparently were not prepared for the conditions they found at the end of the line in Colorado Springs. It was April 27, 1877, and snowing when they arrived. Because of the storm they were unable to find transportation to the diggings until May 2. They were forced to walk the greater part of the way because of weather and roads. Slabtown, where the Oro Mining Ditch and Fluming Company's office was located, was buried in nearly four feet of snow. "Some were furnished quarters in stables, blacksmith shops, a sawmill, Mr. Munger having to walk a mile and a half in snow up to his armpits to find a place to sleep, without supper."

The next morning the men walked the three miles up the gulch to Oro City in search of Stevens. They found him and Wood the following day. Stevens had promised them a six-day work week at $2.00 a day. Room and board would cost them $5.00 a week. Instead of the Detroit offer, Stevens now offered to let them "dig at thirty cents per cubic yard or build rail fence at twenty-five cents per rod." The local miners gave them the horse laugh for allowing themselves to be sucked in by Uncle Billy's promises; but many tried the work at Billy's wages and found they could not even make board and room.

The men got together and decided to demand $50.00 apiece from Wood and Stevens to get them back to Michigan. It was Friday evening, May 11, 1877. Wood and Stevens entered Tabor's store in Oro City, followed by a small army of angry miners from the shores of Lake Erie. Maxcy Tabor, a lad of nineteen, was alone in the store when the harried pair arrived. After quickly explaining that the mob was after their "money or lives," Maxcy helped them bar the door and close the shutters. Wood and Stevens hid behind

Nathaniel Maxcy Tabor, born October 9, 1857, was the only child of Horace and Augusta Tabor. *Photo Source: Colorado Historical Society.*

the safe and Maxcy tended the shop. The mob arrived and began banging on the door with such vehemence that Maxcy opened it to prevent its being broken down. He tried to calm the crowd and told them to "abandon their threats of violence to Stevens and Wood and disperse and go about their business." They promptly went "about their business," someone firing a shotgun into the slush at Maxcy's feet, splattering him with mud. He was pushed aside, and the men crowded into the store firing shot and ball into the ceiling, and all the while threatening to hang Wood and Stevens. They even went so far as to cut a significant length of rope "from a roll they found in the store."

Some versions claim they put the rope around Stevens' neck and swung him a couple times before he gave into their demands. Others have him tied to an old cabin door frame and starved into submission on a diet of crackers and water. All versions agree that the locals did not lift a finger to protect Stevens, and in many stories the gulch populace is seen aiding the abetting. One group of

outraged locals is supposed to have supplied the newcomers with generous quantities of liquor in hopes they might get mean drunk and stretch old Billy's neck.

Billy's neck, however, remained intact. A check was written, a delegation of five men set out immediately for the Fairplay Bank to cash it, while the rest held Billy prisoner. They were back Sunday morning, May 13, with the money. Billy was released, and the men returned to Detroit, and Stevens, we might assume, wore his tie a bit looser.

Abe Lee, one of the most famous of the original gulch characters and discoverer of gold in the gulch in 1860, was back in the area in the seventies, having spent his fortune and looking for a second bit of luck. He was, the story goes, working the Iowa Gulch area in 1876 and awoke one morning to find his horse missing. He set out tracking the animal over the hill to the south of the gulch. While he gazed down at the tracks he noticed an outcropping of black rock. He was curious and examined the rock. After a quick perusal he pocketed a few chunks and continued his search for his horse. Later in the morning he ran into Jacob Long. He told Long what he was doing and asked if he had seen any sign of the horse. Long apparently had not. They then talked mining and Lee gave him a sample of the rock he had found. They talked and hefted and wondered, and then Lee went his way. Later that evening around the fire Long was telling his brother, John, and their partner, Charles Derry, about his encounter and showed them the rock Lee had given him. They discussed the heavy black lump and decided it might be a form of coal and threw it into the fire. It was not coal, but it was lead carbonate. As soon as the mineral began to melt, they knew what they had.

Another story of Long's discovery bears repeating simply because it is a good example of the "anybody-can-get-rich" propaganda of the period. This tale is told from California to the Rockies and from Alaska as far south as miners tell tales. In each version a hunter is necessary, in this case Jacob Long, a rifle, and usually some game. In Long's case, he supposedly shot a deer and the dying animal kicked up some rock that Long recognized as carbonate of lead, hence his discovery. In other cases, one in South Park for instance, the hunter missed and his shot kicked up the ground and paved the way for riches. They make good telling and are very good for impressing greenhorns, but the real discovery was no doubt the result of hard work and was accomplished without the help of a wounded deer.

Jacob T. Long and his brother, John W. Long, came to Colorado in 1860. After trying the San Juans in the southwest corner of the state, they settled in the Leadville area. They supported themselves with hunting, trapping, and gold washing for some sixteen years. Most of their activity seems to have centered in Iowa Gulch. It is not clear how the two Long brothers met Charles Derry, the son of "old man" Derry of Twin Lakes, or the basis of their partnership. It does appear to have been based on a hunting and trapping association. According to Jacob Long, he was out hunting deer and "spied the float" of what became one of the most famous of the early Leadville area producers. The mine was divided equally among the two Long brothers and their friend, Charles Derry. Jacob Long was a man who never forgot a kindness, and that probably accounts for Derry's one-third interest. Another favor he seems to have repaid was to J. D. Dana, an illustrious geologist for whom the mine was named. Jacob Long had taught himself geology, and it seems he named the mine out of the debt of gratitude he felt for Dana and his teaching, which might have led directly to the discovery. The hill where the discovery was made, between Iowa and Empire gulches, was named Long and Derry Hill in honor of the owners.

Long never mentioned Abe Lee, either as partner, participant, or bystander. What, if any, part did Lee play in the discovery of the J. D. Dana? R. G. Dill, an early chronicler of the area, sees Lee making the discovery in 1876 and passing a sample on to Jacob Long, who was "used to making fire assays," and who ran a test on the rock. It led to the location of the J. D. Dana, but no mention of ownership by Lee. Did Long, who "never forgot a kindness," refuse him his generosity? Or did Dill and other writers then and now see Lee as the likely candidate to discover silver since he had discovered gold? The information suggests that he was the Columbus of the period; anything worthy of discovery was discovered by Abe Lee.

The previous summer another enterprise had sprung up in the lower end of California Gulch in Malta. The new industry was a small smelter for treating simple ores and was opened in 1875. Called the Malta Smelting and Mining Company's Works and under the direction of one Emil Leoscher, it ran until 1877. It was closed then for seven or eight months, and reopened by Valentine Beutsch who was employed by James B. Dickson and Company. It had a checkered existence throughout the silver era and, though it was the first smelter in the valley, it never was a major force in the business community.

Wood and Stevens' Premier performer, the Iron Silver Mine, in the early 1880s. *Photo Source: Collections in the Museum of New Mexico.*

III

Anybody Can Do It

Such mines and miners as existed plodded through 1875 and 1876 undisturbed by promoters, ne'er-do-wells, beautiful or near-beautiful women, or the law. Word of the increased mining activity failed to lure the masses and only a handful wandered into the area in response to the cry, "Silver!" Part of that handful, maybe even half of it, consisted of three Irish brothers, not long off the boat and in search of their fortunes. John, Charles, and Patrick Gallagher arrived in the area in the fall of 1876. Being greenhorns and trusting souls they first inquired around Oro City about mining prospects and who to see about information. They were directed, no doubt with a wry smile, to Iron Hill and Uncle Billy Stevens.

We are told that they located Stevens in the vicinity of the Iron Mine, which was then nothing more than a faint hope for the future. The brothers promptly asked Stevens if they might sink a shaft near his. Stevens had spent too much time and money to give the newcomers the full benefit of his efforts. He suggested they go dig under a tree "on the next hill." They must have realized they were being put off, but had no choice but to leave. Unfortunately many writers then and later assumed the next hill was the then un-named Carbonate Hill and have located the Gallaghers there, when in fact they went almost straight north into Adelaide Park, and, on the east flank of Iron Hill, sunk their shaft.

Sinking a shaft in the early days of Leadville mining was hard work, but relatively inexpensive. Hand-driven whims or animal-powered whims were used to lift the ore out. The rock was comparatively soft and usually could be removed with a minimum of blasting. Timbering consisted of cutting the nearby forest and fitting the logs. Water did not trouble the shallower mines. It was only when they began going deeper for the more complex ores that large sums became necessary for pumping. It has been estimated that a man could get into business for one hundred dollars or so.

During the fall and winter of 1876 the Gallaghers staked the Pine, Campbird, Keystone, Charlestown, and Young America. The winter was long, cold, and filled with hard work, but soon after the first of the year they broke into paydirt. One assay on February 26, 1877, ran 934 ounces of silver to the ton and was forty-two percent lead. An added bonus was an average of four and one-half ounces of gold per ton. As their second summer wore on they began to see a sizable profit. The Gallagher brothers proved to the world that anybody could do it, and many did. A few of their stories follow.

Alvinus B. Wood, Uncle Billy Stevens' somewhat silent partner, sold out in 1877. The sale made doubters take notice. They began to wonder at the possibilities of this new metal, especially after they heard Wood received $40,000 for his share. The buyer, one Levi Z. Leiter, late of Chicago, was a retired merchant and one-time partner of Marshall Field. He had no need of further money-making, but became interested in western mining property and, never one to pass a good prospect, invested. It was a fortunate deal. Stevens had extended himself to his financial limits and, while the properties were beginning to yield a profit, Leiter's money enabled them to develop the properties and consolidate much faster, which gave them an early advantage over other mining companies in the area. The Stevens and Leiter mines and properties became the Iron Silver Mining Company and almost immediately began to show excellent profits.

After the windlass came the horse whim, both adequate devices for raising ore from the bottom of a shallow shaft. *Photo Source: Dorothy D. Shelton.*

During that same summer of 1877 two old hands had a bit of luck. Nelson Hallock and Captain Albert Cooper gave up their sawmill and tried mining on the hill just west of Iron. In June of that year they located the Carbonate Mine, the first claim on the hill, and in doing so gave Carbonate Hill its name. They found the digging easy and the weather fair. Everything, in fact, was going their way. On June 20 they were down sixteen feet and hit paydirt. The following April they sold 363 tons of ore and made a net profit of over $40,000. From April to July of '78 they cleared almost $34,000. Suddenly the pair were rich men, and they began looking beyond their high grade hole in the ground. Hallock became active in the early organization of Leadville and served three years as county commissioner, two of them as chairman. Not long after the sale of the Carbonate Mine for $250,000, he moved to Denver where he became president of the Colorado Iron Works. Little is known about his early life, other than that he was born in New York in 1840 and was one of the fifty-niners who came to Colorado on the first great tide.

His partner, Captain Albert Cooper, remained in Leadville a few years longer than Hallock, but the call of the sea took him back to New England and Boston. He was born near Hallowell, Maine, went to sea, and at twenty-one became a captain. In 1876, or thereabouts, he gave up the sea and wested. Leadville drew him as it drew hundreds of others. He was lucky; he made his stake, lived in Denver for about a year, then went home, richer and, presumably, with no need to be wiser.

One old pilgrim who had come up California Gulch long before silver was anything but tableware and worked the area from South Park to Mount Massive, was S. D. Breece. Breece, a likable and highly respected citizen, was active in gulch politics. He served as district recorder for a short time, and was one of the original county commissioners. Even before word of Wood and Stevens' find, Breece had climbed the hill just east of Adelaide Park and located four claims. The most famous was his Iron claim, called Breece Iron. The hill was named after Breece, and the claim put him in easy circumstances for the few remaining months of his life. The mine was unique for two reasons. It was the only open pit mine of note in the district, and was an iron mine. But there was a tremendous market for iron in the area as flux material in the smelting of gold and silver. According to John J. Vandemoer, who came to Denver in 1877 and became a correspondent for the *Mining Record* as well as an occasional contributor to other national journals and area papers, the Breece Iron produced "about seventy-five tons per day," employed about fifty men, and could have "easily" increased production to one hundred and twenty tons a day. It made from seven dollars a ton to twenty-two dollars a ton, but the miracle of the mine was the operating cost. It is said they mined, loaded, and hauled the ore for fifty cents a ton. Anything over that was profit. The Breece Iron was sold to C. R. Bissell in the summer of 1879 for a reported $76,000. Not long after Bissell bought the property, production was reduced due to competition from the Fryer Hill mines that produced, along with their silver, considerable quantities of iron. Later the Breece Iron had a rebirth as part of the Penn Group.

One of the earlier gulch claims Wood and Stevens had not been able to pick up was the A. Y. It was in the bottom of California Gulch near the base of Iron Hill. On October 20, 1869, A. Y. Corman and five other prospectors located the A. Y. Almost a decade later Corman refiled on the A. Y. He was the sole owner according to the relocation entry dated May 12, 1877. In December of the same year he and some associates located the Minnie, immediately east of the A. Y. These two mines failed to produce and eventually fell into the hands of a Jewish merchant from Pennsylvania named Meyer Guggenheim. They became the basis of the fabulous Guggenheim Smelter empire that will be discussed in detail in Chapter VIII.

"The next arrival came in an express wagon," Albert Sanford recalled. Sanford was checking the reservations list for a special railroad car to Leadville. The "next arrival" was on the seat with the driver. He had a carpetbag; nothing else. "He did not jump from his perch, but rather made his descent backward, with a firm hand on the seat, as an old farmer would do." The man was short and stout, dressed in mining duds "that showed stains from mine drippings and candle grease." His trousers were tucked in the top of his boots placer-miner style. He had sideburns, a mustache and "kindly eyes shaded by heavy brows." Sanford had no idea who the man was until someone asked, "How's the Morning Star?"

In June of 1877 two men, Baldock and Bradley, located a claim they dubbed the Morning Star. It showed promise, but the pair were not satisfied. In October of that year Colorado's governor, John L. Routt, the "next arrival," came to look the new camp over. He visited Baldock and Bradley's claim and was told he could have it for ten thousand dollars. He later said he "closed the bargain before coming off the hill." The purchase and the later demands for wages, equipment, and supplies pulled him down to "bedrock, and for a time, with my personal credit nearly exhausted, things looked as streaked as a corn basket." Still, he always had faith in the "ground" and never gave up. He used to make as many trips to Leadville as his official obligations would allow, and when in town he quickly shed his gubernatorial mantel and pitched in and helped the boys.

When his term of office ended and Frederick W. Pitkin became governor, Routt moved to the new camp and went to work full time in the Morning Star. Things began to look favorable, but

Colorado's last territorial governor and first state governor, John L. Routt, spent all of his free time mining in Leadville. *Photo Source: Colorado Historical Society.*

nothing in the form of paydirt appeared. "You know," he later explained, "a miner will never quit until he has put in 'a last shot' and I followed that rule. One day," in April of 1879, "we broke into the 'blanket' of ore and my troubles were over." Early in 1880 the mine was said to be paying in the neighborhood of $70,000 a month; and one body of ore was assayed at 13,884 ounces of silver per ton, though that was not the average for all ore.

In April of 1880 the Morning Star Consolidated was organized with Routt as president. It included the Morning Star, Waterloo, Halfway House, Forsaken, Buckeye Belle, Anchor, and Carrolton claims; twenty-six acres in all. Routt and his two early partners, George C. Corning, Colorado state treasurer, and Joseph W. Watson, who managed the Morning Star in the early years, all became rich men. Eventually they sold out for one million dollars, and it is said that the governor's share was over six hundred thousand. Later he invested in the boom at Creede, Colorado, and added to his already considerable fortune.

George B. Robinson grew up in Kalamazoo, Michigan, and lived the quiet, acceptable life of a successful businessman and banker until his twenty-ninth year. At twenty-nine Robinson, for some unexplained reason, closed out his Michigan enterprises and sailed for Europe. He spent the bulk of 1877 traveling on "the continent," and shortly after his return to Michigan decided to visit the West Coast. He purchased a ticket to San Francisco. West of Omaha the Union Pacific ran into a furious snowstorm and in a few hours the train was snowbound. Robinson wandered about, as did the other passengers, visiting and biding their time until they were under way again. He heard a lot of talk of Denver, and possibly the newly formed town of Leadville. He decided to have a look, and when the train finally made it into Cheyenne, Robinson caught the southbound for Denver.

Little of note was happening in Denver; all the talk was of Leadville, so he bought a ticket for the Cloud City. Several storms and three days later he alighted in the roaring camp of Leadville. He looked the area over for two or three days and decided to invest his small amount of capital in a general store located at Pine and Chestnut. He was a success from the very beginning. "Within a year after locating here [Leadville] Mr. Robinson was carrying the largest general assortment of groceries in the city, and had more freight teams on the road than any merchant in Colorado." He

broadened his scope by erecting a business block on Chestnut Street that at one time was returning $7,000 per month in rentals.

Robinson, like everyone else in Leadville with capital, invested in mining. During the winter of 1878 and 1879 he started grubstaking prospectors and picked a couple of winners. The weather began to break in the spring of 1879 and Charles Jones and John Y. Sheddon made a deal with Robinson that he would get one-half of all they discovered in return for supplies. The pair set out for the newly developed Ten Mile Region, about thirteen miles north of Leadville. They chose a "lime ledge" and located the Undine and Seventy Eight. "At a depth of about thirty feet, mineral from two to three feet thick was found." In the following months the Checkmate, Rhone, Big Giant, Little Giant, Wheel of Fortune, Smuggler, and others were added until a total of ten major properties came under Robinson's control. During the course of events he bought out both of his partners and developed what came to be called the Robinson Group. Around the mines grew up the town of Robinson; named, supported, and founded by George B. Robinson. "He built a large hotel and other buildings, made arrangements to establish a bank, and erected a large smelter."

Success in politics added another feather to the Robinson bonnet, when in November of 1880 the midas of Ten Mile Creek was elected lieutenant-governor of Colorado. Still, even the most successful have their problems, and life in and around Leadville in the eighties was beset with problems even for a lieutenant-governor. Captain J. W. Jacque, competitor in the Ten Mile District, contested Robinson's ownership of the Smuggler. It was rumored that Captain Jacque planned to take over the mine by force if necessary. Robinson stationed guards near the portal of the mine and at various strategic locations about the property. On the evening of November 25, 1880, ironically Thanksgiving Day, he and other members of his staff were looking the property over, and Robinson decided to check on the guard at the portal. It had been suggested the guard was either not at his post or was not doing the job properly. The guard, an Irish lad named Pat Gillian, was stationed inside the portal behind a large, locked wooden door, on duty as he was supposed to be. When Robinson approached the door and, according to some, rattled the chain on the door (others said he called out), Gillian shouted, "Who's there?" Robinson, satisfied, turned to leave, either saying nothing, or speaking so softly that Gillian, only feet away, but behind the door,

GUARDING THE MINE.

From Frank *Leslie's Illustrated Newspaper*, April 26, 1879. *Photo Source: Author's Collection.*

failed to hear him. Gillian, fearing an attack, fired through the door. The bullet hit a nail, driving itself and several pieces of the nail into Robinson's midsection.

Robinson was taken to the hotel where he lingered until the morning of the twenty-seventh when he quietly breathed his last. Before dying, he asked that Gillian be spared, since "he was simply doing his duty when he shot."

At thirty-two, George B. Robinson, promising young businessman and politician, died, the result of one of the West's most foolhardy, wasteful, but exotic practices — claim jumping.

The successes of Wood and Stevens, the Gallagher brothers, Governor Routt, Robinson, Hallock and his partner, Captain Cooper, and a host of others excited the imagination of the world. In 1879 and during the early 1880s, a rash of guide books were published that told the Leadville pilgrim what he would need to survive climate and altitude, and how to find, claim, and work a silver mine. No two guides agreed and none of them were very accurate, due in part, surely, to the fact that few of the authors had done any of the things they were describing. Some claimed the altitude was sure death for all but the healthiest, others recommended the clean bracing air for those with consumption and other respiratory ailments. The equipment they suggested was equally contradictory. The following is as good a sample as any. It is from a guide, ostentatiously titled, *The Silver Fields, Geographical and Historical Sketch of Leadville, Colorado; With Information Concerning the Mines of Colorado and the Mineral Springs at Manitou.* Since it was published in Colorado Springs, Colorado, and written by a physician,

C. E. Edwords, and the Manitou health spa was only ten miles away, it was only fitting to put in a plug for local business, though Manitou surely had no place in a book about the "Silver Fields."

Edwords encouraged the would-be miner "Go to the nearest outfitting point and purchase the following 'outfit'."

1 coffeepot	1 camp knife
1 frying pan	1 bake oven
1 bread pan	1 iron coffee mill
3 tin plates	1 knife and fork
1 tin cup	1 8 lb. breaking hammer
1 tracing pick	1 long handled shovel
2 tablespoons	3 double blankets
1 poncho or rubber blanket	1 good suit of overalls
1 good suit of clothes	1 pair of heavy boots
1 mule or burro	3 steel drills, 18, 26, and 36 inch
1 pair of shoes	
1 6 lb. striking hammer	1 pole pick
4 steel gads, 4 inches long	Powder and fuze

The good doctor forgot to mention that it might be a good idea to get some instruction on how to use the mining equipment, especially the powder and fuze.

Another writer of the period suggested three men work together. The cost of the trio for a two-month "prospecting tour" would cost less than one hundred dollars. "Many of the most valuable mines were discovered on a less expenditure than that." He failed to mention the costs involved if they made a strike, but we'll continue to assume, as did the early prospector, that once you hit it your troubles were over. The less than one hundred dollar investment with a chance at untold millions attracted hundreds and, deserved or not, Leadville had a reputation for being the "poor man's camp." Possibly it was part promotion, but it was also a matter of record that the soft carbonates of the Leadville mines could be worked with a limited amount of labor and money. And everyone seemed to arrive with more than their share of optimism. Those who came to find a mine seemed more than willing to work and endure temporary hardships. One miner, digging with great gusto, remarked that he was "going for carbonates or China."

The first step in getting rich was locating some likely looking site. Very little advice was given for the would-be millionaire. None of the guides suggested a method of search, or where to search, or what to search for, or most important, how to tell a find when you had one. That information was usually available, along with a lot of

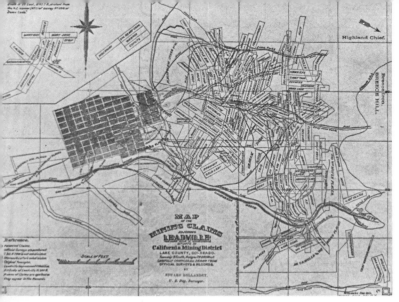

Map of Leadville mines in 1879. *Photo Source: Author's Collection.*

misinformation, from an old-timer; and an old-timer seems to have been anyone who got there before you. But assuming the advice was sound, or your luck was good, and you found what appeared to be paydirt, the next job was staking a claim. Ayers in his guide suggested the argonaut use three-inch-wide stakes and begin by setting one upright in each of the four corners. The law required six stakes — one at each corner and one near the middle of the lateral sides. The discoverer's name, "John Smith lode," and the corner designation, "corner no. 1," should be on each corner stake.

Now, once staked out, the claim is ready to work. Three men working could trade off, one digging, one working the windlass, and one resting. If four were employed, the fourth member cut timber. The average recommended size of shaft was four feet by six feet, and three men working could sink a shaft at from three to five feet per day, timbering as they progressed. "There being every indication that wealth is just beneath their picks," they then built a head frame or "gallows" and hung or fixed a pulley at the top and another at ground level. A rope, later cable, was run through the pulleys and attached to the ore bucket. Then a "mule is hired" to pull the other end of the rope. The system was called a whip. By

Map of Leadville mines in 1901. *Photo Source: Author's Collection.*

using the same hoisting system, but adding a large revolving drum so the mule could travel in a circle, rolling the rope on the drum, the miners had a horse or mule whim. Riding up and down via the bucket was an adventure in itself. Ernest Ingersol told the story of an eastern professor, a student of scientific mining, who was descending the shaft alone in the bucket, the picture of dignity and composure as he disappeared into the blackness below. Suddenly great shouting and frantic pleas to stop the bucket boiled up out of the black abyss. "The engine was quickly stopped."

Those on top called down asking what happened. "I'm hung up by my coattail on a nail," called the professor faintly, from about a hundred feet below. "Hoist the bucket and scrape me off again."

After "making contact," as it was called, the next item of business was a trip to the assayers. An assay would cost between a dollar-and-a-half and five dollars, and would take anywhere from two hours to a day. It was said that Leadville assayers, or at least some of them, did not like to disappoint a customer. On one occasion a fellow took a piece of a broken grindstone to a local assayer and had it tested. It ran over a hundred ounces of silver to the ton. Assay information was presented in ounces per ton for gold and silver, percentages for lead and copper, which was all that was usually tested for. Hence, if an assay came back as the one below, it was clear to the man in the know that the test

ag	au	pb	cu
283	4	56	none

sample ran 283 ounces of silver to the ton, 4 ounces of gold per ton, was fifty-six percent lead, which would mean 1,120 pounds of lead per ton, and that he would not be shipping any copper. The above would be a rich man's assay, or one that could make a man rich. With the assay in hand, proof that he need not look elsewhere, the next very important step was to have the claim surveyed and recorded. Once that was done the miner owned his claim. In the survey process he could change the boundaries, though not the size, of his original claim. A claim was 1,500-by-300 feet. If the long side was east and west and the vein ran north and south, he would simply turn it one-quarter and survey the long side with the general direction of the find. He was required by law to survey so the "discovery shaft" was 150 feet from either side. If some other poor devil happened to be in the road and had not had his claim surveyed and recorded, the first claimant could

simply survey him in. It seemed unfair, but it was based on a very basic economic law; first come, first served. The next man, though, had the option of imposing his will on the next and so on. It does not require much time to understand why Leadville became such a haven for lawyers.

Speed, of course, was of the essence. First in sinking a shaft, then in having it recorded, and finally in filing for a patent (deed). In the first case the one who filed first had first choice. The law was designed to keep the process moving. Within sixty days of staking a claim it was necessary to be down ten feet, have a cross cut below the surface ten feet long, or have dug a tunnel of similar length. Within ninety days a location certificate had to be filed in the court house.

A shaft house, *Harper's Weekly*, June 21, 1879. *Photo Source: Author's Collection.*

The system provided a seeker the opportunity to prospect undisturbed, but gave the legal advantages to the man who found mineral, which is as it should be. It was against the law to file a claim without finding something, but, of course, there were those who attempted to file first, then search. Generally, though, the game was played fairly in the early stages. It was only when miners could afford lawyers that the courts got busy.

The cost of developing a mine was such that a number of prospectors made a living just locating mines and selling them to those who had the money to develop the property. It was said that while Leadville's reputation was built on the production of its mines, "half the good mines in the camp [were] comparitively idle while their owners [were] trying to sell to richer neighbors or to Eastern speculators." One miner was down 135 feet and things looked good. Some money walked up and asked the owner if he would sell a half interest. The owner offered them half for $10,000, if they would close the deal before five o'clock. "At half past four, rich ore was struck." At five thirty the men returned to close the deal. The owner showed them the time and calmly informed them, "The price of a half interest in this mine now, gentlemen, is sixty thousand dollars."

It would seem that with all the work filing and surveying mining property, the one thing that could not happen was to lose a mine, and yet one of the most persistent fables of the American West is the *Lost Mine*. Leadville had her share of hidden, misplaced, or simply lost treasure troves, a few that possibly deserve mention here.

The oldest story of a lost mine dates back to those initial discoveries in the Cache Creek area in the early 1860s. A group of seekers coming over from the Gunnison country in 1860 happened on a real bonanza above Cache Creek in what came to be called Lost Canyon. They worked the mine for a short time in the fall of 1860, then again with great success the following summer. In the summer of 1862 they went back to their diggings, searched, but could not find the vein. There were those who claimed to have found the old vein, but the finds were never confirmed. A score of years, more or less, passed when one night a drunk prospector bought drinks for everyone in a saloon in Granite and proclaimed that he had found the lost mine. As proof he exhibited a "fistful of free gold." He promised to take his cronies to the mine, but first went on a week-long drunk. At the end of the week he could not remember how to get to the mine. The Lost Canyon treasure mine remains lost.

In 1878 a man arrived at the smelter works of Berdell and Witherell with a pack full of high grade gold ore. He wintered in Leadville, quietly, never giving any indication where he came from or where he got the gold. In the spring he quietly left town. Later that summer his body was discovered near the head of Lake Fork by Frank Brown, manager of the Farwell Consolidated Mining Company. He was found in a bank of melting snow, and it was assumed a snowslide caught him. Several went out in search of the mine and tramped the hills west of Leadville for years, but never located anything.

One of the most intriguing of lost mine stories was told by H. L. Denner. It was 1882 and Denner had a string of jacks and was hauling ore from the Continental Chief located high above timberline in the boulder-strewn, upper end of Iowa Gulch. One day a man stopped him and asked if he would haul some ore down from

Weston Pass. Denner agreed and a few days later set out, the man having told him to just follow the main trail and he would be met. All went according to plan, except that when Denner met the man he was requested to get aboard one of the jacks and was blindfolded. A second man joined them and the trio plodded their way up a twisting trail. About an hour later they reached the mine, and Denner was led into a tunnel where the blindfold was removed. The jacks were loaded, the blindfold replaced, and he was then led down to the main trail, blindfold removed, and he and the stranger who employed him went to town with the ore. A few days later Denner was paid, plus a bonus. He repeated the routine several times, always the same way. His questions were rebuffed, though he learned the two men owned the mine and worked two other men.

One day Denner was met on the main trail by the stranger, and it became immediately clear that something was amiss. The man was curt, more tense than usual and continually prodded Denner to hurry. The jacks were loaded as usual, but the other member of the team never showed up. Denner heard the stranger tell the two workers that they were through; that it was time to leave. They, like Denner, were blindfolded and the foursome started for town. When one of the laborers asked where "Jim" was, the stranger informed him that he had gone to town the night before.

When they got to town the stranger paid the men off and saw them on the train, bound for Chicago. He then accompanied Denner to the smelter, where he paid Denner double for the trip. Denner never saw the man again. After some thought he decided something was amiss and set out to find the mine, thinking it would be little trouble to follow the jacks' tracks. As he suspected, the trail was easy to follow until he struck a stretch of granite. The jacks' trail disappeared and he was never able to find it, even though he tried on several occasions. What happened to the lost mine and miners of Weston Pass?

The Homestake region was all but forgotten during the Leadville boom. One lonely prospector, scorning the frantic search for silver east of town, went west into the rugged region below the snow-covered crest of Homestake Peak. There, working and living alone, he discovered what is said to have been a fabulously rich vein of native gold. So rich it was said that "he could pick out strings and threads of it with his fingers." He found "lumps and nuggets as large as peas." He realized he needed help in developing the mine and made plans to return to civilization. First he pulled the timbering out of the mine, set off a large blast in the mouth of the tunnel, caving it in, and then camouflaged the entrance and surrounding area. He then set out for Denver where he became ill and, in the presence of a fellow prospector, died. Before dying he gave directions to the mine and bequeathed it to his nurse, the prospector.

Was there really such a mine or was it the dying dream of an old prospector? The friend set out for the Homestake District and spent years looking for the lost gold mine. He claimed he found several landmarks, but never was able to make the big find, and over the years no one has claimed to have located the lost mine beneath Homestake Peak.

The South Paw Mine might be part and parcel of several stories, for everyone seems to locate and lose this mine, or one like it. It was in the early 1880s when Eric Jones roared into camp and told his partners, John Anson and Heon Hastings, that he had made a big find in a gulch in the vicinity of Mount Elbert. He had gone prospecting up Half Moon Gulch, and, growing desperate, used a method scorned by all but the few who have tried everything. He dropped matches every half mile or so and followed the direction they pointed. The matches led him up a "narrow" canyon. It opened after about three miles, into a "wide gorge enclosed on either side with aspen-covered hills." He noticed the ruins of an old prospect.

Some years before a man named Robert Jeffrey had located a claim in Lackawanna Gulch, south and west of Mount Elbert. He was a loner and arrogant and found himself in conflict with some of the freer swinging young bucks in the Twin Lakes region. After several run-ins he realized that one dark night, alone on the trail, they would surprise him and it would be all over. Jeffrey knew he must act in order to save himself. He disguised the mine and went home to Missouri where, planning his return, he died leaving only a vague description and a crude map to his mine. Years later Jeffrey's nephew tried to locate the claim using his uncle's map, but was unsuccessful. Don Griswold, Leadville historian, suggests that it was never lost, simply located again and refiled on. Since Jeffrey had not worked the claim because of his death, it was deemed abandoned and was eventually relocated as the Miller Lode. But was it? Did Eric Jones using his matches stumble onto the lost mine of Lackawanna Gulch, or another unnamed lost or forgotten treasure?

Jones, of course, unaware of Jeffrey's earlier experience, set out with his friends for the South Paw Mine, the name a compliment to his own left-handedness. Jones led the way as they climbed up the narrow canyon. Suddenly a small rockslide broke loose and gravel and dirt rolled down on top of Jones. One small rock hit him on the head, knocking him from his horse, unconscious. He came to shortly, but knew nothing of his comrades, where he was, or the lost mine. He never regained his memory, and the lost mine was lost again.

Some years later the family of Henry Gaw, a local brewer, was sitting around the fire, while a guest told them a strange story about a lost mine in Half Moon Gulch. The mine was called the Giddy Betsy and appeared to have been located on the north slopes of Mount Elbert. According to the visitor, an old prospector used to visit Oro City, buy his provisions, pay gold for them, then disappear into Half Moon Gulch. He would not be seen again for months. Several times he was followed, but always managed to give his followers the slip. He spent his winters in Denver "in the most regal manner," and was said to have sent considerable wealth to his home someplace in the east. On one occasion, because of illness, he returned home, "his wallet snugly stowed away in his long and abundant hair." He was home only a short time when his health apparently improved and he decided to return to the mountains. At almost the moment of departure he fell ill again and died. It happened suddenly, the result it would seem of overeating, but before his last breath he explained he had a "marvelously rich mine" called the Giddy Betsy, and he managed to draw a primitive map of the area and dictated a letter detailing the route to the mine.

That summer his eldest son and the local minister set out to find the mine. They searched "those sacred hillsides, seeking the retiring but Giddy Betsy." They came every summer for a number of years, but never located the mine. Some years later some smelter hands claimed to have located the out buildings, but Giddy Betsy escaped them, too. It was one of those same smelter hands who, enjoying the Gaw hospitality, told the story, and Henry Gaw wrote it down as he later recalled it.

Years later a mine called the Mount Champion was opened west of Mount Elbert and the gold ore found there was of the same nature as that from the Giddy Betsy. The answer that seems to suggest itself is that the lost mine of Lackawanna Gulch, the South Paw, the Giddy Betsy, and the lost mine of Lost Gulch were either the same mine, or more probably dipped into the same mineral formation as that developed by the owners of the Mount Champion.

At left, the Harrison Reduction Works; at right, August R. Meyer's sampling works—shortly after they opened for business. *Photo Source:Colorado Historical Society.*

IV

The Magic City

Pine trees stood thick in the morning sun on the site that became the greatest silver camp in the American West. Its beginnings were unpretentious. Who was Leadville's first citizen and when did he arrive? One, who himself claimed to be the first arrival, was George Albert Harris. Harris climbed over Mosquito Pass and spent the night of May 7, 1877, behind a log. "He found a few piles of brush, a quantity of stumps and half burned trees, but not a human being." Harris could very well have been the first resident of the city, and his log the first residence, but the man most responsible for establishing the first retail establishment in Leadville, and usually considered the town's first citizen, was an unassuming merchant from Granite, Colorado, named Charles Mater.

Mater, a young Prussian immigrant of seventeen, landed in New York in 1853. He worked his way west in 1860 riding the heels of the Colorado rush, finally settling in 1867 in Granite where he built a general store that did a modest business with local miners and ranchers. In June of 1877 he moved a portion of his stock to the area Tabor called Slabtown, which was just north of the original town of Oro on the rise behind the gulch. There he built a twenty-by-thirty foot log building and established the first mercantile house in town.

The rough trail in front of his store was soon pounded into a road that became Chestnut Street, the new town's first and busiest thoroughfare. Harris, in the meantime, was not spending all of his time behind his log. He began work June 15, 1877, on a structure that was to become the camp's first hotel. He cut and stripped logs, notched them, placed them, and caulked the walls. It was twelve-by-fifteen feet, a story and one-half high, and slept eight to ten men. The number of sleepers probably varied with the occupants' size, how well they knew each other, and how recently they had had a bath.

Shortly after Mater and Harris arrived, H. A. W. Tabor made an investment in the new city. He had returned to California Gulch in 1868 after six years in the South Park camp of Buckskin. In 1877 Tabor had one store up California Gulch at New Oro and another in Malta serving the smelter trade in that area. He robbed his Oro store of supplies and took them to the new town site and set up business just up the street from

Charles Mater, Leadville's first shopkeeper. *Photo Source: Author's Collection.*

Mater. Until Tabor arrived, Mater's place of business was the focal point for the community, but Tabor soon passed his rival since he had a commodity that everyone was interested in. Tabor, the Oro City postmaster, opened a branch office in his new store. Mater's business continued good, but he did not have the crowd standing around, waiting, that Tabor mustered when the mail was due in. By March of 1878 Tabor had scratched out his Oro City and Malta stores on his letterhead, suggesting he had bet his money on the success of the new community.

Another area businessman, William "Billy" Nye, came from Malta. He was good at sizing up situations and spotting future potential. Nye had done well in Malta with what appears to have been the first establishment in that community where a man might wet his whistle. He looked the new camp over and decided food and lodging were sufficient in the community, but "throat nectar" was sadly lacking. Within a few weeks of Tabor's opening, Billy Nye's Saloon opened its doors. Later, remodeled and expanded, it was known as the Bon Ton Billiard Hall.

Next in the line seems to have been Gilbart's Wagon Shop or Miller and Geege's Drug Store, though the order of events gets progressively more confused. Loomis, writing and interviewing in Leadville in 1879, says "Upon the first of August, 1877, there were six buildings upon the present site of Leadville." They probably consisted of Tabor and Mater's stores; the City Hotel, as Harris' log accommodation was dubbed; Jay Miller and George E. Geege's drug store; Gilbart's Wagon Shop; and August R. Meyer's Sampling Works.

As agent for the St. Louis Smelting and Refining Company, August R. Meyer had been keeping his employer, Edwin Harrison, informed about the progress in the new "Carbonate Camp," and early in 1877, backed by Missouri capital, Meyer began building his sampling works. It was this event more than any other that encouraged the building and moving of such local merchants as Tabor, Mater and Nye, and resulted in the birth of Leadville some six months later.

The need for an adequate smelter was great and the clamor loud, so great and so loud in fact, that during June of 1877 the president of the St. Louis Smelting and Refining Company, Edwin Harrison, came to see the area for himself. Harrison was a mining man and builder par excellence. He checked the area over, set up offices on the corner of Chestnut and what was later Harrison Avenue, named in his honor, and "A month later the Saint Louis Smelting and Refining Co. began to erect a smelter."

Harrison surveyed the area and decided his first big problem was getting the ore from the mines to the smelter. So far, the only effective methods were jack trains in the mountains and ox carts in the flat, open country of which there was precious little. He initiated the first extensive road building in Lake County in the summer of 1877. Roads were built or improved into California Gulch and up Stray Horse Gulch to the Gallagher's holdings and Breece's Iron mine. He spent a reported $25,000 to improve the road over Weston Pass to link his holdings in Alma with those in Leadville. Some sources claim he built the road over Mosquito Pass, but there was only a footpath over Mosquito until 1879, when a group formed the Mosquito Pass Toll Road Company and built the first real road over the 13,180-foot ridge. There are stories, no doubt true, of intrepid pilgrims who used the Mosquito Pass route for wagons before 1879, but it was not recommended and was seldom used twice by the same person.

Other early road builders were the Long brothers, Jacob and John, and their partner, Charles Derry. They built out of necessity since their early find, the J. D. Dana in Iowa Gulch, was isolated from the rest of the world. To get their ore out in paying quantities a road was imperative. The first ore that moved out of the J. D. Dana went to Alma via jack train on October 26, 1876. Jacob Long took the train and two tons of ore over Mosquito Pass to one of the town's two small smelting operations. The older smelter, built in 1873, was owned by the Boston and Colorado Smelting Company of Black Hawk. It is likely that the ore went to the new smelter in town, the result of several months' work on the part of August R. Meyer. After completion of the smelting works, Meyer traveled the area in search of good ore, signing contracts with area producers. His company gave special rates to new customers, and it appears that while visiting the California Gulch area he made a deal with Charles Derry and the two Long brothers.

When Long arrived with the ore, he reportedly told the assayer that all of it was found within five feet of the surface. The ore assayed out at over 160 ounces of silver and almost 1,000 pounds of lead per ton. Long wasted no time in getting home. He and his partners quickly set to work building a road into California Gulch so they could make use of wagons instead of the more costly and more difficult jack trains. They spent several months and close to $7,500 building the road.

Road building in those early days was a difficult, slow process. Every stump was a project, every stream an obstacle. Roads were built by men, mules, and muscle. The two most effective tools for road building in the mountains were horse- or mule-drawn "road scrapers" and dynamite. It has been said that barbed wire tamed the West, but it was dynamite that tamed the mountains, if in fact they have been tamed. Without it, mining, road building, and the railroads would have been impossible ventures for a young, relatively unpopulated country like the United States.

By 1878 roads, many in name only, linked Leadville to Stray Horse, California, and Iowa gulches. There was a road running along the bank of the Arkansas down to Granite and Cache Creek. Others went up to Twin Lakes, and over Weston and Trout Creek passes. One road, one of the oldest in the area, traveled the length of California Gulch west of Old Oro, crossed the Arkansas Valley, and eventually wound its way up to the mines at the foot of Mount Massive in Colorado Gulch.

As the community continued to grow with something approaching leaps and bounds, it became clear to all that they had to organize a city government and incorporate. Already disputes over rights-of-way, ownership of land, the layout of the town, and a number of other problems were being referred to miners' meetings, which were equipped to handle neither the volume nor the complexity of the problems. A proper city government with paid civil servants was the only answer.

A meeting of some of the town's dignitaries was called for the evening of January 14, 1878. They met in "Gilbert's [or Gilbart] little wagon shop, on the present corner of Pine and Chestnut Streets, where Robinson's block now stands." The minutes of the meeting, if minutes were kept, have been lost; hence, we do not know the names of all who attended, but most sources agree that there were eighteen. Among those said to have attended were August R. Meyer, Charles Mater, W. H. Bradt, Gilbart, J. C. Cramer, and Nelson Hallock. The first item of business was a proper name for the new camp, though in fact it had been named in a somewhat accidental manner over six months before in the Henderson home in Oro City.

George L. Henderson, sometimes postmaster and sometimes miner and occasional business partner of H. A. W. Tabor's, met with some

One of the earliest photos of Leadville, probably taken early in the spring of 1878. Note the remains of Old Oro in the lower left. *Photo Source: Colorado Historical Society.*

friends in the "fireplace" room of the Henderson cabin. Henderson, Miss Lottie Williams, an Oro City schoolmarm, August R. Meyer and Alvinus B. Wood made up the group. Their purpose was to select a name for the new community that had more dignity and a greater air of permanence than "Slabtown," a name they might submit with their request for a post office.

Some years later August R. Meyer recalled the meeting and claimed four names were seriously considered, "Carbonate, Cerrusite, Meyer and Leadville — and the latter was finally selected." Mr. Wood had suggested Lead City, but it was agreed that it could be confused with "a town of the same name in the Black Hills," and Leadville was accepted as a compromise.

The date of this initial meeting seems lost, but probably was sometime in April or May of 1877 since the Postal Department replied to the request on June 11, 1877, referring to "the application for a new post office at Leadville, County of Lake, State of Colorado." Henderson completed the form July 2, 1877, and signed it. The official designation was made July 16, 1877, with George L. Henderson as postmaster at Leadville, Colorado.

Naming the post office did not necessarily name the town, but by the fall of 1877 the name was in general use throughout Colorado. When the city framers met in January of 1878 they had either to approve "Leadville" or come up with an acceptable substitute. The meeting started with various substitutes.

Meyer apparently suggested "Agassiz," the famous Swiss naturalist, who in large measure was responsible for the development of the natural sciences in the United States. It is possible that Meyer on one occasion or other studied under him at Harvard. The Swiss educator was popular throughout the country and especially in the East. Meyer's suggestion was supported by Bradt, Gilbart, and others, but failed. Meyer then suggested "Harrison" in honor of Edwin Harrison, the president of St. Louis Smelting and Refining Company; but the suggestion failed, possibly because Harrison himself killed the idea if he was at the meeting. Meyer yielded the floor to Charles Mater, who suggested "Carbonateville," but it, too, failed. Then Joseph C. Cramer apparently suggested they stick with Leadville. It was seconded by Nelson Hallock and was approved unanimously. Next the group petitioned Governor Routt to allow them to establish a recognized city.

The necessary legal work was accomplished and Governor Routt issued a proclamation for a special election to be held Tuesday, February 12, 1878. Excitement filled the small community on that cold, grey day in February. The voting was heavy if we can judge from the scanty accounts of the election. H. A. W. Tabor was elected mayor. Clerk and recorder was Mr. C. E. Anderson. The governor's proclamation called for four trustees; but, according to the minutes of the city ordinances, there was a tie between Frank Gay and W. C. Norman, and rather than have a run-off election it was decided to leave the post vacant until the first regular city election, which was to be held in April. Those elected to trusteeships were Charles Mater, the town's first merchant; William Nye, the town's first barkeep; and Joseph C. Cramer, who shortly became part of a trio who supplied Leadville's water. T. H. Harrison was appointed town marshall; T. J. Campbell was the town's first judge; and Mr. A. K. Updegraff, late of Oro City and points east, became city attorney.

Those three sons of Erin, John, Charles, and Patrick Gallagher, who came to the area in the fall of 1876 to seek their fortunes, while neither councilmen nor commissioners, "did right well," as the saying went. By the winter of '77-'78 they had made a small fortune out of the Camp Bird and their other holdings.

In those days it was "the Shanty Irish," the "bog-trottin' Irish," the "no-good Irish," and a good deal worse. It was an uphill fight the Irish had for social acceptability, as any "Mick" of the times could have told you. They were hard working people and those who achieved a modest success coped with it, but the Gallagher's success was of the heady variety of considerable coin. Great wealth, especially for people who previously had nothing more than the clothes on their backs and a couple coppers in their shoe, was more than they were ready to handle.

When the Gallagher wealth began rolling in, the Patrick Gallaghers decided to move from their home near Adelaide Park. The *Leadville Daily Chronicle* spoke with Mrs. Patrick Gallagher. "Och," she said, "Pat isn't Irish at all. He is a Inglishman, but comin' over to Ameriky in a shteamer he got in wid a lot o' Irish, and got their damned brogue; and faith, he can't git over it." When she was asked her plans about moving she exclaimed, "Shure, the Irish up the gulch here are not fit for we'uns to assosheat wid. We are goin' to move down to Leadville and put up a brick house in the latest style, and, be Jasus, we will have an elbow on it."

Another story the *Leadville Daily Chronicle* mentioned about Pat gives some idea, not so much of Pat's ignorance, but of the town's delight in exposing it. First, though, a couple terms might be explained. Porphyry and limestone were common ways of denoting depth and levels of work. Hence, if you were in porphyry, you were in one of the upper levels of mineralization. Limestone put you in the mineralized zone. The story: "How is it, Pat? I hear you are in litigation?"

"What is it yees sez?" asked Pat. "In litigation? No, be gorrah, we are in porphyry, ferninst the limestone!"

During the winter of '77-'78 the Gallaghers sold their property to the St. Louis Smelting and Refining Company for $225,000. Sometime during the next two years they all left the Arkansas Valley to tour the world. Little is known of them or what eventually happened to them, though it is said, "one went to Paris and the others to different parts of America." They traveled until their money ran out, lived the life of kings while it lasted, and seemingly had no regrets. Leadville had no regrets, either, nor time for any. The Gallagher adventure, for that surely was what it was, spread Leadville fever far and wide. It was one thing for a William H. Stevens or an August R. Meyer, trained professional men, to make money. It was quite another for three Irish immigrants, who knew nothing more about mining than how to dig, to get rich. Leadville was indeed "the poor man's camp."

A lot of things were advertised in relation to travel to Leadville. Speed, comfort, and cost were always mentioned, but no one ever claimed that "getting there is half the fun." The trip was costly, long, and punishing. The traveler was called upon at every hill, creek, and bog to get out and push. In summer he choked with heat and dust, and in winter he froze, figuratively for the most part; but there were occasions when stages broke down, were trapped in sudden storms and avalanches, and the passengers found themselves in danger of freezing to death.

The first stage line in the area was Spotswood and McClelland's. The pair had been in business in the high mountains since 1865 with their Denver and South Park Stage Line. In 1873 they linked up with the Colorado Springs area. In 1877 a mail contract to Leadville was offered by the federal government. Spotswood headed east to Washington and got the franchise. During the summer of 1877 Robert W. Spotswood and William McClelland joined forces and made the necessary plans and purchases to extend their Denver and South Park Stage Line over the hill to Leadville. Mosquito Pass was discussed but never used until it was improved in 1879. Weston

On Weston Pass, near the summit, one can still see the old corduroy sections of road. *Photo Source: Author's Collection.*

Pass was the most common route into Leadville from the east, though on occasions of extremely heavy snow, stages had to go farther south to Trout Creek Pass.

The new line used four-horse teams and Concord coaches. The coach carried mail and express and a dozen passengers inside and eight outside, more if they could find a place. The route ran from the terminus of Governor Evans' stalled railroad line in Morrison to Fairplay, then over Weston Pass. The line prospered from the first. It was said that Spotswood's way bills and express "alone" would "amount to over a thousand a day." The demands for space forced the owners to constantly expand. At the height of the staging era with three other lines serving Leadville, Spotswood and McClelland had two stages running each way on a daily basis. One single purchase by Spotswood and McClelland consisted of two hundred head of horses, twelve Concord coaches, and fifty sets of harness.

Other lines that served the area in the late 1870s were Wall and Witter, who used the same passes into Leadville as Spotswood and McClelland; Barlow and Sanderson, who reopened the route along the Arkansas River to Canon City, where they tied into the Kansas Pacific railway system via the Denver and Rio Grande.

Good roads served the new camp from the south and east, but a suitable route north to Denver via Georgetown was lacking. The good people of Georgetown were not willing to accept that

The traffic jam at the "end of track," as people reloaded themselves and possessions onto horse-drawn vehicles bound for Leadville in 1879. *Photo Source: Author's Collection.*

deficiency for long. They were not about to allow all of that Leadville business go through South Park or south by way of Pueblo.

Silas W. Nott, a Georgetown livery stable operator, envisioned a road that would go from Georgetown over Argentine Pass, down the Snake and up Ten Mile Canyon. Later the route was changed and a new road over Loveland Pass was planned. It was said to be 1,500 feet lower than the Argentine passage and would be the most direct route from Denver to Leadville.

Work began in February of 1879, and it was estimated that by working in the winter the road would cost three times as much but would be open for Leadville traffic the following spring. This route is the one generally followed by U. S. 40. It has always been one of the most difficult highways in Colorado, and Loveland Pass the highest year-round highway in the state. Still the promoters claimed the winters would be no problem and planned to use sleighs as soon as the amounts of snow made it possible.

In blinding blizzards and at sub-zero temperatures, two hundred men blasted a road over Loveland Pass, 11,992 feet above sea level, and in June of 1879 Mr. Nott's road was ready. At first, three stages left Leadville and Georgetown

weekly, but business boomed and daily service was instituted before the summer was over.

The route from Georgetown was sixty miles long and took about twelve hours to travel. Fare was ten dollars to Leadville, but because of the lesser demand, only seven dollars to Georgetown. Nott used six-team Concord coaches in the summer and sleighs in the winter, and the route did prove safer and easier than the slightly lower, more torturous Weston Pass route. The following year Nott sold out and moved to Glenwood. That same year the Denver and Rio Grande Railroad put the Leadville staging men out of business, but Nott's road continued to be used and improved.

Riding the stage to Leadville was a short-lived activity, beginning in 1877 and ending in 1880. But that activity was not short-lived for those who had the misfortune of making the trip. It was often said that freighters had the right-of-way over stages, because if a freighter rolled his rig down the side of a mountain, it was his responsibility to get the load back up to the road. Not so with passengers. "All the driver would have to do would be bury his load." Whatever the reason, the problem of slow-moving traffic on narrow mountain roads always plagued the stage drivers.

Tight quarters on a Leadville-bound stage. *Photo Source: Author's Collection.*

On extremely difficult areas where the dangers involved in passing were great, it was the stage driver's custom to unload his passengers, handle the empty rig, and then reload the passengers, who had trotted by the obstacle. Tongue-in-cheek the *Leadville Daily Chronicle* reported that the above method was to insure "there would be survivors to tell the tale."

One method, a bit hard to believe, was reportedly used to pass ore wagons and other slow-moving rigs and consisted of disgorging the passengers, giving them ropes to attach to the top of the stage, and then, with the passengers holding the coach upright, the driver would force his team and the stage around the problem on "two wheels." There is no question that passengers were responsible for helping get the stage to its destination, whatever the price. And, of course, runaways were always a problem. One driver, after being thrown from his stage and run over, strapped himself onto the box. Whatever his fate, he intended to share it with his coach.

One of Leadville's first stage line customers was that young fellow from Holland, John J. Vandemoer. It was early spring when he left Denver for Morrison by rail. As he gained altitude the

clock turned back. It was late winter when he got to Morrison, an hour's ride from the capital. In Morrison he boarded one of Spotswood and McClelland's stages and headed for Fairplay. Using "relays of horses" and traveling the rest of the day and through the night, they reached Fairplay about five the following morning. The stage went on, but Vandemoer elected to stay in Fairplay House and rest and eat.

The next day he boarded the morning stage for the final leg of the journey. They crossed Weston Pass where it was still midwinter. The snow lay about six feet deep and it was bone-chilling cold. On the Leadville side they encountered a group of traveling musicians who had "tumbled down from the road, wagon, horses and all." The whole jumbled mess was mired in deep snow about seventy-five feet below the road. The stage passengers and their driver helped the musicians get unscrambled, checked to see that no one was injured, and helped them to the road. They found one violin was broken but that was the total extent of the damage. The soft snow apparently cushioned their descent. The stage driver promised to see that help was sent; then the stage continued on its way. About three in the afternoon they arrived at the Arkansas River about seven miles below Leadville and followed the frozen stream's left bank until they reached the mouth of California Gulch, where they turned east up the gulch to the Magic City.

In October of 1877 Colorado was due to approve or disapprove a measure for women's suffrage. That bill occasioned a visit to yet unnamed Leadville by one of America's foremost suffragettes, Susan B. Anthony. It was in September when she reached the area and the air already had winter's chill in it; the leaves on the aspens were a bright yellow.

She spoke to the miners in Nye's Saloon since it was then the largest public or private building suitable for a meeting. Governor Routt was in town and "stood by her and spoke also in favor of woman suffrage." The boys in Nye's Saloon, like most men in the mountains, had to be introduced to Miss Anthony and she had to explain what suffrage was, and especially what women's suffrage was. It was a large crowd of willing listeners and generally sympathetic souls. In fact, "when they saw she was coughing from the tobacco smoke, they put out their pipes and made up for their sacrifice by more frequent drinks."

In twenty-four speaking engagements in the area's mining camps, Anthony was able to collect $165 in donations. It was reported that "Miss Anthony found this Colorado campaign the most trying she ever had experienced." The final insult came on October 2, 1877, when the Colorado Legislature voted down the bill for women's suffrage.*

The ladies' vote was not a factor in Leadville's first *regular* election, which was scheduled for April 3, 1878. Tabor was reelected mayor, but anger and uneasiness filled the sober-minded. It was felt that the election was manipulated by the "tough element" and most appointive offices were filled with the men they wanted. No "law abiding citizens could get a law breaker arrested," but good citizens got hauled in and fined the limit if they defended themselves against the lawless element. Harrison left his position as marshal. Some claimed the "tough element" drove him out of town. He was replaced by George O'Connor, a Tabor appointee, who was murdered before the month was out.

But it was 1878 and spring was coming. The passes were opening and newcomers were flooding the town's meager facilities. Business was booming, much to the delight of the merchants, and there was little time or inclination to consider the "tough element." Everybody, new or old, was too busy making money. One newcomer, a William Lovell, like others saw the opportunity to make a few dollars. Bill, as he was known, knew miners and miner's fare and decided the boys in camp would be willing to pay plenty for a change of diet after a winter of venison stew and bully beef. He bought a large number of over-age hens and retired roosters in South Park and with the first break in the weather headed over Mosquito Pass, his birds over his shoulder. The going was rough and the snow still lay deep on the north face and in the trees. He struggled to the top and was caught in a terrible storm. During the night the snow stopped and the frost crept in, and when morning came, bright, clear, and cold, Bill brushed the snow away from his flock, only to find them frozen solid.

Bill considered the prospects and made his decision. He cleaned and plucked the chickens, filled them with snow and headed down the west slope of the pass to Leadville. When he arrived in town he found he had guessed right. There was a ready market for his birds and he did well. Later, when the word got out, the boys began calling him Chicken Bill, and the handle stuck. Chicken Bill Lovell owns the distinction of being the first to introduce cold storage foods to Leadville, but he is seldom remembered for this notable achievement. He had other attributes more noteworthy, if not more notable.

Chicken Hill, the west slope of Carbonate Hill, was named for Chicken Bill, reportedly the first resident. *Photo Source: Pioneer's Museum.*

*April 12, 1893, the Colorado legislature approved an act which submitted the question to the electorate in the general election in November of 1894. It was approved by a vote of 35,798 to 29,451.

44

V

Mr. Fryer's Hill

North of the established mines of Iron, Breece and Carbonate hills lay an area that the experts claimed was barren. To this barren ground came George H. Fryer, who "had previously accumulated and squandered with profiligate recklessness two or three moderate fortunes."

Some years earlier Fryer had done some successful mining on the South Park side of the range and sold a claim on Mount Lincoln to investors in his native Philadelphia for $40,000. After a lengthy and expensive vacation in the east he returned in time for the Leadville boom. Some say he worked in a restaurant, or possibly managed one, in Leadville during the early months of 1878. Somehow he made the acquaintance of Chicken Bill Lovell. Maybe he bought Bill's "cold storage" chickens, though there is no historical evidence to support that. One version of their association was related by William Sweet, who claimed Chicken Bill was prospecting alone in an area north of the developed mining area and "lost his grip" at twenty-six feet and sold out to Fryer for a six weeks' grubstake. Others suggest that Fryer and Lovell prospected together.

Fryer was a bull-headed man, though kindly, and had little or no regard for experts, real or otherwise. Being the perverse man that he was, he decided there was silver in the small hills to the north of the boom area, regardless of what the experts claimed. He prospected, not with Chicken Bill, but with Josiah Eads, who was bought out by an old friend, John Borden, an easy-going likeable sort. Fryer "lived in a squatty little cabin on the side-hill," with a rough dirt floor. A "rough stone fireplace" stood in the corner and "was hardly fit to fry a rasher of bacon." He worked alone and quietly, hidden by the pines, and after

digging "a few yards below the surface," hit good ore.

The mine was called the New Discovery to spite the experts. Borden and Fryer filed the location on April 4, 1878, and a new world opened up. The small knoll, called Fryer Hill, became the richest piece of real estate in the world within a few short months.

Borden sold out soon after the discovery to a team of investor-prospectors, Foss, Bissell, and Hunter, who did well with this and other mines on Fryer Hill. Fryer held on a short time longer, but apparently decided he did not have the capital or will to develop the mine and sold his half to Jerome B. Chaffee for a reported $50,000. Fryer invested in other mines in the area and was said to have "made several fortunes since 1878, and knows how to enjoy them." He was always gruff and curt with men in authority and continued to have no use whatsoever for the experts. Still he was referred to as the "poor man's friend," and never failed to dig deep in his pockets for an old acquaintance down on his luck or "just inches" from the big strike.

In 1880 he moved to Denver where, in 1884, he died, the result of an overdose of morphine. The doctors were not sure, but suspected suicide. Fryer's wealth had dwindled, the result of lavish living and an expensive bride. His grip on life was loosened by progressively heavy drinking. Waking during the night in his hotel room at the Windsor, he appears to have fallen against a radiator and took the morphine "in the wild effort to either secure temporary or permanent rest. He was successful in securing the latter."

Lucky grubstakes did exist, and H. A. W. Tabor had the luckiest. Tabor, as already mentioned, moved stock from his Oro and Malta stores to Leadville and opened a third business that soon eclipsed the other two. He eventually moved all of his stock to Leadville, built a house in the Magic City, and became the town's first mayor and second postmaster. He located his fourth-class post office in a five-by-seven-foot corner of his store. As the camp grew Tabor found more of his time spent in postal work. He was paid by the government according to the amount of stamps he sold. In the early days, mail arrived once a day, and the mail clerks sorted all night to have it ready in the morning. There was no local delivery, everything was general delivery and each morning a long line formed outside the store. Positions at the head of the line are said to have sold for two to five dollars.

Tabor was a generous man and concerned with the welfare of town and citizen. In an effort to improve mail service he hired and paid out of his own pocket more mail clerks. It helped, but the problem was not really solved until the postal service built a regular first-class post office.

Earlier, when Tabor was a storekeeper and postmaster in Buckskin Joe, a man by the name of William Van Brooklyn came in one day while Horace was out. Augusta was tending the store, which was usually the case, since Tabor was a great one for visiting with the boys and gambling, both of which he was surprisingly good at. Van Brooklyn offered to swap his claim for board while he started an express line with "his two mules." Augusta remembered him as a fat man, and her description leaves little doubt that she found him distasteful, so she said, "No." Later he sold the claim for $100 to two prospectors, who took out $80,000. After that incident Tabor vowed to grubstake any who were interested and would dig. He recalled, "Every season I grubstaked men, and was out just that much at the end, for they never found anything."

One day in spring, Tabor remembered, "It was the 15th of April, 1878," two German immigrants walked into his store and asked for a grubstake. The pair are usually described as poor shoemakers whose knowledge of mining was nonexistent. Poor they were, but ignorant they were not.

The apparent leader of the two, August Rische, was born in Minden, Prussia, in 1833. He was nineteen when he came to the United States. After the Civil War he went west and located in Park County where he was employed off and on as a shoemaker. On September 27, 1872, Rische, in the company of W. L. Wilson, J. Marshall Paul, W. E. Musgrove, and George Freassle, stood on

August Rische. *Photo Source: Colorado Historical Society.*

the top of Mosquito Pass and gazed down on the Arkansas Valley. The first touches of autumn had turned the south slope aspens a light gold and the mixture of willows and aspens along the dozens of stream courses in their view ranged from a soft gold to a deep, rich red. Smoke curled up from a large camp of Utes in Tennessee Park. Almost beneath them, the village of Oro, not nearly as populous as the Ute village in Tennessee Park, crowded the upper end of California Gulch.

The group eased their way down the rocky, windswept path toward the tree-covered valley of Evans Gulch. Near timberline they were met by S. D. Breece, Lake County mining enthusiast and area booster, who escorted them to Oro City, giving as they went, his analysis of the bright future of mining in the area. He even took W. E. Musgrove on a side tour of his own Iron Mine on Breece Hill. That evening in Oro the group had a grand reception, and as Musgrove recalled years later, "Our money could buy nothing. Everything was ours without money and without price." The following day, September 28, the group, in accordance with their purpose for visiting Oro City, initiated a "goodly number" of members into the newly formed Oro City chapter of the Independent Order of Odd Fellows, number sixteen.

George Hook. *Photo Source: Colorado Historical Society.*

Two years later, in 1874, Rische crossed Mosquito Range again, this time to try his luck in California Gulch. Dill says he "engaged in mining, taking lessons from Charley Field, S. D. Newman, and William Pierce" in the Printer Boy. He worked several areas and learned the prospecting trade the hard way — out in the field with a pick and shovel. In 1877 an event took place that changed the course of his life. He had an old dog of which he was quite fond. During the winter of '77-'78 he was prospecting with George Freassle, his old lodge buddy, when George in a fit of anger kicked Rische's dog. A violent argument ensued and Rische pulled out. The following spring he formed a partnership with another German immigrant, a local shoemaker named George Hook. Born in Baden, Hook came to America with his parents when he was fourteen. He grew up in the Pittsburgh area and went west, "locating near Denver in 1876." When the mining boom in Leadville began to send its tremors down out of the hills, Hook joined the happy band of get-it-while-it-lasts miners who entered the mountains in 1877. No one knows how Hook and Rische happened to meet, but their backgrounds, two German shoemakers, was such that a meeting was almost inevitable in the still small mining camp. It was Rische who knew the mining trade

and Hook who had made the acquaintance of Mayor Tabor.

On Monday morning, April 15, 1878, Tabor was just opening his store when the two German immigrants walked in. In halting English they explained their plan to him and asked for a grubstake. Their plan had nothing more to recommend it than the dozens of others Tabor had heard. Their knowledge of mining was no better than most, though a good deal better than some. Still Tabor made it a habit, as already stated, of helping any who were willing to dig, so he outfitted the two with picks and shovels, enough food for a week or so, and a jug of whiskey.

After Fryer's New Discovery, the hot spot in the camp was Fryer Hill and the flanking gulches, Evans to the north and Little Stray Horse to the south. The pair set out immediately for Fryer's Hill, and the story goes that they stopped under a tree to have a drink from their jug and decided it was as good a spot as any, especially since it was in the shade. The story, wherever it came from, is good color, but hardly accurate. People who have spent a winter in Leadville know that no one is looking for shade in mid-April. George Hook denied the story later, and claimed they knew where they were going and what they were doing. He explained they were trying to latch onto the same ore body, or off-shoot, of the Fryer discovery. They set up shop almost next door; just a few hundred feet north of the New Discovery.

They worked all week on their prospect, and when their grub ran low they went into town for a second grubstake. The grubstake cost Tabor about seventeen dollars, and after the first he was good for a second, and a third. They gave him the particulars of their prospecting and noted that it looked good, though they had not hit anything yet. Nothing they said seems to have indicated that this was going to be anything more than just another "dry hole" for Tabor.

It must have been about the time of the second grubstake that the pair recorded their claim, for they surely were down the required ten feet and had set out their claim stakes. They wanted to name it the Pittsburgh in honor of Hook's hometown, but there already was a Pittsburg claim to the south of them, so they settled on Little Pittsburg (both spelled without the "h"), and filed.

There were many in the camp who were convinced Fryer's discovery was a freak and the area generally would never produce; Tabor himself had doubts. He recalled that "all who saw them made sport of their foolishness in prospecting there.

Little Pittsburg, Summer, 1878. *Photo Source: Author's Collection.*

But the two Germans kept stubbornly at work and, at a depth of only twenty-seven feet, struck carbonate ore that ran 200 ounces of silver to the ton. The date was May fifteenth, a Wednesday, 1878." Tabor, when he heard the news, put Augusta and Maxcy in charge of the store and took the day off to investigate the mine. Tabor's share, according to the agreement of the grub-stake, was one-third interest. The three worked the mine and on the tenth of June shipped their first ore. All their hopes were realized. They had a bonanza on their hands. The camp went wild and Fryer Hill was crawling with prospectors. During the summer of 1878 the mine continued to produce at fantastic rates.

By the end of the summer they were able to declare a $10,000 dividend for each. In September, Hook, who had never been enamored of Leadville's climate, sold out to his partners before winter set in. He received $90,000 for his share and took a trip to Germany. It is said the partners made back their $90,000 in the next two months. Hook claimed he was never sorry about his early sale, even though he received much less than either of his partners. When he died at eighty-one he was financially sound; a fact neither of the more acquisitive partners could boast. A month after Hook sold out, David H. Moffat and H. A. W. Tabor bought Rische's third for $265,500.

Rische was not made of "sterner stuff." The money went straight to his head, and he went straight to the local merchants. He liked fine clothes and high living. It was no time before he gathered a small army who eagerly shared his tastes and his wealth. He also had a yen for the ladies, and "his virility was apparently exhaustless, and he was prone to test it to the limit."

On one occasion shortly after Rische came into wealth he deposited a considerable amount of money with S. N. Wood, cashier of the First National Bank in Denver, and informed Mr. Wood that he was "goin' to sample dis town today, and see if it is any good. By tomorrow mornin' I'll be broke and come in here for my money. But don't you let me have it. I'll say 'Vos it your money or mine?' You say, 'It don't make no difference. You shan't have it.' Then I'll say, 'D--m your soul, you give me my money or I'll shoot you so full of holes you won't be no cashier no more,' and then you call your janitor and you and him throw me through the door and tell me 'Go to hell, you shan't have your money.' If you don't do that, when I straighten out, I'll make Charley Kontz* my banker.'"

A Chicago tobacconist arranged a marriage for Rische in 1879 to a young lady "of the city." He purchased a hay ranch near Malta and built a fine home. The marriage "was a success, for him at least." In the early 1880s Rische got a touch of political fever. Like so many men of wealth, after years of silence and hard work, he suddenly felt he had something to say to the world; something, surprisingly, that the world had not heard, but was longing to hear. The world is seldom as surprised by the results of this notion as the would-be politician.

Mr. and Mrs. Rische decided that county commissioner would be a fitting position. He needed someone to nominate him and one Sunday afternoon buttonholed his lawyer, Charlie Thomas, who one day would enter politics himself and sit in the governor's mansion. Rische reminded Thomas of all his business, his discovery of the Little Pittsburg, and the fact that he and his money had stayed in Leadville while others had left with their money for Denver.

Thomas was not tempted by the offer. As he recalled years later, "beyond the element of common honesty, the anxious candidate possessed not a single qualification" for the office. Thomas told him he had already agreed to nominate three

*Charles B. Kountze, one of the founders and long-time president of the Colorado National Bank.

other candidates, and he should select someone committed to him alone.

"Not on your life," he said. "Ve talked all dis over and ve agree I must be nominated by some s–– of a b–––– vat can talk, and ve vant you to do it."

Flattered, Thomas agreed, and Rische squeaked into office.

In new county commissioner rooms in the basement of the court house it was immediately clear that they needed more light. It was suggested they purchase a new chandelier.

"Mr. Chairman," Rische called, launching into his maiden speech, "I object to dat. Here me and my friend Kuhlmeyer just been elected Commissioner because we promise the people we reduce expenses. Now, the first thing we hear when we qualify, the Chairman says we must buy a chandelier. Now dis County don't need no chandelier at all. We got along so far without one all right and ve can keep goin' without any. Vot will ve do with it when we get it? You can't get a good one less than a thousand dollars. I know, because I got one for my wife last year. If ve get it, ve got to hire a room to keep it in. And ven you buy it and get a room for it, who in hell have you got what can play on it?"

In November 1878, after considerable trading and selling, the Little Pittsburg Consolidated Mining Company was organized. It consisted of the Dives, Little Pittsburg, New Discovery, and Winnemuck. Jerome B. Chaffee was president, David H. Moffat vice-president, and Tabor, Borden, and others made up the board of trustees.

William H. Lovell, sitting in his cabin on Chicken Hill, a spur of Carbonate Hill named after him, realized there were a lot of people making a lot of money on Fryer Hill and some of it by some right or other should be his. He promptly sunk a discovery shaft and located a claim called the Chrysolite in the saddle between Fryer Hill and Fairview Hill.

Bill had never been one for sustained labor, and when he got down twenty feet or so he began to tire. Chicken Bill was a lot sharper than the usual historical narratives would indicate. The old-timers describe him as crafty and clever and crooked as a dog's hind leg, but Bill was more than that. He was smart. He knew that if he did strike a bonanza he would have to sell because he did not have the money to develop the mine himself. If he did not strike it he was out a lot of work and had a worthless hole to place on the market. Why not sell before investing large amounts of labor? He promptly slipped over to Tabor's Little Pittsburg and stole a good sampling of carbonate ore and dropped it down his shaft. Some say he

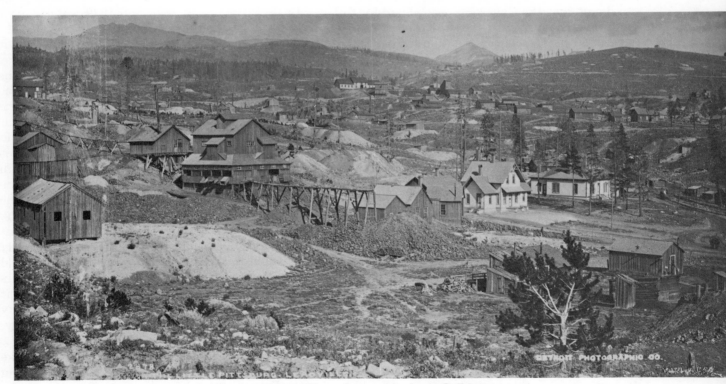

Little Pittsburg Mine. *Photo Source: Author's Collection.*

let it fill partially with water before dropping the ore down. He then made contact with Mr. Tabor and grudgingly offered to sell. Tabor by then was the acknowledged leader of the silver mining fraternity, and the town watched the exchange carefully. Everyone claimed after the sale was made that they knew Bill had salted the mine, but no one spoke up before the sale. Most say Bill received $1,500 for his claim, some claim Tabor paid as much as $50,000. Tabor claimed he paid $900 for one-quarter interest. According to the Lake County Court House records, H. A. W. Tabor purchased from William H. Lovell one-quarter interests in both the Carboniferous and the Chrysolite, adjoining claims just west of the Little Pittsburg. The county clerk's records show Tabor paying $10,000 for the pair, July 13, 1878. The Chrysolite was located May 3, 1878, by Chicken Bill and a pair of surprise partners, George H. Fryer and William Borden. Bill held one-half interest and the other two one-quarter each. What Bill did with his remaining quarter is unknown, or how Fryer and Borden happened to own quarters, though it is likely that they grubstaked Bill, is also a mystery.

Locally the facts of the sale were not generally known. The "fact" that was known and eagerly passed from laughing miner to laughing miner was Chicken Bill's sale of a salted mine to Mr. Silver himself, H. A. W. Tabor. There seems no doubt that the Chrysolite was salted by Bill, and while Tabor never denies it, he claims to have suspected it. "I believed the man 'salted' it but the 'salt' part did not count with me." Then, thinking about it further, Tabor asserted, "I really do not believe that that ore, he put in, had any consideration with me at all."

Tabor apologists have said, whatever the amount, it was a small price to pay to protect the Little Pittsburg's property on the west. We will never know who laughed first, but Tabor got the last laugh. He put a force of men to work in Bill's Chrysolite and in a short time hit a strong vein of carbonate ore. Jonathan Waddle, writing about the situation, claimed, "The joke of it is, if the dam fool Bill Lovell had sunk ten feet further he would have struck a mine that would have been worth a million and a half." Still, Bill was learning a trade and, such as it was, was doing quite well.

Stories about Tabor are as common in Colorado mining communities as Mike Fink on the Mississippi or Paul Bunyan in the north woods, and, while many are about his foolishness and extravagance, a sizable portion are about his beneficences and generosity. "While mayor of the town of Leadville he was indefatigable in promoting every enterprise of a public nature." As a wealthy mine owner he did not forget the boys down below. On one occasion just before Christmas, Mr. Tabor walked into a restaurant and asked the owner if he would give a free meal to a group of "miserable miners." The owner refused. Tabor replied, "You give it, and put the bill into me." The dinner was arranged, and people were fed for miles around. The day after, Tabor came in to pay the bill. "How much is the bill?" he asked the owner. "$5000," the owner replied. Tabor put down the money, and walked out without a word. Did it happen like that? It is not as important as the fact that people thought it did. Tabor wealth and generosity became legend. It was thought both were inexhaustable, but time has a way of whittling away at absolutes.

Another absolute that was short-lived was the Little Pittsburg. The mine was discovered in 1878. Two years later it was clear to many that it was worked out. But what wealth it produced in two years! It was reported that a little over one acre of the property produced $1,800,000. The first load of ore is said to have averaged $200 per ton. The ore ran 200 ounces of silver to the ton, and by mid-summer the mine was producing $8,000 to $10,000 a day. And, of course, before the bottom fell out, Mr. Tabor sold out to his partners for one million dollars even. Owning the Little Pittsburg in 1878 and 1879 was the next best thing to having a license to mint money.

Mr. Tabor's Chrysolite enterprise turned out almost as well, and over the years, probably was an even greater producer, though his part seems to be relegated to having put it all together. The Chrysolite was incorporated and included the Carboniferous, Little Eva, Kit Carson, All Right, Fairview, Pandora, Colorado Chief, Vulture, Solid Muldoon, and Eaton — sixty-six and 57/100 acres in all. Located in the saddle between Fryer Hill and Fairview Hill, not all the properties were important producers, but they surrounded the Chrysolite, protecting it in case the ore body took an unexpected turn and boundary disputes sent the whole operation to court. It was a generally accepted principal that potential litigants could save themselves both money and time by combining into corporations rather than giving their wealth to the greedy pack of lawyers who eagerly awaited a name calling session and the cry, "You'll hear from my lawyers."

The incorporators of the Chrysolite read like a "Who's Who of Finance and Power." Heading the list was Daniel S. Appleton of Appleton and Co. Book Publishers, today's Appleton, Century and Crofts. Next on the list were Henry A. V. Post of Clark, Post and Martin, New York bankers; Leonidas M. Lawson, of another banking firm, Donnell, Lawson and Co.; John P. Jones, U. S Senator from Nevada, and H. A. W. Tabor, by 1879 when the company was incorporated, lieutenant governor of Colorado. William Borden, friend and partner of Chicken Bill and George Fryer, had moved his headquarters to Chicago, but he still held Chrysolite stock. Arthur Sewall, president of the National Bank in Bath, Maine, bought in, as did Charles Whittier and William S. Nichols, both bankers. And for prestige, the company boasted Ulysses S. Grant, Jr.

Such a group expected great things, and they were not disappointed. From the seventeenth of October to the seventeenth of December, 1879, "The net profit realized by the company . . . amounted to $529,501.77."

Mr. Tabor claimed he wanted a mine to call his own, and spent $117,000 to purchase the Matchless from Tim Foley, A. P. Moore, and T. B. Wilgas. It cost him another $30,000 to clean up the various lawsuits against the property. Located in a line almost straight east of the Little Pittsburg, the mine was a real Cinderella. It had been traded and bartered and passed from promoter to promoter until Mr. Tabor bought the property in September of 1879. Water drove the men out in the first attempts and in March of 1880 work was halted. In July of the same year Lou Leonard took over as Mr. Tabor's manager and reopened the mine. Good ore was struck, the property further developed, and suddenly Cinderella came into her own. By the first of the year the Matchless was bestowing two thousand dollars a day on Mr. Tabor. One shipment of ore "gave returns of 10,000 ounces of silver to the ton." Mr. Tabor's Matchless was, indeed, matchless.

Southwest of the Little Pittsburg is the Little Chief. It was located shortly after the Little Pittsburg by four sons of Erin: Peter Finerty, Richard and Patrick Dillon, and John Taylor. Apparently the Dillon brothers, Taylor, and a young man named Dennis Carter sunk the discovery shaft. Carter foolishly traded his share to Peter Finerty for a pair of mules. Finerty and the others sunk one hundred feet in ten days and hit a wonderful body of ore. They took out $100,000 themselves, and then sold to J. V. Farwell of Chicago, a competitor of Marshall Field and Levi Z. Leiter.* Far-

*Field had money invested in Little Pittsburg stock. Some say it was Field's money that bought the Chrysolite. Leiter had earlier bought out A. B. Wood and became Stevens' partner in the Iron Silver Mining Company.

well claimed his Leadville investments did better than either of his Chicago competitors.

Peter Finerty used his money wisely and invested in other mines and continued to do well. Little is known about Taylor, or what happened to him or his share. The Dillons put their money in bonds with a special stipulation that they could not be cashed when they were drunk. It is said that they still managed to squander their fortune on wine, or rather whiskey, which was the miners' equivalent, and women. Later the Little Chief and Little Pittsburg properties went to court over prior rights, and the two ended up in a merger.

The richest of all Fryer Hill mines was located in June of 1878 by George W. Belt and William Knight. Its early history is obscure. It was a slow starter and showed little early promise, but the Robert E. Lee eventually surpassed even the wildest of dreams. In one thirty-nine-day period in 1879 it produced one-quarter of a million dollars in silver. One fellow asked if he might work the mine for one hour in return for ten thousand dollars. The owners declined. Another suggested $200,000 and the right to work the mine for thirty-six hours, but he was refused also. The owners were curious, though, and decided to see what they could do in twenty-four hours. They set to work and after seventeen hours had problems with a hoist and, rather than endanger workmen needlessly, halted the project at that time. The total production after seventeen hours was $118,500! Kent, writing at the time, said "The Robert E. Lee Mine will have to discover coined silver dollars to improve upon its record."

One of the original locators was said to have sold out for fifty dollars and was apparently glad to get it. It then sold in 1879 for $7,000 and at one time James V. Dexter, a surveyor and investor who became one of Colorado's first men of wealth, owned one-third interest. But Dexter, like those before him, was convinced the mine would never pay, and he, too, sold out for a pittance. Finally it fell into the hands of seven lucky men, L. D. Roudebush, Irwin Howbert, James M. Sigafus, Homer Pennock, B. F. Crowell, J. F. Humphrey, and James Y. Marshall.

Good ore was hit in February of 1879, but water and suits kept everyone busy until late summer, when mining began in earnest. By November the true promise of the Robert E. Lee was realized. The following assays are drawn from a number of shipments from various parts of the mine in October 1879: "520 ounces of silver per ton; 708, 767, 882, 1,098, 1,412, 1,516, 2,825, 2,878, 3,014, 5,405 and 10,306!"

The Robert E. Lee in the foreground, the Matchless behind at the left. *Photo Source: Author's Collection.*

Fryer Hill, one of the world's richest locations. *Photo Source: Collections in the Museum of New Mexico.*

Fryer Hill, covering an area not over a mile square, enriched not only Leadville and Colorado, but the whole country. In Colorado David Moffat's Leadville money helped him construct the Moffat Road and Tunnel, one of the state's most famous railroad enterprises. It put Jerome B. Chaffee in the United States Senate and built the Windsor Hotel and Tabor's Grand Opera House in Denver. A host of Denver mansions were built with Fryer Hill money. Certainly the numerous banks and bankers of the Empire State felt the rejuvenating effect of fresh silver in their veins, and Chicago businessmen like J. V. Farwell and Marshall Field must have found the clothing business lacking in excitement after their experiences with the Little Chief, Chrysolite, and Little Pittsburg.

Of course Fryer Hill became the show place of Leadville mining for a time, but Iron, Breece, Carbonate, Long and Derry, Rock and Printer Boy hills, and the valleys in between continued to produce lavishly. And, of course, naming a mine was done with all the care and concentration, minus the reverence, necessary for the launching of a ship. Everything was there but salt water and a bottle of champagne. There were dozens of mines named after wives, sisters, lovers, and lost loves. The area boasted a Minnie, a Clara Dell, a Cora Belle, and a Cordelia Edmondson. Fanny Rawlins and Tootie Gaylord and Lady Adle were honored by admirers as were Little Eva, Little Annie, Little Ellen, and Little Alice. The courtly gentlemen who roamed the hills were kind enough to reserve "big" for the Big Chief. Dolly B could not have been anything but pleased when she found her name tacked on a headframe, and the Modest Girl could not have made anyone unhappy; but there must have been some mixed feelings in Edith's mind when she heard about the Edith Drill Hole. Success or failure often was denoted, if secretly, in the name. Its been said that the C B mine, if successful, was to be named the Carrie Betts after a popular young charmer of the camp. The mine, if a failure, would be christened the Codfish Balls. If you look for Carrie Betts on maps of the mines you will find, where Carrie should be, Codfish Balls.

A few, apparently unimpressed with women, gave their mines their own names, or described themselves and fellow prospectors with names like the Slim Jim, Rough and Ready, Lazy Bill, Rattling Jack, and R.A.M. The R.A.M. locators pushed the recorder for the whole name, but the recorder insisted on initials. The miners insisted that the mine's location on a steep sidehill forced them to slide down to the road in Stray Horse Gulch on the seat of the pants, and Ragged Ass Mine was only fitting. Fitting or not, the recorder would not budge. It was and is the R.A.M.

Harrison Avenue in 1879. *Photo Source: Denver Public Library Western History Collection.*

VI

A Pilgrim's First Glance

The spring of 1879 saw the rush to Leadville take on migratory proportions. One visitor claimed he would never forget his first glimpse of Leadville. "We could look up its length, possibly two miles. It was a crawling mass of horses, mules, wagons, and men. It looked impossible to get through, but we made it in about two hours."

One of the first impressions newcomers got of Leadville was the unending din, the ceaseless sound of money being made and spent. Charles Leonard, an early visitor, recalled Leadville "was the noisiest place you can imagine. The ore haulers and freighters in the daytime were enough, but the dance halls, variety theaters, and saloons at night were worse."

Two years previous Leadville was without a name, virtually without population and covered with pine trees and silence. In 1879 one newcomer noted, "The trees have nearly all disappeared, but the stumps remain, and give variety to the streets."

Nothing in Leadville, not even the land itself, was static. Everything was in a state of flux. One young man, George Elder, a Quaker graduate of Princeton's law school, unsure of himself but eager to make his mark in the new camp, knew that diligence and right living would guide him down the path to success. He viewed the town with amazement and repugnance, but it captured him, like it captured so many others. In one of his first letters home, dated "January 29, 1879, Tontine Hotel," he explained, "You can possibly have no idea of the rapidity of action here. All is push and bustle. The streets are crowded and every other house is a saloon, dance house, etc. I am writing now in the shadow of seven bottles of some odoriferous substance." Lucy, an English observer, viewed the scene with a decided dis-

taste. "Leadville has that striking feature of untidiness common to most American towns."

There seemed no stopping the flow of pilgrims into the bulging town. George A. Hines, superintendent of the Harrison Reduction Works, writing a friend in Missouri, explained, "as you are aware, it [Leadville] has sprung into existence as if by magic, and is fast assuming a metropolitan appearance." He further explained, "it is a good place now to make money," but cautioned, "the climate, singular to say, is quite trying to all newcomers."

The spring of 1879 saw everyone expecting a great flood of newcomers as soon as the passes opened up and the weather encouraged the flatlanders out of their warm lodgings at lower elevations. Our young Quaker lawyer writing home explained, "In a month or so the crowds coming in

Chestnut Street, Leadville's first thoroughfare.
Photo Source: Author's Collection.

here will be so immense that it will be utterly impossible to make your way from Harrison Avenue to the new location of the post office a block below on Chestnut in less than half an hour." Already the problem was acute. "I was 20 minutes coming from the Tontine but then Sunday there is a greater crowd than any other day in the week and it was the sunny side of the street I came up on."

By spring, which at 10,000 feet elevation is sometime between March and June, usually the latter, people were arriving at a rate of one hundred or better per day. Eddie Foy, the famous vaudeville entertainer, who played Leadville several times in its infancy, claimed that "Chestnut Street was a babel — a tangle of human beings on foot, carrying furniture, bedding, window frames, tools and everything imaginable, and of six and eight-mule team wagons, drivers yelling and cracking big bull whips like pistol shots, hauling out ore . . . and bringing back building material, food and supplies."

In the early months the camp's streets were without names and houses were without numbers. The papers published lists of newcomers and where they were lodged. Without the assistance of the press it was virtually impossible to locate a friend newly arrived. By the end of 1878 most of the streets had been laid out, folks had been instructed to number their houses, and, not long after, Leadville's first city directory was published. It was a decidedly inadequate tool for locating an acquaintance, but a good deal more effective than the above method.

The main street in the early days was Chestnut. Harrison Avenue, honoring Leadville's pioneer smelter entrepreneur, Edwin Harrison, soon caught up and passed the earlier thoroughfare. Harrison Avenue ran north and south and became the major north-south artery. Off of it running east and west were Chestnut Street, and a block north, State Street, notorious from the city's beginning. State Street was the home of the most infamous of Leadville's early gamblers, bunco artists, footpads, lot jumpers, and ladies of easy virtue. Of course, the vice in Leadville's early days was far too expansive to be contained on one street, and it spilled over onto Harrison and Chestnut, while the more elaborate houses of prostitution were located in the 100 block of West Park Street, later renamed Fifth Street.

When the Cloud City was originally laid out all streets were named. In the first few months of the town's existence it was deemed advisable to abandon the names of the east-west running streets in favor of numbers. Chestnut Street was

never changed, but it became the first street north, State Street was changed to Second Street, but the old name hung on well into the middle of the twentieth century (see map of Leadville for other early street names).

Lucy noted, "The streets are never swept, nor sidewalks cleaned, whilst the main thoroughfares are only a trifle better than the streets of Chicago." The basic problems were seasonal. Winter was best. The snow covered most of the major holes and ruts, and kept the dust down. Spring saw the streets turn to quagmires. A local paper in 1881 noted, "The annual Leadville regatta will be held over one of the streams flowing down the streets of the city, instead of on the Arkansas as heretofore." Another, not to be outdone, suggested that a little ditching would carry off the water that "makes the pedestrian so damp-disagreeable." Leadville is so situated that the spring trickles that gather on the east side of town run down the east-west streets unimpeded, except by small boys, who every spring dammed the gullies and flooded the streets. By the time the trickles reached the west side of town they were raging torrents that cut away the streets and sidewalks before winding their way into California Gulch and eventually into the Arkansas River.

The mud was so bad that the council attempted to solve the problem by putting smelter slag on the streets, a material still in use for ice covered winter streets, which led Leadville to claim that it was the only city in the world with streets paved with silver. The slag helped, but had to be replenished constantly. In summer the "squirt wagon" was in use. It consisted of several barrels of water and an operator whose job it was to splash water on the streets to keep the dust down. Abe Lee, discoverer of gold in California Gulch, and possibly one of the locators of the J. D. Dana in Iowa Gulch, spent his last days on the squirt wagon, broke.

The hazards of street travel were considerable, but the sidewalks presented even greater dangers. Leadville's walks were constructed from rough cut lumber, where walks existed at all, and true to Leadville's independent frame of mind, each merchant designed his sidewalk to suit his image of what a good boardwalk should look like. Consequently, each varied from the neighboring one. "It is only an eccentricity by daylight, but it becomes dangerous at night," one visitor pointed out. "A man who, walking rapidly along, suddenly steps down ten or twelve inches, usually gets down on his hands and knees the first thing, and then wonders whether his neck is broken."

Looking west from Harrison Avenue down notorious State Street. *Photo Source: Colorado Historical Society.*

After living in the Cloud City for a "spell," the newcomer got used to the variations in the sidewalks. It did not prevent him from stretching himself out face first in front of one or another of the town's numerous business establishments, it only prevented him from being surprised by his fate. "I was walking with a wealthy gentleman, one of the older inhabitants — he had lived in Leadville two years — one evening, when he suddenly executed the maneuver above described. Recovering his feet and his breath, he remarked casually, 'damned sidewalk,' and continued his conversation, as if nothing unusual had occurred."

The town was a jerry-rigged hovel of habitation. There was no uniformity. Tents butted against fine, newly constructed brick buildings. Pap Wyman owned a cabin that sat smack in the middle of newly named Harrison Avenue. A rough slab shack elbowed its space between two fine wooden structures. Lap-siding and board-and-batten prevailed, but were in no way controlling features. Buildings were constructed according to the size of purse, size of lot, and type and amount of materials available. "It is astonishing

how good a house can be made of a big tent." And "a painted cabin meant that the owner had brought his family to town." Lucy observed when on his way to the Chrysolite just east of town that "wooden boxes [houses] are scattered about among the burned stumps of trees and the debris of preserved meat cans." But whatever the accommodations lacked, whatever the climate failed to provide, whatever villainy persisted in the saloons and gambling dens, whatever the problems of getting to and existing in Leadville, the pilgrims were not daunted.

The first arrivals in the Leadville area were refugees of the old gulch fraternity of the sixties and seventies. Next came the boys from neighboring camps. Gradually brothers, cousins, uncles, and friends from back home received letters encouraging them to give it a try. With the discoveries by the Gallaghers, and others no wiser than they, the newspapers caught the fever and soon the world turned toward Leadville like a new Mecca.

One of the first of the professional mining fraternity to arrive was Arthur D. Foote. After spending a lonely winter in the camp he was

A town in the trees. East Third Street in 1879. *Photo Source: Denver Public Library Western History Collection.*

joined by his wife, Mary, in the spring of 1879. Mary Hallock Foote was all the things Leadville was not. She was a lady of long lineage, a writer and illustrator, and charming, feminine, and strangely wise.

On her arrival she recalled, "We knew that we were nearly 'in' when corrals and drinking places and repair shops began to multiply, and rude, jocose signs appeared on doors closed to the besieging mob of strangers: 'No chickens, no eggs, no keep folks — dam!'"

It was late in the evening when they arrived and she did not have time to explore the city until later, but she did appreciate Arthur's home and wrote an old friend that it was "the jolliest little log cabin" and went on to explain the dark wood paneling and oak paper on the inside. "The windows are low and the view is wonderful." Years later, thinking about the view and climate she wrote "the Leadville scene, when it wasn't snowing or sleeting or preparing to do both, was dominated by a sky of so dark and pure and haughty a blue that 'firmament' was the only name for it."

Soon after the city was organized the trustees ordered a census taken. It was admittedly haphazard due to the uncertain aspects of the town and the state of flux of the population, but it was a good indication of what nationalities were represented and in what percentages. According to Leadville's *Daily Chronicle,* January 29, 1879, five thousand and forty souls called Leadville home. It was suspected that another five thousand lived within five miles of town in a number of one street villages and at mine sites. It was estimated in 1879 that "twenty thousand people are tributary to this center, Leadville, for their daily supplies, and ten thousand gather within the city's walls, so to speak, every night." Over half the town's citizens were white Americans (3,651). All city and county offices were held by members of this group in the first few years. The Irish held sway as second runners with 328 pilgrims from the old country. Many of them had come directly from Ireland at the urging, and often with the help, of a friend or relative. Many more had come to America to escape the poverty and want following the great potato famine of the late forties and early fifties. English rule drove still more out. The Irish, like everyone else in camp, celebrated their presence with the names of their claims. The Maid of Erin smiled on the sons of the old sod. There were the three Irish revolutionary leaders honored in the Robert Emmet, Wolf Tone, and O'Donovan Rossa mines. Mary Murphy surely blushed with pleasure when she found a fine Irish lad had named his claim on Rock Hill after her.

Though most of the Irish settled on East Sixth Street, in Stray Horse Gulch, or on Chicken Hill, and put up a tough united front, they were divided among themselves. There were Shanty Irish, Stovepipe Irish, Far Downs, and Cleator Moors. The Cleator Moors, for example, were from Cleator Moor, a coal and iron mining area of Northern England. Previously they had emigrated there from Ireland, and they violently resented being called English.

One of the Irish customs that mystified, and on many occasions amused, the rest of the Leadville population, was the Irish wake. The deceased would lie in state in his home, or the home of a nearby relative if he was without a suitable home, and all his friends, relatives, and enemies would come by to pay their last respects. Usually the visitors stayed for some time, discussing the funeral, the deceased, and occasionally things in general, depending on the qualities of the deceased and his value as a topic of conversation. Usually strong black coffee was served, not infrequently with a bit of Irish in it. On most occasions the gathering was calm and respectful, but once in a while the group became more concerned with the quality of the coffee than the deceased, and the wake became a roaring drunk. On more than one occasion the departed son of Erin was buried with the smell of good Irish whiskey on his breath, the result of some overzealous friend who could not bear to see him go to the hands of his maker without "hav'n a drop in."

The Irish were for the most part a good-natured people, hard working, unschooled, hard drinkers, and good for a joke. Most of the Irish stories nowadays are told by the Irish, but in those days they were told about the Irish. One tale that has been in the area for years seems indicative of their social position in Leadville in the early days. One of the Irish living among the Swedes on Chicken Hill had a cousin visit him from Denver. The cousin, Mike, was a natty young fellow, depressed by the condition of the town. And when he got to his Leadville cousin's house up on Chicken Hill, after walking about a mile through mud and slush, for it was spring, he

was flabbergasted. It was little more than a hovel. Still he got a hearty welcome at the door and a "Come in, me lad, come in." Once inside he relaxed a bit under the friendly warmth of his host. After some time he noticed a door to an adjoining room and asked, "What is it you have there?"

"Ah, it's the cow's room."

"The cow!"

"Sure. That's her room."

"But what about the smell."

"Ah, she doesn't seem to mind."

One old Leadville citizen, Frank McLister, recalled that East Sixth Street was always exciting, especially on St. Patrick's Day. All the good sons of Erin would dress up in their Sunday best, attend the 9:00 o'clock Mass, then walk to their favorite pub where they would fortify their courage. Once fortified, they would line the sidewalk on East Sixth. On the opposite side of the street the Orangemen would be doing likewise. The festivities began with name-calling, and it was not long before the middle of the street was filled with fighting sons of the green and the orange. Muddy or slick, good footing or bad, win, lose or draw it was a grand day for the Irish.

Germans, dissatisfied with conditions in their homeland, in many cases political refugees and escapees from the revolutions beginning in 1848 that swept through Europe, came to America seeking some personal freedom and the opportunity to start over. A good many had been in the country a number of years before arriving in Leadville. Some were second generation. They left their stamp on Leadville with their beer gardens, pastry, the Turners, and the Hamburgh Mine.

Another large group were Canadians. Probably most of them were itinerant miners and merchants looking for the big strike or a firm foothold in a new camp. Of course, their English cousins were not to be left out, especially the Cornish, who came in considerable numbers. Throughout the West they were referred to as Cousin Jacks. The name is said to have come about because to anyone asking about a good worker, nice guy, or honest soul, the usual Cornish answer began, "I have a Cousin Jack. . . ." It seemed every Cornish man had a cousin named Jack.

The Cornish congregated near the smelters in the lower end of California Gulch on the far west side of town in a colony called Jacktown. Many worked in the nearby smelters while others applied their knowledge of the tin mines of Cornwall to the problems of Leadville mining.

The Scots were few in number, but made it known that they were in town. Of course, the town's most obvious Scot was the indomitable Broken Nose Scotty, traditional locator of the Highland Chief and the Highland Mary. Large numbers of Scots always turned out to celebrate the birthday of Robert Burns, and a mine was named for Scotland's poet laureate.

Enough Negroes fleeing the south arrived to form a colony on West State Street that was given the dubious name of Coon Row. The quality of their lives in Leadville seemed, compared to other towns, none so bad. Large numbers lived in the camp, were not restricted in public buildings, owned property, went to the public schools and worshipped apart, but in peace, with their clergymen owning the respect of the public generally. Of course they were subject to all of the tricks and pranks that all newcomers fell heir to, but there is little to suggest that their lot in the Cloud City was worse than in the nation as a whole, and it probably was a lot better.

Jewish people arrived in Leadville with the first rush and were influential in the early commercial history of the camp. Men like Meyer Guggenheim, Levi Z. Leiter, David May, and Charles Boettcher made history in their fields and contributed greatly to the business success of the state and the nation.

Swedes and Norwegians arrived in large numbers in the eighties and congregated on Chicken Hill, forcing their way in among the large number of Irish already on the site. They organized their own Lutheran Church, but there was so much friction between "Swede" and "Norseman" that they went their separate ways, organizing two Lutheran congregations.

One young Swedish lady, Anna Stina, on her way to Leadville, wrote a friend describing the area. "Shortly we were up in the mountains, up in the most beautiful spruce forest, which called to mind the countryside in Varmland." She went on to say a word or two about the "evil men" who easily forgot the old country. Men who "as soon as they are able to say 'yes' and 'no' in a sort of halfbaked English, forget the mother tongue, tramp on all that is Swedish, then take some Irish lass out on roller skates." The American "melting pot" was fired up much too soon to suit Anna Stina.

The list of nationalities included a sizable number of Frenchmen; enough in fact to form and maintain a French Catholic Church. The Swiss and Italians came in small numbers, as did the

Looking east toward Chicken Hill, home of the Swedes. *Photo Source: Denver Public Library Western History Collection.*

Mexicans. Two Spaniards represented Iberia in 1879. Two representatives of Mother Russia, twenty-three Bohemians, and seven Poles formed the first contingent of Slavic peoples, a group that would be swollen by several hundred in the waning years of the nineteenth century as they fled the oppression of the old Austrian and Turkish Empires. The Cornish were joined by a small number of fellow miners from Wales. Ten Danes and one Lapp and five representatives of the Isle of Man complete the list compiled in January of 1879.

One group not represented was Orientals. The town early banned them. "In 1879 Leadville boasted of having representatives of every nation on earth, except the Chinese, residing within the town. Its citizens boasted 'John Chinaman is not allowed by the miners to enter the city limits.'" The miners were suspicious of the Chinese and were concerned about their effect on the economy. It was an accepted fact that they would work for lower wages than the rest of the miners. This caused problems in other camps and the Leadville miners decided to save themselves any problems by eliminating the source. Later events proved that there were plenty of miners of European stock who were equally willing to undercut their fellow's salaries. Hungry men, family men, were willing to do whatever was necessary to provide the necessities of life, and skin color and physical conformation were of no importance. Another factor, real or imagined, preventing the easy acceptance of Orientals was their clannishness. Other nationalities were clannish, it was noted, but not to the same degree. Of course, much of the clannishness was simple banding together for protection, but unfortunately the result enforced the cause. Clannishness begot suspicion, suspicion enforced clannishness. The miner in Leadville, and all over the West for that matter, was suspicious of anyone not open, loud, free with his money, aboveboard, and one of the boys. It was said the Chinese were filthy, smoked opium, drowned their children, and any number of other notions born of ignorance; but the American tradition that newcomers were to "make yourself welcome" rather than "be welcomed" persisted, and the Chinese were never asked to make themselves welcome.

In talking about Leadville's puppy days, Judge Furrow claimed he was the first and only person to bring a Chinaman to the camp. He met the Oriental in Alma and the man told him he wanted to go to Leadville. Furrow warned him, but the man was insistent. He planned to do washing for August R. Meyer and possibly set up a laundry. Furrow continued to discourage him until he offered $25.00 for a seat on his wagon. The money changed the situation. It was 1877 and Leadville was still an unnamed extension of Oro. A number of men rushed up to Furrow and wanted to know what he was about. "They threatened to shoot up the wagon, horses, and Chinaman, and even declared that they felt like awarding me with a similar dose of their aroused wrath." That night the men of town loaded several sections of "gas pipe with giant powder and scraps of iron" and placed it under the abandoned cabin where the Chinaman was sleeping. They tied it all to one fuse and let it go. The explosion woke everyone in camp, especially the Chinaman, who came roaring up to Furrow's quarters, dressed in "negligee attire," his shoes in hand, and his eyes popping. Furrow aimed the gentleman toward Alma and claimed, "I do believe the poor fellow never stopped going until he reached that settlement."

The next morning the judge looked the area over. The cabin had virtually disappeared and the timbers were scattered for "several blocks in every direction." The fact that the poor laundryman lived to tell the tale was nothing short of a miracle.

The really unfortunate visitor to Leadville was the Indian. The old philosophy, "the only good Indian is a dead Indian," was still very much in evidence in the West. Young Elder recalled, "By the way there was a party of Ute Indians in town yesterday looking up some stolen horse stock, but they bore no resemblance to the noble red man of fiction." They were beaten down by that time to little more than a band of wandering thieves who had neither the means nor the courage to steal anything more valuable than the washing off the lines or an occasional horse. Even so, they were more often stolen from than guilty of stealing.

There were no settled groups of Indians in the Leadville area, only wandering bands. Most of them, by the time of the Leadville boom, had been corralled like so many cattle on reservations in western and southwestern Colorado. Still, the attitude of repugnance and distrust persisted. The unfortunate Indian never came in for much generosity and kindness. The *Carbonate Weekly Chronicle*, speaking to would-be pilgrims in January of 1880, suggested they bring a "Sharps rifle which will be very handy to kill elk, antelope and — Utes." They went on to say, "If you are particularly handy with a rifle, bring along a good one and shoot the first Ute you find."

One of the features of the Cloud City was the

independence of virtually everyone. It was expressed in their free swinging, no-hold-on-me gait, their manner of speech, and their relations with others. All men were called by their first names unless tradition dictated otherwise. Some exceptions were Tabor, who was called Mayor, Governor, and eventually Senator. Another was William H. Stevens, who was known around the camp as "Uncle Billy." There were no special provisions for special people. One newcomer was in a cobbler's shop getting a shoe repaired and asked for a chair to sit on while he waited. The proprietor refused him the chair and his services because he was too "fine tone" to sit on the upturned keg put there for sitting. One fellow observed a local miner talking to a rather pompous newcomer, who was strutting down the street. The miner sidled over to the dude and asked, "Mister, how much do you ask for it?"

"For what sir? (in a deep bass voice)."

"Why the town. I supposed you owned it."

The citizens of the Magic City, then and now, have "a high regard for a gentleman, but a hatred of a swell." Letting air out of egos was a special

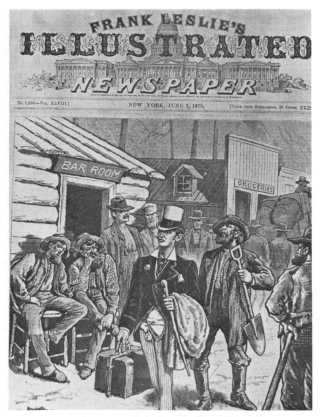

No room for a swell in Leadville. *Photo Source: Author's Collection.*

avocation. Miners had great respect for those who could perform and admired nerve with a kind of reverence "amounting to worship," but they also maintained "a contempt of braggadocio that often results in an impulsive puncturing of both braggart and his boasts."

There was good reason for the attitude of the men in the camp. Many of their comrades had been as poor or poorer than they a few weeks or months before, and in a few short weeks were worth thousands. Today's bum might be tomorrow's newest Carbonate King. The reverse was equally true. Many rich men died a pauper's death. Life was chancy at best, and a Leadville pilgrim was not impressed by family or position. He saw too much present to be impressed with the past, and while he saw it as his sacred duty to keep swells from being impressed with themselves, he also had the job of educating greenhorns.

Imagine Chicken Bill relating the following story to a group of pilgrims: During the winter of 1877 meat became increasingly scarce, and there was no way to ship beef into the camp until spring. Wild meat was all that was available, and the gents in camp ate so much venison and fried potatoes that the venison fat, or tallow, became caked to the roofs of their mouths. Conversation was cut to a minimum, which was bad; but the real crisis occurred when they began to realize their coffee and whiskey were without taste. Many solutions to the problem were suggested and tried, but by far the most effective was covering the top of the victim's head with pine knots and needles and then gumming it in place with generous helpings of pine pitch. When it was firmly in place, they set fire to the mess, which melted the tallow and restored the victim's taste. The cure had a regrettable side effect — baldness. Approximately ninety-seven percent of the miners in the camp were baldheaded by midwinter.

Long about the middle of spring, which usually runs from Monday through Wednesday, which would have made it the Tuesday of spring, a fellow from Kentucky arrived. He was in the hair tonic business. The miners welcomed him, thinking that anyone from the home of Kentucky whiskey could not be all bad. The newcomer was a Republican and left home, so they say, to prevent the Democratic government's tax on his product. Without ado he set up shop and started brewing tonic in a little cabin on the south slope of California Gulch. The tonic was made from potatoes, of which there was still a good supply in camp.

One rainy Sunday evening he was going into

town to peddle his product. He had four jugs; one in each hand and one under each arm. He had to cross the gulch on a rain-slick, barrel-round log and lost his balance, dropping two jugs that broke and ran into the stream. Before long fishermen changed their methods. They would go down on a Saturday afternoon, "stick a red, white and blue pole in the bank, put on a white coat, wave a copy of *Police Gazette* in one hand and brandish a scissors in the other, and yell, 'Next!'" The eager fish would jump onto the bank, and in no time the fisherman/barber would have his "limit of these fine fur-bearing trout with full beards."

The number of young men who wrote home with the story of fur-bearing trout, pirate ships on Twin Lakes, or talking birds has never been estimated, much less computed, but there have been hundreds who not only wrote. but believed.

The weekend was the wildest time of the week. Miners came in from Adelaide, a mining community numbering about a thousand people located at the head of Stray Horse Gulch about five miles east of town; Evansville and Stumpf Town, two small communities located near one another, the first in Evans Gulch and the other in Lincoln and South Evans gulches, tributaries to Evans. Others came in from Oro City #2, a couple miles up California Gulch. They came in from the mines scattered all over the surrounding hills. They came from the various workings at the foot of Mount Massive; Colorado Gulch, Sugarloaf Mountain, and St. Kevin, originally called Sow Belly Gulch until a woman, some say the wife of Thomas Walsh, renamed the area. They all came to town for one thing — to forget the hard, lonely life at the mines, mills, and smelters. And they came armed. "The man who didn't 'tote hardware' in self-defense, if for no other reason, was a curiousity."

Elder remarked in September of 1879, "Murders occur in such a terribly reckless manner that it is uncertain who will be the next victim." Another recalled, "Death by violence became so common that when one man expired from an overdose of liquor the father, in a distant state, rejoiced to learn that his son had died a natural death."

Most had a handgun of some vintage. Many carried old Civil War weapons, others had the newer Colts. "Pistols are drawn so quickly and most of them are these selfcockers that are almost as dangerous to the owner as to his enemies."

Carrying a gun and using one were two different things. Would a young fellow from the settled East, religious, God-fearing, and moral, use a lethal weapon on one of his fellows? Young Elder answered the question. "I carry my revolver about me in the night time and I do not think the small amount of Quaker blood in me would be any hinderance to my swift and immediate use."

The first glimpse of town for most folks was on the swing up Chestnut Street. It was said that stage drivers liked to put on a grand entrance, so the horses were usually given a bit of breather before the driver gave them their heads and a whack on the rump and roared up Chestnut. If the newcomer was lucky he was only choked with dust. If he came to town too early in the spring, which could be anytime before the second week in June, there was a chance that he had spent a large part

A Leadville gaming house as portrayed in *Frank Leslie's Illustrated Newspaper*, April 26, 1879. *Photo Source: Author's Collection.*

of his trip pushing the stage out of mud holes and fighting cold and snow and sleet and wind.

Once in town his first problem was finding some place to stay. He was obligated to haul his luggage around with him because it would not be safe 'unattended. As he walked around he could not help but be struck by the large number of people, all busy, and the large number of vehicles. Ore wagons and carriages were cursed into a tangle with saddle horses, pack trains, delivery vans, and hundreds of people. He quickly found, after stepping into one of the town's 118 saloons, that it was no quieter off the streets than on them. He paid for a beer and learned that change was seldom made for anything under a quarter. If he caught on quickly he emulated the rest of the boys, and drank up what change he had coming. While patronizing the saloon he would most likely ask the barkeep about lodgings.

"You gonna batch or room?" the bartender would be obliged to ask.

A young traveler from the east probably would not have enough knowledge of the area to make an intelligent choice, so he would ask the merits of each and order another beer to insure a reply.

The cost of living was high and remained high until the railroad began to relieve the demand for foodstuffs in 1880. Board and room in 1879 ran from seven to fifteen dollars per week. Hotels wanted two to four dollars a day for a bed. Single meals could be had for twenty-five cents at the small stands along the streets, and upwards of that to a couple of dollars in the better restaurants. Those who could, built a cabin or purchased one and set up housekeeping. Cotton pillows were a little over a dollar apiece, a pair of blankets ran two and one-half dollars and up, while coal oil was selling for four dollars per gallon. A cabin could be had for the price of nails and an ax, plus the time and labor required to construct it. The ideal situation was to form a small party of three or four and set up housekeeping.

The newcomer might make arrangements with the barkeep to leave his luggage, and chances are it was safer there than most places he might choose, especially if he left it with the proprietor rather than one of the drifters who wandered in for a drink and found a job.

A few doors east of his beer hall the pilgrim might encounter his first Leadville grocery, McMillen Brothers, for instance, at 109 West

Little and Pearsall's Meat Market on West Second Street. *Photo Source: Denver Public Library Western History Collection.*

Chestnut. He would quickly realize that it was not cheap to live in Leadville. Prices, of course, changed from time to time, but the following list compiled by Keeler would not be far from those any newcomer would encounter:

Bacon	12½-15¢ per lb.
Beef	6-15¢ per lb.
Pork	15-20¢ per lb.
Bear Meat	12½-25¢ per lb.
Potatoes	4-5¢ per lb.
Flour	$3.25-$3.85 per 100 lbs.
Tea	.75-$1.25 per lb.
Coffee	.25-.45¢ per lb.
Sugar	6¾-8 lbs. for $1.00
Condensed Milk	.30¢ per can

Condensed milk was not only thirty cents a can, it was the only type available. There was also a conspicuous lack of cheeses, eggs, fruits, and vegetables.

Good restaurants were hard to find. One fellow from Missouri put up a large tent and planned to feed the populace. Out front he painted "MEOLS." It was generally agreed by the clientele that the "spelling was a good deal better than the meals." If a young fortune hunter had some financial backing from home, or he arrived in camp with a kick in his pocket, he took his meals someplace besides at home. Those with the resources ate at the Tontine, one of the better eateries in town, for six to seven dollars per week.

One newcomer found himself a cabin owned by a widow lady and set up housekeeping. The "house," he explained to his parents, "is a low log cabin — I dinge my hat on acct of the lowness of the door every time I enter or go out. The walls of the room are papered with Harpers Weekly — Frank Leslie — Waverly — Cin. Gaz. — Rocky Mountain News — Illustrated Weekly — etc." His furnishings were no more of the Ritz than the structure. "I have a straw mattress, no chairs but boxes. Wash stand an inverted box." He was without a mirror, save "the water in the tin basin. No carpet on the floor, etc. — for all these luxuries I pay $2.50 per week."

One of the first problems that visited those who decided to pair up with another fellow and batch was the cooking. It must have been at this time that the old story about a group of pilgrims batching up in one of the gulches above Leadville was first told. It was agreed that one fellow would cook and *anybody* who complained about the food would take his place. The first morning they were all sitting around the table, hunched over their coffee, which was black and oily, and one fellow groaned after taking a sip, "Christ, this is strong

coffee. But," he grinned, "it's just the way I like it."

Those who had little experience with cooking or none at all quickly ran into problems. One aspect that even the more knowledgeable encountered was the effect ten thousand plus feet above the sea had on Iowa and Virginia and New York recipes. Two old fellows got into an argument over the salting of the beans and drew their pistols and both sat watching the pot and each other, and the beans boiled. They waited a couple of hours and then declared a truce and filled their pipes, and the beans boiled. Four hours passed and the beans continued to boil and remain hard. After seven hours they decided to call it quits and eat the still uncooked beans. They both took a bite to see that the other fellow had not been up to some foul play, then laid the revolvers down and began vigorously chewing beans. The moral of the story, if there is one, is that water boils at a much lower temperature at 10,000 feet and tomorrow's beans had best be started today.

Finding lodgings was a problem for everyone. Eddie Foy, the famous vaudeville actor, and his partner arrived in town and set out to find a room. "The task seemed well-nigh hopeless." A number of their fellow actors "were bunking backstage" in the theater. They decided to follow the others' example. They had difficulties securing a blanket for each and a straw tick to spread themselves on. "We didn't try to get beds, but just slept on the floor."

Mass consumption, for in many ways that is what it was, visited Leadville shortly after the town was organized. "During the late political campaign [1878 fall] the Republican Committee erected a very capacious building," which in truth was no building at all, but a tent. It was dubbed the "Wigwam" and after the political doings was used "as a skating rink, and at last was utilized by an enterprising firm as a mammoth lodging house. It was advertised to accommodate 500 men." Other "Mammoth lodgers" were erected, and it was claimed that about 800 men slept in them. The lodgers, like the cheap sleeping apartments, rented beds on an eight-hour basis, and when your time was up there was always someone else ready to take your place. According to the *Daily Chronicle*, "As a rule, at least one of the pair in the first bed above you will be sick, two by your head and three by your feet drunk, five hundred will be swearing and the rest saying their prayers." Mammoth Lodgers left the Leadville scene late in the summer of 1879 due to improved hotels and boarding houses.

Leadville, 1880. *Photo Source: Bancroft Library, University of California.*

One answer to the problem of getting a warm meal. *Photo Source: Author's Collection.*

Thomas Kendrick, owner of the Leadville House at 222 East Third Street, had the dubious distinction of being able to make bedding last and last. His method was simple. He explained that he could not put blankets on the bunks because thieves were so prevalent that they would be immediately stolen. Hence, you were forced to rent a blanket as well as a bunk. The manager had too few blankets so he simply took one off of a sleeping guest and rented it to the newcomer.

It was reported that "good men and women are leaving this city every day simply because they are sleepy." It was explained that it was not due to a shortage of beds, but the "darn noise." It made little difference the type of lodging the newcomer could afford; he could not buy silence. The town operated with vigor twenty-four hours a day, seven days a week, winter and summer. There was no letup.

If our newcomer was able to find adequate lodgings and a good meal he soon felt the urge to explore the Magic City, and set forth.

Woods Opera House on East Chestnut. The whole block was later destroyed by fire. *Photo Source: Colorado Historical Society.*

VII

Boom Town After Dark

It was not uncommon to see small boys going through the sawdust in front of saloons and gambling halls early in the morning. Most establishments had sawdust floors and each dawn they simply swept the old sawdust out the front door and anything on the floor went with it, including cigar butts, wrappers, the grime and crud that goes with such establishments, and occasionally a coin or two. The latter is what attracted the boys, and their diligence was often rewarded, sometimes handsomely.

The newcomer could be entertained on the streets of Leadville for days on end without spending a dime, though few availed themselves of free amusements. In front of most theaters and dance halls a band of questionable quality played and paraded in an effort to attract customers. Ladies of pleasure advertised their wares along State Street and on the south end of Harrison Avenue. All types of wares were hawked with varying degrees of fervor and success by a group of characters that ranged from notorious crooks to newcomers trying to make a stake. One of the more popular items on sale was boxed candy. Another product was soap, which provided a name for one of the West's most notorious con men.

Jefferson Randolph Smith arrived in Leadville in the mid-eighties in a hurry to make a pile before the boom and money moved on. He teamed up with a fellow named Taylor and they set up a shell game. They went into business at the corner of Harrison Avenue and Third Street. The venture was successful, especially for Smith, since he was earning and learning at the same time. After the shell game they tried a new con. They wrapped an occasional $100 bill around a bar of soap, mixed it in with dozens of ordinary bars and advertised. Smith wandered up, purchased a bar of soap, or rather the special bar of soap, unwrapped it, and found the $100 bill. The crowd surged around demanding several bars of Sapolion, their brand. Smith gradually surpassed his teacher and went on to fame in Creede, Colorado, where "Soapy," as he was known, ran the town. Finally when goodness and light began to prevail, he headed north to Alaska where he was killed in a gun battle on July 8, 1898, in Skagway.

Jefferson Randolph (Soapy) Smith. *Photo Source: Denver Public Library Western History Collection.*

Another sure sell item was gold bricks. Con men sold everything imaginable that resembled the fabled mineral. Already mentioned was one of the west's most colorful con men, Chicken Bill Lovell. Bill left Leadville after he sold the salted Chrysolite to Tabor and turned up in Aspen where he mined the pockets of the unwary. But his heart belonged to Leadville. As soon as word got out that Tabor had hit it big in the Chrysolite, "Chicken" set to work planning his return engagement. According to Edmund J. Wells, an acquaintance of Bill's, Lovell located an old copper tank, melted the copper off and molded it into ingots. He buried them for a while to improve their color and then returned to Leadville. There, with the help of a confederate, he sold them in the Clarendon Hotel to unsuspecting tourists as samples of Leadville gold.

Another form of free entertainment was the traveling medicine show. The good doctor — for the shows were always run by doctors who had traveled the world over searching for their advertised wonder cure and had studied either in London, Paris, or Vienna, or all three — the good doctor usually worked with a young fellow or a girl, who either sang, did some dramatic reading, or presented a sketch from some well-known work such as *Hamlet* or *Julius Caesar*. Then the doctor made his pitch. Most of the concoctions were good for nothing but a middling drunk and a ferocious hangover, but some made people violently ill, and occasionally the good doctor lost a patient.

A couple of mud holes away a troupe of tightrope walkers might be drawing a crowd, or a physical giant would be energetically breaking or lifting the most improbable objects. Young Elder recalled, "Every evening for the last week we have been having trapeze and rope walking performances upon State Street by male and female performers. It attracts large crowds every night and between Pine and Harrison Avenue I suppose from 2 to 3,000 people are crowded."

For those who had the money and sought something indoors, there was a carnival atmosphere with something to appeal to every taste. According to Elder, in October of 1879 "another theater opened the other night making five in full blast here now." He went on to question how they made any money with so many on the scene, then answered his own query. "They [the miners] cannot spend their evenings in their rough uncomfortable cabins as there is nothing home-like about them."

The quality of Leadville theater ran all the way from excellent at Tabor's Opera House and Tom Kemp's Grand Central Theater, to the dregs of poor taste in a number of variety theaters such as the Coliseum and the New Theater.

The first theaters in the camp were constructed in 1877 and during the early months of 1878. The Coliseum and the Comique opened first with questionable talent and taste. The dearth of talent generally continued until 1880 when the railroad arrived and top talent could be imported on a regular scale. Of course there were notable exceptions such as Eddie Foy, Jack Langrishe, and Charles Vivian.

Most of the theaters were laid out with a small stage, boxes, a balcony, and a bar, all of which were filled. The theaters were cold and according to one report, the cold was especially noticeable "when watching the girls on the stage — they were fairly blue with it. Eventually the number of bodies warmed the theater." Ben Wood and Tom Kemp realized there should be something for everyone and not just for the rough and ready miners in the camp. Wood remodeled his Chestnut Street Theater, reopened it as Wood's Opera House, and emphasized family entertainment. Kemp did not go quite so far with the women and children, but he did try. On Wednesday afternoons evrything was respectability, for the matinee performance was for women and children. The bar was closed and everything was "order and decorum." Kemp's house was the largest in the camp and one of the most successful. "It contained an auditorium 55-by-100 feet and a stage 35-by-55 feet. Forty-five boxes, 'elegantly furnished,' were arranged in two tiers around the back of the auditorium. Along the front of the building on the second floor were six wine rooms."

The lower class establishments concentrated on the tawdry. McDaniel and Vogus' New Theater advertised in the *Democrat:*

50 WAITER GIRLS
PAY IN GOLD
Promptly Every Week. Must Appear In
SHORT CLOTHES
or No engagement.

The crowds in the variety theaters were drunken, boisterous, and bawdy. The festivities usually began around nine and ran to two or three in the morning. Fights and disturbances were common, but the managers were capable of handling most problems. Shows were often interrupted by a drunken marksman who would attempt to shoot the lights out, hat off, or cork out of. Other shows were momentarily stopped or slowed when some wag dropped chairs or champagne bottles from the balcony onto the crowd on the first floor.

Real, sophisticated theater came to Leadville with the opening of Tabor's Opera House. His establishment was without rival with regard to furnishings, but Tom Kemp kept up the pressure for talent, and on occasion stole talent from Tabor's house.

Tabor, Leadville's popular postmaster-grocer-mayor, joined the ranks of the silver kings in May of 1878. By August of the following year he had gained national fame, was Lieutenant Governor of Colorado, was growing tired of Augusta, his dowdy, austere New England spouse, and was starting construction on his opera house, a house that, when completed, was said to be the finest theater between St. Louis and San Francisco.

The grand opening, Wednesday night, November 20, 1878, was marred by a vigilante hanging across the street. The victims were launched from the rafters of a partially completed building next to the court house. The prospect of open war with the lawless element prevented a packed house, and surely provided the theater goer with a preoccupation that might have detracted from

the event. Still, the patrons filled over half of the over eight hundred seats, and, while they may have been preoccupied, they could not help but notice the grand furnishings. The main curtain was a hand-painted scene of the Royal Gorge and was backed by eight drop curtains* "ready to lend the proper background for any scene the entertainment might demand." The seats were a red plush made by Anderson's, a manufacturer of patent opera chairs. The stage was 35-by-55 feet and was equipped with the popular trapdoor of the period. Below the stage were the dressing rooms, a large one for the chorus and several small individual rooms for the leads, and a very plush one for the star. The house was heated by a massive coal furnace, a first in Leadville, and a leader in all of the West. Lighting was supplied by seventy-two gas jets, the first building in Leadville so lighted. The gas was provided by Tabor's Leadville Illuminating Gas Company, the offices of which were housed in the Opera House.

Jack Langrishe and his troupe of players filled the opening night bill. They were a popular

*Many of these drop curtains are still in the theater and are occasionally used today.

Tabor's Opera House. Note walkway at right to the Clarendon Hotel. *Photo Source: Colorado Historical Society.*

group and had played in many of the mining camps in the area as well as in Denver. The feature attraction was the *Serious Family*, supplemented by a farce, *Who's Who*, which was written by Langrishe for the occasion. Both productions were well received, but it was the opera house that garnered the raves.

While there was little doubt or question about the excellence of Tabor's house, there were numerous questions about Horace himself. Eddie Foy remembered, "When I met him he had passed the million mark, was wearing $600 nightshirts and had a daughter whom he christened Silver Dollar, but he hadn't become the insufferable snob that might have been expected." He goes on to explain why Tabor was liked by the common people. "He was popular because he was still genial among ordinary folks and hadn't forgotten how recently he was a small potato himself." Others, such as Elder, describe him as a "terribly profligate man." He explained to his family back in Pennsylvania that Tabor "owned a house of ill-fame named the 'Mollie May' on Harrison Avenue about three blocks from my office which he has just sold for $10,000 for a court house." A friend of Elder's described Tabor as an "ordinary common looking man, ignorant and illiterate."

It seems fair to conclude that much of Elder's criticism is the result of outraged Quaker blood and ignorance. The house he speaks of was owned by Mollie May and sold by her. There is no reason to doubt that Tabor did hold an interest in the house; but he, like the rest of Leadville, was a product of his environment. He had arrived from Maine some twenty years earlier with some rough edges, and living in Oro City, Buckskin Joe, and Leadville did little to smooth those edges or give the man an Easterner's polish. Tabor, like the rest of the West, had little time, inclination, need, or opportunity for "book learnin'." One incident Foy described illustrates the colorful and possibly endearing quality of Tabor's ignorance — in fact the ignorance of the West. Tabor was doing some political campaigning with a learned orator from the East. At the close of the orator's speech he made a classical reference to a speech on the coming eve, "'Tomorrow night we meet the enemy at Phillippi!' Tabor immediately rose in his place in the audience and said, 'Judge, you are mistaken; it is at Montrose Junction.'" Tabor was not the first nor the last to get caught in the classical trap, but he managed to do it with great gusto.

Eddie Foy had met his wife in Leadville the previous season when she was playing as one of the two singing Howland Sisters. He and a friend took the three women, mother came along of course, to dinner at the Tontine on several occasions. It was not long before Rose Howland and Eddie were married, and Eddie began searching for suitable housing. It was the winter of 1879 and suitable housing was not to be had, but he did locate a vacant room and the young couple moved in. "We were just as happy as if we had been in the Palmer House in Chicago. We were young, and that rare, zippy mountain atmosphere at ten thousand feet above sea level put plenty of joy and kick into life."

One of the most popular performers of the period was a young Cornish lad with a golden voice and a warm, happy heart. Charles Algernon Sidney Vivian was born in Exeter in 1846, the son of a Cornish clergyman. Vivian traveled to the United States and landed in New York in 1867. He and several other young fellows organized a delightful evening group called the Jolly Corks. Vivian was chosen Imperial Cork. The group was organized for simple fun and frolic until one of the members died. His widow was penniless and destitute. Vivian successfully led his fellows through the group's reorganization as a benevolent society. Later the name was changed from Jolly Corks to the Benevolent Protective Order of Elks. The Elk symbol was chosen, according to his wife, when they saw a great elk swimming the Missouri River on one of their many trips out West.

Vivian played successfully in most of the cities and camps of the booming West, and was a well-known, popular performer when he came to Leadville in 1880. He decided to try his own production in the Cloud City and rented a hall where he presented a somewhat condensed version of *Oliver Twist* with his wife as Oliver and himself as the Artful Dodger. The rest of the parts were handled by some skillful double and triple casting. The Vivians, like everyone who came to the silver camp, had a difficult time finding a place to stay. Foy offered them his hospitality. Mrs. Vivian and Rose Foy, Eddie's wife, stayed at the Foys', while Charles and Eddie "bunked on the concert hall stage."

Charles spent much of his free time searching for accommodations for himself and his wife. Meanwhile the show was doing poorly and was forced to close after a short time. The miners just did not seem to go for Dickens, and no matter how artful the Dodger was, it was not enough to bring in the crowds. After closing Vivian went to

The Jolly Corks. Vivian, in front to the right of center, was the group's leader.
Photo Source: Colorado Historical Society.

concert halls like Wyman's Place and did much better. He was a great one-man show. His monologues were popular, and his singing brought down the house, especially his rendition of "Ten Thousand Miles Away."

The winter wind raked the town, the accommodations Vivian located were poor, and sanitation nonexistent. Pneumonia ravaged the camp. Vivian contracted the dread disease. Weak, and thousands of miles away from home, he died in Leadville that winter of 1880. He was buried in Evergreen Cemetery. His casket was delivered by an ordinary express wagon since the town had not had time to purchase a hearse. A band accompanied the large, silent procession, and on the way back to town it began to play Vivian's "Ten Thousand Miles Away" and a shiver slipped through the crowd. The concert halls put on benefits for Vivian's wife and raised enough money for her to go back east. The Elk's Lodges later moved Vivian's body to Boston where a fitting memorial was established. Ironically, Vivian was never a member of the Elks.

The drafty variety halls of Leadville claimed another famous figure. John Baker "Texas Jack" Omohundro survived the Civil War, cattle drives on the old Chisholm Trail, and scouting for the U.S. cavalry, but not Leadville. He was a friend and companion of William F. Cody and Ned Buntline. He was a guide for the Grand Duke Alexis of Russia and the Earl of Dunraven. In 1873 he toured in a show with Buntline, Cody, and Mademoiselle Guiseppina (Josephine) Morlacchi, "the noted danseuse." He was smitten by the lovely, dark-eyed beauty, and they were

married on August 31, 1873. The show, *Scouts of the Plains,* continued, and the newlyweds traveled with it until it closed late in the spring of 1874. After trying his hand at writing, in 1878 Texas Jack opened his own show, *Scouts of the Plains.* In March of 1880 he and his wife were in Leadville, appearing at what was probably the Coliseum on West Chestnut Street.

Texas Jack had limited theatrical ability, but his past and associations were a continued draw. His wife, on the other hand, "was at the time the leading star in her profession." Jack's plans for Leadville seemed to include settling in the Magic City for a while, possibly for health reasons, but more probably for financial purposes. He joined the Tabor Light Cavalry, captured a trio of stage robbers, and in general made himself useful.

Late in May 1880, he picked up a cold. He resisted for as long as his wife would allow, then finally went to bed, expecting to be up and around in no time. A few days later, he, like Vivian, was dead of pneumonia. He was buried in Evergreen Cemetery. A modest headstone marked the grave. In 1908 William "Buffalo Bill" Cody came to Leadville and visited the grave of his old associate. Appalled by the paltry marker he had a bold, granite headstone placed at the site.

Leadville's theaters and concert halls were undaunted by all forms of disaster. Several of them burned, and before the coals were dead a new structure, grander and more gaudy than the last, rose in its place. Elder recounted with disgust the "immense crowds of fancy women who turned out to see the fire" in one such theater.

Texas Jack's grave in Evergreen Cemetery, Leadville. *Photo Source: Author's Collection.*

Advertisements were as garish as the fare. One theater, in addition to bands and banners, burned fires on its roof, a trick in a clapboard town that was sure to draw a crowd.

Another aspect of the theater was the involvement of the local theatergoer. They followed the players' lives and their performances with an eagerness that made the movie madness of the 1920s pallid by comparison. Characters were threatened with pistols. Hamlet often had help from someone in the audience. Advice, derisive or otherwise, was often shouted by an over-zealous patron, and it was not uncommon to have fights break out in the audience. Those who believed in Brutus broke chairs over the heads of Antony's supporters. On one occasion, Bert Laiscell, a tightrope walker and aerialist of some skill, was dropped by his catcher. "I fell like a shot, landing on my head and right shoulder on top of the piano, cutting a five-inch gash in my scalp and smashing a violin to pieces." He got up and climbed back up to his swing. By the time he got there, a dozen or so revolvers were trained on his catcher and angry voices demanded to know who was responsible. The gunmen were asked not to be hasty. Laiscell prepared to try again. "I'm coming again." And to the men with the six-shooters, "If he lets me fall this time, *shoot to kill.*"

The money those early, drafty, heatless, smoky, dingy theaters netted was phenomenal. For instance, it was reported that Theatre Comique rented for $1,700 per month, $20,400 per year, and still made a profit. The estimated daily gross income was $1,200! Not all the paying mines were in the hills.

For those more sporting individuals who did not want the folks on the stage to take all the chances, a plethora of houses invited persons to play games of chance at their tables during the show. Also, for the outdoor types a racetrack was built in 1879. Of course, a fellow with a fast horse could always get a race, track or not.

Some of the gambling halls, such as the Texas House, were finely furnished and were suitable rivals for the grand eastern houses or river boats. There was gambling for everybody. No one was left out. Foy recalled, "They were gambling in tents and even in the open alongside the sidewalk. You could get any sort of bet, from five-cent chuck-a-luck up to a five thousand dollar poker pot." It was said that James V. Dexter, a successful mining man and promoter, and his cronies played for thousand dollar pots all the time in his elaborate cabin on West Third.

One newcomer recounted an experience in one of the gambling halls. "In order not to attract attention I pretended to be interested in some shooting" in the saloon's gallery. He sided up to the bar where three men were standing. One of the men was the "capper." The capper had a large wad of bills "$100, I suppose, under his hand. The next man was his pard and he had several sets of dice and boxes and he was endeavoring to put up the 'greeny' to bet against the 'capper.'"

The pilgrim continued to watch and when he felt a tug at his sleeve he turned. "Haven't I seen you in Kansas City?" He shook him off. "I guess not," and continued to watch the cat and mouse game. "I had not watched them more than five seconds before I felt another twitch and a villainous chap hissed in my ear 'Watch out or you will get slugged.' I turned around and found half a dozen sharps watching me and the game. I remarked that I wanted to see the game when the same fellow said 'Well keep away or you'll get slugged.' I immediately left the concern. What slugged means I cannot imagine as I am not very familiar with the 'sharps' vernacular."

The atmosphere of all the gambling dens was one of unlimited prosperity. In some the games were more carefully controlled by the house than in others, but in all cases the purpose was to separate the uninitiated from his bankroll. The footpads did it quickly with a gun in the street; the gamblers with a toothy smile in a smoke-filled room. The method varied with gambler and gambling hall, but the result was the same. The greenhorn came out with an empty purse. The houses did everything they could do to attract a crowd. The Little Church on the Corner had three musicians stationed in one of the front windows. The group consisted of a violinist, a harpist, and a cornet player. "Each," it was said, "apparently plays any tune that occurs to him, and the result may be imagined. Strangers who hear this music for the first time clap their hands to their ears and rush madly away." If a person stayed around long enough they might get used to it. The older residents "sometimes go in and curse the musicians for a short time, but the relief afforded in that way is only temporary."

Faro was the most popular game and was played in every saloon and gambling hall in Leadville. Good faro dealers were among the highest paid citizens of the camp. Another popular game was chuck-a-luck. This game very probably gave the English language the term "tinhorn gambler," since the dice used in the game were thrown from a horn-shaped container. The betters placed their bets on a number, one to six, and watched. Three dice were thrown, and if one of the numbers came up on one of the dice the player won.

Of course a considerable number of poker tables flourished in every establishment. Drink flowed freely and an occasional bit of dubious entertainment was presented. Also, a wide variety of colorful characters wandered through the bars and gambling dens. Violence often erupted at the turn of a card, or with the exposure of cheating by the night's winner. One of the camp's successful card sharks was a man called the "Professor." As with many gamblers he had his own trademark — gloves. One evening a fellow had a few drinks too

many and determined to find out what the Professor had under his gloves. He watched the gambler and seeing his chance, "he hurled the Professor back in his chair, and after choking him a minute, remarked, 'Now I am going to choke the life out of you if you don't tell me why you wear them gloves all the time.'"

The Professor seemed nonplussed by the whole affair and nodded, "All right." The assailant released his grip, waiting for the reply.

"Because I choose to," and his revolver spoke more loudly. The inquisitive young man fell backward "with a bullet in his shoulder. 'Would any other gentlemen like to ask me any questions?'" All seemed to have lost interest in the gambler's gloves.

And what was it like to walk into a Leadville gambling hall during the summer of 1879? The first impression would have been an air of confusion and hustle. The second feature of any gambling hall that assailed the patron was the noise. A make-shift band played several songs you had never heard and quite possibly neither had the band. Three drunks in a corner would invariably try to harmonize a melody that none remembered, or if they did the outrageous bleating of the band kept them from hitting a harmonious note. Shouts from the bar and tables for drinks mingled with music and laughter and curses and the rattle of dice. The crew assembled before the altar of Lady Luck ranged all the way from the "sharps" with their polished boots, pearl stick pins, gold watches, and slick, curled mustaches to bearded, dust-covered miners with slouch hats and baggy canvas trousers, their red woolens protruding, frayed and soiled at neck and sleeve, from their flannel shirts. A keen-eyed gambler could not tell who had money. Dress was no indication.

Many persons with no home, or none that they recalled, sat and sipped a beer at the bar, or slept in a chair in a warm corner until some prankster kicked the chair out from under them and the fight started. The usual quota of "toughs" capable of licking the whole world slouched at the bar and tripped greenhorns as they came in the door. Greenhorns were always fair game for pranksters and gamblers. It was something of a race to see who got to them first. Usually the fun was not too rough, but a "swell" was something else again. A greenhorn was any newcomer and could be an all right sort, but a "swell!" A swell was someone who put on airs and considered himself a cut above the usual citizen. It was always open season on "swells," and anything short of murder was acceptable, since

A place to sleep was a major problem, as illustrated in this drawing which appeared in *Frank Leslie's Illustrated Newspaper*, June 7, 1879. *Photo Source: Library of Congress.*

whatever he got he obviously deserved. A good many eastern lads who felt their family origin gave them special privileges found themselves groping around in an alley for some portion of their dignity, or at least their pants.

Saloons probably served up entertainment for more miners than any single amusement. There were over one hundred listed in the 1880 city directory for the City of Leadville and all seemed to make a "fair showing." Most neighborhood saloons catered to a particular group, either occupational or national. The Irish, Swedes, Germans, all had their neighborhood pubs, as did the smelter workers, railroaders, teamsters, where friends would gather in the evening to discuss the day's work, politics, and the general conditions of the camp, state, and nation. The neighborhood saloon served much the same social function as the Midwest's general store. Those saloons with entertainment, be it stage shows, women in a variety of capacities, or a makeshift band, tended to be more cosmopolitan than any neighborhood establishment.

One of the more popular saloons of the cosmopolitan variety was Wyman's Place. It was unique because its owner was unique. Wyman's Place, located on the lower end of Harrison Avenue, was run by Pap Wyman, a good businessman, good Christian, and enthusiastic supporter of Leadville. Wyman would not allow married men to gamble, sent them home early, and saw to it that they did not blow their pay on drink. He had a large sign beneath the clock: "Please Do Not Swear." Beneath the clock and sign sat a large Bible. It has been said that those who did not heed the sign spent some time reading from the Bible to atone for their sins, or found themselves in the street. Wyman was a popular fellow and few refused to do as he asked.

Like Wyman's Place, most saloons were named after their owners, and a potential patron could get some idea about the clientele by the name. Obviously, Mrs. Duffy's and O'Reily's served a good brand of Irish whiskey and a lot of talk of the old country. Kirschbert's Colorado Beer Hall usually had a crowd of Prussian gents leaning against the bar, while Tomsick, Usnik, and Zaitz catered to the Slovenians.

Many drank what was served and much of it was of very low quality. Others, with a bit of cash and a desire for a long, full life, spent more and got a better grade. Nationals often ordered and received drinks from their native land. The English, Irish, Scots, and Welsh ordered a variety of beer, stout, and ale. Germans were not forced to go without their kimmel or the Dutch their gin. Wines from Italian and French wineries were available to anybody who could pay the price. Of course there were the domestic brands, such as Old Joe Gideon, Quaker Maid, Ed Top Rye, Elk's Milk, and Hayner's.

The desire for sophistication among Leadville's unsophisticated rich enabled a Denver sharpie to sell champagne bottles filled with an effervescent concoction of brown sugar, water, and yeast to Leadville's carbonate kings for outrageous prices. The most enjoyable part of the whole affair was to watch the boys drink the stuff, rave about its qualities, and get tipsy on it.

Charles E. (Pap) Wyman. *Photo Source: Colorado Historical Society.*

It has been estimated that residents of the Cloud City consumed two hundred kegs of beer per day in the early eighties. The going price was down to a nickel a glass, the result of a price war among the various saloonkeepers. Finally they got together and set the price at ten cents a glass, a price that continued to fluctuate, not below that figure, but above it. A good bartender made $100.00 a month, which was a good deal more than a miner, who worked for three dollars a day, ten hours a day, six days a week. By June of 1879 the town supported in varying degrees of affluence about 350 barkeeps.

Women were introduced in the saloons as waitresses in June of 1879 and, since women were somewhat rare in the Cloud City, they were very popular. They were called "beer juggers" and were paid five cents out of every dollar they took in. All were encouraged to partake. "For Wine, Women, and Fun walk straight ahead." In the Carbonate Beer Hall a sign suggested "patronize the bar." The doors swung open and "inside were gathered about forty men, taking their pleasure with infinite sadness."

Of course anything out of the ordinary was sure to bring in customers and as a result the management of Leadville's one hundred plus saloons encouraged and supported anything from snake charmers to brass bands. "The man who shot apples from his wife's head with a Remington rifle, in the Keystone Saloon last evening, drew a crowd of humanity and a bag of silver." In addition to the bands, magicians, shooting exhibitions, the saloonkeepers, if they had the room, provided dancing. The going rate fluctuated, but twenty-five cents a dance seemed to be the usual price. A girl who knew her business usually managed to sell a few drinks as the evening wore on as well as collect for the dancing she did. Regrettably, the situation forced on most of these girls was deplorable, and for many it was the final step on the road to prostitution. Elder commented on the situation in a letter home during the fall of 1879. "In your last letter you refer to the possible disappearance of the Dance Houses. Well when I came here there was but one in operation. There are now six in full operation and all within the space of one block and on the same street." It got worse before it got better.

The dance hall girls were described all the way from religious to tawdry, depending on who was describing and who was being described. "If you step across the threshold you will soon be approached by a painted syren who in the seductive parlance of the place will extend the courtesies of

77

the place by 'Say, ain't yer going ter treat?' Decline and the fair Hebe will politely inquire, 'What kind of fellow are you anyhow! Guess yer nothin' by a snide.'"

Some of the girls were no more than twelve or thirteen years old. They came from all over the country. Some were orphaned, others ran away from unhappy homes only to find greater unhappiness. Still others started husband hunting and were forced into the dance halls to live. All seemed to be running; some after something, others from something.

Sweet tells about a charming girl, "not over 16" dancing with a man with a wide-brimmed hat, a chew in his jaw, and a massive cigar jammed in his mouth. They were good dancers, and he watched them waltz around the room. As he watched, the man next to him explained the girl was from a Missouri river town. She was "ruined" by an unscrupulous fellow and ran away from home. Her family thought she had thrown herself in the river and mourned her loss.

Competition was the order of the day and when the girls in the Red Light Dance Hall heard the ladies in the Bon Ton claimed shorter skirts a Donnybrook loomed. About three in the morning the Red Light sisters met in the wine room for a few drinks and a council of war. "Speeches were made . . . a vote was taken and the unamimous voice of that scarlet outfit was for 'war to the knife, and the knife to the hilt.'"

They marched on the Bon Ton, located across the street, and "stormed the breast-works." The action was shortlived, but bloody. "The air was thick with wigs, teeth, obscenity and bad breaths."

Back in the Red Light short minutes after the fray they surveyed the damage. "One girl had a finger badly bitten, another had about half of her hair pulled out, a third one had an eye that looked as if John L. Sullivan had snubbed it." Several of the girls were hauled off to the "cooler" by a courageous policeman. It was never determined who, Bon Ton or Red Light, had the shorter skirts.

The lowest rung on the social ladder was crowded with an army of variously painted and gowned harlots. There were those who haunted

INTERIOR OF A DANCE-HOUSE ON STATE STREET.
COLORADO.—A NEW ELDORADO THE WONDERFUL MINING TOWN OF LEADVILLE.—From Sketches by our Special Artist.

A State Street dance-house. *Photo Source: Denver Public Library.*

the saloons, dance halls, and cribs on State Street and those who ran the "fancy houses" on West Third and West Fifth streets. Tiger Alley, north of State Street and Stillborn Alley south of State Street, rang with every form of human corruption and debasement. Tiger Alley was probably named for the gambling establishments that butted against its soiled void, since gambling was known as "bucking the tiger." The number of bodies of men, women, and children found in Stillborn Alley, especially unwanted infants born of the wretches who inhabited the cribs along State Street, surely gave the alley its name.

Since prostitution was never legal, it could not be taxed, but it was real and needed to pay its way. The local police came up with a procedure that satisfied the ladies, their customers, the courts, and for a while, the general public. On the twentieth of each month each madame paid a fifteen dollar fine, and each "boarder" coughed up five. The only problem the police faced was payment on time. The girls had the "bad habit" of 'standing the officers off,'" the chief of police reported. And since the "police depended mainly upon this revenue for the payment of their salaries each month they were much disgusted at the delay."

There was no doubt about it. Prostitution was an accepted business enterprise in Leadville, and if the public was outraged it maintained remarkable silence and composure. Duane Smith, author of a number of works on western mining and mining camps, claimed that Leadville, of all the mining settlements "was the only camp which seemed to take real pride in its depravity." Smith's remark appears harsh, but probably is impossible to refute, especially when one is reminded that as late as the 1960s Leadville proudly boasted the continued, almost enthusiastic, operation of the Pioneer Bar, said to be the oldest operating house of prostitution in Colorado.

It has been reported that there were over two hundred prostitutes in the State Street brothels. This makes no allowance for the street walkers, nor the madames like Frankie Paige or Sallie Purple who moved into more fashionable quarters north of the red light district. Unfortunately, the good prostitute, like the good fairy, was seldom seen or heard. Stories of ladies like Red Stockings have spread a silken shroud over the real lives of these soiled doves. With few exceptions the Leadville whores died a miserable, disease-racked death while still relatively young. They died alone and broke after lives of violence, drunkenness,

and unhappiness. There is nothing quite so poignant as the old, haggard lady of the night; a lady who once had men flocking to her side and now has nothing. One observer noted, "The women are the most forlorn looking pieces of humanity I have ever seen. One of them down at the 'Red Light' committed suicide last night by taking poison." He went on to explain, "It does not make any difference how many of them die, there always seems to be a perfect scramble to fill their places."

While the community tolerated the bawdy house and even took pride in the quality of the town's wickedness, the "soiled dove" remained more soiled than dove. Still, it was possible, though difficult, to rise above one's reputation, if not above one's station, and earn the respect, albeit a grudging respect, of the greater portion of the community. One such madame was Mollie May.

Mollie arrived in Leadville in 1879 and by 1880 was housed next door to her arch rival, Sallie Purple. The two madames competed for press and people for their houses, Mollie at 129 West Fifth and Sallie at 133 West Fifth. On one occasion the pair got into a fight over "the merits of Connaught and Tipperary as birthplaces." They shouted insults between the two houses as

Mollie May is buried directly beneath this giant evergreen in Leadville. *Photo Source: Author's Collection.*

they prepared to do battle. Guns and ammunition were stockpiled and war began. "The girls and guests in both houses joined in the fray, pumping lead into the two houses." No damage was done, and after an hour or so they went back to their regular business, possibly renewed and refreshed by the change in routine.

Mollie was a generous contributor to local charities such as the hospitals and churches. On one occasion she adopted a child and faced the "better people's" outrage with outrage of her own. She was allowed to keep the child, and while it is not known what became of it, Mollie did leave a considerable legacy when she died in 1887, and it is assumed she saw to it that the child was provided for.

Mollie's funeral was one of the largest the camp ever saw. It was a great event. Too bad Mollie missed it.

Think of her mournfully;
Sadly—not scornfully—
What she has been is nothing to you.
No one should weep for her,
Now there is sleep for her—
Under the evergreens, daisies and dew.

Talk if you will of her,
But speak not ill of her—
The sins of the living are not of the dead.
Remember her charity,
Forget all disparity;
Let her judges be they whom she sheltered
    and fed.

Keep her impurity
In dark obscurity,
Only remember the good she has done.
She, to the dreggs has quaffed
All of life's bitter draught—
Who knows what crown her kindness has won?

Though she has been defiled;
The tears of a little child
May wash from the record much of her sin;
Whilst others weep and wait
Outside of Heaven's gate,
Angels may come to her and lead her in.

When at the judgment throne,
The Master claims his own,
Dividing the bad from the good and the true.
There pure and spotless,
Her rank shall be not less
Than will be given, perhaps unto you.

Then do not sneer at her
Or scornfully jeer at her—
Death came to her and will come to you.
Will there be scoffing or weeping
When like her you are sleeping
Under the evergreens, daisies and dew?

VIII

The Wheels of Progress

The railroad reached town in July of 1880 and it was not long before the town had an abundance of professional people with a variety of skills, diplomas, and recommendations. "Lawyers rushed to Leadville in increasing numbers, until, as one wag put it, you could not throw a club across Chestnut Avenue without hitting two or three of them." Over 120 lawyers made Leadville their home, while almost half that number of doctors attempted to correct, medically, the effects of alcohol, altitude, cold, and 120 lawyers.

One early legal aspirant was young George R. Elder, late of Lewistown, Pennsylvania. He arrived in Leadville on January 28, 1879, and spent his first night in camp at the Tontine Hotel. After searching for a couple of days he found an office, "13 ft. by 10 ft. and the floor very roughly made as also the walls," for twenty-five dollars a month. He planned to take his meals at the Tontine, which was one of the better eateries in town, try it for a month, and then see if he could improve on the situation and cut the costs.

He set up his office and waited for his library to arrive. The eternal pessimist, he wrote, "I have no great expectations but I shall stick by my office and try to merit success."

He moved out of the Tontine and took a room in a cabin owned by an Irish widow lady from "the renowned city of Dublin." His office was "absolutely the coldest place" he knew of, and he went out and bought a stove and pipe for $9.25, but he still was unhappy with the room. He continued to search for a location large enough that he could live in it as well as use it for his office. Late in February he located suitable accommodations and moved in. It was primitive, but it was home.

Gradually business began to come his way. "I have already filed two complaints in the county court and have one suit before a Justice of the Peace." His books arrived, his notary's commission provided him with a small income plus the opportunity to meet many people and encourage further business. One month after he hung his shingle he was able to report favorably to his father that he had made $21.00, and felt it "quite a fair showing" for an unknown. He did not allow his head to be turned by new affluence. "I intend to stick closely by my office and study hard."

After a busy summer and a lot of hard work, the following winter found him prospering. "I began a suit yesterday against another of the 'bonanza mines of the camp,' 'The Little Lulu vs. the Little Ellen.'" He was also engaged in litigation in the Waterloo, another local mine. One of the methods of payment in suits was mine stock and his holdings in some of the mines paid good dividends. In addition he purchased shares in several claims. By December of 1879 he could boast "five large suits in the District Court at Jan. Term." Another means of increasing his income was open to him but he disdained it. He wrote his father that Nash and Thompson, associates of his, were "loaning money at 5% per month ... If that is not Shylock with a vengeance, what is?"

Young Mr. Elder went on to hold several county offices and positions of trust and honor in the new camp. He married and settled down to stay.

"It is stated as a fact that cats will not live at this altitude." The *Daily Chronicle*, when they printed that statement, never made clear whether the cats were unwilling or unable, but their point is clear, nevertheless. Living at altitudes in excess of ten thousand feet was not recommended for cats or humans. The Leadville camp had the most rigorous climate and was the highest mining camp of note up to that time, and there were many who felt it was not "fit for man nor beast." But a decade after the birth of Leadville the mood had changed and local doctors were extolling the virtues of high altitude living and the "surplus of ozone."

According to the Tenth Census, published in June of 1880, the most common cause of death in 1879 was rheumatism, followed by "Crippled, Maimed," which appears to indicate those who died as a result of accidents in mines and in construction. Pneumonia was the third largest killer in the camp. "Blowed up in a mine" accounted for one death, while "Altitude" accounted for two as did "Shot Wound" and "Sore Throat." One person died of each: "Sore Foot," "Sore Hand," and "Sore Eyes," while one unfortunate succumbed to an "Old Army Wound." Gunfights in Leadville, as throughout the West, were not the deadly disease television has made them out to be. The census, missing one ward and not overly accurate, still lists only two people as dying of "Shot Wounds"; and it is not clear if these were self-inflicted, accidental, or the result of a "shoot out." Climate, diet, housing, hard work, and hard liquor accounted for most of the deaths, either directly or indirectly. And doctors.

It is not difficult to understand why some sixty-one physicians and surgeons were listed in the 1881 *City Directory*. They were as varied as their names and credentials. Many had graduated from the great medical schools of the east, others had a degree from the "School of Hard Knocks" and sold medicine to the highest bidder. Of the sixty-one doctors listed in 1881, only twenty-three could produce diplomas from "recognized medical schools."

A dozen or so dentists had settled in the Carbonate Camp by 1880, and one name stands out among the rest; that of Henry Rose. He and his family served the dental needs of the people of Leadville for over three-quarters of a century.

Young Henry Rose arrived in Leadville during the summer of 1878. He was unable to locate an office immediately, so he set up practice on the sidewalk at the southeast corner of Chestnut and Harrison Avenue. There, under a street lamp, on a folding chair, he began practice.

His hours were six in the evening until ten. There was little business during the day because the miners and prospectors were all busy. After work, though, things picked up. According to his grandson, Dr. William Rose, he used a kerosene lantern for additional light, and the bulk of his business consisted of extractions. All sterilization was done with whiskey, and those who wished anesthetic had a shot of the same. It is not clear whether the anesthetic went with the price of the extraction, was extra, or the patient provided his own.

Doctor Rose continued his work under the street lamp for some three months before he

Offices of Leadville's first newspaper, the *Reveille*. *Photo Source: Author's Collection.*

found suitable accommodations. Once properly housed he did a variety of dental duties, but the one that impressed him the most were the Negroes who came in for caps of gold. One Leadville Negro had six gold caps on his uppers and in the center of each he had diamonds encrusted. Several had designs of hearts, diamonds, spades, and clubs that let the enamel show through.

In January of 1878 Leadville was without a paper of its own. Papers from the other camps and Denver were slow in arriving and had little information of local interest. Before 1890 twenty-six different mastheads would make their appearance. The local miner's union had its own called *The Crisis*. The Democrats and Republicans would support several; the German population had its *Deutsche Zietung;* the people of Chestnut Street supported the *Chestnut Street Boom*, or *Broom*, depending on the source. The *Dome City Blade* cut its swath, and the *Free Lance* attacked almost everybody. But it was young "Dick" Allen, Richard S. Allen in print, who was first.

On the east side of Mosquito Pass, Allen ran the *Fairplay Sentinel* and could not help but hear the sounds of money being made on the other side of the ridge. During the fall and early winter of 1877-1878 he made plans to haul his plant to the new camp, and shortly after the first of the year he made his move. Some sources claim the first issue of the *Reveille* came out in August of 1878, but it seems likely that he was in business much earlier. According to the *Engineering and Mining Journal* of March 30, 1878, "Leadville now possesses a newspaper, the *Lake County Reveille*, the first number of which appeared on 23rd of February of the present year." Allen started modestly with a weekly morning paper and "he would have done well if his habits had been steadier."

82

Competition soon arrived to plague the fledgling paper. Allen's neighbor, William F. Hogan, from Alma, Colorado, a mining camp a few miles north of Fairplay, arrived in the fall of 1878 with a "shirt-tail full of type" and dreams. Hogan hauled the plant from his *Mount Lincoln News* to Leadville, picked up Democratic supporters such as Nelson Hallock, a locator of the Carbonate Mine, and set out to drive Allen's Tabor-supported Republican number off the streets. The first issue of the *Eclipse* came off the press in the fall, and since the paper was both morning and daily it presented an immediate threat to the *Reveille*. Allen got a bit of encouragement from the *Georgetown Miner* in late November. "Dick Allen, of the Leadville *Reveille* is a brick. He started the pioneer paper in that town, and he doesn't propose, now, to be outdone in the race for supremacy; so he announces to the world that on the 1st prox.—next Monday probably—he will issue the *Reveille* as a daily. Good luck to you, Dick, for old acquaintance sake."

Allen's plan seemed to work since the *Miner* noted in their December 21 issue, a short three weeks after the change in the *Reveille*, that "The Leadville *Eclipse* of the 12th came to us printed on wrapping paper."

Edward M. Hawkins came to Colorado from Joliet, Illinois, in 1876. He bought into the *Sunshine Courier* when the Sunshine camp promised the moon. He and his partner, John B. Bruner, ran the paper for some time, but the ore pinched out, the moon set, and their clientele left for greener pastures. They closed up shop, tried their hand at mining, and eventually ended up in Leadville. Hawkins became city editor for the *Eclipse*. Bruner arrived shortly after Hawkins, and they decided to try a paper of their own. "The outlook for our newspaper enterprise seemed very good," Hawkins recalled, and he was particularly unimpressed by the current competition. "The *Reveille* and the *Eclipse* did not promise great opposition. Dick Allen was a man of parts, but his success had apparently turned his head and he had fallen into bad habits, at the same time neglecting his business." Hawkins had worked for Hogan's *Eclipse* and knew the situation there. "Billy Hogan was at best a figurehead, and his paper did not amount to very much."

The Daily Chronicle staff from left to right, C. C. Davis, James Burnell, and Col. John Arkins. *Photo Source: Colorado Historical Society.*

But trouble was in the wind. While Hawkins and Bruner waited for the South Park Railroad to unscramble the freight jam at the end of the line at Bailey, a trio of Denver-based newsmen were also looking the place over. "They brought a carload of paper, a cylinder press," $13,000 worth of equipment, and announced their intentions to begin the publication of an "up-to-date daily newspaper," which they dubbed *The Daily Chronicle*, later the *Leadville Evening Chronicle*.

Hawkins took one look at the new competition and rerouted his equipment to Fairplay where he and Bruner filled the void left by Allen's departure.

It was in the fall of 1878 when James Burnell, one of the triumvirate who created *The Daily Chronicle*, was first dispatched to Leadville to weigh the chances of success for an afternoon daily. He returned to Denver. His estimate was favorable. The three, James Burnell, Colonel John Arkins, and Carlyle Channing Davis, decided to resign their positions with the *Denver Tribune* and set up shop in Leadville.

Davis recalled that Colonel Arkins secured a sagebrush-covered lot, 25-by-67 feet, for $175. His title consisted of a "Squater's quit-claim deed." They built a slab shanty, 20-by-30 feet, and began the furnishing. It took them four months to locate enough bricks for a chimney, and when they finally had their stove set up, they found they could have had the bricks mailed to them cheaper than the local price they paid. They tried to secure Associated Press dispatches, but failed, so they did the next best thing. They hired a Denver associate to glean important bits from the Denver papers and send them up as "specials." They used a cypher or code and telegraphed messages over Mosquito Pass, and with the help of Arkins made major stories out of a few words.

The paper was without a subscription list when it hit the streets. Davis reported that he was willing to settle for an initial sale of five hundred copies. Before the day was out, street and over-the-counter sales totaled over nine thousand, which was more than the total population of the camp. By the first of May the new paper was averaging five thousand street sales per day and had two thousand more subscribers on newsboy routes. They quickly drove the two pioneer papers off the streets.

In large measure the success of the *Chronicle* was the result of level-headed management, creative thinking, and a lot of hard work. For instance, their Western Union line over Mosquito Pass occasionally blew down, fell down, or was knocked down by winter snowslides. The *Chronicle* editors would accompany Western Union crews in blinding snowstorms and bone-chilling cold to help repair the line so the news could continue to flow. Neither did they forget the value of a good selling job. Their newsboys, according to Davis, used to shout such come-ons as, "Here's your *Evening Chronicle!* All about the shipwreck in California Gulch!" On one occasion Davis saw a small delivery boy and he asked, "Where do you get your papers, young fellow?"

"Oh, I buy 'em of Johnny Green."

"Oh, you buy them of Johnny Green! What do you pay for them?"

"Five cents."

"What do you sell them for?"

"Five cents."

"Well, you don't seem to make any profit at that rate. What do you do it for?"

"Oh, just to get to holler."

One aspect of John Arkins that became near legend was his niggardliness. One of Denver's famous literary figures, Eugene Field, described his penurious policy as being so severe ". . . in regard to the uses of paste, towels, and the leavings of lunch that he starved out 500,000 dependent roaches."

Launched at the same time as *The Daily Chronicle* by the same trio was the *Carbonate Weekly Chronicle*. It was a wrap-up of the past seven days and was a very popular mailer that found itself in mining clubs, club rooms, banks, and investment houses on both sides of the Atlantic. It did as much as any single vehicle to tell the Leadville story to a waiting world.

During the early months of the paper's first summer, Burnell caught a bad case of mining fever and sold out to his partners and headed for the Red Cliff region. Colonel Arkins hung on until April of 1880, but was forced to sell out because of ill health. He moved back to Denver where he bought into the *Rocky Mountain News*, Colorado's pioneer paper, and became its editor for a number of years. Burnell eventually rejoined him as business manager.

Three local Republican businessmen got together during the summer months of 1879 and formulated plans for a new publishing company. The trio was determined to establish a first-rate paper to support the party point of view and supply stiff competition for the *Chronicle*, though the Davis paper was Republican. The three directors, William H. James, Robert G. Dill, and William H. Bush formed their corporation, The Leadville Herald Printing Company, early in the fall of seventy-nine. It was filed for record on

October 3, 1879, and according to Dill, their first publication hit the streets on October 21, 1879, a Tuesday.

R. G. Dill. *Photo Source: Author's Collection.*

Dill was the newspaperman in the group and became the editor. William H. Bush, the second member, was a successful Leadville businessman by 1879. He owned the Clarendon Hotel and was a business associate of H. A. W. Tabor. The third member of the group was the Honorable William H. James, mayor of Leadville. With Bush and James' money and prestige, plus Dill's know-how, the new paper was an immediate success and had the backing of the Republican majority in the county.

Two Republican papers was too much for state Democrats. John M. Barret, manager of the *Rocky Mountain News* and one of the leading journalists in Colorado, interested W. A. H. Loveland, the owner of the *News,* in a Leadville venture.

Loveland and Barret organized a company with Loveland the major stockholder. The rest of the stock was picked up by leading Leadville Democrats. They hired M. J. Gavish to edit the new enterprise and published their first *Democrat* on January 1, 1880. Barret was the general manager, but he remained in Denver. All went well until the miners went out on strike in mid-summer, 1880. A disagreement between Leadville owners and Loveland forced the latter out of the venture and left it in Leadville hands. John L. Bartow was hired to take over the editorship of the *Leadville Democrat,* and the situation stabilized but the paper remained weak, an easy prey for Davis' pioneer *Chronicle.* In 1883 the Democrat's paper began to "exhibit that tired feeling." Debts mounted, the board of directors fell to bickering, and when Davis made an offer that would let everyone out free of debt, the offer was eagerly accepted.

After a fierce battle with Tabor and the Republican-owned *Herald,* Davis managed to buy out the last major competitor. He combined the *Herald* and the *Democrat* forming the *Herald Democrat,* a daily, and continued the *Carbonate Weekly Chronicle.* Leadville continued to see a wide variety of papers come and go, but the *Herald Democrat* and the *Carbonate Weekly Chronicle* outlived all comers and are still being published today.

No story of Leadville journalism would be complete without Orth Stein, who went to work for Carlyle Channing Davis in 1880. He invented his first assignment on the train to Leadville. Stein, the "eldest son of one of the first families in Indiana," visited local doctors, posing as a young medical student looking for a possible place to practice. He found that one doctor's diploma was really a "working card in the plasterer's union." It was filched by Stein and later printed in the *Chronicle.* Several boasted no experience in medicine and no training. Others laughed greedily when fees were mentioned. There were several doctors in need of a doctor shortly after the *Daily Chronicle* hit the streets.

When there was no news, Stein was at his imaginative best. He created a vast cavern north of town, his Cyclopean Cave, complete with stalactites, stalagmites, underground pools, a bottomless lake, and even an underground river. It was an enduring piece of fiction. Even today there are people who swear they "know a fella" who "knows a fella" who has been there.

Others of his enduring tales concern an abominable snowman, a great underground wreck of a ship that seemed to have an early Egyptian registry, a mummified body, a sea serpent in Twin Lakes, and the discovery of a man's remains with chains about his neck and bowls of food just out of his bony reach.

Orth Stein's Cyclopean Cave. *Photo Source: Denver Public Library Western History Collection.*

Unfortunately Stein was of somewhat loose construction. Davis in one breath claims, "I here record a conviction that his peer as a reporter has never yet been born"; and in a second breath, he was said to "prefer infamy to fame. . . ."

After a couple of years in Leadville, Stein went to Kansas City, where under the name John Bell, he worked for the *Star*. The eternal triangle caught up with him, and in a fight over a chorus girl, Mattie Hartlein, he killed a variety theater owner named Fredericks. He was charged with murder, convicted and sentenced to be hanged. With death waiting, his family came to his rescue. According to one source, his mother used her wealth and the family's social status to save her son from the hangman. Davis claims that Stein's maternal grandfather (or uncle), Godlove S. Orth, saved him. Chances are it took both to free the lad. He was granted a stay of execution and while waiting for his second trial was welcomed back to Leadville by Davis. He immediately ran up a number of large debts and had a hound of creditors after him. "I soon was forced to recognize," recalled Davis, "the painful fact that the man was hopelessly lost."

The second trial brought an acquittal. The last Davis heard of Stein, he had stolen his mother's jewels and money and fled his hometown of Layfette. Other sources see him leading a life of ever-increasing degeneracy until he died, ostensibly from consumption, in New Orleans in 1901.

What happened to Orth Stein? What caused the precipitous decline of Leadville's greatest newsman? Davis washed his hands of Stein with the statement, "There will be no profit in pursuing him through a subsequent career of crime, or waste time in guessing what particular jail or penitentiary claims him for a guest."

Before leaving Leadville for Kansas City, Stein went to Denver to take a job on one of the large dailies. He had been in town almost a week when he heard that a group of Leadville cronies were staying at the Palace Hotel. He set out that same evening on foot for the Palace. As he reached the corner of Fifteenth Street and Blake he was set upon by a would-be assassin, who struck him a severe blow just above the right eye. Stein struggled to draw his pistol, unconsciousness overcame him and he fell to the sidewalk.

"It was this unfortunate experience on the streets of Denver that seems to have been a turning point in the life of Orth Stein." Many of his friends claimed his periodic declines, criminal behavior and inability to get and hold a job all stemmed from "cerebral injuries received during his beating." It can be argued equally well that the man who on the one hand exposed the malpractice of a host of Leadville doctors, and on the other duped a whole community time and again without explanation or apology, was of mixed parts from the outset. The basic appreciation of right and wrong and any responsibility for the well-being of others might have been lacking in Orth Harper Stein. But, oh, what a yarn he could spin.

The safe in Tabor's store, according to Gandy, was the town's first semi-official bank. The first official one was founded in early April, 1878, and was dubbed the Lake County Bank. A year later it became the First National Bank and moved into a new stone building on the southeast corner of Harrison Avenue and Chestnut Street. The town's second bank, the Miners Exchange, opened in April, 1878, a few days after the Lake County Bank. The most important aspect of the Miners Exchange Bank was that two of its founders were A. V. Hunter and George Trimble. These two Missouri gentlemen worked for James McFerran in his Colorado Springs People's Bank, both married McFerran daughters, and both grew rich in Leadville finance. They were backed by their father-in-law in their first Leadville banking enterprise. In early October 1881, the brothers-in-law sold their holdings for a tidy profit. Then, after all the boom-day banks had folded, in 1884 they got back into the banking business; first as the Trimble and Hunter Bank and later as directors of the already successful Carbonate Bank.

A third banking venture of note was Tabor and Rische's Bank of Leadville. It opened first in a corner of Geegge's Drug Store on October 15,

The Carbonate National Bank, Monday morning, October 1, 1888. At left of picture, Vice-President A. V. Hunter, bearded; President D. H. Dougan, seated; and J. C. Mitchell, the Cashier sporting the bow tie. *Photo Source: Colorado Historical Society.*

Photo Source: Author's Collection.

1878. Frustrated employees in an effort to answer all questions with a single statement prepared a sign "which hangs just beside the cashier's window at the Leadville Bank in Geegge's store, reads as follows: 'This is not the express office, nor the stage line office, nor the Little Pittsburg office, nor the telegraph office, nor Mr. Tabor's office — Damn!'" Those young gents who could not stand seeing anyone get the last word walked up to the window and asked, "Is this the mayor's office?" At this point it seems safe to assume that the cashier found a simple "damn" inadequate to cover the situation and resorted to somewhat stronger language.

Not long after the Leadville Bank had opened, Tabor and Rische began construction on a new building which, when complete, was according to Ayer, "the finest building in Leadville." It

was winter when the staff of the Leadville Bank moved into their new quarters across the street from the Lake County Bank on the corner of Harrison and Chestnut. The first floor housed the bank that was elegantly furnished with a black walnut counter, French glass front, and heavy glass plating on the interior. The second floor housed business offices, the most spacious and "tastiest" of which was occupied by Mr. Tabor. They handled between $75,000 and $90,000 in over-the-counter business every day. Still, some of their credibility was destroyed on February 6, 1879. George Fisher, cashier of the Leadville Bank, was hard at work on the morning in question when a portion of the wall began to lean streetward. The wall continued to sag, a crowd formed, police were called and roped the area off. A large timber was hauled to the scene, but no one had the courage to place it so it went unused. About 11:30 A.M. the wall crashed into the street. It seems a portion of the wall, cemented together in the late fall, had frozen in place rather than set. A warm day in February brought the section down. It was quickly repaired and business continued as usual.

Leadville in 1879 and 1880 was a retail merchant's dream. Everyone consumed, was willing to pay the price, and, for the most part, could afford to pay the price. For those who were latecomers, the cost of getting into business was considerable. First was a location. If you could purchase a lot, which was doubtful, you would find yourself paying upwards of a thousand dollars for anything suitable on Harrison Avenue or Chestnut Street. The same lots a year previous in 1878 ran from $50 to $100. Rents were high. A good store site on one of the major streets ran "from $200 to $300 a month," and that for a one-story structure 25-by-40 feet. Office space, if you could find it, went for $30 to $100 per month.

Most of the retail workers who came to Leadville expected to go into business for themselves. There were almost as many grocery stores listed in the Leadville City Directory in 1880 as saloons. The list of barbers rivaled that of the doctors and every type of retail endeavor was represented. Tobacco shops proliferated, as did bakeries (eighteen). The town boasted five "Booksellers and Stationers," a bowling alley, a candy factory, a cracker manufacturer for those who required something in their soup besides yesterday's leftovers, and an ice dealer.

A soap manufacturer, Miller and Periolat, located at 123 West Second Street, supplied, no

Tabor's Bank of Leadville.
Photo Source: Colorado Historical Society.

doubt, some of the necessities for the Turkish baths up on East Second Street. John B. Hill made vinegar, horseradish, and pickles at his place at 230 East Third Street. Another vinegar producer was located at 404 West Sixth. Bucktown, just west of town, also had a soap works. "Reef, Prince and Knuckles had a big store at 231 West 3rd. This store used to have herds of cattle driven into Leadville to be slaughtered in Slaughter House Gulch."

Charles Boettcher, one of Leadville's successful young merchants, came to America from Germany when he was a lad of fifteen. After successful ventures in the hardware business in Cheyenne, Greeley, Fort Collins, and Boulder, he decided the new camp of Leadville was ideally suited for hardware, and he left Boulder for the Cloud City. Boettcher secured an excellent site for his store on Harrison Avenue between Third and Fourth streets. The structure that Boettcher built was two-story brick with a full basement. It was equipped with an elevator that served all three floors. The basement and third floor were used for storage and the first was the business hub of the growing Boettcher empire. In back of the store was a large tin shop that provided not only the Boettcher store with a variety of tin goods, but also the rest of the hardwares in town. Boettcher's hardware, by 1881, was employing twenty-six men, twelve of whom worked in the tin shop. His stock was so great that, in addition to the two floors of storage, a two-story warehouse was built on West Fourth.

Boettcher, like many other Leadville business leaders, realized that Denver was gong to be the major city in the state and eventually he moved his holdings to the capitol. There he was the driving force behind the Colorado Portland Cement Company, which eventually became Ideal Cement. At the same time his interest in the Colorado sugar industry led to the eventual creation of Great Western Sugar Company.

One of the West's most successful merchants was a likeable little German Jew named David May. May was born in Kaiserslautern, Bavaria. He worked with his father in their store, but realized his chances of success in Germany were limited to someday taking over the family business, and he wanted more.

David May had an uncle who was established in the clothing business in Cincinnati. Fifteen in 1863, May left home and family for the new world, filled with hope and fear and keen anticipation. He found work with his uncle and did well, becoming a partner in the business. All this was halted by a bout with pneumonia. He recovered, weakened, his lungs threatened by tuberculosis. His doctor told him he would surely contact the dread disease if he did not go west to Colorado and rebuild his exhausted lungs in the dry western air.

May left for Manitou Springs, planning a limited stay to regain his health. With a group of clothing merchants who were visiting the area, May traveled to Twin Lakes to do some fishing. When the group arrived at the lakes they heard the stories about the new camp of Leadville and, being merchants first and fishermen second, they abandoned their fishing trip and traveled the additional fifteen miles to Leadville. Accommodations were limited in the Magic City, and they found themselves sleeping in a hayloft. After looking the camp over, the rest returned to Manitou, but May stayed on.

He was not in town long before he met Jake Holcomb, a victim of malaria, who was out West, as was May, trying to regain his health. The pair staked a claim they were sure would make them rich. But wealth eluded them. However, they reaped a benefit more valuable than money. The hard work, clear dry air, and the simplicity of their task restored their health. By winter May was clear on one thing. Mining might restore his health, but it was not going to line his pockets. He and Holcomb, after pooling their thoughts and resources, bought out the "meager stock of a clothing and implement merchant" who had lost all he had in worthless mining ventures. The new store featured the riveted overalls manufactured by a Californian named Levi Straus. They advertised the product as "California Riveted Duck Clothing." Another product that was to form the basis of the May fortune was "Pure Medicated Scarlet Wool Undershirts and Drawers," or, as the miners knew them, "long johns."

Business was good and May wanted to build a new, larger building, but Holcomb and a silent third partner were cautious. May determined to go it alone and built a new structure on Harrison Avenue and on January 1, 1878, opened the Great Western Auction House and Clothing Store. Eventually he formed a partnership with Moses Shoenberg. It was a faithful union, for it provided him with a lifelong friend, and in the summer of 1880, a wife. Rosa Shoenberg, dark-eyed and winsome, won the love and affection of thirty-two-year-old David May and fell heir to a fortune.

May and Shoenberg did business at a number of sites in the 1880s. Always stiff competition for Leadville's "leading dry goods store" owned by

DRY GOODS!

CLOTHING.   CARPETS.

Daniels, Fisher & Co.

—OFFER—

EXTREME BARGAINS

TO CASH BUYERS OF

Dry Goods, Clothing and Carpets!!!

OUR SPRING STOCK IS NOW COMPLETE IN ALL

DEPARTMENTS

Is Five Times the Largest We Have Ever Shown.

301, 303 HARRISON AVENUE.

Photo Source: Author's Collection.

W. B. Daniels, W. G. Fisher, and Joel W. Smith, they at one time operated two Leadville outlets plus a number of stores around the state. May D and F department stores are contemporary proof that Leadville competitors finally resolved their differences and merged.

In 1879 David May, always concerned about people, was one of the founders of the Hebrew Benevolent Association in Leadville. In 1881 May, a Republican, was elected Lake County treasurer; then was reelected in 1883. It was his first and last venture into public office.

In January of 1885 May bought out Shoenberg, and the modern May Company was born. May Company stores spread across the state and his eldest son, Morton J. May, was "destined to succeed to the presidency of the nation-wide May operations."

While the saloons and beer gardens did a great business slaking thirsts, three breweries were busy providing the substance to put out the fire. Feuerstein's brewery and Koch and Lichter's brewery were located north of town on the Ten Mile Road, while Henry Gaw's Columbine beer was manufactured and bottled in his plant located in California Gulch "opp Lake Co. Sampling Works."

Henry Gaw was one of the first to locate in the new camp, arriving with his family in the spring of 1878. A native of County Down, Ireland, he knew the value of a good beer. His family left Ireland for Montreal, and it was there that Gaw began to learn the brewer's trade.

In 1875 the Gaws, with three daughters, Clara,* D'Arcy, and Polly, and a son, Will, set out for Colorado. They settled first in Idaho Springs, about thirty miles west of Denver on Clear Creek, gateway to the high Rockies. Shortly after their arrival Gaw bought out a local brewery and set to work. The plant seemed to be prospering, when late in 1877 or early 1878, fire wiped him out.

He sold his gold watch, gathered his family, the few undamaged vats, and set out for the Magic City. Breaking frozen ground in March, 1878, Gaw began construction of Leadville's first and most famous brewery. By 1880 Gaw was producing 120 kegs of Columbine Beer per day and shipping it all over Colorado.

Not so popular with the men, but a hit with children and women, was soda water, a forerunner of the modern soft drink industry. Isaac Hougland made and bottled the popular drink at his home on West Third. Frank Schmidt and F. M. Aldinger had a larger operation located on the back of the lot at 112 East Chestnut.

In a town that was as male oriented as Leadville, it was difficult to find respectable jobs for women. The two standbys were boarding houses and washerwomen. Out of the forty-five boarding houses listed in Leadville in 1880, twenty-five percent were owned by women, and there is no telling how many more were managed by women. It was the most popular form of housing for single men, and the boarding house institution flourished in Leadville well into the 1940s.

Nine laundries served the town's needs in 1880, but the bulk of the washing was done by washerwomen, or if you prefer, laundresses. Since the town had made it clear that Orientals were not welcome, the Irish washerwoman controlled the market. Prices were high, $1.50 to $3.00 per dozen for shirts, especially when it was a practice to lose a shirt or collar — always one of the newer ones.

Probably the most famous laundress was Mrs. Sarah Ray. She located lots at the corner of

---

*Clara Gaw married a local metallurgist from Wales, named Harvey Norton, in 1899. When Mr. Norton died in the 1920s, Clara continued to run his Leadville assay business throughout the '20s and '30s. She, with others, organized the "Leadville Historical Association," responsible for preserving most of what remains of Leadville's past.

Gaw Brewery, home of Columbine beer. *Photo Source: Author's Collection.*

Harrison Avenue and Second Street early in 1878, built a slabsided shanty and hung out her sign — "Lundry." Business was good and with her profits she erected a two-story brick building. Lot jumpers tried to take her "claim" from her, and she is said to have stood off some of the town's most notorious characters with nothing more than a broom and a whip of a tongue.

Another washerwoman, not as successful as Sarah Ray, but every bit as colorful, was "Crazy Jane." She used to pick up the laundry in the saloons around town and if she could find a listener, which was not difficult in afternoon saloons, she would tell them about her husband, the pirate. According to Jane, he stole her, a lovely young maiden, from her parents and carried her away on the high seas. Unfortunately, he was captured, presumably by the British, and hung from the yardarm of a man-of-war. When she heard the news, she set out for Leadville. Why Leadville? That was never made clear.

The more refined ladies who found themselves in need of support went into millinery and dressmaking. Nine such shops were located in the Magic City in 1880, and every one of them was owned by women. Later, a large number of respectable women found employment in the public schools, others set up and taught classes in music and elocution, and still others became instructresses of the dance.

Jewish merchants found a home and a fraternity in the pawnbroker busines. Nathan Cohn, A. Goldsoll, Meyer Goldstein, Morse J. Levi, Sol

Levy, and Joseph Samuels controlled the market. E. L. Wheeler, author of the Deadwood Dick dime novels, set one of his adventures, *Deadwood Dick's Leadville Lay,* published in 1889, on the doorstep of a fictional Leadville pawnbroker named Rachel Cohen. The tension mounts as Dick and his faithful companion, Billy Bucket, unravel the mystery surrounding the comely-looking Jewess.

Freighting was one of the most important industries in the Cloud City and, while stage drivers were the elite and not unlike modern airline pilots in prestige, the largest fraternity, and by far the loudest and zaniest, were the freighters. Men like Shorty Dunn and Al Dickens were the idol of every boy who could holler and

Wallasey's, a typical Leadville laundry. *Photo Source: E. J. Callahan.*

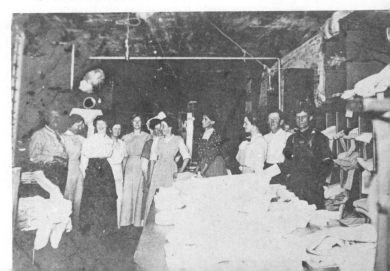

spit. Whispering Jim Lowery, it was said, "could be heard 10 miles away — more or less."

Those freighters who hauled into Leadville, either from the railheads or from surrounding communities, were a separate fraternity from those who hauled ore from the mines. In both cases some owned their own rigs, and they made good money. Those who worked for someone else tended to enjoy their work and the prestige that went with being a muleskinner, freighter, or ore hauler, but they did not get rich.

Freight rates into the new camp were, in the first few years before the railroad came to Leadville, changeable, but always bordered on highway robbery. Freight from Denver went for $50 a ton in the summer — more in winter. There are records of "4, 5, 6, and even 10 cents a pound" from Denver, and on at least one occasion a local merchant was forced to pay 25 cents a pound for a load of liquor, "then an absolute necessity — so considered — in the new camp," which, if you figure it out, comes to $500 per ton. One historian tells of a Leadville clergyman who had some books sent to him from England. "The books reached Denver from London at a cost of $22.00; the bill for forwarding from Denver to Leadville was $36.00. The clergyman refused to accept the books and left them at the freight office 'for the perusal of the company's employees.'"

The freighting of Leadville ore by 1878 employed almost six hundred teams and a corresponding number of skinners. Ore haulers were paid by the ton, and most rigs hauled between 15,000 and 17,000 pounds, depending on the road conditions. Wagons weighed around 3,000 pounds empty! Most roads to the railyards and smelters were downhill, with an occasional short climb. Drivers often worked their rigs in pairs, and "doubled." Doubling was a method of using both teams to pull a load to the crest of a hill, unhitching both teams and pulling the second load up, then hitching up to their respective wagons and continuing.

Haulage costs were based on distance. Those from the east side of town, such as the Sixth Street shaft to the Rio Grande yards at Twelfth and Poplar, went for fifty cents a ton, and they usually hauled lighter loads with two-horse teams. Longer trips required more horses and greater loads were hauled. The long trip from the Continental Chief in Iowa Gulch, some ten miles distant, cost $2.50 per ton.

It was the driver's job to care for his team and wagon, to load and unload the ore, and to haul it. If he was lucky he hauled from ore bins that were elevated, and gravity would load all or part of the load. Usually, though, he was forced to hand-load at least some of the ore and often all 17,000 pounds had to be hand-shoveled. His day, according to Ivan Crawford, whose father was a Leadville muleskinner, was of his own design. He was not required to work a certain number of hours, but rather to make a certain number of trips, the number usually based on the distance to be traveled. He wanted to get started as early as possible, so rose around four or four-thirty. He fed, curried, and harnessed his team, had breakfast, and by six he was on the road. "Frequently on short hauls, the trips would be all completed and the team back in the barn by two or three o'clock, perhaps even a little earlier." When he was out of town, he took a lunch and fed his team oats in a nosebag and often some hay. In winter his lunch had to be thawed on some "shafthouse boiler."

Usually, four-horse teams were employed. They consisted of two "wheelers" that worked on either side of the oak tongue immediately in front of the driver and were the mainstay of the operation. They usually weighed between 1,400 and 1,600 pounds. The "leaders," the front pair, were smaller and more agile, weighing between 1,100 and 1,300 pounds. They were hitched on most rigs to an "iron rod extending underneath the wagon tongue back to the axle joining the front wheels." In six-horse hitches a "swing pair" was added between the wheelers and the leaders. The leaders then were hitched to chains that connected to the iron bar of the swing team. It was the job of the wheelers to provide much of the power and do the backing when necessary. The leaders were important in the maneuvering of the rig.

The wagons were solidly built and set on four wheels that were two and one-half or three inches wide. Each felly and spoke was of wood, usually oak. The wagon beds generally ran eleven feet long and three feet wide with a bed nineteen inches high with additional sideboards that increased the bed height to around three and one-half feet. Chains were stretched across the bed to keep it from spreading.

Winter gave wagons, teams, and drivers most of their problems. The wheelers in winter were equipped with sharp steel spikes on their shoes called caulks, to keep them from slipping. Crawford describes the method of "rough-locking" used by haulers to slow the progress of wagons on steep hills. It consisted of "wrapping a chain with links square in cross-section about the rear wheel, fastening this chain to another which was connected with the front axle." The wagon was then driven forward, rolling the chain around the face of the rear wheel until it was tight, and locked the wheel. The square links dug into the icy surface, and if done correctly, it required considerable effort for the team to move the wagon even downhill. The great danger was a lock that failed to hold or a chain that broke. If the rough lock turned loose, driver and team were in for a hard ride that often resulted in a dumped load, injured team and driver. Crawford recalled a time when he and his father were hauling from the Continental Chief down snow-choked Iowa Gulch. Suddenly there was a "loud pop" as the rough-lock broke. The left side of the wagon missed a bridge, and they rolled into the creekbed. Young Ivan jumped clear, but his father was partially buried in ore. The team received cuts and scratches, but everyone managed to come out of the affair with only minor injuries.

While the smelter at Malta was the first in the area, it was August R. Meyer, through the good offices of the St. Louis Smelting and Refining Company, who introduced the smelting industry to Leadville. Meyer, after shipping ore from the Rock Mine early in 1876, was empowered by the company to establish the A. R. Meyer and Company Ore Milling and Sampling Company. "The firm began operations in Leadville early in the fall of 1876." The following year Meyer's reports brought Edwin Harrison to Denver in June 1877. Harrison, president of the St. Louis Smelting and Refining Company, is said to have been a quiet, unassuming man of considerable charm. He was tall, lean, and quietly industrious. Born in Washington, Arkansas, in 1836, his father, a successful merchant, moved to St. Louis when Edwin was only four. His father sent him to the best schools and by the time he was twenty he had studied in France (was fluent in French), in Belgium, and at Harvard under the renowned Professor Agassiz. When, at forty-one, he visited California Gulch he was already a powerful figure in the industrial and smelting world and was president, not only of the St. Louis Smelting and Refining Company, but also headed up the Iron Mountain Company (owners of Missouri's Iron Mountain ore deposits), his own Edwin Harrison Company, and Chouteau, Harrison, and Valle's rolling mills.

Ore wagon near the Presbyterian Church on West Eighth. *Photo Source: Author's Collection.*

It was no problem for a man with Harrison's holdings and reputation to raise the funds for the construction of a smelter in California Gulch, nor for one of his experience to size up the situation and strike with energy and enthusiasm. A two and one-half acre site was selected, probably by Meyer, and construction began, apparently in May, which would indicate the decision to build had been made before Harrison arrived in Denver. Meyer, who had recently been appointed general manager of all Colorado operations, and Harrison planned and built the Harrison Reduction Works during the spring and summer of 1877, and by October the first furnace was in blast. Ore was weighed and sampled at Meyer's Sampling Works, then smelted in Harrison's Reduction Works, or if superior grade, shipped immediately to the St. Louis Refinery.

The company's first and continuing problem was not ore; there was plenty of that. It was coke. There was no coal in the area and while charcoal could be manufactured from the surrounding forests, coke, a by-product of coal, was necessary, even if the total need could be reduced with local charcoal. To supply that need August R. Meyer hired "sixteen teams of oxen to haul the products of their smelter over the mountains to Colorado Springs and return with El Moro coke."

The area's first smelter, the Malta works, located at the mouth of California Gulch in the summer of 1875, was designed to handle lead, primarily from the Homestake and Printer Boy mines, and from the outset had difficulty. The plant itself was deficient, and coke, of course, was in short supply.

The plant was eventually incorporated in March of 1877 by a group of Ohio investors, who put up too little and expected too much, and like most poor boy operations the resources were average size and the dreams — well, they were dreams. They hired Emile Loescher, of whom little has been written, though he seems to have been well qualified, and at least one man in the area, Maurice Hayes, territorial assayer, had a high opinion of him, calling him a "gentlemanly and efficient manager."

Being a gentleman and efficient was not enough for success in the upper Arkansas in the late seventies, and the plant, after a checkered history in which it was closed more than it was open, was sold in the spring of 1878 to one J. B. Dixon and his family. Brothers and their wives all pitched in and got the plant ready to reopen, which it did on September 1, 1878. It was refitted and with Loescher still at the helm, began doing

business. According to J. T. Loomis, who was looking the area over, the rebuilt plant produced its first bullion on October 12, 1878.

The operation struggled on for another eighteen months, and finally the competition forced them to close. Too many problems with the plant, a greater distance than most smelters from the mines, inability to get coke, and probably poor, or at least uninspired, ownership contributed to its demise in the spring of 1880.

Meyer's Sampling Works was the first, but was not the only sampling works for long. In the waning months of 1877 Nathaniel Witherell and Theodore Berdell set up an office in Malta and began purchasing ore for the Omaha Smelting and Refining Company. They paid good prices and according to the *Engineering and Mining Journal*, "The miner here gets the advantage of competition." Their connection with the works in Omaha seems similar to that of Meyer and his relationship to the St. Louis Smelting and Refining Company. Not long after they established themselves at Malta they entered the smelting business as officers in the La Plata Smelter.

The most successful of the early sampling works was established July 3, 1878, by Edward Eddy and William H. James. The two partners followed similar paths. Edward Eddy, the younger of the pair by two years, was born in Cornwall in 1840. He studied the mineral industries of Britain and, when twenty-one, sailed for America. His first permanent home was in Georgetown, Colorado, where he met Mr. James, then superintendent of the East Terrible Mine, who gave Eddy his first job in the Colorado mining industry. James was from Wales, came to America with his parents when he was eight, and studied the watchmaker's trade. Lured by stories of gold near Pike's Peak, he and his young wife set out for Colorado when he was twenty or twenty-one. For a decade he flirted with mining — ventured and lost, repaired watches, then ventured and lost again. In 1871 he became the "super" at the Terrible, and it was at that point that Eddy entered his life for the first time.

After a short time the East Terrible Mine was sold to European investors, and James went to South Park where in 1873 he was engaged in hydraulic mining. Eddy saved his money, invested it wisely in mining ventures around Georgetown, and a few years later moved up the gulch and built the Silver Plume Sampling and Concentrating Works in the town of Silver Plume. In 1875 James left South Park and went to Lake County as the superintendent of the Printer Boy. He traveled around much of the state as mining man and as representative from Lake County to the state Constitutional Convention. In February of 1878 Edward Eddy came to Leadville to look the new camp over, and he and James surveyed the area's prospects, forming a partnership that was the beginning of the Eddy and James Sampling Works.

The new plant was in operation by July 3, 1878, and was described as a "very neat sampling works, with a fine plant of new machinery." Eddy and James shipped ores to a number of smelters and acted as agents for several smelters such as

Mather and Geist's new plant in Pueblo. In addition to the sampling business, James, always active in politics, became mayor of Leadville in April of 1879, a post he seems to have filled with an easy charm and considerable distinction. His affable manner was a welcome contrast to the brisk, often crude methods of operation in the Magic City's first months.

The sampling business was good, and a number of ore buyers and sampling works faded in and out of the picture in the next two decades. But by far, the most important works were the three mentioned above, all of which tied themselves to a local smelter within two years of their organization.

The rush to get in on the sampling business was more than matched by the rush to open smelters. With the Malta smelter getting by and the newly opened Harrison Reduction Works increasing their capacity during their second summer to two furnaces, the mines began to produce much more than local facilities could process. So a third smelter opened on September 23, 1878. The operation was the product of James Benton Grant's initiative and knowhow, and his uncle's money and contacts.

James Benton Grant's ancestors came from Scotland and settled in the Carolinas. Like many Carolina families that wested, some settled in the south, some went north. James Benton Grant's branch of the family settled in Alabama in 1848, where in January of that year he was born. With only a quick taste of the antebellum South, James and the rest of that unreal world of planters and slaves were plunged into the Civil War. When the war ended James sought out his namesake and uncle, Judge James Grant of Davenport, Iowa, one of the members of the Carolina Grants who chose to go north when the family split. Judge

James B. Grant. *Photo Source: Author's Collection.*

Grant Smelter. *Photo Source: Pioneer's Museum.*

Grant welcomed the young southerner, befriended him and sent him to school. He went first to the Agricultural College at Alma, today's Iowa State University, then to Cornell, and eventually to the School of Mines at Freiberg, Germany. While finishing his studies in metallurgy he traveled throughout Europe and on completing his formal education came home to the United States via the Far East. His voyage the long way round took him to many of the famous mining regions of the world.

Back in the United States he stopped in Colorado, first at Mill City, then at Central City, where he engaged in assaying for a short time. He then accepted an offer from the Pueblo and Oro Railroad to explore the Leadville potential and determine if the new camp would justify the construction of a railroad from Pueblo, the state's growing industrial center. His survey assured the Pueblo capitalists that the Leadville mines were among the richest and most extensive he had seen. The survey also gave him the opportunity to explore on his own. He passed his assessments on to his uncle back in Davenport, and not long after he finished his work with the railroad entrepreneurs, set out for Davenport himself. The result of his Leadville trip was the Grant Smelter, incorporated as James B. Grant and Company, and located three blocks west of Harrison's works between Leiter Avenue and Maple Street on the south side of Front Street. The plant was fully a block long when ore bins, loading docks, offices, and the smelter itself were included.

Shortly after the Grants set their enterprise in motion, a trio of gentlemen who were already prominent in the sampling and ore purchasing industries established another reduction works in Leadville. Nathaniel Witherell and Theodore Berdell, along with their "silent partner" Charles B. Rustin, the onetime president of their parent organization, the Omaha Smelting and Refining Company, finished their first large building in June of 1878. Others followed in rapid succession and by October 1878 they were in operation. The plant, just west of the city limits, was an immediate success and continued to grow until by December of the following year they had four furnaces in operation. In June of 1879, as a result of a search for additional capital, a group of New York money men entered the enterprise. Berdell, Witherell and Company was reorganized as the La Plata Mining and Smelting Company.

During the winter of 1878 two prominent German smelter men, Gustav Billing and Anton Eilers, began making plans to sell their interest in the Germania Smelting and Refining Company near Salt Lake and open a plant of their own in Leadville. Shy, quiet, somewhat distant when first introduced, Gustav Billing did the leg work, examining the prospects and reporting back to Eilers. Once decided upon, the project moved rapidly ahead, and by May of 1879 the Billing and Eilers Smelter, located just north of what became Stringtown, was in business. The Utah Smelter, as the Billing and Eilers plant was locally known, was a success from the start, no doubt the result of excellent management and top flight equipment. By the end of their first year of operation they were the third largest producer in town, following the Grant and La Plata works.

A number of other smelters fired their furnaces and a few are worthy of mention. One of the more active and aggressive firms was Cummings and Finn, located in Big Evans Gulch. Another Big Evans firm, and there were plenty, was the Elgin Smelter, located just west of Cummings and Finn. The Elgin was a small, but well-equipped, plant, and under a variety of managers was for a number of years a successful producer.

In the spring of 1879 a group of Illinois merchants and railroad men of substance organized the American Mining and Smelting Company, not to be confused with the later American Smelting and Refining Company. The plant was one of the most aggressive competitors in the camp. It bought from all quarters and continued to prosper even though it sat between two Leadville giants, the La Plata on the east and the Billing and Eilers plant immediately to the west.

La Plata Smelter. *Photo Source: Author's Collection.*

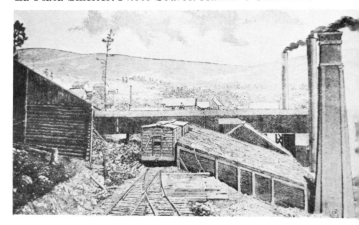

Some of the mines decided to try their hand at smelting and the Little Chief and Adelaide both built plants. They were poorly planned and poorly run and folded shortly after they commenced. Other projects that had short histories and grand plans included the Lizzie, an early pioneer whose only possible claim to fame was the anticipation in their choice of name of Henry Ford's four-wheeled Lizzie, the Abby Smelter, Frankie Ballou's Union Smelter, Manville Smelting Company, and Tabor's Chloridizing and Amalgamation Mill, which burned not long after it opened. Dozens of others, to greater and lesser degrees, helped give Leadville in the early eighties the largest smelter production in the state. One source lists forty-four smelters and reduction works in Leadville from its first plant at Malta in 1875 until the American Smelting and Refining Company's plant closed in 1961.

A smelter was a difficult undertaking, but making it pay, and continue to pay, was even more difficult. A successful smelter had to have qualified management, skilled workers, and top equipment.

The operation consisted of three major parts. The assaying of ores to determine processing methods and value of the ore, the smelting of the ores, and the business operation that consisted mainly of purchasing and selling the ore. Of the latter, purchasing was the all-important function. Supplies of ore had to be maintained or the furnaces were shut down. Ore had to not only be purchased at a competitive price, but had to have the proper mix of minerals to insure the most profitable smelting.

Assayers were employed by the smelters, by mining companies of size, and in a number of independent assay offices that served the needs of individuals and small mining operations. Fourteen assay offices were listed in the *Leadville City Directory* of 1880. Most had at least two assayers in each office and a couple of helpers. Many had larger staffs. Compared to the four listed in 1879, the single year's growth was phenomenal.

Assaying was a kind of miniaturized smelting. The ore was pulverized and divided into the quantities necessary for each test. Each step was carefully controlled and measures were extremely fine and accurate. In testing for lead and silver, which was the most common and most important test during the eighties, the assayer used a very delicate balance and usually measured out one-tenth of an ounce. The desired amount of ore was then mixed with lead and borax to provide a flux, poured into a scorifier (a small cup made of fire clay), and then placed in a small furnace.

After about thirty minutes the vessel was removed from the furnace. It contained a heavy black liquid that was poured into a container and allowed to cool. When cooled it would contain, hopefully, a small button of silver and lead at the bottom. To separate silver and lead, the button was placed in a cupel (a small cup made of bone ash). Once in the cupel the ore was reheated. After

The American Smelter, not to be confused with the American Smelting and Refining Company. *Photo Source: Western History Collection, University of Colorado.*

Edward Mondy, Leadville assayer at work. *Photo Source: Author's Collection.*

fifteen to thirty minutes the lead was absorbed by the cupel and the remainder, a pinhead, was pure silver. The amount of silver remaining in the cupel determined the richness of the ore; the amount per ton. A pinhead of silver would make the ore assayed run about two hundred ounces of silver per ton; very rich ore!

Assays run by smelters were done the same way, but a sample of all ore hauled was necessary to get an average. Occasionally there was a disagreement between mine and smelter over the content of the ore. In case of such a disagreement, the two would hire a third, unbiased, assayer, both agreeing to accept his verdict.

The operating smelter must have been the closest thing to hell that most men could envision. It was either hot or cold, depending on what part of the plant you were working in, and always noisy and gaseous. With over a dozen smelters working in Leadville by 1880, the whole town was covered by a blanket of noxious black and yellow smoke that made modern pollution appear mild by comparison. Old-timers claimed they could predict the weather by the way the smoke was behaving. If it rose high and straight the weather was going to be good, but if it slid back down the outside of the stacks and over the rooftops of cabins and shacks surrounding the smelter, a storm was on its way.

The smelter, while often operating on a grand scale, worked on a very simple principal, that of specific gravity. The ore, once the assay was run, was mixed with predetermined amounts of coke, iron and limestone flux, then melted. If the mixture was poorly proportioned the results could be costly. The lead and silver were allowed to settle to the bottom of the vessel where they were drawn off and poured into ingots. The slag, or waste material, was drawn off at a higher level, poured into slag pots, large conical vessels, and dumped on the slag pile. That, simply stated, was smelting.

Mention should be made of milling. It was a poor man's substitute for smelting. They both attempted to do the same thing — separate the chaff from the wheat — but smelting was far more efficient and far more costly. Milling was a water process not unlike the old sluicebox method and was used primarily with gold ores. The ore was crushed and washed over a series of riffled water tables. In many mills tables were made to vibrate to increase the washing action. The lighter material, waste, washed aside, and the remaining material, called concentrates, was trapped behind the riffles. The problem faced by all mills was how to increase the percentage of silver or gold in the concentrates without losing too much in the process. A little silver or gold, whichever was being milled, was lost with each washing. Chemicals such as mercury and cyanide were used, which increased the catch of precious metals but poisoned the mountain streams and rivers so thoroughly that many still have not recovered from the muck that was released into them.

One of the misleading factors concerning mining was the notion that if silver was selling for a dollar on the New York market, that was the price the miner was paid. Not so. Silver was bringing around $1.08 per ounce on the New York exchange in 1879. The rates in January, 1879, in Leadville were as follows:

For ores carrying 50 to 60 ozs. silver per ton, 44 cents per oz.
For ores carrying 60 to 70 ozs. silver per ton, 55 cents per oz.
For ores carrying 70 to 80 ozs. silver per ton, 61 cents per oz.
For ores carrying 80 to 90 ozs. silver per ton, 65 cents per oz.
For ores carrying 90 to 100 ozs. silver per ton, 68 cents per oz.
For ores carrying 100 to 120 ozs. silver per ton, 71½ cents per oz.
For ores carrying 120 to 140 ozs. silver per ton, 73 cents per oz.
For ores carrying 140 and over ozs. silver per ton, 75½ cents per oz.

If the ore ran twenty-five percent lead or better they paid 40¢ "for each unit" and deducted the same amount if it ran under twenty-five percent lead.

Another system used was to buy silver at ten cents off the New York quotation, and lead at twenty-five cents off the New York price, and then add a fifty-seven dollar a ton "working charge." Certain metals found in local ore were assessed a penalty. If, for instance, a local mine owner shipped ore with a high zinc content he was penalized because of its presence. Later, around the turn of the century, when methods of smelting zinc improved and the market increased, zinc became the staple of Leadville mining.

Competition in the smelting industry helped the miners, and by 1889 smelters were paying for lead that ran fifteen percent or better and were giving better deals on silver and other metals, though the penalties were still in force.

The rush to build smelters in 1879 was almost equaled by the failures a year later. Gage-Hageman, the Lizzie, the California Smelting Company, Ohio and Missouri Smelting Company, the old Malta smelter, and Raymond, Sherman and MacKay all folded within a few months of one another. They did not go under as a result of a single cause, but all seemed to have one thing in common; they had to produce continually to survive, having no margin for serious error. As a result several went flat, and bigger smelters were seriously hurt by what was called the "coke famine." During the winter of 1879-1880, for long periods of time snow halted the flow of freight into Leadville. One of the commodities in high demand was furnace coke, necessary in the smelter operations. Some, like the Grant Smelter, had a good supply on hand, others were big enough and had resources enough to curtail operations and weather the storm, but most of the small, marginal operations folded, or were so weakened that the next wind of adversity wiped them out. One of those unkind breezes was the continued decline in the price of metals throughout the 1880s.

During the first decade of the smelting industry in Leadville several operations were born, altered, some successfully and others fatally, but some eight firms stand out. The Arkansas Valley Smelter, known to most old-timers as the A. S. and R. (American Smelting and Refining Company), the short-lived but highly successful Grant Smelter, Billing and Eilers, Harrison's plant, Cummings and Finn, the American Mining and Smelting Company, the up and down, on-again-off-again Elgin operation north of town, and the La Plata.

The most successful, the Grant Smelter, was the first to go through the reorganization process. Judge Grant, after rendering invaluable service and providing the funds for his nephew's plant, sold out on January 1, 1880, to Edward Eddy and William James. Young Grant bought a share of the James-Eddy sampling works, and suddenly they all were partners. The smelter was then remodeled and expanded, making it the largest by far in Leadville. The trio invested in a number of local mining properties and continued to expand their production and holdings until May 24, 1882, when a fire completely wiped out the Grant Smelter. Undaunted, and no doubt a bonus in disguise, they built again, bigger and better in Denver.

Another merger was forthcoming about a mile down the gulch. Billing and Eilers closed down their operation during the summer of 1880 to convert to electric lighting and add a number of refinements to their already outstanding plant. After the Grant Smelter burned, they became the camp's number one producer. Prior to the fire, though, Billing and Eilers dissolved their partnership on January 1, 1882, with Billing retaining the plant and Eilers getting a bundle of cash, the amount of which was known only to the principals.

On April 10, 1882, Billing entered into an agreement with August R. Meyer, now of Kansas City. With a group of Kansas City, Leadville, and St. Louis money men, they formed the Arkansas Valley Smelting Company. The corporation was filed for record on June 27, 1882. The company was incorporated at $500,000 in capital stock. All stock was held by the first board of directors, who were:

Shareholders	No. Shares	City
August R. Meyer, v.-pres.	11,000	Kansas City, Jackson County, Missouri
Frank L. Underwood, pres.	9,000	Kansas City, Jackson County, Missouri
A. W. Armour	2,000	Kansas City, Jackson County, Missouri
Edwin E. Wilson, secretary	1,000	Kansas City, Jackson County, Missouri
Theodore Plake	5,000	St. Louis, Missouri
John Harrison	2,000	St. Louis, Missouri
Arthur H. Meyer	2,000	St. Louis, Missouri
Horace A. W. Tabor	5,000	Denver, Arapahoe County, Colorado
Gustav Billing	8,000	Denver, Arapahoe County, Colorado
Charles T. Limberg	5,000	Leadville, Colorado

Denver was designated as the principal place of business, and while not a stockholder, James B. Grant was named the company's agent. In Leadville, Charles T. Limberg was the agent and was hired to manage the concern. August R. Meyer, first selected vice-president, later was chosen president. He seems to have been the guiding light from the inception of the project.

In January of 1873 part of the Hixon family, as unaware of August R. Meyer as he was unaware of them, arrived in Denver aboard a freight car. Their arrival was announced when the car jumped the rails and crashed into a warehouse. The rest of the family arrived in a wagon, traveling from Missouri to Denver. They located on a "starvation" farm near Cherry Creek and attempted to survive. In 1877 or early in 1878 the oldest of the eleven children, Emma Jane Hixon, then twenty, left family and friends and set out for Leadville where she got a job as post mistress in Tabor's post office. She came to the attention of Meyer. The courtship was brief and on May 24, 1878, the pair were married in Tabor's home in Leadville by Joseph Adams, "minister of the gospel." Mr. Tabor and one M. L. Clark were listed as witnesses.

Meyer had a home built for his bride which, for a time, was the envy of all Leadville. Meyer's home, known today as Healy House, is owned by the Colorado Historical Society and is a public museum, open during the summer. In 1881, after spending a very productive five years in the Magic City, Meyer moved to Kansas City where he became active in the smelting industry and in local politics.

It is difficult to list, or even determine, all of Meyer's contributions to Leadville. Horace Tabor was and is *Mr. Leadville*, but Meyer's contributions in organizing the town, introducing industry, and providing a hundred minor services over the years tend to go unnoticed. From laying out the town to organizing the Arkansas Valley Smelter, August R. Meyer's future and the future of Leadville were intimately entwined.

Meyer's Arkansas Valley plant faced not only local competition, but, like all Leadville plants, found out-of-town competitors grabbing an ever increasing share of the business. Denver and Pueblo began to emerge as the industrial centers of the state, and as rail traffic improved it became more and more profitable to process the raw ore in the above centers rather than fight the elements in Leadville. Two of the earliest competitors in addition to the new Grant Smelter in Denver, were located in Pueblo — the Pueblo Smelting and Refining Company, and Anton Eilers new smelter, the Colorado Smelting Company. And even stiffer competition was on its way.

It was October 20, 1869, when six men, A. Y. Corman, David Ringle, John Nelson, John McKinna, George Martin, and M. G. Huntzucker,

The Arkansas Valley Smelter, gemstone in the American Smelting and Refining Company's empire. *Photo Source: Colorado Historical Society.*

The A.Y. and Minnie property. *Photo Source: Author's Collection.*

laid claim to a property named the A. Y., after Corman's initials. They seemed singularly unimpressed with the prospects of their California Gulch property and did not get around to filing on the location until July 16, 1870. The claim was never seriously worked and was considered abandoned when A. Y. Corman refiled by himself May 12, 1877. Late that same fall Corman located the Minnie, December 28, 1877, named for his wife, and with more urgency than in the past the claim was filed for record January 2, 1878.

The two claims were worked by Corman and a variety of partners, but lack of funds and lack of initiative left them both full of promise and water. To complete the story it is necessary to leave Leadville for a brief European visit.

Meyer Guggenheim was born February 1, 1828, in Langau, Switzerland, a short distance from the capitol at Bern. Meyer, like his father before him and his father's father before him, were subjected to the continuing ebb and flow of prejudice against the Jews. Nineteen-year-old Meyer convinced his father, Simon, that America held a promise of greatness for the Guggenheims. The family set sail for America in 1847. Simon Guggenheim, Meyer, his three sisters, his stepmother, Rachel Myers, and her seven daughters by a previous marriage, all landed in the new world, penniless and without language, home, or employment.

They settled in Philadelphia, and it appears that the conduct of the family fortunes fell to Meyer, the only son. For the first four years of his life in America, Meyer practiced the tailor's trade as he had in Switzerland. In 1850 he married his stepsister, Barbara Myers.

In the next thirty years, through hard work and a natural ability to manage and develop opportunities, he moved from a modest "essence of coffee" business with his brother-in-law, Leman Myers, through stove polish, soap, general merchandising on to railroad stocks and the importation of East Indian spices and Swiss lace. In 1881, after thirty years, he quit the tailoring trade. He had amassed a small fortune and had a family of seven boys and three girls. This Jewish Horatio Alger had only just begun. He had schooled his sons so that they could fill responsible roles in his growing economic empire. Then something happened that changed his whole direction.

Charles H. Graham, "a big man with a white beard, refined and distinguished," was a Quaker from Germantown, Pennsylvania, and business associate of Meyer Guggenheim. Graham got the mining bug and left his grocery business and headed west, arriving in Leadville during the boom. The years and the life had begun to tell on A. Y. Corman, and he began to entertain thoughts of selling his two California Gulch properties. Albert F. Harsh, a Philadelphian, purchased an interest in the A. Y. from Corman. Another merchant from Philadelphia, George F. Work, picked up the remainder along with Charles Graham and Thomas Weir.

Work and Wier were short of funds and gave notes to Harsh for the interest on their shares. When the notes came due they did not have the funds. Graham turned to his old business associate, Meyer Guggenheim. Guggenheim came up with the funds, which gave him one-half interest and Harsh and Graham each one-quarter in the A. Y. It cost Guggenheim five thousand dollars to get into the mining business. Shortly after his initiation, he and Graham bought the Minnie from Corman on November 10, 1880.

Meyer Guggenheim was a small, worn man with an uncanny ability to smell a good deal and pick the best man to exploit it. He came to Leadville late in the summer of 1880 and investigated the properties and promptly employed Charles Hill as superintendent. That fall, some two months after he left the Magic City, he received a telegram from Harsh, "RICH STRIKE FIFTEEN OUNCES SILVER SIXTY PERCENT LEAD."

The strike was in the A. Y. Ore was soon found in the Minnie. By the summer of 1882 the properties were yielding $2,000 a day. It was not long before the Guggenheim sons, especially the three youngest, Benjamin, William, and Simon, were engaged in some aspect of the mining operation. The A. Y. and Minnie continued for a decade or more to produce handsomely for the Guggenheim family, and "Meyer squeezed the last cent from his mine." He got better freight rates from the railroads, worked the smelters for all they were worth, and dealt ruthlessly in the courts with all pretenders.

Benjamin, "a charming Edwardian swell," was unlike his elder brothers in that he was socially eager and unimpressed by his Jewish heritage. While in Leadville in 1888, pursuing the family's financial concerns and his social interests, he met Edward Holden, sometime smelter operator and promoter. The association provided the "in" that the elder Guggenheim needed. Meyer invested heavily in Holden's plant in Denver, and Benjamin and Simon went to work in the plant to learn the smelter trade first hand. With the Guggenheim money behind him, Holden retired from his Denver operation and organized the Denver Smelting and Refining Company, a company, at that time, in name only. He and Benjamin looked several cities over as possible sites for their new smelter. Denver was considered too far from coke, coal, and lime. Leadville was too isolated. Pueblo won. The name of the company was changed from Denver to the Philadelphia Smelting and Refining Company, honoring the Guggenheim home base.

Holden became upset with the constant family interference in the development and operation of the new smelter, and especially with William, the youngest, whose dreams of grandeur outstripped all the others of the family. Holden felt there were problems enough without the meddling of the uninformed. The new plant's major difficulty was with its new hearthless furnace, which was being called "Guggenheim's folly." But Meyer, always able to get to the core of the matter, bought out Holden rather than listen to him, put his sons in the administrative positions, and hired August Raht, "a product of the German mining schools," who got the operation on a sound footing in short order.

In the following decade the Guggenheim family began importing Mexican ore and flooded the U.S. silver market with cheap Mexican silver. To halt the flood the industrialists in the mining states combined with others to force the passage of the McKinley tariff. It hurt a lot of people, but not the Guggenheims. They simply built a pair of smelters in Mexico and began dumping their Mexican silver on the world market.

On March 7, 1899, the greatest threat to the Guggenheim position in the smelting world was initiated. Most of the major smelters and big money men in the industry combined to form the American Smelting and Refining Company, a trust of international significance. The Guggenheims were asked to join, but were dissatisfied with the role they were asked to play, so stayed out. During the following year, through excellent management and shrewd business measures, the Guggenheims managed not only to outproduce the trust, but they bought enough interest in the organization that they could not be ignored. That first inglorious year for the American Smelting and Refining Company saw their twenty plants producing a profit of $3,500,000, while the Guggenheims with their three plants produced a profit of $3,600,000.

It was time to take stock. Leaders of the

THE GUGGENHEIM FAMILY

BENJAMIN   MURRY   ISAAC   DANIEL   SOLOMON   SIMON   WILLIAM

MEYER (THE FATHER—NOW DEAD)

Meyer Guggenheim and his sons. *Photo Source: Colorado Historical Society.*

trust realized that a trust without the Guggenheims was no trust at all. The Guggenheims were invited in on the most favorable terms. They were given stock in the corporation worth $36,000,000, five of the sons were elected to the board of directors, and Daniel, a board member, was also selected chairman of both the board and the executive committee. Men like August R. Meyer, Anton Eilers, and James B. Grant sat down with the Guggenheim family, and the trust became one of the most powerful economic enterprises in the world.

In Leadville, the merger brought Meyer's A. V. plant and the old La Plata, which became the BiMetalic smelter, into the American Smelting and Refining Company's grasp. The Arkansas Valley plant out-lived all other Colorado smelters and finally closed its doors early in 1961.

To supplement coke, Leadville's smelters used charcoal as a fluxing agent. By 1885 a number of local merchants, including the local sheriff, were engaged in the process of cutting native trees and "cooking" them until they were nearly pure carbon. The process, after a series of trials and errors, was quite simple. Cone-shaped, "bee hive," kilns were constructed, usually out of brick, although a few stone kilns were constructed. They were usually built so that they could be served by the railroad and were situated against a hill making it easy to feed them from the top as well as from the side. They averaged twenty to thirty feet in height and fifteen to twenty feet across at the base. Wood was cut from the surrounding hills, hauled to the site, and stacked floor to ceiling in the kiln. The wood was stacked loosely so that air could circulate, then hot coals were placed around the base and all doors were closed and sealed with mortar. Around the base of the cone were three rows of openings that could be opened or closed by simply placing a brick in the space. These vents were used to regulate the flow of air. Once the process was set in motion the cone was whitewashed to prevent any uncontrolled leakage of air. Fire was never allowed to break out, and the oxygen flow was regulated to permit the wood to smoulder until virtually everything was burned out, except the carbon. Finally all vents were closed and the smouldering process died out after about a week. Another four or five days were required to let the kiln and contents cool.

It is said the smelters required ten bushels of coke to every ton of ore, and it would appear the need for charcoal was even greater. One of the "Kings of the Kiln" was George H. Hathaway, who, during the heyday of the charcoal era, oper-

This old charcoal kiln has become a barn. It is one of a few still standing in the area. *Photo Source: Author's Collection.*

ated over one hundred kilns in the area. One writer reflecting on the industry estimated that at one point 2,500 men were employed in charcoal production. Wages were exceptionally high for charcoal workers. Men chopping timber received from one dollar to one dollar and two bits per cord, and a good man and a sharp ax could pile up from four to six cords in a day. A man and team hired out to the charcoalers for eight dollars a day.

Contemporary reporters claimed that as many as seventy-five bushels (each about fourteen pounds) of charcoal could be obtained from a cord of good wood, and a bushel brought anywhere from six to ten cents. While pockets were lined with cash from the charcoal industry, it was one of the worst offenders where the land was concerned. Not only did it inundate the area with smoke, but it left the land barren and without the cover necessary to prevent erosion. By 1889, when coke totally replaced charcoal, the timber in the Leadville area was almost completely cut off. Acres and acres of trees had been cut for mine timbers, housing, and, most of all, charcoal.

IX

The Rough Element

Leadville's first marshal, T. H. Harrison, served only a few days when threats from the growing crowd of villains convinced him that life would be longer and more rewarding someplace else. George O'Connor was the town council's choice to replace the prudent Harrison, and as a result of the first regular election on April 2, 1878, he became town marshal. His reign lasted a short three and one-half weeks.

On Thursday night, April 25, 1878, O'Connor was making his rounds when he encountered one of his junior officers named James M. Bloodsworth. Earlier in the week O'Connor had criticized Bloodsworth, known to his fraternity as "Texas," about his habit of frequenting the dance halls and gambling dens. O'Connor warned him "that if he did not behave better," a complaint would be filed with the City Council. Texas stood about five-ten, weighed around one hundred and fifty. His hair was brown and generally he was quiet, though apparently not sullen. He accepted O'Connor's reprimand without rancor and gave no one cause to sense the hatred that festered in his soul. But vengeance gripped him, and he carefully laid his plans. He gathered a number of weapons to take with him, and had two or three lunches prepared in advance. Then on the evening of April 25, after doing the town, he met O'Connor in Billy Nye's Saloon.

"I hear that you called me a coward and a guy."* Bloodsworth accused the marshal.

O'Connor denied the charge. When "Texas" repeated the accusation, O'Connor replied, "the man that said so was a liar."

Bloodsworth, in an excited voice, remarked,

"any man who tries to run over me gets off wrong, and if anyone says that I did so and so he is a dirty s–n of a b–––h."

O'Connor tried to calm him down and started toward him. That ended the discussion. "Texas" drew his revolver and fired. The first shot hit the marshal in the stomach, the second, just below the heart. Bloodsworth fired three more shots into his victim "then fled down the street, stole the sheriff's horse and left." It was said to be the best horse in Leadville.

The town was outraged. Mayor Tabor offered a six hundred dollar reward for the "arrest and return of the body of James Bloodsworth."

"Texas," about twenty-four years old, was stylish in his dress, and it was thought he would not be difficult to find. A Leadville man was sent after him, a man said to be "equal to the emergency." Equal or not, Bloodsworth was never heard of again, and it was assumed he managed to lose himself someplace in Texas.

O'Connor lived "several hours" but was doomed. Even before he died, Mayor Tabor called a special meeting of the city council. At that meeting Martin Duggan was appointed City Marshal. Duggan was a County Limerick man, born there November 10, 1848. When still a young child he and his parents sailed for America. He spent his boyhood on the streets of New York. At sixteen he started west and finally, working all the way, he arrived in Denver in the fall of 1860. He worked as a miner and freighter in a number of Colorado communities before arriving in Leadville early in 1878.

Duggan had his work cut out for him. The "roughs" had ridded the town of two marshals in the two months since incorporation, and they wasted no time in giving Duggan the word. "I

---

*"Guy" apparently used here to describe someone who is a fancy dresser. Possibly also implies femininity.

105

rec'd a written notice from the roughs to leave town & if I stayed 24 hours I would follow Geo. O'Connor. Paid no attention to notice but took every precaution to always be on my guard." Duggan realized that he had not only the "roughs" to contend with, but also "there was some quarrelsome, shooting miners" in the town who had lived in the area for years and were not about to allow some newcomer to tell them how to conduct themselves.

From a twentieth-century point of view, Duggan was a poor choice. He was not overly concerned with the letter of the law or the rights of the accused. His methods were those of the "roughs," and his success was born out of his superior strength, determination, and absolute fearlessness. One chronicler of the period described him as "medium height, but of compact, massive build. He had sinews of steel. His features were good. He had a square face, with broad forehead and pleasing expression. His hair and complexion were light and his eyes blue. He was a man that you would look at twice as you first met him."

Duggan wasted no time in establishing himself as the law. One evening, shortly after he took his one hundred and twenty-five dollar a month job, a group of drifters and ne'er-do-wells had taken over the Tontine Restaurant on West Chestnut. In the group was a locally wanted man. Mart confronted the group, spotted the man, and ordered him out.

The man declined, and waited.

Duggan gave him the alternatives. Go and live. Stay and die.

The man looked to his crowd of supporters, who were staring at the floor, looked back into Duggan's cold blue eyes, and went along peacefully.

A local black named John Elkins, Charlie Hines, and a number of other men had spent the whole of Sunday playing poker in the Pioneer Saloon, then located on East Chestnut. Around midnight the game broke up and Hines and Elkins, along with the rest of the players assembled at the bar for a drink. An argument broke out between Elkins and Hines and fists began to fly. They were separated by friends, but during the course of the evening they met again and the fight was resumed. Elkins drew a knife and even though friends of the pair piled on them, Elkins slipped out of their grasp and buried his knife deep in the mid-section of Charlie Hines. In the midst of the confusion, Elkins escaped.

Hines was taken to a back room, and it was soon rumored that the poor man was near death.

Crowds began to form and before long the cry, "Lynch the Negro" was heard throughout the east end of Chestnut Street, and a lynch mob began to form.

Marshal Duggan was home in bed when one of his officers began pounding on the door. The officer explained about the stabbing and informed the marshal that officers had located Elkins "in a house he occupied with a Negro woman." Elkins had given up immediately. "I got my clothes on as soon as possible," Duggan recalled, "and sending the officer to assist in guarding the jail I started out alone to get ahead of the mob who by this time I could hear coming down the street." The crowd rounded the corner by the jail, which was located at Front and Pine, a little over four blocks from the Pioneer, and found Duggan waiting for them, a cocked revolver in each hand, standing beneath a "dance hall lamp" in the middle of the street. "I told them I would kill the first man who attempted to pass the lamp post."

According to Duggan there were about two hundred men in the mob. A few rabble rousers shouted, "on to the jail" and they were "jerked out of the crowd and jailed." The crowd stopped and Duggan later remarked, "I managed to make them understand that some of them were sure to be killed if they persisted in interfering with the law."

Hines recovered and a year later was working for the local police. Elkins was quietly released from jail and fled town.

In April of 1879 Martin Duggan's appointment was up. He decided not to accept a second appointment and was succeeded by P. A. Kelly. Duggan went to Flint, Michigan, with his wife, to visit her family.

As soon as Duggan left town the "rough element" began again to assert itself. One area of endeavor was lot-jumping. The price of town lots had risen to outrageous proportions as the city developed. The land on Chestnut Street, still the town's major thoroughfare, had originally been purchased from the U.S. government for $2.50 an acre. Early in 1879 lots with seventy-five front feet were selling for $10,000. One fellow is said to have made such a purchase, then sold fifty front feet of his original seventy-five for the same amount the following day.

It rapidly developed that the difficulty was not in getting the land, but in hanging onto it. "It was tacitly understood that the actual construction of a building should give an undisputed title to a lot." But what was "tacitly understood" and what actually happened did not always coincide.

106

Leadville's finest, 1878. *Photo Source: Denver Public Library Western History Collection.*

"City lots were actually grabbed by these gangs when houses were being erected on them." The workers were driven off the building, the structure was torn down with axes and the lumber thrown in the street, along with anyone who protested, and a new shack would be thrown up in its place with new lumber "to become a stronghold for toughs, all of whom were walking arsenals."

A group of lot jumpers, as they were called, "broke into a small dwelling one night, threw the owner into the street dressed only in his nightclothes," and took possession of his belongings, house, and lot — lock, stock and barrel. Their methods varied but always included a lot of muscle and very little finesse. Often they would simply appear like a pack of hungry wolves, mill about, intimidating the owner until he fled. On other occasions, such as the one mentioned above, they would physically evict the owner from his land. Another method mentioned by one observer was to stand back at a safe distance and pour volley after volley of bullets through the doors and windows until a white flag appeared, the man fled, or he was hit severely and could not put up a fight.

A second group of brigands, even more deadly than the lot jumpers, were the footpads. During the early spring and throughout the summer and fall of 1879, an epidemic of daring holdups plagued the Magic City. Honest men were advised to stay off the streets after dark. If they were compelled to be out, then they were instructed to walk in the middle of the street, a drawn revolver in their shooting hand. A local paper ran a regular feature called the "Holdup Record." One Leadvillite, writing back east, declared, "I do not believe there is a town or city that contains as many cut-throats, thieves, and black legs of all kinds than Leadville."

Sister Florence (Mary Florence Cloonan) came to Oro City as a young girl in March of 1876 with her mother, sister, and four brothers. Her father had arrived ahead of them. As a youngster she watched Leadville burst into existence, and while still a child had two run-ins with footpads. On one occasion she was on her way home. The streets were being worked on and she was struggling to get atop a pile of dirt and away from the construction, which hosted a rather heavy stream of muddy water, when she heard the ominous

"Hands Up." She told them to take whatever they wanted, but to help her atop the bank away from the creek when they were done. "The men grinned slowly, put away their guns, and one gave her a dollar after he had lifted her up to the footpath."

On another occasion, Sister Florence and her father were walking in the vicinity of Ninth Street school "one cold winter day" when someone in front of them shouted "Hands Up." The robbers held three groups of two at gunpoint. They first fleeced two pair of men before they came to Sister Florence and her father. Sister Florence recalled she was "glad, because she longed to know how her father would act in a holdup."

The robbers stood before them and one of them, looking at little Florence, asked, "Whose daughter is this?"

"My daughter," Florence's father replied.

"Pass on, then." And "one of the hold-ups reached down to a small hand and put a dollar in it." The other small hand was in her father's overcoat because of the cold.

By late summer, 1879, merchants and townspeople were getting desperate. On September 1, 1879, the Merchants' Protective Patrol was organized. Eight men were hired by local businessmen and deputized by the sheriff. Their job consisted mainly of checking doors after hours, looking for anything suspicious, and protecting property. Also merchants were outfitted with police whistles. Since there were no phones, the police whistle served to alert the officers that a policeman was needed.

"Most men here carry sums about them varying from $50 up to the hundreds of dollars so that the field is a very lucrative one for highwaymen. Their usual method of operating is to watch men who have plenty of money and follow them to their homes and when they get them on retired streets they point their revolvers at them and make them shell out."

Of all the footpads, the most famous, or infamous if you prefer, was an arrogant pup by the name of Patrick Stewart. Stewart's fame was accidental, ill deserved, but nigh on to eternal.

On the night of November 15, 1879, a Saturday, Carl Bockhaus, "a little German barber," closed his shop around ten-thirty and started for home, a sizable amount of cash on his person. He carried a revolver in one hand and whistled away his fears as he walked. "When nearly opposite the residence of Mr. John Arkins, on lower State Street" two men, Stewart and an associate, jumped out of the shadows and commanded him

to raise his hands. His next two moves are confused, and his stories differ, but he either pulled his cocked pistol from his coat and fired, or in raising his hands fired his first shot. With each telling the tale becomes more self-defense by design, and less by chance. Stewart's accomplice was killed, and it appears to have been by the barber's first shot. Stewart's cohort was said to have later been identified as Clifford; wanted in Texas for the robbery of a stage near Fort Worth. A later shot, not necessarily the second, wounded Stewart, who by that time was legging his way down State Street. Bockhaus, after his desperate shooting spree, fled in the opposite direction. Both he and Stewart ran into the waiting arms of Leadville's police.

Bockhaus, gasping, related his story to the dubious officer and the pair returned to the scene of the crime. Bockhaus was sure his first shot had found the mark, and when they arrived a resident in the area opened his front door and informed the growing crowd that there was a dead man on his back porch.

The following day Carl Bockhaus was a hero. He "was carried all over town in a chair upon the shoulders of a large crowd and a banner was borne in front marked 'Terror to Highwaymen' and 'Foot Pad Exterminator.'"

Stewart claimed he was trying to help the barber, but the story did not take and he was jailed. In jail he was defiant. He claimed he was going to get the plucky barber, and expected to be out soon, and would not make the same mistakes again. The day after the shooting a crowd of from four to five thousand people gathered at the jail, "and speeches were made about lynching" Stewart, "but nothing was done."

While Stewart languished in jail, dark doings were afoot. A vigilance committee was formed, the membership of which remains a mystery to this day. Their plans included Stewart and a local "real estate man" by the name of Edward Frodsham, said to have been the dean of the lot jumpers and evil stem to stern.

Frodsham came to Leadville early in 1879. He was a jeweler by trade, but there is no evidence that he ever practiced his craft in the Cloud City. Prior to coming to Leadville he had made Wyoming his home and had served time there in the state penitentiary at Laramie for murder. The record of who he killed or the circumstances are not clear, but he was sent to Laramie State Penitentiary from Evanston, Wyoming, in May of 1876 to serve a ten-year sentence. "In some manner, however, he secured an interest on behalf of the people of Laramie and he was pardoned

December 31, 1877, by Governor John M. Thayer, after only serving a year and a half of his original ten-year term."

He settled then in Laramie and began working at his former profession of jeweler and watchmaker. In June of 1878, while frequenting Susie Parker's notorious house on Front Street, he got in a fight with a cattle dealer named Taylor. The pair stepped out in the street in front of the parlor house and shot it out. Both men were hit and not expected to live, but Frodsham made a miraculous recovery, while Taylor did as expected — died. Frodsham seems to have beaten any charges that were preferred against him on a plea of self defense, and wisely fled Wyoming. While there are stories about him in the Cortez area, his next confirmed stop was in Leadville where he was listed in the *Leadville City Directory* of 1879 as "Frodsham, E. real estate dealer, res. Tenth avenue, bet. Harrison avenue and Pine street, Capital Hill."

For the times he was a tall man; five-eleven, dark complexioned, brown hair and grey eyes, slim, with small scars on his left cheekbone and just under the jaw. By all accounts he appears a cold, but handsome, man. He was born in England, probably in Manchester, and according to one source he was brought to this country at the age of seven with his parents at the behest of Morman missionaries. "He was educated in Zion for a preacher, but became a jeweler."

Frodsham does not seem to have been in town any length of time at all before he got into the real estate business. "Within a few weeks he had earned for himself the distinction of being the most intrepid lot-jumper that ever contested the right of a squatter in Colorado." In spite of his reputation there were few public outcries against him and "his gang," and it appears that most of his dealings had the air of legality about them.

R. G. Dill, editor of the *Leadville Herald,* was a close observer of the events of November 1879. He surely knew many of the participants in the vigilance committee, and possibly was a participant, though he never acknowledged a personal involvement. Certainly he was in basic agreement with the vigilantes, noting that the notorious real estate agent "walked the streets of Leadville as unconcerned as if he had never raised his hand in violation of the law or of the rights of others." He also pointed out that "it was no secret that if he [Frodsham] should be once lodged in jail he would be 'taken care of.'"

Someplace in a back room or in the privacy of a local home, outraged citizens bemoaned the disintegration of law and order. They were concerned for the victims, but there was also the concern for the future growth of the city. They could not hope to make Leadville the hub of the state if the streets were not safe and a man's property could be taken from him while he stood and watched.

Out of those discussions came the idea and the will to act. A vigilance committee was formed, claiming to be seven hundred strong. All it needed was a victim. Patrick Stewart, a footpad of some reputation, languished in the county jail; but the vigilantes were looking for bigger fish.

It was said that certain members of the police force were in with the rough element, and Marshall P. A. "Pat" Kelly's name was mentioned often. Still, the vigilance committee in order to successfully carry out its plans needed the help of some members of the police force. It seems they received that help on the evening of November 17 when Undersheriff Watson arrested Edward Frodsham. The charge was listed as "Riot," which is, in today's jargon, disturbing the peace. Two days later on the nineteenth of November a note "To remain in custody until fine and costs are paid," was added in the sheriff's jail record. Most contemporary news accounts claim Frodsham was arrested on November 19 and denied bail. The sheriff's records, however, clearly state that Frodsham was arrested on the seventeenth, and we must assume that he sat in jail for two days before the vigilantes sprang their trap, which suggests that bail was denied, not a few hours, but two days. It probably was not set until fine and costs were established, and when Frodsham asked to post bail on the nineteenth he was told it was "too late."

The county jail apparently was always locked from the inside, and on the interior of the jail was "the cage," a cell within a cell, with all four sides visible and the top several feet lower than the ceiling. Stewart and Frodsham were being held outside of the cage, "Frodsham because he generally gave bonds and then refused to go into a cell, and Stewart because his arm was in a sling," the result of the German barber's heroic defense.

Everything was ready; the time had arrived. The vigilance committee set the wheels of mob justice in motion. They set out from Latey and Black's carpenter shop, located in the alley between Second and Third streets, a half-block west of Harrison Avenue, and traveled in small groups to the county jail at Fifth and Harrison. There, at the corner, they divided into action groups, each going to his appointed task. Small groups congregated on the corners approaching the court house block and effectively sealed off the area. Another group went for Undersheriff Watson, whose account of the event has appeared three different ways, two versions of which came from Watson. Dill took care to note that "Undersheriff Watson was not in the affair of his own free will, as that would be inconsistent with his duties as a county officer."

In Dill's familiar account published in 1881, he explained, "Shortly after 1 o'clock, on Thursday morning, November 20, the Under Sheriff of the county was on his way home.... As he turned down the street leading to his residence, these men closed in upon him, and he suddenly found himself a prisoner." Earlier, in his account in the *Herald,* Dill reported that Watson "was *awakened* in bed."

Matt Rix, surely a pseudonym, possibly for John Bonner, city editor for the *Chronicle,* claimed that "Sheriff Watson had been drawn home by a decoy—the report of his child's illness."

Whatever the truth, Watson, either by prior arrangement or the result of careful planning, was captured by the vigilantes. His captors wore black masks and many were in black gowns. He was told to surrender his keys, but he generously informed them that the jail was locked from the inside. He was assured no harm would come to him if he cooperated and was escorted to the jail. The undersheriff was told to ask admission from the guard on duty at the door. To insure his complete compliance, Watson was placed in front of the group so that if the guard fired Watson would receive the full force of the blast.

The guards recognized the undersheriff's voice and immediately opened the door. The instant it was opened, the vigilantes rushed the door and secured the immediate interior. "Resistance under the circumstances was impossible, and the doors leading into the cells were thrown open."

Frodsham knew immediately what they were about and scrambled to the top of the cage, where he put up a desperate fight, "tearing off masks, scratching, biting, and pounding his adversaries at every turn." Finally he was dragged to the floor and subdued. "As he fully realized that there was no hope for him, he merely requested permission to write a letter to his wife." He was told that there was no time for writing letters. He was then bound hand and foot and dragged from the jail to the frame of a small adjacent building that was under construction. Its purpose does not seem clear, but one local witness said it was to be a kitchen. Some reports claim that Frodsham at-

tempted to cry out and a handkerchief was shoved into his mouth, the rope was slipped over his head, and he was pulled fighting, struggling, over the ridgepole on the unfinished kitchen.

The men then returned for Stewart. There has always been some question if Stewart was part of the plan, or whether he was an afterthought. In either case the result was the same. Stewart was bound and dragged down the hall to the door. He begged a chance to write his mother. "You can write your letter in the morning," was the savage reply as he was forced out of the jail. As he stumbled into the cold night air he cried out, "I die an innocent man." No one heeded his claim, and he was dragged to the rude kitchen building where he, like Frodsham, was hanged.

The vigilantes remained at the jail long enough to be sure their victims were dead, then vanished.

Dawn found the two bodies twisting in the cold morning light, the ground littered with black masks. An ominous hush settled over Leadville; citizen and blackguard waited the next move in the grisly drama that began in the wee hours of a dark November night.

When the bodies were cut down, the following note was found pinned to Frodsham's back:

> Notice to all lot thieves, bunko steerers, footpads, thieves and chronic bondsmen for the same, and sympathisers for the above class of criminals: This is our commencement, and this shall be your fates. We mean business, and let this be your last warning. . . . and a great many others known to this organization. Vigilantes' Committee. We are 700 strong.

The message was followed by a list of undesirables who were encouraged to leave town.

As word of the lynching spread, the streets became crowded with the curious. The threat of open warfare hung in the air. A detachment of militia was stationed at the Clarendon Hotel on Harrison Avenue and another on Chestnut Street. "It is rather warlike to see arms stacked up and patrols guarding them," Elder remarked in a letter to his parents on the twenty-third. The miner's union volunteered to help police the town in the event of an outbreak of violence, but fortunately they were not needed. They might have created more problems than they would have cured.

"In the evening you see firearms on all sides, every third man carries a Sharps, Spencer, or Winchester rifle and every man has one or two revolvers in a condition for immediate use." That first evening after the lynching, November 20, Tabor's new opera house opened its doors to a

Certificate of Attendance.

State of Colorado,
County of Lake. } ss.

I Hereby Certify, *That* H W Law *was summoned* and served as Juror *during an Inquisition held on the body of* E Frodsham & Patrick Stewart on the 20th *day of* Nov. A.D. 1879

John Law, *Coroner.*

Attendance, 2.50
Mileage, ——

nervous, half-filled house, many of the patrons staying away for fear of being caught up in the violence that seemed ready to sweep the town.

The town toughs met in secret meetings, organized an antivigilance committee and swore vengeance on those who had dared take up arms against them. A note was sent through the coroner to Bockhaus, the little barber who wounded Stewart and killed his accomplice, which said he best leave town or he would be killed. It was signed "A Friend." A wave of threatening letters swept town, many written, not by toughs, but local citizens out to settle former wrongs and private grudges. Citizens getting even with a neighbor who had a mean dog, or whose kids were a local menace, managed to increase the terror and keep the pot boiling. Still, according to Dill, the original goal of the vigilance committee was achieved. Those people listed on the note pinned to Frodsham's back "were absent from their accustomed haunts," and many others of dubious reputation, in spite of their vow to retaliate, seem to have gotten the message and beat a hasty, but quiet retreat.

It was hard to assess the lasting effects. Surely those who participated and their sympathizers were convinced that the town had benefitted from their actions. Elder, though, felt it was of little use. "The holdups continue their work and the example of last week seems to have had no effect upon them," and he expected to see a few more strung up before the point was made. "Monday night no less than three men were held up and robbed. One of them had only 15¢ on his person and he was badly beaten and wantonly shot at three or four times. He was wounded in the leg."

Dill, the newspaper editor, did not remember it that way at all. "The remedy was a desperate one, but it was demanded by an outraged public sentiment, and was entirely effective." Was it? As we will see, it did not halt or even discourage violence, and seemed, as Elder observed, to have no effect on the petty thieves and the holdups. But it does seem to have crushed the will of organized crime, and those who were engaged in the creation of a powerful underworld element fled. What remained was good, clean violence, dishonesty, and lust—the kind of crime police were, and are, best equipped to handle.

And the vigilantes? Who were they and what happened to them? Today, scores of years later, not one person has been identified, not one name can be listed on the roll of vigilantes. It was and remains one of the Magic City's lasting enigmas. Those nameless men who appeared out of nowhere on the night of November 19, 1879, and disappeared as quietly and swiftly as they had appeared, never to be heard of again.

One look at Frodsham and Stewart swinging in the breeze and the city council wired Duggan and asked him to reconsider his decision to resign. Duggan later explained, "They did not believe that anyone else could prevent the roughs from running the town." Duggan returned and was reappointed marshal in December of 1879. He served out the rest of Kelly's term, but refused to accept another. Edmund H. Watson, undersheriff during the Frodsham affair, became the new city marshal in April of 1880. Duggan went into the livery stable business and indulged in his favorite pasttime, horses and horse racing.

About six weeks before Duggan left the force, one of the wildest nights in Leadville's none too quiet past erupted at about 9:00 P.M. on the evening of February 27, 1880. A tremendous volley of gunfire filled the cold night air, and local citizens rushed out of their homes and rooms. The bars and gambling houses emptied. Some thought they were being attacked by an army of Utes. Others suspected the renewal of vigilante action. The shots, sounding like "a pitched battle between two armies," came from the southwest slope of Carbonate Hill just above town. Newsmen and curious citizens immediately set out to find out what was going on.

The war was being fought at the O'Donovan-Rossa between two groups of claimants. The night was clear and cold, and the headframe of the mine stood out stark against the star-filled sky. The fight centered around one Patrick Gilbert, Irish immigrant via English prisons, who had located the mine the previous May. Gilbert selected a small spot of unclaimed land just west of several major producers on Carbonate Hill, and then sold a half-interest to Burt LaSalle, a local mining man, with the understanding that LaSalle would sink a shaft to ore contact, and he and Gilbert would split equally anything they found. LaSalle then peddled his half to Moses Blair, who in turn sold the same busy half-interest to T. J. Prindle and Company, an organization made up of Tom Prindle and Charlie Harper, saloon owners. Prindle put a Mr. Benneford to work on the claim. Sometime around the first week of September, 1879, Prindle "abandoned" the project.

The claim lay idle, so Gilbert "disposed of a one-half undivided interest to Messrs. W. S. Griffiths and George C. Bates," and they hired John D. Morrisey and Willett Rose. It was the same half-interest that Gilbert had originally sold to LaSalle. There were no problems until Saturday, February 21, 1880. At sixty-five feet contact was made. It held "rare promise," and "turned out a good assay." The following day Prindle heard how he had missed a bonanza by abandoning the claim. He wasted little time in trying to reclaim his lost fortune. During the week the owners, or at least the possessors, of the mine changed hands several times, and the final exchange was what disturbed the quiet night of February 28.

Morrisey had regained control of the mine the previous evening after the local sheriff's department had tried and failed. He had about a dozen armed men who were prepared to stand off an attack. It was not long in coming. Patrick Gilbert supported Morrisey, both men being Irish and proud of it, and they had decided it was a question of honor as well as money. Prindle, claiming he had not abandoned the mine, rounded up an army of his own and attacked.

The fight raged off and on throughout the night, and it is surprising there were no deaths. Two men were wounded slightly, one from each side. The next morning the sheriff's department was able to end the war and jailed a number of Morrisey's troops. Prindle's men were unknown and escaped.

A reporter, after examining the area and talking with some of the participants, was amazed by the volume of fire. "The windlass and rope bore the marks of fully fifty balls, while the curbing above the snow resembled a splintered sieve more than anything else." One participant recalled having fired at least ninety-five shots, and those defending the mine had to lay their rifles in the snow from time to time to cool the barrels. Those in the mine escaped serious injury by standing on a platform about five feet down in the mouth of the shaft. "An occasional ball would glance down but nothing more serious."

John D. Morrisey. *Photo Source: Denver Public Library Western History Collection.*

John D. Morrisey was the acknowledged hero of the short war, and the *Carbonate Chronicle* noted that he "would rather indulge in a genuine knockdown than a good dinner at anytime." The war finally was settled in the courts, but Morrisey continued to make news and is remembered, not for his part in the town's violence, but for his ability to do violence to the English language.

Morrisey was born in Connaught, Ireland, during the desperate years of the potato famine and, like thousands, grudgingly foresook the shores of Erin for America. He worked in a number of jobs and finally came to the attention of Diamond Joe Reynolds, an energetic millionaire on the Mississippi. Reynolds was attracted by the hard-working, jovial Irish lad and decided to help him. Morrisey was illiterate, and Diamond Joe considered sending John to school, but decided he was too old for that and, instead, sent him to Colorado as his special agent. It was not long before John arrived in Leadville and found a mine, or rather a pair of mines, the Crown Point and the Dome (originally located by Stevens and Wood). John became Diamond Joe's manager, but his illiteracy worked against him. A hired secretary got John involved in a highgrading scheme that was quickly discovered by John's benefactor. Diamond Joe was lenient, gave John a second chance, but he muffed it. John Barleycorn and fair weather friends, jealous of John's benefactor, poisoned his mind against Diamond Joe, and Morrisey died alone and forgotten in the county poorhouse. The stories of Johnny Morrisey, funny though they may be, have a kind of sadness and poignancy that can only be portrayed by telling a few.

When John was a successful mine boss, his crew gave him a great gold watch. He could not tell time, but was an expert at disguising the fact. When asked the time, John would pull out his fine gold watch and aim it at the questioner. "Here, look fer yourself. Ye wouldn't belave me if I told ye."

As a major mining figure in the camp he was called to Denver on business as well as to other mining camps. Hotels were a major problem. He devised a number of methods to avoid signing hotel registers such as "Me fist is frose and I kud'n howl'd a pen." On one occasion he arrived at the hotel desk, a handkerchief wrapped around his hand, and "Just write me name for me, young feller. I jist slammed the cab door on me hand and hurt it."

Inter-Laken, a beautiful resort, was constructed on the south bank of the lower of the two Twin Lakes, and the management was considering the addition of gondolas from Italy for the use of the guests. The cost of importation was prohibitive and Morrisey's opinion was sought. He was told the problem, mulled it over a bit, and

Rules and Regulations by which Each Renter will be Governed.

1. No one except the Renter or his Deputy, to be designated on the books of Trimble & Hunter, or in case of death, his legal representative to have access to the safe.

2. Renters will not examine their boxes or papers in the Vault, but will use desks provided for that purpose outside.

3. No Renter will be permitted to enter the Vault except in the presence of the Vault keeper.

4. All rents payable in advance, and Renters held responsible until the key is returned.

5. In case of loss of key by the Renter of a Safe, the lock will be changed at the expense of the Renter, including a new lock.

6 Trimble & Hunter reserve the right to terminate a rental at any time, on written notice to the Renter or his Deputy, and the Renter will thereupon withdraw his papers and surrender the key and receive back *pro rate* the money paid.

Having read the above rules, I accept them as binding on me during my occupancy of a Safe in the Vault of Trimble & Hunter, and I hereby designate No One *as my Deputy.*

LEADVILLE, COLORADO, Oct 10" 1885 John *his* Morsey mark

Note the spelling of Morrisey and his "x." *Photo Source: Denver Public Library Western History Collection.*

gave his solution. "Why, hell, jist get a couple and let nature take its course."

And the stories go on and on, but the sadness of Morrisey's situation was the sadness of a generation of immigrants who populated the West. They were the butt of innumerable jokes, but managed to laugh them off and lend a willing hand wherever help was needed. In his continual quest for learning John fell in love with and married a Central School teacher, Miss Molly Brennan. But there was no saving "Jack." He was in an impossible position, a superintendent who could not read. Before it was over Morrisey lost everything, even his self respect.

Word of Leadville violence spread around the world and caught the ear of one of the East's most famous reforming clergymen, Reverend DeWitt Talmadge. He had made headlines the previous year when he personally inspected the slums of New York and later denounced the conditions from his pulpit at the Brooklyn Tabernacle. He came to Leadville prepared to make headlines again.

The Talmadges arrived on the evening of July 26, 1880, via the newly completed Denver and Rio Grande Railroad, and settled in separate rooms at the Clarendon. "When," according to a local reporter, "night has drawn her somber veil over scenes of crime and shrouds those who travel its labyrinthian pathways, from the slumbering eye of Justice and morality," the pride of the Presbyterians set out around 11:00 P.M. to see sin in the raw. He had a single companion whose task it was to expose the minister to Leadville's seamy side. Their first stop was the Board of Trade Saloon. He was informed that a man was shot there the previous Monday night in a gaming argument. Talmadge took a quick look inside and they proceeded on. Their next stop was Pap Wyman's. Another quick look and they headed for the Texas House, one of the richest of the Magic City's gaming houses. They entered and while looking the crowd over Talmadge was recognized by one who had seen him earlier. Every eye turned on the preacher. "He quailed under the curious gaze and beat a hasty retreat." They visited three other gambling establishments before turning down State Street. First stop on the infamous street was the Odeon dance hall. He was invited to participate by the floor manager, who failed to recognize the Reverend. Talmadge declined, and as soon as he could locate his guide, who had wandered off amidst the charmers, the pair left. They stopped at several other hot spots on State Street before returning to the Clarendon shortly after midnight.

Once safely back in New York, Talmadge preached against the sin in Leadville, but made no attempt, then or later, to clean up the Magic City. Possibly he noted the eager character of Leadville sin, and decided discretion is, indeed, the better part of mining camp valor.

Crime came in all shapes and sizes in Leadville. There were the deadly assassins, the passionate, the careless, and the comic; all creating havoc, confusion, and a reputation for the Magic City that still hangs over the town. The crimes ran the gamut from murder to pranksterism; the guilty and innocent were not spared because of age or sex.

One young man, smitten with love, almost found himself smitten by a small revolver. "A little less than a week ago a young, good-looking and 'well fixed' businessman of this city had an experience which will probably forever cure him of the sin of flirting with strange females." The young man was sitting with friends in the lobby of one of Leadville's better hotels where he roomed, when the stage arrived. A lady alighted, who was such an extraordinary beauty that "the attention of the crowd was attracted at once." The young man, determined to make her acquaintance, put several questions to the proprietor. He was informed that she was from a distant city and in town to meet her brother who was going to accompany her to San Francisco.

The young gentleman reflected on the stranger, who had "large dark eyes that it was no trite misnomer to term liquid." She had "regular features, perfect complexion, a wealth of wavy brown hair, voluptous form," and she was in Leadville, obviously with nothing to do until her brother arrived.

The young man, emboldened by her beauty, introduced himself. He was charmed by her immediately, and congratulated himself on his good fortune when she agreed to accompany him to the theater. The evening went well, and the young man suggested plans for the next day.

Sunday morning he accompanied her to church, then they went for a buggy ride to Soda Springs, a popular picnic area a few miles west of town at the foot of Mount Massive. It was late when they arrived back in town, and the young lady went straight to her room. The young man lingered in the lobby before retiring to his room, which was just down the hall from the lady's. He was surprised to find her door slightly ajar. He walked closer and the whole room was exposed to his view. His lady was standing next to the bed. "She was in the ravishing deshabille of that one formless garment in which all women are said to

One of Leadville's better hotels, the Clarendon. *Photo Source: Colorado Historical Society.*

be equal.'' He hesitated a moment. "Here seemed plainly and unmistakably an invitation.'' Hesitating no longer, he stepped inside the room and "slipped an arm around the silent woman's waist." Instantly the lovely lady leaped back, and "leveled a cocked revolver" at the young lover's chest.

"How dare you insult me, you scoundrel! Give me five hundred dollars or I will blow your life out!"

The young gentleman knew he could never explain his presence in her room at that hour of the night and realized that if she shot him under the apparent circumstances, "she would be commended instead of condemned."

Trying to buy time, the youth claimed he did not have the money on his person, but if the lady, now a questionable term, would accompany him to his room he would give her the money.

"No, sir! The money here and now or I will blow your brains out."

"But," pleaded the merchant, "I haven't got the money with me." And he explained that it was in his dresser.

She thought it over and ordered him to walk before her to his room. As they walked to the room, he felt the cold steel of the revolver at the base of his neck, and surely realized that this was not a desperate lady, but a cold, calculating professional.

Once in the room the young man bent over his dresser and at that moment the woman made her first mistake; but it was all that was necessary. Peering after the gentleman, she let her pistol hand drop and in an instant her victim had her arm and the gun.

"Now you infernal blackmailer, go!"

She was caught, and "for an instant turned deathly pale, and tried to stammer some words."

"Go, I tell you."

Not waiting until he changed his mind, she left immediately. Later, when the gentleman inquired of her whereabouts, the hotel clerk informed him that "the stranger had met her brother during the night and taken the later train." He was not surprised.

There is a theory existant in western history circles that the "Wild West" was in fact a rather dull place, and the fabled violence of the West has been more a creation of dime novels, cheap movies, and sensational television programs than any reflection of the true West. And while that is

115

probably documentable as far as the West is concerned, generally it was not the case in Leadville during the summer and fall of 1880. The town was busy, loud, lively, and violent.

The headlines of just one randomly selected paper, the September 11, 1880, edition of the *Carbonate Weekly Chronicle*, will give some idea of the kind of activity common on Leadville's streets, and in public places.

LYNCH LAW
Why the Guns Were Stolen from the Armory

AN ASSASSIN'S BULLET IN HIS BRAIN

CROOKED COPPER
He Says He Had Done Wrong and Will Tell All

GAY GARROTERS
Attempted Hold-Up on State Street Last Night

RED RIOT!
Carnival of Crime in Camp

Edward Jones Mortally Wounded Last Night

A FAMILY FIGHT

FIRE FIEND AT WORK IN OUR MIDST

POISONED!
A Horrible Murder at South Arkansas

TODAY'S TRAGEDY
Doctor MaGee Commits Suicide Last Night

And this last, which must be a record for long headlines: "A Double Tragedy—Without a Parallel in Crime's Record, Enacted on East Sixth. John M. Wollery, A Mining Contractor, Attempts the Life of Nannie Berry In a Moment of Unguarded Passion, Discharging Two Pistol Shots Into Her Person. He Presses the Instrument of Death to His Temple, Sends a Bullet Crashing through His Brain, and Expires in His Own Doorway. She Was Not Only the Sister of His Wife, But for Two Years His Mistress in Secret."

Each of the foregoing headlines had a lengthy story following it that was, in most cases, every bit as grisly as the headline claimed.

In September, the *Chronicle* tallied local deaths in an article called "Their Boots On," and in it they listed those who died of unnatural causes. From March to mid-September there were eighteen citizens who met their Maker as a result of shootings. Five suicides were recorded, while one man was run over by the stage, another drowned, several died in mining accidents, and one was killed in a sawmill accident. A number were found dead, no cause of death determined. One unfortunate, William Donahue, was "killed by whiskey."

From October to December 31, 1880, 426 persons were jailed for larceny, while 111 found themselves behind bars for vagrancy. They roomed with another 95 who were there for assault and battery. Thirty-four people were jailed for murder during the last three months in 1880. Substantial numbers of local residents found themselves in the "crowbar hotel" for forgery, resisting arrest, adultery, bigamy, rape, insanity, robbery, and riot. The jail even had an inmate suspected of treason. Another was doing some time for "obscene language." All told, the jail had 1,095 guests from October 1, 1880, until New Year's Eve, 1881, when a goodly number no doubt were invited back.

It was the fourth Monday of November, 1880. Fresh snow lay on the ground, but by all accounts it was a nice day. Sometime after lunch Mart Duggan received word that Winnie Purdy wanted a sleigh. Mart, now a respectable businessman, fitted her out with a "smart little cutter" and a pair of matching blacks, and set out for Winnie's establishment among the fashionable houses of ill repute on West Fifth.

As Mart neared the corner of Pine and Fifth streets he encountered Louis Lamb, who, witnesses reported, Duggan almost knocked down with his sleigh. Some sources claim that the pair had already had words down near the Kentucky Whiskey Depot on West Fifth and the fire was burning when they met again.

Three carpenters were working on a house next to the Leadville Lumber Company on the northeast corner of Fifth and Pine and witnessed the whole thing. According to them, Duggan and Lamb exchanged hot words, and Duggan shouted, "You're a G———d son of a b———h!", and turned his team toward Fourth Street. The incident could have, and should have, ended there. But Duggan, his Irish temper boiling, turned round and returned, turning up Fifth Street toward Winnie Purdy's. Fate showed her hand. Lamb had continued up the street and was in front of Winnie's when Duggan reined in his

Rubble from bank construction fills the street, Pap Wyman's cabin sits in the middle of Harrison Avenue, and the boys at the Little Church Saloon on the corner at right watch the passing parade. *Photo Source: Colorado Historical Society.*

horses. Lamb chose that inopportune moment to demand an apology of Duggan, and Duggan refused. Lamb went for his gun. The men on the house saw Duggan jump from the sleigh and fire at Lamb from behind the rump of his near-side horse.

Lamb's pistol was loaded and cocked but never fired, for Duggan's shot hit him in the mouth, killing him instantly. Lamb lay in the snow, the stub of a pipe protruding from his vest pocket. Passersby pulled him up onto the porch, while Duggan climbed into his sleigh and waited. He later turned himself in to his old friend, Police Captain Charles Perkins.

Night fell on November 22, 1880, with Martin Duggan a murderer. All the time he served as marshal, in spite of rumors, he never was forced to kill a man in the line of duty. At the inquest the judge stated, "we consider that said shooting was done in self-defense." Mrs. Lamb swore undying hatred of Martin Duggan and vowed to wear her "widow's weeds" until Duggan was dead and she could personally deliver them to Mrs. Duggan.

One of the camp's toughest characters was a woman by the name of Kate Armstead, a black-Sioux mixture that spelled trouble for any who crossed her. She lived at 137 West State Street, known locally as "Coon Row," and ran a house of very ill repute. It was said of her that she had

absolutely no concern for anyone but herself. To illustrate, the *Denver Tribune* explained "when one of these degraded, debased creatures [her ladies] became incapable through a constitution broken down by drink and disease, to take the part allotted to her, Kate thrust the poor wretch out of doors and let her die in the gutter." On one occasion when one dying member of her household sought refuge in another house nearby, Kate was said to have "dashed a bucket full of lye over her half inanimate form."

The life Kate was forced to lead was no more generous toward her than she was toward others. If Kate was tough, it was a necessary ingredient to survival. One morning Kate was in one of her hovels and a big "mulatto" by the name of Andrew Lewis slipped into her room and slammed the door. He was drunk. She ordered him out, "a quarrel ensued, resulting in his drawing a razor and attempting to cut her throat." In the battle that followed Kate received a gash from "the shoulder to the elbow," and several cuts in her mid-section, the worst of which "ran through the left breast, cutting down to the ribs, leaving a gaping wound into which the two hands could have been thrust."

A short time after he fled, Lewis was captured in a vacant cabin in the vicinity. Kate, on the morning of July 3, 1881, was found "hovering between life and death, with a decided chance for the latter." But Kate, tougher than the proverbial old boot, survived.

The area of town where Kate operated was as notorious as any in Leadville's history. The numbers began to dwindle in the Row in 1881, but the buildings, a tangle of "irregular shanties" and two-story buildings fronting on State Street, remained. Kate looked the situation over and decided she would leave also. She sold her holdings to another black named William H. Jones, who ran a small saloon next door to Kate's, known locally as Coffee Joe's. Kate moved to Red Cliff and was there a short time when she returned to Leadville, claiming that Jones had defaulted on their agreement. "A dispute arose over this point, and she left the place, swearing she would burn it down before she went away from the city." Jones was concerned, knowing Kate was more than capable of carrying out her threat.

Around midnight Jones closed up Coffee Joe's and retired to his room in the back, "and without any preliminaries of disrobing he crawled into his bunk." He had been in bed a few moments when he was aroused "by a singular crackling noise in the alleyway between the saloon and the old Armstead house." He noted later that he could detect the odor of coal oil. The fire destroyed not only Coffee Joe's, but all of "Coon Row." The damage was estimated at $5,000. Few people mourned the loss of the Row. Kate Armstead disappeared and was not heard of again.

In the spring of 1882, the *Denver Tribune* ran an article called "Life At Leadville" that serves to show the glee with which the capital viewed Leadville life and problems. The first item of interest was Leadville's newest evil, that of opium smoking. It was generally known that the "gambling fraternity are all more or less addicted to it," but the evil was spreading. One location near the corner of Poplar and Fifth streets was "frequented by women who move in decidedly upper circles." The police, it was reported, were reluctant to raid the den because of the local nobility who frequented the place. They were afraid of who they might find. The next item introduced was a "racy bit of scandal" that concerned a prominent businessman who spent some of his free time with his wife and the rest with a "variety actress." The wife found out about her husband's paramour and matrimonial hell broke loose, the result of which saw the actress on a train to Chicago until things quieted. When the coast appeared clear the thespian returned, but her stay was short. The wife found a gun and set

out to settle the score. She was prevented from killing the actress by friends, but her point was made nevertheless. The crime was prevented, "but not a scene that is the talk of certain circles in the city."

While Leadville ladies were engaged in opium smoking, their men frequented the Leadville Mining Club, which was said to have the highest stakes poker game in a town noted for its high stakes. The occasion the *Denver Tribune* relates is one in which a local mining superintendent sat down and sixty minutes later got up, $750 poorer. Later he related his losses to a local gambler, and cursed his luck. The gambler asked him if he would like a little revenge. The super agreed, and the gambler introduced him to what the "fly" fraternity called a "shiner." A shiner was "nothing but a silver dollar on one side of which a concave mirror about the size of a man's fingernail is set." The coin was polished to such a degree that the mirror was not noticeable. It was then laid upon the player's "pile of notes and coin," and the cards dealt over it. The dealer, when finished, had a good idea what everyone was holding.

Later that evening the super tried it out at the table where earlier he had lost his bundle. The players were impressed by his skill, and at the close of the game he had the crowd in such a state of "dead-brokedness" that they were forced to charge their drinks. "Since then the Mining Club has experienced a season of financial depression which seriously lamed their political potency in the city election."

The story of Leadville society smoking opium might go down with a struggle, while the Leadville lady's threatened shooting of an actress is not hard to swallow, but the story about Leadville's leading gamblers being fooled time after time to the degree that they were out of mad money, and that the election results were affected by their inability to buy their candidates, has the distinct ring of make-believe. Still, it made good copy, and there was no reason for accuracy as far as Leadville was concerned. After all, the truth about Leadville was often harder to believe than fantasy.

It seemed that everyone who was anyone during the late seventies and eighties eventually came to Leadville. Among the less desirable notables were Tom Horn, Frank and Jesse James, the Daltons, Bat Masterson, Wyatt Earp, and John Henry Holliday, better known as Doc. According to the *Carbonate Weekly Chronicle*, September 4, 1880, "It is currently reported that the notorious James brothers are now and have been for some weeks ostensibly engaged in working a mining claim in the near vicinity of Leadville." The reporter took his life in his hands when he went on to assert that it had been some time since the James gang had committed a robbery, and since winter was approaching and they were no doubt short of funds, "it is safe to believe that somebody will, in all probability, before cold weather sets in, have to contribute to their support; and . . . it would not be strange if that honor should be conferred on some of our wealthy corporations or citizens."

The reporter's hunch about the James brothers' residency appears to have been true. The *Daily Democrat* in December reported that they had been positively identified by an old Missourian from Independence. The reporter telling about the James brothers' presence in the Magic City claimed to have interviewed Jesse in Charlie Lowe's saloon, known as the Alhambra Hall, at 106-108 West Chestnut. Little is known of the activities of the James brothers while they were in the area, but they never did anything to call attention to themselves, and they left as quietly as they arrived.

The same cannot be said of Doc Holliday. Holliday, the West's most notorious dentist, might have visited Leadville with Bat Masterson in 1879 when the pair joined forces with the Atchison, Topeka and Santa Fe Railroad in what was known as the Royal Gorge War. William Jackson Palmer's Denver and Rio Grande was in a life or death struggle with the Santa Fe over who had the right to lay track in the Royal Gorge, the easiest southern route to Leadville's rich silver mines. The Santa Fe and Rio Grande both recruited a stable of guns to insure their success, but the courts had the final say. The Rio Grande got the right-of-way.

If Doc did not make it to Leadville on that first trip to Colorado, he did make it to the Cloud City on several occasions in the early eighties. In November of 1883 Doc seems to have settled in Leadville, and in 1884 he was listed in the local directory as John Holliday, residence 219 West Third. He dealt faro for Cy Allen in the Monarch Saloon, two blocks east of his residence, at 320 Harrison Avenue.

Doc Holliday was tubercular, and the disease

Hyman's Saloon, to the left of the Tabor Opera House, was the home and place of business during much of Doc Holliday's Leadville sojourn. *Photo Source: CMHC, Lake County Public Library.*

was well advanced and slowly killing the notorious gambler. What he saw in two mile high Leadville other than almost continual games of faro is hard to understand. In a nearby gambling hall, called the Casino, worked John Tyler, who was once thrown bodily from the Oriental Saloon in Tombstone by Wyatt Earp, while Doc looked on ready to come to Wyatt's aid if necessary. In Leadville Doc tried to antagonize Tyler, but Tyler was no fool. He had no taste for an eye-to-eye confrontation with the deadly dentist. But he did have a taste for revenge and "began to campaign behind the tubercular gambler's back." Finally one of Tyler's buddies picked a fight with Doc. Doc won the fight, but lost his job.

Tyler apparently was not satisfied. Doc, now near destitution, was given a rent-free room over Hyman's Saloon and a five dollar loan by Billy Allen, one of the bartenders in the Monarch, one-time chief of police, and friend of John Tyler. During this period Doc caught and recovered from a bout with pneumonia which, considering his tubercular condition, was miraculous. A broke, dying Doc Holliday was unable to pay his five dollar debt to Allen. Allen let it be known that Doc would either pay up, or he would whip Doc. "Billy finally set Tuesday, August 19, 1884, as the date by which Doc would make payment or suffer the consequences." Doc did not pay, and Billy came to collect. Billy was no doubt given confidence by the redoubtable John Tyler, by the the fact that Doc had stopped wearing a gun, and by the fact that he was down to an emaciated sheath of 122 pounds.

"When Allen blustered through the swinging doors of Hyman's Saloon Doc was standing behind a cigar case at the end of the bar. Doc's hand dropped below the counter to pick up a short-barrelled Colt a friend had previously placed there for Doc's use." Within seconds the fight was over. Doc fired twice. The first shot hit the door frame, the second hit Allen's gun hand. Bystanders prevented a third, probably fatal, shot from being fired.

The police hauled Doc to jail, and he was released on bail, eight thousand dollars that the good folks of Leadville put up. Constable Kelly, a friend of Allen's, was dissatisfied with the results and decided to change the course of history. He, in fact, ended up making history.

Doc was wearing a gun when Kelly found him. In his most professional manner Doc asked Kelly if he was armed. Kelly went for his gun, which was his final act. Local men took him away to die, and again Doc was arrested. He was eventually cleared of both charges, Kelly and Allen.

Doc moved from Leadville but continued to visit the camp off and on for the next year or so. He finally left the camp for good in May of 1887 when he boarded a Carson stage bound for Glenwood Springs, where he planned to take advantage of the healing qualities of the sulphur baths. Some five months later, on November 8, 1887, John Henry Holliday drank his last glass of whiskey and whispered his amazement at dying in bed, "This is funny." He was buried at Linwood Cemetery.

After the Duggan-Lamb shooting, Martin Duggan continued to struggle along in the livery stable business, but finally in 1882 the business failed. Unquestionably his killing of Louis Lamb had an adverse effect on his business. That, plus the fact that the boom and rush were over and business generally was suffering, probably account for his failure. He tended bar around town, worked off and on as a deputy for the sheriff's department, and for a while worked in Douglass City.

Douglass City was a wide open railroad construction town located just below the east portal of the Hagerman Tunnel, where James John Hagerman's Colorado Midland Railroad pierced the Continental Divide on its way to Aspen. Duggan, said to have been a deputy sheriff at the time, served drinks in one of the small settlement's many bars.

In 1887 a "Hebrew came into the dance hall with some jewelry to sell to the dance hall girls." They all bought some and were very pleased with their purchases. The girls were admiring their good fortune when Duggan came in and told them it was all phony and asked where the fellow was who sold it to them.

The girls all broke down in torrents of tears, but one of them pulled herself together long enough to look out the window and exclaim, "He's comin' down the road." Duggan recognized the merchant as the robber of a jewelry store in Pueblo and set out after the man. There was a scuffle in the street, but Duggan subdued the man and brought him into the dance hall. There he had the girls lay out the jewelry they had purchased on a pool table and tell how much they had paid for each item. Duggan then made the merchant repay each girl. Duggan considered the situation and decided to "let the Hebrew go free — if he would buy drinks for the crowd." The money and drinks arrived, and the Jew left for Leadville.

Once in Leadville he immediately filed a complaint against Duggan with the justice of the peace for robbery and assault. The justice sent word to Dugan to arrest himself and come to town. Duggan, the girls, and William McCallum, a witness, all headed for Leadville the next day.

"Duggan, who said that he would be his own worst witness, took the stand first." The other witnesses followed. Duggan was fined ten dollars for assault and court costs. Duggan, enraged, told the "Hebrew" to pay the fine himself and told the judge to forget the court costs. Duggan in a rage was a sight to behold. The "Hebrew" was not interested in beholding it any longer and fled. Charges and fines were dropped, and Duggan and his witnesses went back to Douglass City.

Douglass City faded fast once the tunnel was completed, and by late 1887 Duggan was back in Leadville, where he went to work for the Leadville Police Department. "But times were changing," and tough lawmen like Duggan "often proved an embarrassment to the town council, who had to answer for his actions."

After roughing up a local jeweler, S. W. Rice, in March of 1888, Duggan was fined $25. Duggan refused to defend his actions and soon resigned, embittered by his experiences. Some two weeks later Mart, apparently drinking rather heavily and in a quarrelsome mood, was with friends in the Texas House. He had been having a running argument with William Gordon, one of the house dealers, and had threatened to run him out of town. Bailey Youngson, owner of the Texas House, took his dealer's part, and Duggan volunteered to meet both of them in the street and "shoot it out."

Finally his friends got the better of him and talked him into going home. A few minutes after he left, shortly after four in the morning, "police officers making their rounds heard a shot." The officers in the vicinity rushed toward the sound and converged on a spot near the front of the Texas House where they found Martin Duggan lying in a pool of his own blood.

He had been shot at close range just behind the right ear. Amazingly he was still alive, and doctors ordered him moved a few doors down to Bradford's Drug Store. Shortly after daybreak he regained consciousness and requested a glass of water. His mind was clear, and he looked at a

The Texas House, with the awning in the center of the picture. *Photo Source: Colorado Historical Society.*

nearby window, "It is light," he said. His wife asked who did it and Duggan, clearing the blood from his throat, said in a clear voice, "Bailey Youngson shot me." Later in the morning he said he did not know who shot him, but knew it was "one of the gang."

Martin Duggan, one of the West's most fearless marshals, continued to hang onto life until shortly after 11:00 A.M., April 9, 1888. Ten years almost to the day from the time he became marshal of Leadville, Martin Duggan died. Youngson, along with two of his employees, George Evans and James Harrington, were arrested, but the latter two were soon released. Youngson stood trial and was acquitted for lack of evidence. But Duggan's death ruined him. Shortly after the shooting the town was so enraged that it elected a reform slate of city officers, and they closed the gambling halls in Leadville. Of course, private games continued to flourish in back rooms, but the heyday of the gambler was over in Leadville.

The closing of the gambling halls crippled Youngson's business, trial expenses nearly broke him, and when, not long after the shooting, the Texas House burned, he threw in the towel. Once the trial was over, he left Leadville, his health impaired, his financial world in ruins, and his reputation destroyed, to settle in Salt Lake City.

The death of Martin Duggan brought down the curtain on lawlessness in Leadville. Local merchants, mine owners, and smelter operators tried to reopen the gambling establishments, but the council stood firm. The Leadville fling was over, and responsible government reflected the will of the people of Leadville. The saloon keepers and gambling men ceased to run the Magic City, but while the violence was gone, the magic continued.

The story of Martin Duggan should have ended with his burial in Riverside Cemetery in Denver alongside his parents, but the last chapter remained untold. Who murdered Martin Duggan? Was it Bailey Youngson? Was it "one of the gang," as Mart had finally indicated? Most were convinced that Youngson was guilty.

The question remained a mystery for almost twenty years after thirty-nine-year-old Mart Duggan was laid to rest. Sixteen years after Mrs. Louis Lamb danced in front of the Texas House and delivered her widow's weeds to Mrs. Duggan as promised, an article appeared in the *Rocky Mountain News* on May 27, 1904, which unraveled the mystery and cleared Bailey C. Youngson.

George Evans, arrested with Youngson and later released, was apparently hired to kill Duggan by an unknown group "who desired his death on account of old grudges." After killing Duggan, Evans fled, eventually to Nicaragua, where he was killed in 1902 in a shoot-out "with a Spaniard whom he had offended."

Martin Duggan is never mentioned in the gallery of heroic western marshals, but his impact on Leadville, when the town was running wild, surely marks him as one of the great western lawmen, and deserving of the title, Marshal Duggan.

X

Society of Sorts

Bringing the word of God to Leadville when it was sure that it had already heard it—the word was *Silver*—was no easy matter. Henry Lucy, talking about his first visit to the camp, claimed he could only find one church. He admitted it was simply a personal observation, but then noted, "some of the citizens from whom I made inquiry doubted the existance of a church." Others were sure "there was one round about."

The Methodists and Catholics arrived in Leadville first and settled across the street from one another at West Third and Spruce. Probably the Catholic priest, Father Robinson, settled in the camp first.

Henry Robinson was from Salem, Illinois. He journeyed to Denver in January 1872, and was ordained on January 21, 1872. In September 1874, Henry Robinson was sent to Fairplay, and while there he frequently visited the settlement in California Gulch. His church in Fairplay was very popular, as was the young priest. Then in 1876 Father Robinson moved to nearby Alma, and in February of 1878 he moved to Leadville.

Recalling his first visit to California Gulch, Father Robinson noted the small number of residents in the area. "There were a few houses where Front Street now is." A few more houses were located in Upper Oro. Robinson's first Mass was celebrated at Thomas Starr's house in Old Oro, where a box placed on a table served as an altar. Twelve people attended that first service, and the Father recalled with a certain satisfaction that there were only fifty Catholics in the whole district.

The coming of the Sisters of Charity of Leavenworth, Kansas, to Leadville is an epic in itself. Two sisters from the Mother House in

Leavenworth visited the camp in the fall of 1878. They were there to raise money for their hospital in Denver. They asked Father Robinson if they might canvass his area and Robinson, even though he was trying to raise money for projects of his own, willingly gave permission and

One hundred years old, Annunciation Church, little changed since the consecration in 1879. *Photo Source: Francis Bochatey, Leadville's* Herald Democrat.

123

traveled around with them, helped them raise money, and found them lodgings with Miss Anastasia McCormick.

The Sisters were overwhelmed by the miners' generosity and with the hustle and bustle of the new camp. The miners "expressed a wish that the Sisters would build a hospital in their midst." One superintendent, as he gave the Sisters his contribution, told them, "If you come to live amongst us, I will make this donation a hundred fold." After the Sisters' departure, miners and local doctors continued to petition them for help in establishing a hospital in Leadville.

The Sisters of Charity finally decided that they should do what they could for the miners of the Cloud City and three Sisters, Bernard Mary Pendergast and Crescentia Fischer from the Mother House and Francis Xavier from Saint Joseph's Hospital in Denver, were entrusted with the mission.

Snow delayed the Sisters' December departure from Denver and the trio did not arrive in Leadville until shortly after the first of the year, 1879. It was around seven in the evening when their sleigh quietly stopped in front of Father Robinson's church. Their driver went to the door and found Father Robinson at home, but ill. He invited them in, and they discovered their first patient "pale and emaciated, wrapped in a buffalo-robe, and sitting by the side of a drum-stove," which had one very long stick of wood in it, the stove door partially open to accommodate it. On the top of the stove sat a small bucket of water. The good Father was unable to rise, but invited the Sisters in and explained he was just recovering from pneumonia. The Sisters doubted his remark about recovering.

Miss Anastasia McCormick arrived shortly after the Sisters and immediately took them under her wing. Father Robinson received kind and careful attention, recovered, and assisted the Sisters in planning and raising funds for the new hospital. By the first of March the building was virtually complete, except for the finish work, doors, windows, and furnishing. On Saturday evening, March 1, the Sisters were on hand to examine the work, when a patient was brought to them. The Sisters explained that they were not prepared to receive patients, but the man's companion replied that "he would leave him anyway, as he might as well die *there* as on the street."

It was dusk and the Sisters decided they must do what they could for the dying man and asked some workmen to board up the windows in the room where the man lay on a bed of shavings. St. Vincent's Hospital opened that day and has continued to serve the people of Leadville from that day to this, though the location has changed.

Father Robinson's first church, the Sacred Heart, located at West Third and Spruce streets, was, from the day it opened in 1878, too small. Plans were immediately formulated for the construction of a much larger home for Leadville Catholics. Property on the corner of East Seventh and Poplar was secured and construction of Annunciation Church was begun in 1879. The first Mass was held in the still unfinished church on New Year's Day, 1880.

One of Leadville's most colorful and most successful divines was Thomas A. Uzzell, known locally and throughout the state as "Parson Tom," a nickname given him by the Englishmen in his congregation.

Parson Tom came to Leadville from Indiana Asbury University (now De Pauw) on February 1, 1878. He followed the usual route of early clergymen going first to Fairplay where he preached his first sermon, November 1, 1877. He remained in Fairplay until the last of January 1878, when he decided to move to Leadville, where his congregation had already determined to go. He caught a ride with a freighter headed for the Magic City and alighted as the long gray shadows of dusk began to settle on February 1, 1878. His first problem in Leadville was that of hundreds just like him—where to sleep. There were no lodgings available, so he rolled out his bedroll in an abandoned "dry goods box," and settled down for the night.

The next day Uzzell set out to find suitable lodgings and finally located a twelve-by-sixteen-foot cabin behind the Grand Hotel. Once he had a cabin, he had a church, and so set out to find a congregation. To all who would listen, he announced his intention of founding a Methodist Episcopal Church in the Cloud City. He spread the word on the streets, in the saloons, in the gambling houses, and to all he met. After letting the town know his location, time and intent, he returned to the cabin and cleaned everything out of the building. He then placed candles in the windows and on three walls. He fixed the slab door "so that it would swing open and shut without tumbling down," and then waited.

The crowd that gathered at dusk filled the little cabin to overflowing. Uzzell estimated that forty souls, standing shoulder to shoulder, heard that first Protestant service in Leadville. He continued to hold services in his cabin every night for the next four weeks and at the end of that time he was able to form a church society of thirty members, "three of whom were women."

Thomas A. (Parson) Uzzell. *Photo Source: Colorado Historical Society.*

mile from town, looked over to a companion and observed, "Bob, I'll be darned if Jesus Christ hasn't come to Leadville, too."

In the early years of Leadville, a number of faiths were represented. In 1880 the *City Directory* listed seven Christian faiths, Baptist, Catholic, First Christian, Congregational, Episcopal, Methodist, and Presbyterian. In 1900 the roll was the same except that the First Christian had in 1881 ceased to exist, and the Lutherans had established themselves. A Jewish congregation, boasting some of the town's leading merchants, constructed Temple Israel on corner lots at Fourth and Pine, said to have been the gift of H. A. W. Tabor. Black Americans established the African Methodist Episcopal Church at 124 East Ninth Street in 1881. A second black church, the Second Baptist Church, was located in 1885 on the shady side of West Fifth between Pine and Spruce. The following year it was gone. The earlier church, the African Methodist Episcopal, served its congregation well into the twentieth century.

Churches, and especially those people who went to church, had a lot to do with putting a halter on the Carbonate Camp in the 1880s and finally civilizing at least the outward appearance of Leadville in the nineties. And more than any group it was the work of intelligent, educated women, who would not allow their men to exist in a world of drink and temptation, nor would they

The next task was to build a proper church. Meetings were held from the time of the formation of the church society until June 1. They met in "barns, saloons, private houses and wherever a place reasonably large enough to accommodate the people could be obtained." Money came from a number of sources, the least of which was not the gambling-saloon fraternity and the ladies of easy virtue. All of Leadville helped him build his church. William H. Stevens, owner of the famous Iron Silver Mining Company, gave four lots to the Parson on the corner of Spruce and Third streets and threw in $200 in cash. H. A. W. Tabor gave the chandeliers and Captain Albert Cooper, locator of the Carbonate Mine, gave the bell. The Parson, wanting to surprise the townsfolk, did not tell anyone that the bell had arrived and had been hung. The whole town was pleased Sunday morning when Tom, using the new bell, called the people to church. Dill remarked, "Old Independence bell never got a worse shaking up than this one." The sound was so unique and so loud that a miner at the Iron Silver Mine on Iron Hill, a good

Annunciation's spire in the distance. The neat white carpenter gothic church right of center belongs to the Baptists. *Photo Source: Colorado Historical Society.*

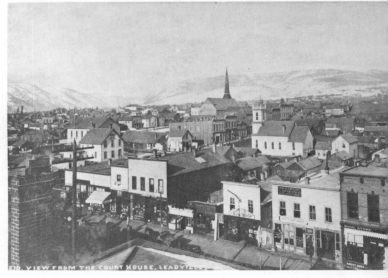

see their children raised in a world without refinement.

It was no accident then that Leadville had a teacher before a mayor, a school before a city hall, and an educational program with funds before a city code, budget, or government.

When Colorado was made a territory, county superintendents of schools were appointed for each county. In 1877 the county seat of the continually reorganized and resurveyed county of Lake was in Granite, some seventeen miles south of the new camp of Leadville. In July of 1877 E. R. Naylor, county superintendent of schools, received a petition from residents in the Magic City asking that a new school district be formed. George L. Henderson, always a quiet advocate of the civilized life, was "authorized to post notices calling for a meeting on July 14, 1877." As a result of the meeting, it was determined that there were enough people in the area to support a school, and a board for a third class district was elected.

August R. Meyer chaired the organization meeting and W. H. Bradt served as secretary. The three-man board elected at that meeting con-

sisted of F. M. Hills, president; W. H. Bradt, secretary; and George L. Henderson, treasurer.

Louise H. Updegraff, wife of Oro City's foremost lawyer, was the first teacher* hired by the newly formed board. Even though the district was formed in July of 1877, it was not until February of 1878 that school opened in a "log shanty," said to have been a commodious, seven-by-nine-foot, mud-roofed structure behind the Grand Hotel. One cannot help but wonder if it was not the same log building used by Parson Tom. There could not have been too many log cabins behind the Grand Hotel that were available for the making of history.

Thirty students were enrolled in Mrs. Updegraff's "log shanty" school, which makes reports on the building size seem a bit out of order. Mrs. Updegraff was paid forty dollars per month. School lasted three months. The school treasury was exhausted at the end of that time and school was forced to close.

*Miss Lottie Williams organized and ran a private school in July and August of 1877, which was the first recorded attempt at such an enterprise in Leadville.

Looking east up Chestnut Street with Grand Hotel at right of center, Carbonate Hill in the background. *Photo Source: Colorado Historical Society.*

The original records of that first board of education were lost and little is known about the operations of those first years. Sometime during the 1877-1880 period the district number was changed from eleven to two, and it would seem the change was made at the same time Chaffee County and Lake County were split and the county seat of Lake moved to Leadville in February of 1879. The school population rose from those original thirty pupils early in 1878 to a whopping 1,513 in 1880. Growth that was common over a couple of decades occurred in Leadville in a year. The original school district could not begin to handle the problems, and the public demanded reorganization. "On April 13, 1880, the decision was made to change the classification . . . from a third class district to a first class district." On May 3, 1880, a school election was held. None of the original three ran, so six new board members were elected. Since the minutes and financial proceedings of the earlier board were not passed on to the new board, and none of the old board served on the new board, there was very little carry-over. The result was the virtual starting over again with regard to policies, planning, and curriculum development. Confusion reigned.

The new board's first job was to provide adequate facilities for teachers and students. The population rose so rapidly that "schools were established in different portions of the city, in rented rooms; so that during the winter of 1879-80, there were in Leadville twelve schools in successful operation."

An election was held July 14, 1880, to determine whether the public favored the purchase of lots and the construction of a proper school building. The vote was affirmative. Lots on the corner of Chestnut and Spruce streets were donated to the district on August 2, building plans were submitted and those of a local architect were chosen. Bids were opened on August 9. Additional property was given and purchased until the district owned the half block immediately west of Spruce Street between State and Chestnut streets.

Construction on the new school, to be called Central, began in October of 1880. It was a two-story brick building complete with gas lights and telephone, but had neither running water nor toilets. "Several teachers who taught in Leadville Schools during the early 1900's reported that toilets were located outside, and water for drinking was dipped from a bucket located in the school." The building was accepted by the school board in May of 1881.

The school district still was short of space and on May 3, 1881, purchased four lots in the 200 block of West Seventh and moved the old high school building from the property next to the newly constructed Central School. It was remodeled for primary children and became the Seventh Street School.

On June 1, 1880, a committee was formed to locate a site for two more schools. Lots were purchased on Carbonate Hill for the erection of what became the Carbonate Hill School. It was a frame building and considerably smaller than Central School. Carbonate Hill School was finished in time for classes in the fall of 1881, but Ninth Street School, the other building contracted for, was not finished until January 17, 1882. Located on the corner of Ninth and Poplar, it was similar to Central School in design, having been designed by the same architect, and was brick.

Going to school for a child in the early boom years of Leadville must have been an experience unequaled anywhere. Mothers whose children went to Central School gave long lectures about the evils of State Street and instructed their young to look neither right nor left and not to speak to anyone. Young boys and girls found themselves walking to and from school in ethnic neighborhoods where their ability to fight or flee was a real necessity.

Carbonate Hill School. *Photo Source: Colorado Historical Society.*

The school day began at 9:00 A.M. for the scholar, earlier for the teacher. In 1879 the student had an hour and one-half for lunch and was finally dismissed at 4:00 P.M. After the first of the year, 1880, he lost one-half hour of his lunch break, but got out of school at three-thirty. The system was revised again by 1883 when the scholar once more enjoyed an hour and one-half for lunch. All students in 1883 reported for school at 9:00 A.M. and left for lunch at noon. They were expected back, lunched and eager, at 1:30 P.M. Primary students were dismissed at 3:30 P.M., and everyone else at 4:00 P.M. All students got a recess of fifteen minutes in the morning and again in the afternoon.

Discipline then as now was a problem, but somehow the pranks of 1880 seem more imaginative and less malicious; if not then, now. Willie Morris, who attended Mrs. Updegraff's "log shanty" school, had a reputation for being an unworthy citizen. On one occasion Willie and Inez Hill, a charming young lady classmate, armed themselves with a brace of revolvers and set upon the school near the end of their lunch. When they arrived, Mrs. Updegraff was still away at lunch, so they set about intimidating the rest of the students. The awesome pair were successful except for one brave or careless young man who fled the scene, but not in panic. He went right to the school board members, told them the news, and suggested they might want to be present at the massacre, or even take steps to prevent it. Several board members followed the brave lad back to the school and unarmed the desperate duo and restored order. Mrs. Updegraff arrived at that moment, and the students gleefully caught her in the street before school and told her the whole grisly tale, no doubt adding a few colorful touches of their own. Mrs. Updegraff's first response was to swoon, but one of her charges shouted, "'mud,' and thinking of her new gown she thought she wouldn't faint." Willie got his revenge some time later when he threw a string of lighted firecrackers through an open window, which relieved the tedium of the educational process for one day at least.

Rules laid down by the school board in 1883 with regard to students were not overly restrictive. They asked that the students not throw "snow-balls, stones, or other missiles upon the school grounds, or in the street in the immediate vicinity of the school-grounds." Students were also expected to "walk quietly up and down stairs and through halls." One aspect of public school education that seems always to be on the public mind is punishment. Possibly Tom Sawyer's experiences convinced several generations of Americans that "the thrashing" was part of the school curriculum. Not so in Leadville in 1883. The official school rules stated, "Corporal punishment shall not be inflicted without the approval of the Principal or Superintendent; and in all cases of corporal punishment or suspension, the parent and Superintendent must be promptly informed by letter, stating the case in full." By 1899 the rule was stiffened by stating that, "Corporal punishment shall, under no circumstances, be inflicted without the approval of the Superintendent."

The teachers in 1880 were without job security or recourse. "Teachers are not hired by the year or month in Leadville, the board reserving the right to dismiss a teacher at any time. No written agreement is made, and the teacher's position depends entirely on the work they do in the schools." In 1880 most teachers were paid eighty dollars per month, with an additional ten dollars for those who did their own janitorial work. A music teacher was hired for $100. There is little evidence of a criteria for arriving at salaries, other than what will it cost to get who we need, but the earlier habit of changing the salaries each month in accordance with cash on hand seems to have been abandoned early in the eighties. Teachers and students got a week off at Christmas. It was rather remarkable that the board decreed "that the teachers be allowed full salary for the time." It must have been a manifestation of the Christmas spirit, since it was not their habit to consider, much less grant, compensation for anything less than a complete job. For instance, in the spring of 1881 the schools were closed in April and did not reopen until May 16, due to an outbreak of scarlet fever. Certainly the cause of the closing or the decision to close was not the teachers' doing, but they were not paid during the closing and were forced to shift for themselves until notified by the board that the schools were reopening and they were again needed.

The social requirements for Leadville teachers, unlike most other Victorian communities in the United States, were nonexistent. The *Rules and Regulations of the Leadville Public Schools,* published in 1883, included no rules restricting the freedom of teachers, or addressing in any way the off-duty hours of faculty. The district asked that school begin on time, that teachers be in their rooms twenty minutes before the appointed starting time and remain fifteen minutes after student dismissal. They expected the staff to prepare monthly reports, keep the room at "seventy degrees, Fahrenheit," or below during the winter months, and refrain from resorting to corporal punishment. The total number of rules for teachers in 1883 was twelve and all concerned themselves with teachers' duties.

By 1899 the rules had been expanded to forty, and were more restrictive, but still did not address themselves to off-duty conduct. But they did tell teachers that they "shall not visit each other's room within the hours of duty, except on business of the school which cannot be postponed, and all reading and writing outside of the regular school work is strictly forbidden." Teachers were further admonished to "avoid sarcasm, ridicule, and every appearance of passion," in the governing of their classrooms.

In 1882 Saint Mary's, a Catholic parochial school, opened for the youngsters of that faith. It was operated by the Sisters of Charity of Leavenworth, Kansas. The Sisters reported that on opening day the Catholic students in the public schools went to school, "demanded their books, and left." All the Catholic students left the public schools to attend their own school, "and assuredly each and everyone must have thought he owned it, from the noise made on entering the hall of the building." The building and staff were expanded from six rooms and three Sisters when it opened, to twelve rooms "with music rooms attached and nine class-teachers, and two music teachers."

The Episcopalians also established a school, called the Leadville Academy, in 1887. In 1888 the name was changed to Professor Austin's Select School, and it continued until some time in 1893 or 1894. The records of the Episcopal Church are not complete and it is hard to say how closely Professor Austin and the local church worked.

Earlier, in 1880, Colorado College in Colorado Springs promoted a boys' school, called the Leadville Academy, but it appears to have had no connection with the later Episcopal school. The *Prospectus of the Leadville Academy*, dated "Leadville, Colorado, August 16, 1880," promised the services of Professor Kershaw, an "eminent teacher for several years in New York and vicinity, fitting boys for college." The Leadville Boys' Academy was slated to open in the social rooms of the Congregational Church, September 8, 1880. Tuition was $1.25 per week, but the demand was not there, and the project apparently died in infancy. In addition to the established

schools, the town supported to varying degrees a host of voice, dance, diction, and music teachers.

The Leadville public schools, once out of debt, hired Edward C. Elliot as superintendent. Elliot was a native of Nebraska and became one of the outstanding educators in the country. He served as superintendent of the Leadville schools from 1898 until 1903, when he left to complete his doctor's degree at Columbia University. While he was superintendent the school district launched its biggest building program to date. The erection of the Leadville High School was decided by voters on April 15, 1899, and they agreed to accept a bonded indebtedness of not more than $45,000. There were a number of irregularities in the first election, and a second election was held October 2, 1899, and again the voters approved the idea. The building was finished almost a year from the date of the original election, April 19, 1900. It was open to the public for two days, then students and faculty moved in and set up shop on Monday, April 23, 1900.

Teachers, miners, merchants, the ladies at the boutique and the men at the Miners' Club, everyone who was anyone, was getting ready for the Leap Year Ball, December 31, 1879. The novelty of young ladies picking up their gentlemen guests and "ministering to his every whim" excited lads and ladies, and gave some fathers cause for concern. At ten o'clock everyone was introduced and the grand march filled the ballroom of the Clarendon Hotel. Ladies and their guests, between twelve and one o'clock just after bringing in the new year, were treated to an "elegant supper." Dancing then resumed until four in the morning when a halt was called to the festivities, and ladies escorted their gentlemen home.

The Leap Year failed to bring the proper results, and the editor of "Our Society" column lamented, "There have been fewer marriages solemnized here during the present week than at any other time in the history of the city. It looks as if the boys are all waiting for the girls to avail themselves of the privilege accorded by leap year and pop the question. Pop, girls, pop!"

The dress for any Leadville outing, whatever it lacked in eastern elegance and sophistication, could not be bested in cost. The town supported four diamond firms, and the local paper estimated they had, "at lowest calculation, a combined stock of two hundred thousand dollars in diamonds." And everyone wore diamonds. The *Chronicle* in reporting on some of the major gem wearers decided it "would be an easier matter by far to list those who do not wear the precious stones. . . ."

Owning diamonds was no fun unless the owner had occasion to wear them, and Leadville provided plenty of occasions. The social calendar for one week began with the Apollo concert on Monday evening, Tuesday saw everyone attending the Caledonian concert and ball, on Wednesday evening it was the Altman-Schloss wedding, a major social event since both were important social leaders. Thursday everyone who was still able attended the Tabor Cavalry Ball, and the survivors sallied forth Friday evening for the F F F F's ball. That concluded the formal events for the weekdays, but that did not include the usual round of receptions, teas, dinners, card and game parties, and social and fraternal gatherings and meetings. And the weekend had not even arrived yet.

The most popular entertainment was a dance. Organizations and individuals held dances to celebrate every occasion. Every holiday—national, regional, religious, or ethnic—was just cause. St. Patrick's Day brought forth a host of green costumes and no small number of fights, the Railroad Workers had their annual dance. The Fourth of July, Thanksgiving, Christmas, May Day, and, of course, New Year's were all celebrated with a dance. There were masked balls, phantom balls, Firemen's, Miner's, and Leap Year balls.

With all the dances it was obligatory that all learn to shuffle with the best of them and learn all the new dances. Professor G. A. Godat was at everyone's service. The professor turned the most backward wallflower into a princess, the heaviest footed miner into a prince. It all took place at the Academy School in the New Turner Hall at the corner of West Fourth and Pine. At the completion of his course for ladies, "they are enabled to participate in the intricate dances with skill and grace." Apparently men were more difficult to teach, since the going rate for sixteen lessons for gentlemen was twenty dollars, while the ladies received the same instruction for sixteen dollars. There were lessons for couples, families, children, and private lessons at $1.50 per hour.

While Godat was the master of the dance, the most popular musician was Professor Henry Simon, a leading member of the Turnverein, and dancing master in competition with Godat.

Popular music of the day included, in any dance program, Strauss waltzes, selections from Gilbert and Sullivan, John Phillip Sousa's "Only A Dream," and a waltz called "When the Leaves Begin to Fall." And dancers filled the floor for the ever popular waltz, polka, and schottisch. Couples eagerly gathered when the quadrille was called, and braver souls danced an athletic sounding number called the "Gallop." Other popular dances included the "Lanciers," "Rage," and the "Newport." In honor of the Cloud City, someone

Programme.

1.	Grand March............Wolfe Tone Guards
2.	Quadrille.............Our Friends in Ireland
3.	Waltz.......................Blue Danube
4.	Lancers......................Our Guests
5.	Waltz-Quadrille......Tabor Highland Guards
6.	Plain Quadrille.....Knights of Robert Emmet
7.	Freeman's Dance...........Harrison Hooks
8.	Schottische.............Leadville Guards
9.	Waltz.......................Tabor Hose
10.	Quadrille................Georgetown Boys
11.	Heel and Toe Polka ...Emmet Guards, Central
12.	Virginia Reel.............Mountain Boys
13.	Quadrille................Prof Simmons

--⊹·⊰ SUPPER ⊱·⊹--

Programme.

14.	Quadrille-Lancers.........Our Lady Friends
15.	Waltz.....................Ladies' Choice
16.	Schottische ....Daughter of the Regiment
17.	Sicillian Circle............Knights of Labor
18.	Waltz-Quadrille..................I. O. B. B.
19.	Polka..........................I. O. O. F.
20.	Monie Musk................Masonic Order
21.	Waltz.................Knights of Pythias
22.	Virginia Reel....................A. O. H.
23.	Varsouvienna.................Denver Boys
24.	Quadrille.............Leadville Merchants
25.	Waltz...............Our German Friends
26.	Tucker and Medley............Good Night

PROF. SIMMONS, Promoter.

An October 1879 dance program. *Photo Source: Author's Collection.*

developed the "Silver King" quadrille. Most dance cards consisted of from fifteen to twenty-five printed selections, but extras were common.

Most of the big dances included refreshments. The punch and cookies of a later era would have been looked at with chagrin by the pre-twentieth century hoofers of Leadville. The menu often consisted of exotic foods imported from abroad or from the East. Oysters on the half shell, lobster Newburg, and pickled lamb's tongue were not uncommon. Fresh salmon from Alaska and a rather exotic local product, "smoked buffalo tongue au beurre Montelier," both appeared on one menu. Desserts bloomed in profusion. Some of those that either seem more mouthwatering, or impossible, were Neapolitan ice cream in molds, tutti fruti ice in pyramids, white grape ice, sweet salad of pears in wine, ornamental fruit jellies, English and American plum cakes ornamented, Madeira wine, and an assortment of fruits, candies, small cakes and, to top it off, French coffee. Leadville's first Leap Year Ball boasted some thirty-seven dishes, a gourmet feast for those with the appetite or courage to try them all.

Novelty dances were always the rage, and one of the most popular was introduced by the Leadville Turnverein early in 1880. The Turner's contribution to Leadville social life was the masked ball, and some of the costumes were sensational, especially when one considers those bachelors working ten hour shifts and then preparing for a ball as Louis XIV, or Falstaff. Ladies liked the princess look, but there was always a fair representation of maids, Dutch and Quaker being the most popular. Another popular dance was introduced by Professor Godat and called the Phantom Ball. The guests were expected to dress as the "proverbial phantom." Apparently one of the amusing aspects of this dance was the gentlemen's inability to tell whether his prospective partner was male or female. Henry Simon was not to be outdone by Godat and introduced the Hard Times Ball. Admission was ninety-nine cents and everyone dressed for the occasion, men in business suits or bib overalls, while the ladies came gowned in "calicoes or worn housedresses." It was a very popular event with the younger set, and everyone crowded the floor for the "Tramp Quadrille."

Whether it was the Leap Year Ball, or the Hard Times Ball, dress was an important consideration. Charles Boettcher, a popular man-about-town, appeared at the Hard Times Ball wearing an "elegant pink leather collar beautifully studded with tenpenny nails; vest cut square in the corsage and at the back; no coat; cream tinted slippers, spotted with red ink; bouquet of dandelions and lilies." At one point in the history of the city's social life, beads became an important article in every woman's wardrobe. It was noted by one reporter that ladies, when dancing with all their beads, sounded "like a bag of beans when it is shaken."

Paris often suggested a number of "questionable" practices, some of which might have invited the curious, but it was England that provided the social forms and patterns for Americans in the waning years of the nineteenth century. It mattered not so much what you did, as how you did it. The form was everything. Today, for instance, we think of the Victorian tea as if it were an institution, when in fact it was several institutions. There was "high tea," which was really an evening supper; "five o'clock tea," which could be given at anytime in the late afternoon, not just at five; and the kettledrum, afternoon reception, and morning reception, all teas of a sort.

One of Leadville's leading families, the Leonards, gave an afternoon tea for a family guest, and it was "one of the most brilliant affairs that has taken place in the city this season." The Leonard tea attempted and succeeded in doing something different. "A very happy idea was that of not having the usual hot house flower decorations, but of filling every niche and corner of the rooms with our beautiful wild flowers." Adding to the effect, and possibly obscuring the fact that wild flowers wilt very rapidly in most instances, the Leonards darkened their rooms during the afternoon tea and served their guests by gaslight.

The summer of 1888 saw Leadville's ladies adding a new aspect to the afternoon tea — colored teas. They were already popular in Denver and in the East, and Leadville adopted the idea with enthusiasm. Mrs. George Goldthwaite is said to have introduced the fad with a Rose Tea. Miss Cora Smith gave a Green Tea, Eva and Lotta Schloss had a White Tea and other ladies of Leadville completed the rainbow of teas with pinks, lavenders, and yellows. The colored teas called for a decor that matched the color of the tea.

Flowers, as always, were in great demand and had a special language of their own. For instance,

if one was graced with a bouquet of red roses, the message was beauty. If a young lass was a flirt, she might get the message in the form of a bouquet of dandelions. Bachelor buttons declared "hope in love," while candytuft proclaimed one's indifference. Daffodils were used to announce chivalry, and dead leaves, sadness. Pumpkin denounced the recipient as coarse, and African marigold condemned one as "vulgar minded." A book on social forms, *Our Deportment,* published in 1882, listed over four hundred plants, each conveying a special message.

The clues and subtle messages of the Victorian era found their greatest expression in romance. Fans, gloves, flowers, parasols, and handkerchiefs all, when properly handled, conveyed a message. A handkerchief resting on the right cheek said "Yes" to the young man watching for the signal. Holding one's gloves loosely in the left hand said, "I am satisfied." For the lady who was not satisfied, she might hold or lay them and smooth them out gently, telling an admirer that she wished to be with him. She could even do something to arrange such a situation by striking them over her shoulder. The man in question read the message, "Follow me." Fan language was a lot like handkerchief language, and the messages were much the same. A quick open and shut fan told a man he was cruel. Fanning rapidly told the man that the lady he was pursuing was engaged. Fanning slowly said she was married. Twirling the fan in the left hand said, "I wish to get rid of you." All spoke inducements, enticements, prescribed action, and provided warnings. A lady with a parasol could warn a lover, "Be careful, we are watched," simply by twirling it. Folding it up, a lady might tell a young man to "Get rid of your company" while simply closing it told the gentleman that the lady wished to speak to him.

The question that easily comes to mind and is very difficult to answer is: To what degree were the various forms of sign language practiced? They certainly were experimented with, since most Leadville families of prominence publicly followed the forms, and many of the books of deportment and social behavior that have been consulted were from early Leadville families. It seems likely, judging from what we know of Leadville and its people, that every effort was made to conform to the acceptable (acceptable by Leadville and, later, Denver, standards). The language of fans, gloves, and parasols was probably played with by the young, more than adhered to by them. Flowers, cards, proper dress, visiting times, and suitable decor were no doubt adhered to more religiously, especially in the 1890s when Leadville's social structure was more stable and leading families were not just rich, but educated and informed.

Those early leaders consisted of a stable of young gentlemen who went on to become the leaders in the state. Young Charles Boettcher, who would become one of the state's financial wizards, seemed to make it to every social event in the city's early years. The A. A. Blows, the A. V. Hunters, and the W. F. Patricks provided social leadership as did the Boehmers. David May, concerned with hard work and financial success, was, nevertheless, a frequent party goer, as was the Schloss family. In the early years of the camp August Rische and Horace Tabor cut a wide swath, but their style was soon considered vulgar and common by "nice" people, who preferred more reserve and humility, at least in others.

While dozens of pretenders pranced through Leadville's social circles, the scepter of social acceptance resided in the firm grasp of Roswell Eaton Goodell. Mr. and Mrs. Goodell had five daughters, Annie, Mary, Jennie, Clara, and Olive, all of whom bore unimpeachable social credentials. In addition to a lineage traced back to John Alden and Priscilla Mullins, they were gracious and attractive and cultured — the belles of Leadville. Writers referred to them as the "famous Goodell Sisters' of Leadville," and the "American Beauties of Leadville." The Magic City witnessed one of its greatest social events when Mary Goodell married Leadville's young smelter owner, James Benton Grant, in a lavish ceremony in the newly finished Saint George's Episcopal Church. The pair were wed January 19, 1881, and it was said that Grant provided the funds necessary for the completion of the church so it would be ready in time for the ceremony.

The Goodells gave Leadville a model to follow. "Since the founding of Leadville, the home of Colonel and Mrs. R. E. Goodell has been the synonym of hospitality and good cheer, and invitations to attend gatherings there have always been considered social prizes." R. E. Goodell served as postmaster of Leadville for a number of years and was the prime mover in developing Evergreen Lakes for social and sporting occasions. But his lasting fame were his daughters and his hospitality. At the Goodells "There is a heartiness ... that banishes restraint and makes each and all feel 'perfectly at home.'"

Teas and dances certainly filled a lot of Leadville's social calendar, but when the weather per-

R. E. Goodell. *Photo Source: Author's Collection.*

mitted, and often when it did not, citizens of the Cloud City engaged in a wide variety of outdoor activities. In the summer, picnics and wild flower picking excursions were popular with people of all ages. Conventions, business and fraternal, voided the streets of citizens periodically, as whole trainloads of military orders, fraternal groups, and mining men left the Magic City for Glenwood Springs, Denver, Chicago, and points east.

The Boulevard, Leadville's fashionable route west to the summer spas at Evergreen and Soda Springs, was said to be so smooth that it had nary a "straw to impede" the wheels of one's carriage. It was a popular evening or Sunday afternoon riding or driving route in the summer and fall, and also provided access to the race track, where the Magic City's horsey set gathered to watch, wager, and be watched.

One of the most popular stops on the Boulevard was Evergreen Lakes, originally called Law's Lakes, after their owner, Dr. John Law. Oriental gardens covered the grounds and J. Henry Hunts' Suburban Hotel attracted many local as well as out-of-town guests. A short distance north of Evergreen Lakes was Soda Springs, named for the mineral springs located near the mouth of Colorado Gulch. Cal Summer's

Mount Massive Hotel at Soda Springs competed with Mr. Hunt's establishment, with both encouraging picnic groups and clubs to come and enjoy the excellent mountain scenery.

The most popular summer hideaway for local citizens was Twin Lakes, located some fifteen miles south of the Cloud City. The area had been a remote, but popular, camping and fishing site for easterners and Front Range residents a decade before the Leadville boom, but accommodations were primitive. In 1880 the railroad passed a few miles east of Twin Lakes on its march to Leadville, and the tourist business boomed. Within two years four hotels were in operation along the lakeshore. The most famous of these mountain hostelries was the Inter-Laken, a delightful blend of informality, primitiveness, solitude, and comfort. Many a Leadvillite spent several days each summer in the gracious, unhurried seclusion of Inter-Laken.

One did not have to go to Twin Lakes to find entertainment, however. There were always the citywide celebrations and the loudest by any set of standards was the Fourth of July. The first big Fourth of July celebration in Leadville was in 1879, and the townspeople made the most of it. The plan called for picnics and a parade by Masonic and Firemen's groups. Children were forbidden the use of firecrackers for fear that they would burn the new city down, but there was plenty of noise provided by dozens of bands competing for the nervewracked audience.

While the Fourth of July was the loudest celebration, Christmas was the gayest, at least for most people. But there were those who suffered at Christmas time as they suffered most of the days of the year. Frank Vaughn, local poet and newspaperman, looked at Christmas in 1882 and asked about the young man with no ties:

> But of the young man, out to have a spree;
> 'Twixt wine and frolic swift the hours flee,
> Until dead drunk and in a sorry plight,
> The kindly cooler holds him for the night.
> He who will dance the fiddler must pay—
> A sore head follows up his Christmas day.

The gambler fared no better, rising

> . . . with the noonday sun,
> Cheerful or blue, as he has lost or won;
> He sees before him but a day of care—
> An eight hour shift within the dealer's chair.

And so Christmas comes riding the crest of a winter wave,

Inter-Laken Hotel. *Photo Source: Denver Public Library Western History Collection.*

Cyclists on a trip around "the Loop" posed for their picture at the Leadville Fish Hatchery. *Photo Source: Author's Collection.*

Dark, dismal, drear—the blinding sleet
Is wind-whirled down the silent street;
And 'gainst the horizon, inky black,
The night sky lightens at the back
Of mountains, grim and gaunt and tall
Beneath the midnight's somber pall.
But hark! the chime of distant bells . . .

And Christmas passed, year in and year out, generally happy, usually gay, and always white.

Winter or summer sporting events could always be counted on to draw a crowd. And the largest crowds always gathered to see the Leadville Blues versus anybody. The cry of "batter up" was a sure sign that summer had arrived and baseball, even at two-mile-high Leadville, was about to begin. The Leadville Blues were a professional team and played throughout the state. In 1882 the Blues had a phenomenal record. After beating virtually everyone in the state, they made a tour of the midwest. Their season record was forty-nine wins out of fifty-two starts. Not bad for the hometown team.

Summer called for a variety of physical competitions. Every beau had a belle he wanted to impress with his physical prowess, and pulling a chicken wing apart and offering the more succulent half to the girl of his dreams would not suffice; hence picnic planners usually included a number of foot races, jumping competitions, and wrestling matches. Rock drilling contests always drew a crowd, and were not only summer activities, but indulged in whenever and wherever miners got together. Leadville teams traveled throughout the West meeting, and usually besting, the pride of Georgetown, Butte, Deadwood, Central City, and other mining camps of the region.

Hiking and mountain climbing were popular activities and early Leadville scrapbooks abound with photos of groups sitting atop Mount Massive, looking as if they had simply alighted, rather than climbed there. One of today's mysteries — how did those ladies climb to the top of a fourteen thousand foot plus mountain wearing those long skirts and arrive, every hair in place, looking as if they had just stepped out of the bandbox?

In the late eighties Leadville and the West found a new toy called the bicycle. A local club of male cyclists was formed in 1889 and "by May of 1893, bicycling had taken its place as a leading sport." In the early years of cycling in Lake County it was a male sport, but the ladies did not allow that haughty attitude to persist for long. By the early nineties a local journalist reported "the cycle craze broke out with something like fury, affecting all grades and conditions of men and extending in somewhat milder form to the fair sex." It was further noted that locally there were five types of cyclist. "The good and the very good, the bad and the very bad and the incorrigibles. Compassion for the kindergarten pupils, however, who are doing the best they can and do not deserve to be shot at. . . ."

One place a cyclist could peddle his machine and be in keeping with the new sporting attitude, was to local tennis courts. Tennis seems to have wandered onto the local scene in 1888 and by 1889 had become a mania. The same year that bicycle enthusiasts were organizing their first organization, tennis players were getting together to form the "Lawn Tennis Club." The town soon boasted three private courts and one public facility.

135

When the weather forced the sporting populace indoors, the Leadville Athletic Association had a well equipped gymnasium on West Fourth, complete with horizontal bar, swing rings, and the rest of the paraphernalia of a gymnastic set-up, where an athlete could wear himself out in feats of near quiet desperation. They also had a boxing ring and a bowling alley. Dr. Dougan, a successful businessman and orator, had so intimidated the pin boy that he wore a steel ribbed mask when the Doctor's "gattling gun" delivery started balls on their way toward the pins.

Skiing did not become a sport of any appreciable dimensions in the mountains until well into the twentieth century, but other winter activities were quite popular. Great groups of younger ladies and gentlemen, for instance, took their toboggans out on the clear, cold winter days and made eager use of the Capitol Hill toboggan slide. The number of interested tobogganers dwindled in the early nineties, and the slide was closed down in 1892. Curling was imported with the Scots, and the baseball fields and Evergreen Lakes were used for competitions.

"Miss Carrie Betts and Miss Rockwell are becoming the most proficient skaters in all Leadville. They seldom practice, but for all that they are the pink of perfection, to speak in connection with so cold a subject." From the town's organization to the turn of the century, skating was far and away the most popular winter activity. Over the years the city had a dozen or more popular skating rinks.

Leadville society, as society throughout the West, attempted to emulate the East, but just below the surface lurked a touch of what might be called hypocrisy. An eastern "dude" with eastern manners was not acceptable to the bulk of western folk unless he could also drink and ride, unless he was one of the boys. Stories in the West about the bilking of eastern gentlemen abound. It was the West that took the greatest pride in its own primitiveness and even though there were attempts to bring culture to the West, it was not the opera house that eastern visitors were shown. In Leadville they invariably were given a tour of State Street and told that it was the wickedest street in the nation, were taken down in a mine,

The Blue Ribbon Comedy Company, one of many such groups designed for member edification and public entertainment. *Photo Source: Dorothy D. Shelton.*

and were given a saloon tour where they were expected to drink whiskey neat.

A possible explanation for the westerner's eagerness to impress the easterner was the easterner's willingness to be impressed. The eastern half of the country and western Europe were hungry for stories of the American West, for paintings of it, for photographs of it, for anything that could give them a mental picture of the West.

In Leadville, like many cities of the West, people found themselves on the one hand trying to live down a reputation, partially deserved, partially manufactured, and at the same time supporting a legend they knew to be true in essence, but false in detail. The literary and artistic societies that were organized in Leadville, like those organized in other western towns, struggled not only with their own frontier temperament, but also with those who expected to find a frontier. No easterner worthy of the name came to Leadville expecting to find, nor wishing to find, total refinement. He was not disappointed.

That small coterie of artistic individuals, women for the most part, who struggled to bring some essence of refinement to Leadville fought an uphill battle. Artistic groups like the Apollo Club gave musical presentations, most societies encouraged art, music, and poetry. The Tabor Light Cavalry sponsored plays, and local musicians and playwrights produced works like the "Hagerman Pass March" and a popular local drama, *The Streets of Leadville*.

Most of the Leadville literature and music has been lost, mercifully, but two artistic efforts should be recalled, one because it has become an American institution without a "home," and the other is an author almost forgotten with the rush of time, who was one of the best chroniclers of the West, and surely one of the most perceptive Leadville has ever had.

In 1885 a group of young miners lived at the "Junk Lane Hotel," a small cabin on the outskirts of Leadville. The name was given the cabin by the occupants, Bob Swartz, Bill McCabe, and Bingham Graves, and a "fourth companion" known only as Jim. The group mined, played occasionally for dances, and wrote and played their music throughout the long winter nights. It was during the winter of 1884-1885 that C. O. "Bob" Swartz wrote the music to "Colorado Home," and he and his companions added the words and made musical history at the Junk Lane Hotel.

Colorado Home*

1. Oh, give me a home where the buffalo roam,
   And the deer and the antelope play;
   Where seldom is heard a discouraging word,
   And the sky is not cloudy all day.

Refrain: A home, a home, Where the deer and the
   antelope play;
   Where seldom is heard a discouraging word,
   And the sky is not cloudy all day.

2. Oh, give me the hill and ring of the drill,
   In the rich silver ore in the ground;
   And give me the gulch where the miners can sluice,
   And the bright yellow gold can be found.

Refrain:

3. Oh, give me the gleam of the swift mountain stream,
   And the place where no hurricanes blow;
   And give me the park with the prairie dog bark,
   And the mountains all covered with snow.

Refrain:

4. Oh, give me the mines where the prospector finds
   The gold in its own native land;
   With the hot springs below, where the sick people go
   And camp on the banks of the Grand.

Refrain:

5. Oh, show me the camp where the prospectors tramp,
   And business is always alive;
   Where dance halls come first and faro banks burst,
   And every saloon is a dive.

Refrain:

6. Oh, give me my steed and the gun that I need
   To shoot game for my own cabin home;
   And give me the light of the campfire at night
   And the wild Rocky Mountains to roam.*

It would be easy for Leadville to claim all the credit for "Home on the Range" on the basis of Bob Swartz's letter, and there seems little doubt that he penned the song and he and his friends wrote verses, but was the music his? Probably not. The basic verse has been traced back to Kansas where it was published in a local paper in 1876. In 1867, it was being sung in Texas. No doubt it is a true folk song with folk origins. It remained for Bob Swartz and his cronies to convert a cowboys' song into a miners' song and formalize the music.

*This is as recorded from Bob Swartz's letter to his mother and father, Mary W. and Charles S. Swartz, February 15, 1885.

*On Monday, November 19, 1945, the Honorable Robert Fr. Rockwell, representative from Colorado, addressed the speaker of the house, and requested that the Leadville origins of "Home on the Range" be recognized and inserted into the Congressional Record. He went on to read Bob Swartz's letter home, written in February of 1885, and read the verses and chorus into the record.

Mary Hallock Foote's "cabin on the ditch." *Photo Source: John Martin.*

And, like the music and musicians of Leadville, "It was the Leadville books and stories . . . that gave Mary Hallock Foote her reputation as a western writer." Of all the writers who have attempted to commit the Magic City to paper, possibly the most effective was a well-bred eastern lady named Mary Hallock Foote. Mrs. Foote, descendant of an old New York family, married Arthur Foote, scion of the famous Beecher family. After a short sojourn in California and a year in the East, the young bride followed her engineer husband to Leadville in 1879.

At her cabin on West Eighth, the literary folk of Leadville came to call. She visited with Samuel Franklin Emmons, famous government geologist of the West, of whom she wrote he "wore riding clothes of Indian-tanned buckskin made by his London tailor." She noted "he was tall, spare, rather harsh featured but distinguished looking, a somewhat hawklike profile deficient in chin, black hair, marked eyebrows, an open-air color on his thin cheekbones." And "he was as fond of people as he was rocks, which is," she conceded, "saying much for an eminent geologist."

Another caller at the Foote cabin was the already famous Helen Hunt Jackson. Dining at the Clarendon Hotel, the Jacksons and Footes whispered beneath the roar of the mob, and Mrs. Jackson "assured us earnestly — she warned us — that we could not stay; the place was too unnatural. Grass would not grow there and cats could not live." The Footes accepted the advice, but failed to heed it. When Helen Hunt Jackson came to call on Mary in her cabin on the Stevens and Leiter Ditch, she had to wait on the porch until Mary was dressed since their cabin had only one room. Mary, thinking back on it, remarked,

"fancy asking Helen Hunt to wait on one's porch!"

A host of mining men of all castes came to call. One, Rossiter W. Raymond, who Rodman

Samuel Franklin Emmons. *Photo Source: Author's Collection.*

No doubt this Mary Hallock Foote illustration, *Scribner's Monthly,* October 1879, depicts the inside of her cabin at 216 West Eight Street. *Photo Source: Author's Collection.*

Paul, editor of Mrs. Foote's autobiography and noted western mining historian, describes as "the single most influential person in shaping the development of mining engineering into a respected profession," came to call at the Footes' cabin on the ditch. When he returned to the East he found everyone stricken with the grippe and soon was in bed himself. Looking longingly back at Leadville, the dry clear air, and the hospitality of the Footes, he wrote them:

> "Let princes live and sneeze in their palaces of ease,
>   Let colds and influenzas plague the rich,
> But give to me instead, a well-ventilated head
>   In a little log cabin on the Ditch!"

When Mary Hallock Foote came to Leadville, she was already known for her artistic work. Her letters home prompted her old friend and member of the *Scribner's Century* staff, Richard Watson Gilder, to suggest "that anyone who could converse so well could also write." The result was a series of popular sketches and eventually short stories and novels. Mary Hallock Foote the artist became Mary Hallock Foote the writer. Still, while her fictional works like *The Led-Horse Claim* and *The Last Assembly Ball* were popular successes, it was as an observer of people that made her exceptional. Her autobiography, *A Victorian Gentlewoman in the Far West,* edited by Rodman W. Paul, and her personal correspondence portray Leadville as it was exposed to the eye of an artist and keen observer. The Leadville scene and populace have seldom been so skillfully painted as in the sharp, concise personal narrative of Mary Hallock Foote.

At left, the King home was under construction. George E. King designed the Tabor Grand Hotel. At center is the Ward home, and next door, the Foote cabin. *Photo Source: Colorado Historical Society.*

Harrison Avenue, one of Leadville's better streets. *Photo Source: Colorado Historical Society.*

XI

Trials of Growing Up

The Leadville Post Office was organized in July of 1877 with George L. Henderson as postmaster. The post office moved about with the frequency of changing weather, but its most famous home was in Horace Tabor's store, and the second postmaster, Mr. Tabor, is without a doubt Colorado's most famous postal employee.

During Tabor's short stint as postmaster (February 19, 1878 until December 13, 1878), the postal business began to boom. It was said during the rush that "One letter is received daily for every two inhabitants, and almost as many are sent out." In January of 1879 postal business amounted to an average of fifteen hundred letters arriving and one thousand leaving each day. The *Daily Chronicle* noted that four thousand people were waited on every day at the Leadville Post Office's general delivery window. Young George Elder wrote his mother in February 1879, and explained, "If you knew how patiently I am compelled to wait for letters at the P. O. you would be amply rewarded for writing as you do. I have frequently formed the last man in a string containing 50 men and those were only from A to L — the M to etc. were equally represented. I can go to the office at any time in the day and find 25 men ahead of me." It was not uncommon to sell positions at the head of the lines for "from one to five dollars." Many solved their mail problems by investing in a box and thus avoiding the crowds at the general delivery windows. The demand for boxes became almost as great as the demand for general delivery, and because of the shortage several shared the same box.

By 1880 the load had swelled to an average of nearly six thousand letters received daily and some three thousand mailed. Around eight thousand people were waited on daily and the two general delivery windows of '79 had swollen to four by the following spring. Sixteen hundred boxes served probably two or three times that number of patrons. It was not uncommon for postmasters to pay some of their employees out of their pockets because they could not wait for Washington to okay a new position. And only three years before, the mail for the "sand mines"* near Oro City was delivered to Charlie Mater's store where it was kept in a cigar box until picked up.

By 1881 the city had regular mail delivery and that, plus the fact that the population had stabilized considerably, ended the massive crowds at the general delivery windows.

Leadville, like all western mining camps, had one overriding fear — fire. It was a constant concern, but, as usual, the need was more evident than funds to solve the problem. The immediate solution in most communities was the volunteer company. Leadville's first volunteer group was organized by the man who had the most to lose at the time, Edwin Harrison, the Magic City's first builder. On June 20, 1878, the Harrison Hook and Ladder Company was formed, and by midsummer they "had purchased a truck and other equipment and were ready for duty." The city displayed an uncommon touch of generosity in August and purchased 150 buckets to support the new fire company.

The second company formed was established by the man who had, by then, the most to lose. H. A. W. Tabor's Hose Company was born during the cold days of February 1879. Tabor bought

*Sand mines was an early nickname for Leadville's soft carbonate ores.

the equipment and was given a lifetime membership for his generosity.

Two additional volunteer companies were soon organized. The first, organized by William H. Bush, later an associate of Mr. Tabor, called the W. H. Bush Hose and Fire Company Number 2, was chartered November 5, 1879. "Most of its members were formerly members of Denver's crack Orcher Hose Co. and the new group was the most promising in Leadville." This crack group soon developed a bad case of hurt feelings because the city council failed to provide the attention the company felt it deserved, and to which it probably was entitled. So the members all resigned and their equipment was given to the city.

The deceased Bush Hose was quickly replaced by the Humphrey Hose Company Number 2 on August 6, 1880, and continued active until the end of the volunteer fire company era. It was said that John F. Humphrey's move was purely political. The incumbent mayor organized his fire company to help boost his chances in the upcoming election. If that was the case it was a waste of time, since he lost.

While all of the companies of volunteers were organized by prominent citizens, their benefactors' support was neither total nor eternal. Usually after the company was underway and had the basic equipment, all further additions came out of the firemen's pockets, or were purchased as the result of successful fund raising events such as the Firemen's Ball, a popular event in many a western community. Most of the volunteers' free time was taken up with preparation for competitions with other volunteer groups and a variety of social and fund raising events. Little real effort was put into fire fighting.

The city council, while not providing funds, did give constant advice and finally began to put restrictions on the fire companies. The fire laddies' reactions could be predicted. They resented city council interference. The council, to encourage excellence and calm the lads, authorized the payment of one dollar and fifty cents to every man who participated in drills. That was appreciated, but they also fined those who missed the drills a dollar and a half, and that did not set well. Internal friction, competition, and council interference considered, it appears as if the town had reasonable fire protection.

Still, at the back of everybody's mind was the danger of the "big" fire. And it was not long in coming. What might have been the end of Leadville, almost before it began, took place late in May 1879. A forest fire broke out on the north side of the town and almost encompassed the northern, western, and eastern city limits. The mayor called upon everyone to help fight the fire before it could enter the city. Hundreds turned out. Their efforts at building backfires and trenching were assisted by a providential change in the wind's direction that drove the fire back the way it had come, and the city was saved.

In September 1879, a group of buildings burned across the street from the Clarendon Hotel. "It occurred about 12:30 A.M. and was over in one hour. The firemen did splendidly although if there had been the slightest wind the whole avenue would doubtless have been destroyed." Other near misses continued to worry the council and as 1880 dawned they continued to enact more restrictions on the fire companies.

In addition to the fire companies, the town almost from its inception enacted a number of measures to insure safe construction. Fabric signs lighted with kerosene lanterns were made illegal, flues had to conform with city standards, and an attempt was made to force all persons in the city to build brick flues and replace existent flues with brick within twenty days. The measure was impossible owing to construction methods and the availability of brick, but as noted, the measure indicated "an awareness of the danger of fire."

On a later occasion the city fathers authored an ordinance that no building exteriors could be constructed of anything except brick, and all additions on existing wooden structures would also have to be of brick. Two months later the measure was rescinded as impractical.

The city fathers, in their attempt to make the city fire proof, failed to look seriously at the fire companies themselves and the possibility of city financial support. Instead they attempted to legislate fire out of existence. Of course, many of their measures were practical and necessary, such as restrictions against open burning, improper sign lighting, unsafe flues, and storage of combustibles, but they seemed convinced that if they made fires illegal, fires would cease to exist.

While the council legislated, the fire companies themselves were creating one of the great hazards to the welfare of the community with their competitive attitude. It was not uncommon to have all fire companies answer a call, arrive in a matter of minutes, and let the building burn while they fought over who was going to fight it. To combat the problem the city finally appointed a fire chief and an assistant to take charge at fires and bring order to what was a chaotic situation. W. H. Bush was their choice in 1879. His assistant was Lou C. Leonard. In 1880 G. H. Fonda was appointed chief and Lou Leonard reappointed assistant. In 1881 there was a clean sweep in the city elections and Herman Kantsler and Sanford McKusick became chief and assistant. They held those positions until 1882. But the problem persisted and one writer noted, "During the next two years [1880 and 1881] fires became even more popular and if one didn't start, someone started it just to see the action."

With the installation of a city water system, fire plugs were installed in strategic positions throughout the city, and by December 8, 1879, the *Herald* reported that seventeen were installed and ready for use. By the end of January it was reported that "four out of every five fire plugs" were frozen and the remainder were "freezing rapidly." The situation was rectified the following year by digging the lines deeper, but the fight to keep water running in the frozen lines was a losing battle during the winter of 1879-1880.

One of the most difficult problems the fire companies faced was the reporting of fires and alerting their volunteers. Originally the method consisted of a centrally located fire bell, but during the winter of 1879 the bell got so cold and brittle it was feared that it might break if it was rung. The answer to the problem was a new fire alarm system, which was installed in March of 1880. It was a "telegraph-type" system and linked the station with ten fire alarm boxes located throughout the city in strategic locations. When a call came in the officer on duty could then ring the fire bell and call the men to the fire. Because of the positions of the boxes, the firemen on duty had an idea of the fire's location, while the rings of the bell signalled the location to the volunteers. When the Presbyterians were hanging their bell in their new church they inadvertently sounded the call for a general alarm fire, and confusion reigned supreme.

Early in 1881 Fire Chief G. H. Fonda requested the city go to horse-pulled fire machines, rather than using men. He pointed out that Leadville's hilly, snow-covered streets provided special hazards, and also pointed out that much of the equipment was in bad repair and in need of

Leadville fire laddies and their equipment. *Photo Source: Colorado Historical Society.*

replacement. The city council did not act until the following August 1881, but when they did it was with vigor and money. The new equipment consisted of a horse-drawn engine complete with a device that dropped the harness on the horses, making the buckling of a few straps all that was necessary, and automatic doors.

As with all fire companies, certain horses became legends, and the Leadville company had a legendary team named Tom and Frank. The pair were housed in the fire house at 704 Harrison. Everyone, young and old, stopped by to visit the famous pair, who held the all-time Leadville speed record. Tom, the great bay, together with his teammate, Frank, "held the speed record from the fire station to the corner of Fourth and Harrison — 60 seconds flat." It is doubtful if the modern engine could cover the same distance today in as good a time.

Another resident at the fire station was the fire dog, whose task was to keep other dogs from attacking or frightening the horses while racing to a fire. Spot was far and away the most famous of Leadville's fire company mascots, and one reporter explained to an admiring public, "Spot was a dog of really remarkable intelligence. When a fire alarm sounded he would run to the side of the stalls and wait there till the horses were under harness. Then he would take his position at the doors and keep ahead during the run . . . keeping other animals out of the way." Spot met his death in the line of duty. The fire horses were racing down the street in a demonstration, when a large dog charged from the sidewalk and Spot tore into him. It happened so quickly that the firemen and team could take no evasive action, and the heavy wheels of the fire truck passed over him.

"At ten minutes to four o'clock this morning . . . three shots were heard on Harrison avenue. . . ." The shots were immediately followed by those dread words — "Fire! fire! fire!" Late risers on that Friday morning, May 19, 1882, rose to find approximately all of the south side of East Chestnut Street in ashes. The First National Bank at the corner of Harrison Avenue and East Chestnut was all that was saved. Between the bank and the corner of Plum Street nothing remained.

The fire seemed to have started in the back of the Palace of Fashion and quickly spread to the Windsor Hotel next door. The flames also ignited the Brunswick, a hotel east of the Palace of Fashion, and from there continued east until halted at the end of the block. The brick walls of the bank stopped the fire's progress in the west.

The local volunteers were successful in preventing the fire from jumping Chestnut Street, and the city stopped south of East Chestnut. The fire was contained and burned itself out by late morning.

Losses were estimated at half a million dollars. It was feared dozens had perished, and rumors circulated rapidly to that effect, but fortunately only one body was discovered. It was badly burned, but the victim was eventually identified as Arthur Ballou, the brother of Frankie Ballou, a local miner. Mr. Ballou had been visiting Leadville from Colorado Springs and was staying at the Windsor when the fire broke out.

At the inquest a local veterinarian, Thomas O'Connor, testified that he was "attending to three cases of pneumonia in the stable of O'Connor and Ballou" when he noticed "three persons passing through the alley towards the Palace of Fashion." He saw the door at the back of the Palace of Fashion and the shadowy forms of men enter the doomed building. It was around one in the morning. During the next two hours he continued to see men coming and going and at one point, thinking they were robbers, "went to Wyman's and Delmonico's looking for a policeman." At three-twenty he roused his assistant, who dressed immediately, and the pair stood in the alley, O'Connor calling his companion's attention to the dim light in the back of the store. The pair saw another man leave, then they walked around to Delmonico's for a drink. O'Connor and his assistant returned "immediately" and while there was a "brighter light burning in the store," he assured the inquest that there was "no conflagration."

O'Connor was sure that the men he saw going to and from the store were responsible for the fire, and even gave physical descriptions. The men who lived in the back of the Palace of Fashion, all of whom should have witnessed the comings and goings O'Connor revealed, testified that they were not sure what happened. Fred Butler, one of the store's owners and lodgers, noted "the distance of [the] nearest gas jet was overhead and was all of fifteen feet distant from the place of the fire."

Butler and the other witnesses who were in the Palace of Fashion all agreed that there was little initial smoke. The fire seemed to start on the floor and none smelled kerosene. The inquest failed to come up with a cause and was forced to rule out arson for a lack of evidence. Most were not convinced that someone, possibly the management of the Palace of Fashion, had started the

Hotel Windsor in 1879. The Palace of Fashion was housed just to the left of the hotel. *Photo Source: Denver Public Library Western History Collection.*

fire. While O'Connor had testified to seeing people coming and going at the Palace of Fashion, his description of the men he witnessed in the store's vicinity did not fit the description of those living at the Palace of Fashion.

Pressure began to build and reports of a weak financial position at the Palace of Fashion encouraged the city to act. The employees of the Palace of Fashion were charged with arson. But the big news had shifted from the fire to the fire department.

It was rather broadly hinted around town that the fire departments had set the fire themselves to see which volunteer company was the fastest. Others accused the volunteers of incompetence and dereliction of duty. Many who witnessed the arrival of the fire companies felt their flamboyant attitude was the cause of much of the eventual damage. When the companies arrived, most thought the fire a minor one; one that would be quickly extinguished. "Consequently several of the firemen in a sportive mood laughed, joked and kidded members of the other companies." One jolly member of a crew saw a friend in the crowd and turned a hose on him. It was not long before the reality of the situation dawned on everyone and a call was sent out for every available fireman. Many who answered the call had been drinking for a considerable time and were much the worse for wear.

Alderman C. C. Joy, newly elected and eager, happened on the scene and verbally and physically tore into a number of the volunteers. After the fire the volunteers, praises ringing in their ears and coins jingling in their pockets, accolades and gifts from a grateful public, wrote a public letter. The volunteers, filled with righteous indignation, proclaimed for all to read:

To the Honorable Mayor and
Council of the City of Leadville:

GENTLEMEN—At an indignation meeting of the Fire Department of the city of Leadville, held this 20th day of May, 1882, it was unanimously voted to express our deep indignation at the remarks and treatment received at the hands of Alderman (?) C. C. Joy. Your ordinances require us at all time, especially at a fire, to be under the directions of our chief engineer and his assistant.

We therefore ask of you whether the expressions given utterance to by said Alderman, calling the fireman "a set of drunken s--s of b------s," and his actions in knocking down and kicking one of our members, is an expression and the feeling of your honorable body. If this be the case, you cannot consistently expect us to any longer remain members of the Leadville fire department.

Respectfully submitted,
Harrison Hook and Ladder Co., by
C. E. Wyman,
Sam Jacobs,
           Committee.
H. A. W. Tabor Hose Co., by
M. Dawes.
F. H. Officer,
           Committee.
Humphrey Hose Co., by
Matt Medill.
Harry B. Kantner,
           Committee.

The fire departments knew they had the city council on the carpet and there seemed no question that they had the support of the citizens and the press, but when the council assembled Tuesday evening, May 23, 1882, it was clear that the vote of censure of Alderman Joy was not going to be automatic. The council went into a fifteen minute executive session that dragged on to thirty-five. When they emerged motion was made to end the volunteer system and immediately establish a paid fire department. Somehow the council, "on the carpet," managed to pull it out from under the volunteer firemen. The motion was voted upon immediately and passed nine to two. The era of volunteer firemen ended.

Later, the press, talking with the mayor, Dr. D. H. Dougan, asked if he was in agreement with the council's action. "I was in full sympathy with the movement." When he was asked if the volunteers had not performed in a satisfactory manner, the mayor referred back to the firemen's letter, and especially their casting the gauntlet at the council's feet when they said, "If this be the case, you cannot consistently expect us to any longer remain members of the Leadville fire department." His reply stated the city's case. "They have assumed a position and made a plain business proposition before the council." He noted that they did not ask for an investigation into Joy's conduct, rather they requested the council endorse their point of view. "Out of common self respect the council could not do this, hence they did as they did."

The city council did initiate an investigation of their own, and their findings were devastating.

We find upon careful investigation of the alleged attack upon Andrew King that he and several other members of the fire department were intoxicated at the time and that after Alderman Joy had arrested said King and turned him over to Officer White an attack was made on Alderman Joy by a number of firemen who raised spanners and other weapons in a threatening attitude whereupon Alderman Joy struck said King with his fist, he having got loose from the officer in the meantime, and that Alderman Joy did not kick said King and that any statement as to the kicking is false and untrue. We further find that the arrest of said King by Alderman Joy was for breech of the peace by using foul, obscene and abusive language at the time when Alderman Joy was trying to prevent a number of intoxicated firemen from gutting and robbing the saloon of William Roberts on Chestnut street, and endeavoring to prevail on the men to return to duty at the fire. That said intoxicated firemen did steal and take by force from said Roberts 600 cigars, a lot of liquor and beer. We further find that quite a number of firemen were in a gross state of intoxication at said Windsor Fire and that the communication addressed to your honorable board emanates principally from that class.

To the large number of the members of the fire department who have always been honorable, faithful and efficient, we recommend that the thanks of the council be tendered believing that they are entitled to such consideration at our hands. We would respectfully recommend that the threat to resign on the part of the respective companies be accepted and that we find the conduct of Alderman Joy on the occasion referred to worthy of commendation rather than censure.

The City of Leadville had a new fire department, and while a number of people were outraged by the council's swift and decisive move, it was done and there was no turning back. The new fire department consisted in large measure of the same equipment and men, only they were now financed and controlled by the city. The new department consisted of "one fire marshall, one hook and ladder company of seven men, two hose companies each of four men with a foreman for the hose companies and one for the hook and ladder company." The fire marshal was paid $125 a month, $80 for foremen, and $75 for the newly hired firemen, most of whom were the pick of the volunteers.

The employees of the Palace of Fashion, charged with arson and with the threat of murder charges hanging over their heads for the death of Arthur Ballou, began to prepare their defense. The citizens of the Cloud City were still reeling under the press of sudden change when the fire bell rang again.

It was late Wednesday evening, May 24, 1882, only five days since the devastating Chestnut Street fire and less than twenty-four hours since the creation of the Leadville Fire Department, when the fire alarm rang in Box 21 — the Gas Works. Crowds rushed to the southwest corner of the city, guided by "the volumes of smoke." Turning the corner of Chestnut Street and Leiter Avenue, the crowds halted. There before them was the massive works of the Grant Smelter completely enveloped in flames. Smoke and flames so completely surrounded the smelter and its support buildings that the "big smoke stack could not be seen for nearly half an hour."

The new department set right to work and the fears of some that the old fire boys might interfere were for naught. They soon had several streams of water playing on the blaze, but for the first "ten minutes" it "seemed to make no impression." Efforts were increased and the public, after its first shock, pitched in and helped. "Aldermen, citizens, ex-firemen and boys" all volunteered and "no one's good services were refused."

Within an hour the building was a mass of smouldering rubble, the fire was contained, and no one was injured, but three hundred men were out of work, the Leadville smelting industry was severely crippled by the loss of a half million dollar facility, and the economy of the Magic City was staggered by the loss of a ten thousand dollar a day business.

Arson was the cry, but the cause of the fire was quickly discovered and explained. At about twenty minutes to twelve the smelter crew had left the plant to eat their midnight meal. A watchman was on duty. "About five minutes later a loud report was heard and the watchman discovered the flames coming through the floor." Furnace number 3 had become clogged with molten slag, gas was trapped inside the furnace, and the pressure quickly blew out the tuyeres (pipes) allowing the flames to shoot out of the furnace and ignite the building. The watchman who discovered the result of the explosion could do nothing and was fortunate to escape with his life.

Almost a year after the Chestnut Street fire, the employees of the Palace of Fashion came to trial. It was mid-March 1883, and political candidates and nominating committees were preparing for local elections. The trial of the employees was being reported by the local press in an almost soap opera fashion, when on March 16, 1883, the public read a sworn statement by J. (Jack) H. Brogan, who was at the time a resident of the State Penitentiary in Canon City where he was serving time for setting the torch to Leadville's Famous Shoe Store the previous summer. According to Brogan, he was in bed asleep on the night of May 18, 1882, when he was awakened by Bryce Blair and Walter Wilson. The pair wanted him to come with them to the Comique "to call the dances." Brogan declined, but they insisted, so he went along.

Once downstairs, Blair told Brogan that "he wanted to put fire to the Windsor and Palace of Fashion." Jack claimed he did not like the idea, but went along. Blair had two beer bottles of coal oil, a cigar box, and a candle.

"Blair waited for a light from the smelting works* in the rear of the Palace of Fashion, to see to go in under the building, and then he proceeded to scatter the coal oil on the floor and side of the wall on the underside of the floor and base of the building of the Palace of Fashion." He filled the cigar box with paper and liberal quantities of coal oil, lit the candle and placed it upright in the cigar box, then carefully placed his fuse under the building near the area he had covered with coal oil. Blair crawled out from under the building and they "all went over to the Central Fire Station." All three were volunteer firemen. Brogan and Wilson stayed at the station. Blair was the bookkeeper at the Windsor Hotel, which suggests a strong motive. The arsonists were brought to justice, and a large banquet was held in honor of the acquitted employees of the Palace of Fashion.

One of the city's first tasks after its formation in the winter of 1878, was to determine boundaries and how the new community should be managed. One of their first acts was selecting a street commissioner. On May 1, 1878, the city fathers agreed to pay $100 per month to the newly appointed commissioner. He set about laying out the streets and dividing the city into blocks. One of the major problems was solved by a number of merchants when they gave the city a right-of-way, one hundred feet wide, that ran north and south and at right angles with Chestnut Street. The new street was named Harrison Avenue, honoring Edwin Harrison. The town's rapid growth prompted C. E. "Pap" Wyman, colorful owner and operator of a number of liquor dispensaries, to remark in 1881 that people had thought him crazy in 1878 when he located his property "as far out of town" as Harrison Avenue and State Street. "I was away up in the sage brush then."

The new street commissioner not only had to deal with sagebrush streets, but had to fell trees in the right-of-way, pull stumps, and fight with property owners who had built buildings in the middle of what was to become a city street. Many suggested the road go around them. All claimed the time honored precepts of prior occupancy, squatters' rights, and "possession is nine-tenths

---

*When they dumped molten slag at Harrison's Reduction Works, just south of Chestnut Street, it produced a flash of light, then continued to glow for several minutes.

of the law." None prevailed and all were eventually evicted. Another problem the city street builders encountered were wells, some of them quite deep, smack in the middle of a planned street. They were covered, but many continued to open up for years afterward. Another problem then and now were abandoned mine workings. Even today it is not uncommon for a portion of a citizen's backyard to disappear, an alley to sink, or a small dark hole to appear someplace in town that will require several dump trucks of dirt to fill.

By the end of 1878 the city was laid out and the city council ordered every citizen to number his property. For the first time since the birth of the city it was possible, at least in theory, to find a place of business if you had its address.

One of the most pressing and persistent problems of the street crews was trying to halt the mud in winter and hold the dust down in the summer. They were largely unsuccessful in both endeavors, but not for want of trying. What seemed like an ideal solution to both problems was the use of smelter slag on the streets. The heavy black sand gave the streets a nice uniform color, refused to be mud, and seemed likely to hold the dust down. Prior to the laying of slag, "Four thousand dollars were spent by the new city government the first month for grading streets, constructing bridges, and cleaning the streets and alleys of accumulated filth." Then came the slag. "The cost of grading, dumping of eight inches of slag from the smelting works and covering it with gravel was $35,253; $30,088 of which was to be paid by the property owners on the streets."

It is little wonder that those same property owners were upset when the gravel sank to the bottom and wagon wheels pounded the slag into a fine powder. What was once an ordinary brown dust became a heavy black mist following every wagon and riding every breeze. A mountain shower would settle the dust for a time, but it was quickly dry. Businessmen took the situation in hand during the fall of 1879 and hired a water wagon (squirt wagon) and sent a man out to slop water onto the streets to keep the dust down. It worked well until another group of businessmen hired a wagon of their own. Leadville being Leadville, in no time a rivalry grew up between the two squirters and both attempted to out-water the other. In a matter of hours what had once been a dusty street was converted into a black bog. The

The streets of Leadville were a staging area for all manner of enterprises. Here a pack train is about to depart. *Photo Source: Denver Public Library Western History Collection.*

148

final solution was achieved when the streets were paved.

One of the simple pleasures citizens enjoyed, if they did not happen to be in the path, was a runaway. A most colorful runaway took place when the Coliseum Theater advertising wagon encountered Colonel Wood's advertising dog. The team took one look at the playbill-covered dog rattling in the breeze and promptly left town. On another occasion the questionable music of the band at the Coliseum Theater sent the half-loaded stage coach of the South Park Line careening down Chestnut Street. But the most popular runaway had to have been the one that took place on May 8, 1879. One of Houghland's beer wagons was turning the corner from Chestnut Street onto Harrison Avenue when the inside front wheel caught under the wagon and bounced, rattling the load and spooking the team. Off they went careening and bouncing, strewing beer the length of Harrison Avenue, much to the crowd's delight. The team forsook the street and raced up the sidewalk. The driver fell from the seat onto the tongue, and still scrambling for the reins, fell under the wagon. The racing beer wagon passed over him, missing him completely. People from one end of the "Avenue" to the other had the opportunity to sample a free bottle of Houghland's beer. Possibly the advertising more than made up for the loss.

The pedestrian took his life into his own hands when crossing a street in Leadville, and he really was not too safe on the sidewalk, as the Houghland beer wagon story will testify. Once in a while the pedestrian had the last laugh. One afternoon in the late fall a pair of speeding wagons, scattering pedestrians left and right, encountered each other in the one hundred block of West State Street. "Jameson's Mineral Water wagon came to a rapid collision with Herd's cord truck. The glass wagon went to atoms, the wood wagon went on end; the horses broke loose and went to Malta."

Nineteenth-century America was looking for a solution to the ever increasing problem of traffic in the cities. The most popular early answer was the street railroad, or as it came to be known in the twentieth century, street cars. Leadville seized upon the new method of urban transportation and within a year of the city's incorporation at least seven organizations were working on plans and raising funds to get their project underway. Most never got past the talking stages, but there was enough excitement to prompt R. G. Dill to declare in the *History of the Arkansas Valley, Colorado*, "Several attempts have been made during the past two years to organize a street railway company . . ." but all ". . . have failed to come to a definite conclusion except the last. . . ." He goes on in optimistic terms to explain, "It is anticipated that the road will be in operation by early fall, probably by the time this reaches the eye of the public."

After a pair of false starts and two ordinances later a street railroad did in fact materialize during the summer of 1881, but it was the City of Leadville, rather than the bevy of promoters, that forced the project to a successful conclusion. On April 2, 1881, the city council, led by Mayor John Humphrey, passed an ordinance granting L. M. Dorr, superintendent of the City Railway Company, the last in the long line of aspirants, "the right, privilege and license to build, construct, equip, operate and maintain a street car railway, to be operated by horses or mules. . . ." It then went on to name the dozen or more streets they could operate on and the conditions under which they could operate. Such items as expansion of facilities, method of constructing tracks, and a charge limit (10¢) were all detailed. The firm was granted a twenty year franchise, "provided, that the said L. M. Dorr, his heirs or assigns shall, on or before May 1, 1881, have expended at least the sum of two thousand five hundred dollars ($2,500) in stabling, ties, rails, or actual construction on said street railway, and shall on or before August 1, 1881, have constructed and began operating at least one (1) mile of said railway."

That put the fat in the fire. If the City Railroad Company was going to get the job done they had to act fast, and they did. On Friday, August 5, 1881, an army of leading citizens were on hand to witness the grand opening and ride the new road. The route was along Harrison Avenue from Chestnut Street to the corner of Eighth and Harrison, up Eighth to Poplar and then north to the Denver and Rio Grande station.

The cars were capable of carrying over forty passengers each, and the company had four of them, white with lively blue tops and green ends, pulled by small mules. Their stock and equipment were housed at 704 Harrison Avenue* in the middle of the line, a location that later was considered a handicap, the end of the track being a better location for stables and maintenance.

Shortly before the street railroad got into

*The building was later used by the Fire Department and served in that capacity until 1975.

business the Herdic Coach Company started. It was a nineteenth-century counterpart of the urban bus system. The company had six coaches capable of carrying eight persons and in many ways was more practical for Leadville, as winter soon proved. The basic route of the Herdic's was from the Clarendon Hotel to the Denver and Rio Grande station, but since they could go where they pleased and were not restricted by rails, the routes were subject to change.

During the summer months the street railway seemed to be doing reasonably well, but the seeds of disaster were sown with the first snow. As the snow multiplied, it became obvious that not only was the company poorly prepared for winter, it was also financially weak. The company found their cars were too heavy for the small mules and the wire brooms that were attached to the front of the cars near the wheels were embarrassingly inadequate for removing snow. Unable to move the snow, they purchased a pair of sleighs, again too large for the mules, and attempted to slide over their problem. The snow melted, rendering the sleighs useless, but the weather failed to warm up enough to melt the ice on the tracks. The City Railway Company was unable to adequately serve their customers. The following July 1882, saw them officially fold their tent and retire.

The Herdic Coach Company continued to perform its duties for a while longer, using sleighs and carriages according to the dictates of the weather, but they soon went the way of the street railroad. The livery stables continued to serve the public and make money doing so, evidence that even then the American people were not interested in cheap public transportation, but rather preferred to be able to go where and when they pleased, and were willing to pay for the privilege.

The most exciting and most efficient form of travel in the world of the nineteenth century was the iron horse, the railroad. The people of Leadville prayed, pleaded, and demanded a railroad. In the end they got three. "The first road to commence stretching out toward Leadville was the Denver, South Park and Pacific." The road was planned during the Oro City days before the advent of the Magic City; the resources were not available, nor was the idea practical at that time.

Freight rates from Denver and points east drove merchants on both ends of the route to eagerly support any railroad scheme that proposed a stop in Leadville. And, of course, railroad men were eager to tap the mines and smelters of Leadville. William Jackson Palmer's "Baby Road," the Denver and Rio Grande, was in Colorado Springs, Pueblo, and Canon City the year of Leadville's birth. The Denver, South Park and Pacific, awakened from its slumber by the mining activity in the high Rockies had worked its way up Platte Canyon, following the North Fork of the South Platte River and in 1878 reached "Pine Grove, then Estabrook." The race was on and the Leadville pot of silver lay in wait for the victor.

The Rio Grande's push out of Canon City met with opposition from the Santa Fe, who also saw their route west through the narrow canyon of the Arkansas. The result was the Royal Gorge War, a combination of armed threats from both sides and a legal battle that finally went to the

Almost a hundred miles of track were laid by Leadville's railroads to serve the mines east of town. This trestle was located about a mile east of town in Stray Horse Gulch. *Photo Source: Author's Collection.*

Supreme Court. In the final round, the "Baby Road" won and immediately set out for the upper Arkansas and Leadville. On July 22, 1880, around 10:00 P.M., the Denver and Rio Grande rolled into Leadville, almost three hours late. In spite of the rain and the hour, the celebration would have made a presidential inauguration appear dour by comparison. In fact, the town had a president on hand to aid in the festivities. General and Mrs. Ulysses Grant and their entourage entered the Magic City on the first train for a frantic five-day visit, a part of their round the world tour.

The general and his family were met at the train by hundreds of well-wishers, a company of mounted police, two cavalry companies, five infantry companies, the volunteer fire departments, thirty veterans of the Civil War, a one hundred gun salute, and the ever ready, ever present, bands — five of them. Before retiring, the general said a few fitting words from a speaker's platform erected for the occasion in front of the Clarendon Hotel.

The railroad's impact on the community was immediate. Prices on a number of goods dropped; the freighting industry was crippled, forcing many teamsters to become ore haulers or into the short haul business from Leadville railroad docks to the mines and communities in the area. Another important feature of the railroads was the introduction of luxury items not available in quantity before.

On the heels of the Denver and Rio Grande was the Denver, South Park and Pacific. By early 1879 they were pushing through South Park, working by torch light, twenty-four hours a day. They arrived in Buena Vista shortly after the Rio Grande, were unable to secure a suitable right-of-way, and eventually negotiated a deal with their competitor whereby they were allowed to use the Rio Grande's tracks. The agreement was designed to last five years; traffic and maintenance would be split fifty-fifty, the Denver, South Park and Pacific would pay a rental for use of the Rio Grande's trackage, and the "gross profits were to be pooled" and divided equally.

By 1883 dissension over the unequal use of the tracks between Leadville and Buena Vista drove the two lines to a split. The Rio Grande handled seventy-five to eighty percent of the freight and in spite of the 50-50 split established in the "Joint Operating Agreement," the Denver and Rio Grande wanted a share based on actual haulage. The South Park wanted their half of the maintenance reduced according to the amount they used the road and began in 1883 to build their own route into Leadville from Como, over Boreas Pass, via Breckenridge and Dickey, up Ten Mile Canyon, over Fremont Pass and down to Leadville. The Denver and Rio Grande had "anticipated this move" and by the end of 1882 had completed their Blue River Line from Leadville to Dillon over the Arkansas River — Ten Mile Canyon route proposed by the Denver, South Park and Pacific. Undaunted, the Denver, South Park and Pacific, now owned by the Union Pacific and called, simply, the South Park, set to work laying track. When they reached the Ten

Denver South Park and Pacific RR's yards. *Photo Source: The Kansas State Historical Society, Topeka.*

Denver South Park and Pacific atop Fremont Pass. *Photo Source: Collections in the Museum of New Mexico.*

Mile Canyon area they ran into a number of conflicts with the Rio Grande over right-of-way. For the most part, the two lines ran along opposite sides of the narrow gorge. The South Park, its line finally completed up Ten Mile, conflicts for the most part resolved, announced the termination of its service from Buena Vista as of February 6, 1884.

When the new High Line, as it was called, neared Leadville, an unanticipated problem reared its head. Sam Boise, owner of the Ingersoll Placer, and Richard Finch and Miles Southward, owners of the old Crown claim, sought an injunction against the railroad for crossing their property without permission, and for damages. Before anything could be done to halt the line, the "builders of the South Park took advantage of the darkness of the night of February 1, 1884, put a force of 300 men to work, and when the property owners awakened on the morning of the 2nd, the tracks of the South Park had been laid."

The South Park finished the High Line twenty-four hours before their self-imposed deadline of February 6, 1884. The race was over, but the results were not clear. It was another eight months before the lawyers could unscramble the knots between the South Park and the Rio Grande. Finally, on September 30, 1884, traffic

began to move on the High Line. The new line reduced the mileage to Denver from 171 to 151, making it the shortest, though not the easiest, route to the state capital.

"While enjoying a brief respite at Manitou's restful resort, under the shadows of Pike's Peak, I fell in with Major Jerome B. Wheeler, active head of the great New York dry goods house of R. H. Macy and Co." Carlyle Channing Davis, Leadville's famous newspaper editor, goes on to tell how he injected the idea of a railroad from the Aspen mines to Leadville's smelters. Major Wheeler "seemed much interested in Leadville" and wondered about the economic opportunities in the camp. "I made suitable reply, and then rather timidly unfolded my railway scheme."

The result of his vacation, according to Davis, was the Colorado Midland, though things did not go according to his original design and what he hoped would be a boon for Leadville turned out to be a losing proposition. His plan, as he proposed it to Wheeler, consisted of a line from Aspen to Leadville. He did not suggest a line from Colorado Springs to Leadville, knowing that such a line would make it easy to bypass the Leadville smelters in favor of those along the Front Range.

All sources, save Davis, have the Midland

The Colorado Midland railroad trestle over California Gulch. Central School at left. *Photo Source: CMHC, Lake County Public Library.*

idea originating in Colorado Springs. Morris Cafky, author of *The Colorado Midland*, sees H. D. Fisher as the prime mover, and gives none of the credit to Davis or Wheeler. J. J. Lipsey, in his *The Lives of James John Hagerman*, notes that Hagerman and Wheeler had a number of problems, most concerning Wheeler's mining property in Aspen and his control of coal deposits near New Castle. But out of those problems comes some evidence that supports Davis' none too modest claim of initiating the whole Midland project. James John Hagerman, a well-to-do Michigan capitalist, arrived in Colorado Springs a very ill tubercular patient in October of 1884. The Colorado Midland had been incorporated since November 23, 1883. Hagerman's health began to improve almost immediately and by June he was an officer of the paper corporation along with Wheeler who "had invested heavily in Aspen, Colorado."

Unfortunately, Davis gives no indication when he met Wheeler in Manitou Springs, but he did claim to have interested Wheeler to the degree that he accompanied Wheeler on a scouting trip of the Aspen area. According to Davis, Wheeler "satisfied himself as to the probable existence of extensive coal deposits, and before leaving bought an option on a controlling interest in the Aspen Silver mine."

There are too many unanswered questions, but it is possible that Wheeler seized upon Davis' plan for an Aspen to Leadville railroad, bought Aspen mining property, sold his idea to Fisher and other Colorado businessmen, who may well have been thinking along the same lines, and together they formed the Colorado Midland Railroad Company.

It is abundantly clear both from the company's name and their incorporation papers that by the time they organized they were planning a road from Colorado Springs into the midlands of Colorado. Hagerman and other leaders of the company decided to proceed with the Leadville-Aspen leg first, since it would immediately begin to generate capital. But, because the Denver and Rio Grande "refused to make any concession in rates on rails and other material," the new company was forced to complete the Colorado Springs leg first so they could haul building materials to Leadville.* Still, they had a crew of almost a thousand men working in the Leadville area at the same time they were driving tracks west up Ute Pass out of Colorado Springs.

As the Midland neared Leadville, the perpetual railroad problem reared its ugly head — right-of-way. Right-of-way was to railroads what prior claimants' rights were to mining, and both kept an army of lawyers in clover for years. The Denver and Rio Grande owned a piece of property that lay in the proposed path of the Midland's downtown approach to their station and yards. After repeated efforts to purchase the land, it became clear that the Rio Grande intended to use the property to halt the progress of the Midland, or at least impose a costly delay on the new railroad. Mr. Davis, who had followed the Midland's

*Unlike the Rio Grande and the Denver, South Park and Pacific, the Midland was a standard gauge road.

153

progress with a keen eye, was invited by George Cook, the Midland's Leadville agent and mayor of Leadville, to meet him on the contested ground "at one minute after 12 o'clock, midnight."

By 12:05 men were at work laying track on the contested land. The mayor had made sure that the police were stationed well away from the area and since it was Sunday the courts were closed. It was impossible to get an injunction against the Midland, had one been sought. By morning the Midland track was laid. "The site was guarded for a few days," but the Rio Grande seemed willing to fight it in court rather than in the streets of Leadville. Eventually the Midland, Davis assumed, paid a "fair price" for the property, but it remained in Colorado Midland hands and became the site of their passenger station in Leadville.

On the cold rainy afternoon of August 30, 1887, large crowds gathered to watch the track layers build their way across the California Gulch trestle and into town. Finally the men, cold and wet, quit at Chestnut Street. The following morning, Wednesday, August 31, the Colorado Midland completed its line into Leadville. The city would be served with passenger service, but all freight traffic from the west would bypass the city. Davis' fears were realized. The Aspen ores went to smelters along the Front Range.

But the Midland's task was not nearly complete. They still had to cross the fourteen-thousand-foot Sawatch (Saguache) Range and push their rails into Aspen. The major link in that last bit of line was the Saguache tunnel through the continental divide. Later it was renamed Hagerman in honor of the company's indefatigable president. Work on the tunnel's approach had begun in 1884, and the tunnel construction itself began in 1886. The bore was completed the following year in June.* The tunnel construction itself was brutal work, and several men were killed on the job.

The completed tunnel was 11,528 feet high and was snug against the crest of the continent, just north of Mount Massive in a saddle near the upper end of Busk Creek. The bore was 2,060 feet long, high enough and wide enough to accommodate standard gauge equipment, and it was reached by crossing a series of spectacular trestles and going through tremendous snow fields near timberline. The maintenance and snow removal problems were almost insurmountable. Cafky reports that "as many as six hard-working locomotives were sometimes required to shove the Leslie plow through the white wastes." It

*Again the Rio Grande got into the act and started laying track up the Roaring Fork from Glenwood to Aspen and actually beat the Midland into the city.

The Colorado Midland's depot, a grand example of railroad Victoriana. *Photo Source: Colorado Historical Society.*

The tents of Douglass City are dwarfed by this giant trestle on the approach to the east Portal of the Hagerman Tunnel. *Photo Source: Author's Collection.*

cost the new road in the neighborhood of $70,000 annually to maintain the tunnel and its approach.

Rail travel, though much better than Old Dobbin, had its shortcomings. One traveler telling about a trip on the old South Park line, which had become the Colorado and Southern, noted, "This is a narrow gauge road and has not changed a great deal. The coaches still have a coal stove in one end of the car for heating purposes; it takes this train about 12 to 14 hours to make the trip from Denver to Leadville and is rarely on time." It is fair to point out that the C and S was always a bit more Spartan than its competition. The Denver and Rio Grande was not much better with its eight to ten hours. One story that was told on one occasion or another about every railroad in the West seems appropriate here, since it may well have originated with the old, notoriously slow, Denver, South Park and Pacific.

After what seemed an eternity of jolting and bouncing across the white wastes of a Colorado winter, a rather attractive young lady asked the conductor how much longer it would be.

"Some time yet, madam."

"But I'm going to have a baby."

"I'm sorry, madam, but you shouldn't have considered traveling in your condition."

"I agree, but I wasn't in this 'condition' when we started."

Before the railroad industry fell upon hard times, service was much better, and in 1894 some sixteen passenger trains served the people of the Magic City every day. Rates originally were quite high, especially considering wages. For instance, it took $12.50 to buy a ticket to Denver in 1880. A miner would have to work over four days at $3.00 a day to make enough for a one-way fare. By 1899 competition had pulled that 1880 price to Denver down to $1.25. A drawing room cost $7.00 on the Midland and other lines' rates were comparable.

155

Railroad competition was keen and any device they could come up with to cut cost and increase efficiency and business was quickly seized upon. In 1888 both the Rio Grande and the Midland announced plans to speed up their Western Slope accesses by building tunnels. The first bore, the Denver and Rio Grande's tunnel under Tennessee Pass, would cut "four miles" of tortuous curves and "hard pulls over the Continental Divide." Construction began in January of 1890 and to speed the process they not only tunneled from both Lake County and Eagle County sides of the 2,600-foot bore, but also sank shafts along the course of the tunnel and worked from the center out. "Daylight through the bore was achieved in mid-August and by early November, the tunnel had been cleared and lined with redwood."

Leadville people understood the rationale for the tunnel, but regretted the loss of scenery, especially the opportunity to view the Mount of the Holy Cross. The first train through the new tunnel consisted of a "standard-gauge engine with palace and baggage cars attached" to test the new tunnel and newly laid standard gauge track west. "The run proved successful, signaling the way for coast-to-coast, broad-gauge service."

The Midland's tunnel plans, which consisted of a new bore hundreds of feet below Hagerman tunnel, received an even greater outcry from outraged nature lovers. The new route promised an end to the "wonderful views obtainable from the car windows." It was suggested that the new route might be used in winter, but the old route could be opened in summer for passenger service.

It was not that the Midland was insensitive to the scenery, but they were more sensitive to winter maintenance costs. The new tunnel would be almost five times as long, but would eliminate the difficult curves and massive trestles, so endearing to the tourist and so maddening to the railroad company. *Harpers Magazine* appreciated the view and the problems in 1888 when a Mr. Howard wrote, "The Midland's climb over the Continental Divide, at the Hagerman Tunnel, is a wonderful thing in the way of railroading, but it cost a dozen enormous fortunes. This is not a narrow-gauge road that goes zigzagging up one side of a lofty mountain range and down the other, but a standard-gauge road, with sumptuous passenger coaches and 65-ton locomotives."

The Busk-Ivanhoe Railroad Tunnel Company, Incorporated, was organized in June of 1890. Construction began the following month. It took a little over three years to drive the tunnel and "twenty men were killed in the process." In spite of the difficulties, the bore, 9,394 feet long, almost two miles, was finally completed on October 18, 1893. The first train roared through the tunnel on December 17, 1893.

The Western Union Telegraph line is said to have arrived in Leadville in December 1878. A two-wire line was expected in June, but construction techniques being what they were, the city did not have telegraph service until a line was completed over Mosquito Pass in the fall of 1878. The line was installed by Western Union "chiefly for the purpose of bringing to the camp the latest market quotations on silver." The construction problems were many, but the problems of main-

Hagerman on the Midland's Aspen line. *Photo Source: Author's Collection.*

taining the line were almost insurmountable. Much of Mosquito Pass is above timberline, and the winter wind blows with fierce, unfettered force, ripping lines and poles down, and tearing at repair crews with knife-like sharpness. One workman, caught in a sudden storm, was forced to crawl along the ground over the icy, windswept crest of the Pass "in order to save himself from being blown over the precipice." The traffic on that first primitive line was increased to the point that Ayers, writing in 1879, could claim "the telegraph and post office are, next to those in Denver, the most important in the state."

By 1880 the city had two telegraph companies; Denver, South Park and American Union Telegraph, which controlled the railroad telegraph; and Western Union Telegraph Company, struggling with the Mosquito Pass line. The latter line's receipts in 1880 amounted to over $40,000, and four operators were kept busy around the clock. "Press reports alone ... amounted to 1,496,342 words."

Almost immediately the telegraph had a worthy rival. The telephone arrived in Leadville in May of 1879, just a little over three years from the date of Professor Bell's immortal, "Mr. Watson, come here; I want you." Many of Leadville's conversations lacked the simple dignity of that first conversation, but to everyone's amazement the contraption worked. The telephone was introduced to Leadville by Western Union. "On May 15, 1879, the two plants of the Malta Smelter Company below Leadville were connected by telephone." Mr. Tabor immediately saw the value in the new device and with some other leading businessmen organized "The Colorado Edison Telephone Company," notarized July 16, 1879, and filed for record the following Monday, July 21, 1879. The company was organized in Arapahoe County with principal offices in Denver and Arapahoe counties. It could legally do business in Arapahoe and Lake counties.

The new enterprise went to work August 1, 1879, and placed their first phone in the office of Berdell and Witherell's Smelter. The exchange opened on Monday morning, August 25, with fifteen connections. By the first of the year, two hundred and fifty locations were connected by telephone, and two hundred more were on the waiting list.

Tabor, president of the Magic City's first telephone company, with his associates, reorganized the company the following year for the purpose of "operating and maintaining the 'National Bell Telephone Exchange System' in the City of Leadville." The newly organized Leadville Telephone Company was notorized on July 24 and filed for record on July 28, 1880. Tabor remained president and a director. George Fisher, cashier of Tabor's Bank of Leadville, was one of the two directors while A. G. Hood, manager of the earlier Tabor enterprise, was the other director. The Leadville Telephone Company's first official act was a five dollar increase in rates from fifteen to twenty dollars per quarter. The new business took over room 20 in the Quincy Block for their office and rented additional space, plus the roof, for $2,000 a year. On the top of the building they mounted a tall, rather primitive mass of wood and wire from which telephone service was strung to all segments of the community.

In the early days of the telephone, wires were strung from every conceivable fixture. They were draped over rooftops, from buildings, trees, and poles. Gradually they were replaced with fifty-five to sixty foot poles with row upon row of "ten-pin" crossarms. Cold weather added a host of problems. In addition to lines tangled and twisted by the wind and poles that simply laid down before winter's onslaught, the breath of the users froze the telephone diaphram. To combat the cold, patrons stuffed wool into the mouthpiece.

Telephone in the Magic City provided a kind of unexpected magic. The street argot; the jargon of the ladies of ill repute, who by the way were among the first subscribers; and the language of miners and smelter operators and railroaders rendered the use of "lady" operators out of the question. The ladies could neither understand all that was being said to them nor, agreed the men of the community, should they.

Maintenance of the lines in the days before proper equipment, especially for climbing poles, was hazardous business. "It was considered a brave act" to mount a pole, wrap one leg around it, and proceed to mount a ten-pin crossarm. The greatest risks, though, were saved for long distance operation. Wires were strung along the Western Union route over Mosquito Pass during the spring of 1881, but the problems were so great that it was finally abandoned. The project was reintroduced in 1888, and better equipment seemed to suggest the promise of success. It threaded its way from Leadville to Denver via Mosquito and Loveland passes and was the "most celebrated" line in the state. "It was the only one in the world built in high altitude over lofty mountains." The winds, snow, and electrical storms at the high altitudes where the line was

Harrison Avenue decorated with bunting, power poles, and the telephone company's "ten pin cross arms." *Photo Source: Colorado Historical Society.*

strung played havoc with the original, rather ordinary construction. "The number of poles over Mosquito Pass was doubled and larger wire used, but storms played with them as with dry leaves." They kept adding poles until they stood one every seventeen feet, and heavy cable replaced the earlier wire. It did not solve the problem. Finally the solution required the line be buried. Leadville was finally connected by telephone to the rest of the world.

The origins of the Leadville water system are somewhat confused. In the early days, domestic water was provided by a number of peddlers who sold water by the barrel, the price ranging from thirty-five cents to seven dollars per barrel. No doubt the season determined the price. The city council approved the construction of a domestic water system as early as May of 1878, but, due to a lack of funds, nothing was done. The issue was discussed again in July and finally a call for a

special election was issued for November 12, 1878. While the city was going about its plans for a water system, local businessmen were also busy and had formed the Leadville Water Company. The city, after considering the possible courses of action and the value of two water systems, signed a contract with the new company on January 7, 1879. The contract was drawn for twenty years and required the city to pay $125 for each fire plug installed up to ten, and $85 for each additional plug.

The new water company elected J. S. D. Manville, secretary, H. W. Lake, treasurer, and Joseph C. Cramer, superintendent. Cramer was one of the early residents of Leadville and had been active in organizing the town. He served as a trustee, as councilmen were called, and was serving as town clerk and recorder when he accepted his new position as head of the Leadville Water Company.

158

Evans Gulch Reservoir, linchpin of the Leadville Water Company's system (above). *Photo Source: Colorado Historical Society.*

Work, in spite of the January snow and cold, began almost at once and was pushed with a diligence usually lacking in purely civic enterprises. One problem did emerge. "When the pipes were being laid, soft solder was scarce in the camp" and threatened the early completion of the project. But a solution was immediately at hand. Leadville's water lines were soldered with silver bullion.

Two reservoirs were dug. One, the smaller of the two, was just above town on Carbonate Hill. It was fed by a larger one located in Evans Gulch about two miles east of town. The water from the "Big" Evans reservoir was transported to the 60,000-gallon Carbonate Hill storage via an eight-inch pipe. According to the *Colorado Miner* in

Georgetown, watching the progress with keen interest, "in excavating the water works reservoir at Leadville some very promising indications of mineral were observed." No major strikes were reported, but in Georgetown the feeling was that "It is probable that there is more money under than in the water works."

When the installation was complete, the city had some forty-eight fire hydrants, and those people willing to pay for it had running water. In the first test of the new system it was reported that there was not a single leak after "a severe first test," made April 1, 1879. Apparently silver was a more than adequate substitute for solder.

By 1880 the twenty thousand plus citizens of the Cloud City found themselves surrounded by

Leadville Water Company's staveline to the Arkansas Valley Smelter. *Photo Source: Colorado Historical Society.*

their own refuse, the result of the deplorable practice of simply hauling their trash to the edge of town and dumping it. A virtual forest of rotten, stinking outhouses filled alleyways, backyards, and dotted the backs of business houses up and down the main streets. Some of the citizens dug cesspools, but they were few and, due to their construction, not much of an improvement over the ever-present privy.

Even the dead were not free from the malodor. The old cemetery on the lower end of West Chestnut had been neglected, and the *Leadville Democrat* reported an "almost unbearable odor" rising from the graves. Some of the graves, it was reported, were in "such condition that parts of the coffin are exposed and myriads of flies swarm."

Two obvious problems sought immediate attention: a city dump and a sewer. The merchants were so distressed by the situation that they volunteered to construct a sewer at their own expense. The city fathers managed to make a mockery of civic need and decision in their bumbling attempts to establish a city dumping ground.

And all the while the trash continued to pile up. The city council was agonizing over the problem of location. Everyone agreed there should be a city dump, but not near them. They also agreed it should be conveniently close to the city. Rather than striking out with decision and selecting a site because of its suitability, they listened to the critics and pondered. Finally, long after the decision should have been made, they selected a site just north of the city limits. They also created the office of city scavenger and gave him police powers, hoping rather than believing, that one person with police authority frowning at a negligent citizenry would restore the quality of the environment. They also used the chain gang, but they were incapable of cleaning as fast as the populous littered.

Finally in 1886, eight years after the founding of the Magic City, work was started on a sewage system. Charles N. Priddy, then superintendent of the water company, was given the contract. Thomas W. Jaycox was the civil engineer in charge of the operation. The businesses along Harrison Avenue, those in the vicinity of West

Interior of a Leadville electric power plant. *Photo Source: CMHC, Lake County Public Library.*

Chestnut, and a few residences along the route were served, but the rest of the city was still without the services of the sewer, and it was not until after the Second World War that a sewer system that served the whole community was installed.

One civic improvement that seemed to proceed without a hitch was the gas lighting. It was, of course, obsolete in a decade, but it survived into the twentieth century. Again the hand of Tabor was seen stirring the growth genes of Leadville; the result was the Leadville Illuminating Gas Company. The company filed its articles of incorporation on March 18, 1879, with the state. Local filing was done on April 4, 1879, with G. R. Fisher, cashier of Tabor's bank, Dennis Sullivan and Charles L. Hall as the incorporators. According to Gandy, an early Tabor biographer, "Tabor bought a majority of the shares, amounting to $75,000." Prior to the organization and incorporation of the gas company, the city had conducted a special election in February, and by vote of the people had the authorization to establish a "Gas Works in the City of Leadville." Shortly after the filing of the incorporation papers, an agreement with the city and the new gas company was arrived at, and work began immediately. The project was completed the following fall, and on November 18, 1879, the yet unopened Tabor Opera House was bathed in the soft glow of the newly installed gas lights.

The city, in its ordinance, stipulated that "for the convenience of the public, at least one hundred street lamp posts and lamps" would be installed. They were not going to be accused of being wasteful, though. The lamps were only to be lighted from twilight to dawn and only on nights "when the moon shall not be shining."

On May 13, 1881, Leadville citizens were treated with their first glimpse of the wave of the future. The Billings and Eilers Smelter installed their own generator and illuminated their property with electric lights. A local reporter described the light bulb as "a star of such brilliancy that one could not look at it for more than an instant." Its light was so intense that he could see the "tiniest pebble on the ground, the flakes of dust on the clothing, every notch on the ragged bars of bullion. . . ."

The success of electric lights was assured in the city, but unlike most projects, early electrification was not something that required a community effort. In 1883 Charles Boettcher's Leadville Light and Power Company was organized and the following year the new lighting system began to replace the gas lights on Harrison Avenue. For years, both sources were used, but gradually the romantic gaslight gave way to the safer, more effective electric light. The Boettcher-led organization supplied the Cloud City with electric power unhampered by competitors until 1894, when a group of local citizens organized the Citizens Electric Light Company and built a plant on the corner of Fifth Street and Leiter Avenue. Boettcher tried to stop the company by court action, but a vote of the people in April of 1894 allowed the new company to operate. By 1897 the two companies had merged, Boettcher seemingly relinquished control, though remained a stockholder, and the newly organized Leadville Light Company, with a variety of adjustments, continued to serve the community until 1924, when it became a part of Public Service Company.

DOWN THE SHAFT

The life of a miner was hard, lean, and chancy. *Photo Source: Author's Collection.*

XII

Reality Comes to Stay

In June of 1879 the *Daily Chronicle* reported that the silver ore in the Little Pittsburg ran all the way from 100 ounces to 2,200 ounces per ton. Tabor, of course, had sold out for one million dollars, but his old partners, led by Jerome B. Chaffee and David H. Moffat, using the unheard of production figures, Tabor's success, and the legend of wealth that Leadville had come to be, promoted the mine and the sale of Little Pittsburg stock. They were able to capitalize the mine for twenty million, which, had the mine been able to do all it was said to be capable of, would not have been excessive.

Throughout 1879 the Little Pittsburg continued its fabled production and in mid-January the company paid $850,000 to its stockholders. Its stock was selling at a very gratifying thirty-five dollars per share, though that figure moved up and down in the thirty dollar range, depending on the vicissitudes of the market.

The Little Pittsburg, while surpassed by a number of other famous Leadville producers, was for the investor the symbol of Leadville wealth. In February of 1880 a ripple of fear spread through those in the upper echelons of the Little Pittsburg hierarchy. Chaffee and Moffat, both in

Jerome B. Chaffee. *Photo Source: Author's Collection.*

David H. Moffat. *Photo Source: Author's Collection.*

163

New York singing the praises of the Little Pittsburg, Leadville, and silver eternal, received word from their manager that unless new ore was found the Little Pittsburg's days of glory were numbered. The first crisis to be faced was the word that dividends would have to be suspended while exploration for new ore bodies was initiated.

Word got out that the Little Pittsburg was out of ore and by mid-March the stock had dropped to $7.50 per share. A good many old, practical Leadville miners, "while marveling at the wonderful results of its operation, shook their heads." They had always felt that the "deposits on Fryer Hill were not of a character to insure permanency." Unfortunately, these old mining sages were not heard from until after the event, and had they spoken out before they would have been shouted down. And what of the team of Moffat and Chaffee? Both men publicly bemoaned their losses and according to Duane Smith in his fine Tabor biography, "Chaffee flatly stated he was the 'heaviest loser' in the crash." Later it was revealed that the pair beat the deadline and unloaded some 51,000 shares of Little Pittsburg stock early in March before the bottom fell out. Both men denied any wrongdoing and claimed to be the victims of circumstance, ignorance, and youthful innocence. It did not wash, at least not in Leadville.

Frank Hall, Colorado historian, claims the Wall Street crowd was congratulatory, rather than angry. They claimed Moffat was the first westerner to fleece the eastern money fraternity, and he was praised for "his superior shrewdness in standing from under."

While many predicted the return of the Little Pittsburg, history records a sad demise for Tabor's famous mine. By the end of the year the value of its stock had dropped to a dismal $1.95. That was a tremendous shock to those who had bought shares in January at thirty dollars plus prices. It also had a devastating effect on the stock of all Leadville mines. Most investors assumed that if the Little Pittsburg, the prime mine in the Leadville district, could fail, what was to stop other, lesser properties from doing likewise. John J. Vandemoer, important correspondent for a number of mining journals as well as newspapers, wrote in October of 1880, "One valueless claim sold in a district will hurt that whole district. The Little Pittsburg affair gave the mining interests of Colorado, and especially Leadville, a blow, from which it has not yet recovered. I do not mean to say the Little Pittsburg mine was valueless, but it was undoubtedly stocked at too high a figure."

In 1879 miners were making three dollars per day on the average. By the summer of 1880 some few mines had increased wages to four dollars a day. Eight-hour shifts were the exception, but were being worked in some mines. C. C. Davis, in his account of the strike of 1880, attempts to gloss over his support of the mine owners and his role in bringing the miners to terms by explaining that "Miners and smelter hands had been receiving the full Union scale, from $5 to $8 a day," and asserting that there was no reason for a strike at that time. After the Little Pittsburg failure, the whole of Leadville mining was shaky, which is understandable, and Davis asserts that had the miners' "new demands been made six months prior, they doubtless would have been acceded to without demur." His contention that the strike was ill timed is *sound*. His contention that the mine owners would have agreed to wage increases in January of 1880 "without demur" is equally *unsound*. There is nothing in the history of Leadville silver mining or western labor history to suggest that mine owners would have been generous then, or at any other time, and events after 1880 tend to bear this out. Leadville mining recovered, but wages remained the same in most mines, three dollars per day, until 1893 when they *dropped*.

Joseph R. Buchanan, a Leadville labor leader, suggested that the arrival of the railroad contributed to the unrest by introducing large numbers of cheap labor, forcing the wage scale down. Certainly that was a fear, but a strike for higher wages was not a solution to the problem of large numbers of cheap labor. In fact, it could have had just the opposite effect, that of forcing management into hiring the cheap newcomers. Also, a fact that Buchanan in his *The Story of a Labor Agitator* failed to take note of was that the railroad arrived in Leadville after the strike, and not before.

What, then, caused the strike of 1880? A number of factors were present and wages were not the single, nor possibly even the most important, factor. The eight-hour day was the exception in most western mining districts, and while such Colorado counties as Park, Summit, Chaffee, and Gunnison were paying four dollars per day, the opportunities in those nearby districts were not great enough to entice large numbers of Leadville miners to pack up and leave. Some of the cause might lie at the door of fate itself. Many of the miners in the Leadville mines had come to get rich and instead found themselves working for someone who was no better than they, just earlier or luckier. As the big mining company control became more pervasive, the individual saw his chance of riches slipping rapidly away, and he was trapped by a system that he had come to the Magic City to beat. The Chrysolite and Little Pittsburg mines, the Little Chief holdings, the Robert E. Lee, the Morning Star Consolidated, and the Stevens and Leiter Iron-Silver holdings "produced approximately two-thirds of the silver output of the district."

The big mine owners and managers controlled the local mining industry almost totally, the business community to a large degree, and local government when the need arose. The miners, for their part, generally attempted to stay out of local politics. They even organized a semi-secret society called the Elephant Club, an organization that had as a basic tenet the boycotting of local and state elections. In January 1879 they organized Leadville's first union, hoping that through group action they could enact the changes that industry and government appeared unwilling to consider. The Miners' Co-operative Union was associated with the Knights of Labor, but, since both were secret associations, little is known of their membership, organization, or affiliations.

The Leadville union was the first of its kind in the hard rock mines of the state and is said to have been the second association of Knights in the state. Michael Mooney was the leader of the local union at the time of the strike, but it is unclear whether he rose to that position through acclamation in the early hours of the strike or was duly elected president. The Leadville Miners' Co-operative Union was listed by the Knights of Labor as "Cosmopolitan" number 10,005.

Most of the problems that precipitated the strike seem to have germinated in the Chrysolite,

A Chrysolite mine crew about the time of the miner's strike of 1880. *Photo Source: Author's Collection.*

and the first of those problems was a medical plan that management planned to impose on the miners for their own good. The plan called for a two dollar deduction for family men and a dollar for bachelors. The deduction would come out of their pay, weekly. In return for allowing the company to do this, the company would then be released from all liability for damages or injuries. The miners opposed the plan, first because of the liability clause, and second because they claimed they had no option. It was either sign or quit. The company issued a disclaimer on the latter, but the conflict intensified and finally the managers simply dropped the idea. The mine owners detailed in very terse terms the miner's rights in this and later conflicts. If a miner was unhappy "it was his privilege to quit."

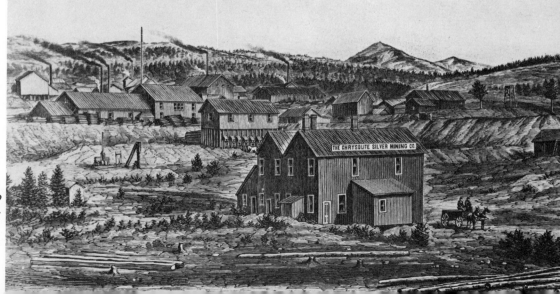

Photo Source: Colorado Historical Society.

Shortly after the medical debacle, the Chrysolite management instituted a series of policies that, with the aid of hindsight, appear to have been designed to bring about a confrontation. First was a no smoking order that included no "talking or loitering by miners on duty." Many of the foremen were unwilling to enforce the rules and quit, others were accused by management of not carrying out the policies and especially of not "measuring the men's work accurately and that the miners were idling" while on shift.

Rumors circulated that the mine managers were talking of reducing wages from three dollars per day to two dollars and seventy-five cents. While the rumor added fuel to the fire, it was the restrictive measures instituted in the Chrysolite that brought the men out of the mine.

As the day shift approached the Chrysolite workings on Wednesday morning, May 26, 1880, there was nothing to suggest this would not be like any other Wednesday. But deep in the depths of the mine the night shift was determining a course of action, and when they came up at 7:00 A.M. they greeted the day shift with the news that the strike was on; no one was going to work in the Chrysolite that day, or presumably until their demands were met. The day shift agreed and immediately joined the night shift. After a short discussion they marched on the Little Chief, a short walk to the west.

The general manager of the Little Chief and Chrysolite was Winfield Scott Keyes. When the strike broke out he was in Denver, preparing to leave for California to visit his family. When news reached him he cancelled his trip and returned home. In the meantime his mine superintendent at the Little Chief, George Daly, was the first member of the owner-manager fraternity confronted by the striking miners.

Michael Mooney, leader of the miners, along with others met George Daly "at the mouth of the shaft." Daly was informed that the miners wanted a four dollar a day wage standard in the district and the right to choose their own shift bosses. Later the demands would include a standard eight-hour day for all mines, but the mines under Keyes' control were already working eight-hour days. When the miners approached Daly, it appears they did not have a written set of demands, nor had they communicated with other miners in the district.

Daly, in charge of all General Manager Keyes' mines in his absence, told the miners that he would have to check with the directors in New York, but that he would recommend against approval. In the meantime he closed the Little Chief and all the other mines under his control. That evening the New York directors replied, agreeing with Daly's actions and turning down the miners' demands. In the meantime the striking miners, their six hundred man force from the Chrysolite now swollen to almost three thousand with the workers from the other Fryer Hill properties under Keyes-Daly control, met on Fairview Hill, just west of Fryer Hill, around one o'clock in the afternoon to discuss their course of action. At the conclusion of the meeting a band, which appears to have been a necessary ingredient in any public gathering in Leadville, led the strikers to Carbonate Hill where the miners there joined the growing army. They split into two groups on Carbonate Hill, one group visiting the mines on Iron Hill, the other continuing on east to the mines of Breece Hill. As evening approached, the miners, six thousand strong according to one report, marched down California Gulch to the music of an energetic brass band. They turned north at Harrison Avenue and gave the citizens of the

Carbonate Hill from the north. *Photo Source: Author's Collection.*

Cloud City a look at the wave of the future as they marched up the Avenue to Capitol Hill. There, standing part way up the hill, Michael Mooney instructed the men to retire for the evening, respect persons and property, and report the following morning to a site near the Little Pittsburg.

For some unknown reason, the old Miners' Co-operative Union abruptly changed its title to the Miners, Mechanics and Laborers' Protective Association. It seems likely that the old designation did not fit the organization's new role nor the persons served, hence a name change. It does not appear to be a new organization.

The following morning, Thursday, May 27, 1880, the miners assembled as instructed and prepared to march down Harrison Avenue in another show of force and good order. After the march they reassembled on Fryer Hill and hammered out a set of demands. First they demanded a one dollar a day wage increase for all employees and "that no man shall be allowed to work for less than $4 per day." Second, "that the hours for work shall be eight hours, top and bottom." Third, no one could be "in or about any mine" unless agreed with the above conditions. Fourth was a pledge to protect their own from possible retribution for participation in the strike. Last was a resolution supporting the Chrysolite request that would allow miners to select their own shift bosses.

During the Fryer Hill meeting it was agreed that no man would work until the demands were met. Arrangements were made to send copies of the resolutions to the mine managers and also see that the community was made aware of the strikers' demands. While the meeting was in session it was noticed that the Chrysolite pumps were still running. The miners demanded that Daly stop the pumps. Without the pumps the mine, and others in the immediate vicinity, would have been flooded, causing considerable damage to underground workings and equipment and necessitating expensive refitting and cleaning after the strike before any production would be possible. It was an ill-advised demand for the miners and did them considerable damage among moderate elements in the community. Daly, for his part, would not be intimidated. He refused and ordered his properties barricaded.

The following morning mine managers got the word from their respective owners; there would be no acceptance of the miners' demands. Charles Thomas, local lawyer and eventually governor of Colorado, along with a number of influential citizens, called a meeting of managers and union spokesmen. It was hoped that the community might act as a negotiator for the two parties. The miners were congratulated on their restraint and model behavior, Mooney spoke moderately for the miners and Daly was, apparently, equally moderate. Like a modern summit meeting, praises were exchanged along with smiles and well wishes, and everyone went home feeling better. The next day it was clear that nothing had changed, and all parties remained in the same position as previously.

Saturday morning, the twenty-ninth, the mine managers received word that they should start up operations on Monday with either new help or local miners not in sympathy with the strike. Sunday was Memorial Day. Strikers marched and "it was noticed that their numbers had materially diminished." They were accompanied in the parade by several local militia companies and veteran groups.

On the thirty-first, Monday, the Chrysolite, Little Chief, and the mines of the Iron-Silver Mining Company reopened with skeleton crews. They were protected with armed guards and "arrangements were made to board and house" the returning miners. Other mines in the area decided to do likewise. After all, Mooney, when asked if returning workers would be attacked, emphatically said, "No." The smaller mines, unable to afford guards to protect their men, found that Mooney's saying it did not make it so. Miners on their way to work were "waylaid," "intimidated or maltreated." More and more the strike evoked the bitterness that eventually came to characterize western mining's labor relations well into the twentieth century.

The first third of the month of June saw the glamour disappear from the strike and with it the parades, bands, and banners. They were replaced with minor breaches of the peace and meetings of angry, exasperated men. The union moderated its demands, but management held firm. Negotiating continued, but the dialogue seems to have become a monologue with a group of doomed strikers trying to move a group of mine managers who knew time was on their side.

On June 8, Mayor John F. Humphreys attempted to get the two parties back to serious bargaining. The owners in the persons of Daly and Keyes came prepared with something of a compromise, which was a new posture for them. They requested the miners go back to work at the old wage and they, Daly and Keyes, would attempt to use their influence to get an eight-hour day in the other mines. For them it would have been total victory, since the strike had started on their properties, and they already had the eight-hour day. The miners refused the proposal, insisting that some salary increase must be included. Two days later the miners proposed a $3.20 a day wage. The owners refused. Neither party would budge. The time for talking had ended. During the week prior to the union proposal, local merchants had become increasingly alarmed at the number of threats and the tension that spoke of impending violence. Several citizens' meetings were called and on June 10 or thereabouts (the date is somewhat difficult to pin down since much of what was accomplished was done under a veil of secrecy) a group of citizens met, determined to change the course of events.

C. C. Davis claimed inspiration in the form of his advertising solicitor, W. L. Cooper, who visited him with the "fairly shouted" suggestion, "Davis, *you can stop this strike and save Leadville.*" Davis apparently mulled over the statement and decided there might be something in it and within an hour he had, "in writing," a hundred signatures of "prominent citizens" who would attend a meeting in Hallock's Hall, built and owned by Nelson Hallock, codiscoverer of the Carbonate mine.

The crowd, swelled by concerned citizens who had heard of the meeting, filled the building and spilled into the street. "Using a six-shooter for a gavel" Davis called the throng together and announced his intention of moving the group to Tabor's Opera House. While Davis does not mention him, it appears that Tabor was one of the leaders of the citizens' group.

A short time later the group reassembled in the Opera House, filling it to the scuppers, and again Davis called the group to order. After considerable discussion, and we can imagine the far-ranging type of discussions there must have been, a motion was passed that a group of one hundred form an executive committee to "take charge of the movement." The one hundred selected retired to Lieutenant Governor Tabor's private quarters in the Opera House and, while it really does not apply at this point, the size of Tabor's "private quarters" cannot help but impress a modern apartment dweller.

The first order of business seems to have been naming the group the "Committee of Safety," and we might suspect that the similarity to the infamous French Revolutionary committee that sought out counter-revolutionary elements and instituted the Reign of Terror in Paris in 1793, was no accident.* Davis was chosen chair-

*The French version was called the Committee of Public Safety.

Carlyle Channing Davis. *Photo Source: Colorado Historical Society.*

Nellie, Mrs. Carlyle Channing Davis. *Photo Source: Colorado Historical Society.*

man. Then those present signed a pledge apparently prepared by the group, either at that first organizational meeting, or soon after, which bound all to "organize ourselves into a Committee of Safety, whose objects shall be maintenance of order, the punishment of crime, and to take cognizance of all lawless acts that may transpire within our midst and come within the objects of this organization."

It was unfortunate, but the Committee of Safety jumped into their work with a kind of politico-religious fanaticism that saw them fighting for God and country, stringing cliches one upon another, and even borrowing from the Declaration of Independence when they stated, "we the members of this organization, hereby solemnly pledge ourselves, our property and our sacred honor. . . ."** It was clear from the outset they were enjoying the strike much more than the strikers.

The organization had a president (Davis), a secretary, and an executive council of five. In concert the executive council had almost dictatorial powers. They referred to themselves as a citizens' committee concerned with the protection of life and property. Citizens were led to believe that this was a merchant group. It was really the joining of business and mining interests in a protective association bent on the perpetuation of the status quo through the use of the extralegal tactics of vigilantes. Davis even admitted without a blush that their organization was "patterned after the famous San Francisco 'Vigilance Committee.'" The Leadville membership included a number of mining men, prominent among them were Tabor, George B. Robinson, and W. S. Keyes. A number of the elected officials of local government were signators. The police were there, justices of the peace, and a number of city aldermen. The total was an impressive list of Leadville power and influence.

Davis saw his job as the "protection of life and property, and the ridding of the community of its turbulent element." The "turbulent element," of course, were the strike leaders. His first act was to hire a number of Pinkerton detectives to infiltrate the union and keep the committee informed of their plans. He then wrote a long letter to the governor describing the origins and organization and purpose of the Committee of Safety. He told the governor that the civil authorities, sheriff, mayor, and chief of police "were believed to be in sympathy with the strikers." He went on

**The Declaration version, which somehow sounds more dignified, "we mutually pledge to each other our lives, our fortunes, and our sacred honor."

to suggest that it might be necessary to declare martial law. The governor replied that he wished Davis to "exhaust every resource before calling on him." The movement now had the tacit approval of the governor.

They went to work immediately. Military companies were organized, and strike leaders were ferreted out, escorted to the city limits, and told to vanish. It was made clear that if they appeared again in Leadville it would be upon pain of death. Most vanished. Arms were ordered and expected at any day. Miners who wanted to go back to work were guaranteed their safety. One of the first targets of the Committee of Safety was the strikers' paper, *The Crisis*. It was published daily in the press room of the *Leadville Democrat*, the only paper to show any sympathy to the striking miners. Shortly after the committee organized, three of those responsible for the paper's publication, Robert Higgins and Howard "Hop" Lee, printers at the *Democrat*, and John Sorensen, a printer at the *Herald*, all received neatly written notes, the handwriting attributed to the *Chronicle* editor, C. C. Davis.

Sir, You are hereby ordered to leave Leadville before sun-up to-morrow morning, to return no more. Disregard this notification at your peril.
By order
Committee of 100

Michael Mooney received a similar letter and was forced to leave town a few days later. Sorensen and Higgins took the prudent way out and left town immediately. "Hop" Lee claimed he was in camp "before any of that 'Law and Order' gang," and was convinced he had "done no man a wrong." He armed himself and defied the committee; the "100" proved to be more bluff than action.

Not only did Governor Pitkin approve the extralegal force and its actions, he answered C. C. Davis' call for "arms and ammunition" by dispatching the Pitkin Cavalry from Denver with the munitions to supply Davis' twelve hundred volunteers.

On Saturday, June 12, it was expected that the governor's shipment of arms and ammunition in the company of the crack Pitkin Cavalry would arrive in the early afternoon. Davis claimed that rumor had it that the miners were going to parade as a show of strength, but there is little evidence that such a plan was afoot. Rather, it sounds like a feeble excuse for what almost turned into a bloodbath.

Davis and the other members of the Committee of 100 planned to march their forces down

Harrison Avenue in the company of the governor's forces in a display of unity and power, hoping to overawe the strikers. Davis, in the company of Leadville's famous storekeeper, H. A. W. Tabor, made a short speech from the balcony of the Tabor Opera House. He recited the background of the strike, the need and determination for law and order, and the law-and-order party's determination to protect property and those who wished to work. He feared for his life as he spoke, as well he might.

His speech was greeted, by most, with deadly silence. The mood that greeted the law-and-order parade was much the same. The streets were lined with grim faced miners and anxious, determined merchants. Nothing was absent save an incident capable of exploding the situation into a violent confrontation. The cavalry was late, having broken a wheel on one of their wagons on Mosquito Pass, and the parade began without them. A brass band led the way with the commanding officers of the committee following. Behind them another band, then the "enlisted citizens" of Davis' army. The figures for the army vary. Dill claims they numbered around 600, but the *Democrat* reporter saw an "army of about 1,500 men."

At one point, Colonel A. V. Bohn, not lacking courage but short on good sense, rode into a crowd of miners in pursuit of a striker who "referred to the commander in an epithet of an outrageous character." Bohn was industriously beating the offender over the head with a light sword

Colonel A. V. Bohn in civilian attire. *Photo Source: Author's Collection.*

when the police pulled him from his horse, arrested him, and hauled him off to jail for safe keeping, thus halting a chain of events that might have been the "incident" capable of setting off the charged emotions of the throng. Those same policemen, whom Davis felt were incapable of preserving order, were the only thing between Davis' army and the striking miners. They were successful and maintained the peace until the cavalry arrived later in the afternoon and cleared the avenue, instructing the populace to go home and remain there.

The confrontation, intentionally or unintentionally, had the desired effect. Governor Pitkin was bombarded with telegrams from citizens and from the Committee of Safety foretelling the most grievous consequences unless martial law was declared. The governor pondered for twenty-four hours, consulted his lieutenant governor, H. A. W. Tabor, who certainly was not an impartial third party, and on Sunday, June 13, declared Leadville under martial law. The city grew quiet and waited. On Monday three to four hundred local residents were sworn into the Colorado National Guard and asked to serve until a bona fide military force could arrive and police the camp.

Martial law rang the death knell for the strikers. On June 18 they voted to go back to work on the old terms. On the twenty-sixth, martial law was revoked and Leadville returned, as much as was possible, to normal. It was the first major labor disturbance in the Leadville mines. It was not the last.

Causes for the strike have received much more attention than the effects. After it was over many were convinced that it was initiated by a small group of Mollie MaGuires, labor agitators born of the strife in the coal mines of Pennsylvania. The most persistent rumor was that Keyes and Daly had concocted the whole thing. Mary Hallock Foote, whose husband, Arthur, was manager of the Adelaide properties, recalled, "years afterward I was told that it was an operator who brought on the strike." She explained that the operator, who appears to have been Keyes, wanted his mine to shut down while "he gained time to sell his own stock in it before the price went down." Prior to the strike, production in the Chrysolite had fallen and its usual $200,000 monthly dividend had fallen to $100,000 in April. According to Walter Church in his *Some Facts Regarding Leadville*, published in 1881, the Chrysolite stock dropped during the first half of 1880 from $47 a share to $3.75! After the strike it was found that the great Chrysolite ore body was exhausted, and while other ore was later discovered, it, like the Little Pittsburg, never returned to its earlier prominence. One old-timer, Steve Philbrick, writing years later, left no doubt as to what was in the public mind. "Gossip said that the Chrysolite mine was not going to amount to anything, so Mooney was paid $5,000 to get the men to strike."

R. G. Dill, writing about the strike the following year, probably came as close to the truth as anyone when he said, "The causes . . . will probably never be fully understood." The three who could possibly tell us what really happened, Keyes, Daly, and Michael Mooney, threw little light on the question. Keyes and Daly were never heard from in any substantive way, and both left the camp before the year was out. Michael Mooney returned and worked in the mines for a time. He was asked what the causes for the strike were, and he could not answer save to say that it was not a premeditated thing.

In retrospect, the Leadville miners' strike of 1880 seems, in spite of the rumors, to have not been the work of one or two men, or the result of a preconceived plan, but rather a sudden, angry expression of the seething hatred fomenting in the minds of Leadville's overworked, underpaid, hard-rock miners. Five thousand dollars in the hands of Michael Mooney, which in view of the fact that he returned to work in the mines seems improbable, might appear adequate to start a strike, but ten and twelve hour days, six day weeks, at three dollars and less per shift, seems a greater motive.

If Keyes, Daly, and other mining men managed to feather their nests as a result of the strike it is not surprising. Throughout history resourceful men have seen ways to turn a buck in the worst of times. The real loser was Leadville. "In 1880 the public not only lost faith in both mines (the Chrysolite and the Little Pittsburg), but temporarily lost confidence in all Leadville mines." New capital for exploration and development froze solid, and for several months the Leadville district felt the effects of the Little Pittsburg collapse, the disastrous miners' strike, and the questionable dealings in other Fryer Hill properties. Still, there was a bright side to the whole mess. Mining in Leadville took a rational turn and investments were based on real values, rather than the inflated dreams of a few promoters and fast buck artists. Engineers and miners were listened to with care, rather than being dismissed as crepe hangers and doomsmen.

The decade separating the seventies from the nineties comprised years of growth and civic accomplishment. They were also years of change. The Leadville of Chicken Bill and Broken Nose Scotty became the Leadville of Dr. D. H. Dougan and of A. V. Hunter and of George Trimble, bankers. Polite, conservative society replaced the fist-full-of-cash optimism of the boom.

Miners' wages held at the three dollar level, and every other laborer's wage was built upon the miner's. A Sunday closing move in 1883 met with considerable success in all areas except the saloons and gambling houses. In 1883 the Little Jonny was down 120 feet and destined to become one of the most famous mines in western history. The following year the "Jonny" was shipping lead-silver ore.

In January 1883, Colorado's most famous mine owner sat in the eye of one of the state's greatest scandals. On January 31, 1857, Horace Austin Warner Tabor married Louisa Augusta Pierce in Augusta, Maine. In Oshkosh, Wisconsin, Elizabeth Bonduel McCourt had four months earlier celebrated her second birthday. In 1880 in Leadville the threads came together. Between

Elizabeth Bonduel McCourt Doe, better known as Baby Doe, as she must have looked when she arrived in Leadville, a twenty-five-year-old divorcee in 1880. *Photo Source: Colorado Historical Society.*

1857 and 1880 Tabor had become one of the wealthiest and most influential men in the West. Elizabeth McCourt had married Harvey Doe, a local boy, June 27, 1877, in Oshkosh. They left soon after the wedding for Central City, Colorado. In the company of Jacob Sandelowsky she visited Leadville in December of 1879, returned to Central City, divorced Harvey, and returned to the Magic City in the early spring of 1880. Tabor's life was never the same.

Stories of their first meeting are a dime a dozen and all different. No one really knows how or when or where they met, and other than for curiosity's sake, it really is of limited consequence. The fireworks started soon after, though. By the middle of the year Tabor was keeping steady, though still discreet, company with the ex-Mrs. Doe. Tabor moved out of his wife's home in July of 1880. He tried to get Augusta to agree to a divorce, but she refused. He became desperate and ordered Bill Bush to secure a legal, but quiet, divorce for him. Bush, Tabor's right hand man, secured a quiet divorce in Durango, but it was not legal. Either unaware that the Durango decree did not take, or in defiance of law and convention, Horace and his "Darling Baby" were secretly married in St. Louis, September 30,

1882. His pursuit of a divorce continued with such vigor that he seems an American West version of Henry VIII, with his lieutenant, Bill Bush, suffering just as Wolsey — both were dismissed because of their inability to provide their lords with a legal divorce.

Augusta found out about the Durango divorce, but did not find out about the illegal marriage until it was too late to use it against her husband. The first Mrs. Tabor applied for separate maintenance and listed a number of charges against her husband. The list soon appeared in papers all over the state. She claimed her husband's worth was in the neighborhood of nine million, plus he owned a number of properties with which she was not familiar. Tabor denied the figure. The court accepted Tabor's accounting, which placed the total at a much lower figure. The exact amount of Tabor's worth has never been agreed upon, but Don Griswold, a very knowledgeable student of Leadville's past and people, has placed Tabor's wealth in the neighborhood of three million dollars.

The public viewed the Tabor scandal and divorce, January 2, 1883, with relish. The women of Denver flocked to the support of Mrs. Tabor and most of their husbands, willingly or unwill-

Tabor Grand Hotel, shortly before opening in 1885. *Photo Source: Colorado Historical Society.*

ingly, dutifully tagged along. The Tabor name no longer was found at the top of guest lists. Mr. Tabor had sacrificed his social status, when social status was indispensible, for his youthful bride. To the wealthy, aging silver king it must have seemed a small price to pay.

In addition to a second marriage, Tabor had one more goal — United States Senator. Henry Teller had vacated his senatorial position to accept a cabinet post in President Arthur's administration. Tabor, calling on all his financial resources and past favors wrangled a thirty day appointment. He was sworn in on February 3, 1883, in Washington. He served until March 4 when the new Congress met. On March 1, 1883, Elizabeth McCourt Doe became, legally this time, the second Mrs. Tabor. The lavish ceremony was held in the Willard Hotel. There was a conspicuous lack of women, but the men paid their respects to the beautifully gowned bride and her giddy groom. Even President Arthur was there. Washington society was outraged, and a number of wives had the last word when a short time after the wedding the *St. Louis Times* broke the story of the illegal St. Louis marriage. Redfaced, Washington gasped a sigh of relief when the senator from Colorado and his bride finally left town.

The year 1885 saw Leadville's Tabor Grand Hotel open its doors to the public. The same year saw California Gulch produce $60,000 in placer gold. Ten years before it was said to have been worked out. The following year saw mining men bemoaning the declining mineral market and complaining about the problems of water. It was suggested by James V. Dexter, successful mining man and promoter, that mine owners construct a drainage tunnel from the Malta area under the city of Leadville to the mines east of town. The benefit would not only be the unwatering of the mines east of town, but it would also drain the water from the downtown district* and provide an inexpensive, downhill ore pass. There was no telling what good ore might be encountered or what new areas developed as a result of such a tunnel. Unfortunately, the cost of the project was prohibitive, so a number of shorter, less costly unwatering plans were promoted, and a number completed, but while they helped some mines, all came in too shallow to be of universal help. But the plan, and its dozens of variations, was discussed off and on for the next seventy-five years, and the idea is not dead yet.

*Mines developed in among the dwellings on the east side of the city of Leadville.

As the decade of the eighties closed, owners began digging deeper in an attempt to hit second and third contact ores. Two problems faced most operations of this type. First, the new ores proved to be more complex and difficult to smelt, and usually were of a poorer quality. Second, the water, a problem in the eighties, became an overwhelming burden for the deeper mines in the nineties. It was not uncommon to hit water that flowed into the workings with such force and quantity that miners were in danger of drowning before they could be lifted out. On January 25, 1890, a large charge of dynamite was detonated in the Gnesen mine near the crest of Rock Hill that unleashed a flood of water that swamped men and equipment, over-turned cars, and ripped up rails. Men were hurriedly evacuated ahead of the advancing waters. A similar situation occurred in the Olive Branch. Within a few hours the water had risen from the 700-foot bottom of the shaft to within 150 feet of the surface. In some cases it took months to pump the workings dry again.

The original idea of developing mines under the eastern half of the city, thus creating the downtown district, usually is attributed to Samuel Franklin Emmons. Emmons suggested in his first major work on the area, published in 1886, that the basic geological formations that predominated east of the city continued beneath the city, buried under two hundred to three hundred feet of glacial "wash."

In 1889 the Leadville Chamber of Commerce, unable to interest anyone in an experimental project that would test Emmons' theory, began the work themselves, but they quickly ran out of funds. Fortunately, though, they were able to interest private capital in completing the project, and a deep shaft was sunk on the Lucy B. Hussey property just east of the city limits between Third and Fourth streets amid a variety of homes and cabins. Good ore was struck, and by 1891 ten shafts had been sunk and four made impressive strikes. "The Downtown district became the center of mining activity in 1892 and continued to be the center for the next three years."

But the real problem of the nineties was price, not production. In 1890 the federal government had attempted to bolster the failing silver market with Senator John Sherman's Silver Purchase Act and the McKinley Act authorizing the government to purchase 4.5 million ounces of silver monthly with the issuance of $54,000,000 in paper money annually. The cheap money advocates and silver interests won that first round.

The McKinley Tariff, as it was called, was hailed as a boon to western mining since it made the purchase of foreign metals almost impossible, forcing up the price of domestic metals. It also closed a number of domestic smelters that had been buying foreign metals and could not afford to pay the increased cost of American metals.

In Leadville, as throughout the West, the artificial market slowed the slide, but could not halt it. By 1891 the average silver price had slipped to ninety-nine cents an ounce. By 1892 it was at eighty-seven cents. The silver advocates developed a host of arguments for free silver coinage, bimetalism, and the fact that overproduction had nothing to do with the failing silver market, but the banking interests in the East had another idea, and it was gold. The West, in an effort to combat the arguments and political pressure from eastern and European capitalists, formed Silver Clubs bent on telling the silver point of view and electing silver candidates. The Leadville Silver Club, one of over two hundred in Colorado, was organized in 1892.

In the spring of 1891, word reached the Magic City that Republican President Harrison and his wife were arriving. The city's leaders immediately began the usual Leadville welcome, which included speeches, parades, parties, and the indispensable host of bands. The hope was, of course, that the president, visiting the silver West, would become more generous toward the silver interests. Little Republican help was forthcoming, however, and Populism's successful sweep through the mining and agrarian West continued to accelerate. The People's Party (Populists) nominated James B. Weaver, a reform, free silver advocate, for president in 1892. Unfortunately, it was the East, not the West, who elected the new president. And the new president was none other than Grover Cleveland, a Democrat and a staunch advocate of the gold standard.

The new administration wasted little time. Cleveland believed the country's fiscal woes were directly attributable to the government's purchase and coinage of silver. A special session of Congress was called by the president on August 1, 1893. The votes were finally tallied in October after a fierce senate battle. The Sherman Silver Purchase Act was repealed. Whatever the underlying reasons, the country was plunged into a depression west of the Mississippi, and Cleveland's fight against bimetalism was considered the cause.

Many indicators foretold the coming of financial disaster, especially a host of unhealthy signs from Europe and the shaky structure of the over-extended, underproductive U.S. railroads. C. C. Davis, Leadville's leading newspaper editor, who always saw the operations of the world emanating from Leadville, and Leadville emanating from his office, declared, "The fact that Leadville could produce $30,000,000 to $40,000,000 in silver a year had alarmed the bankers of the world." The reasons for the financial collapse of Leadville mining, and in fact mining throughout the West, requires more explanation than Davis has supplied. First, and most importantly, was the general worsening condition of the nation's economy. The second obvious cause was the closing of Britain's India mints, on June 26, 1893, and on that decision's heels, the repeal of the Silver Purchase Act. The collapse of the silver market was not simply because the West was producing too much silver, which of course it was, but in addition the traditional markets were closing.

Immediately after the closing of the India mints, silver fell from an already devastating low of eighty-two cents an ounce to sixty-two cents. There were "between seventy and ninety producing mines in the district [Leadville] in 1890." By the summer of 1893 only eighteen remained profitable. The price of silver eventually hit bottom in March of 1894 at sixty-one cents an ounce. As the number of mine closings continued, more and more men were thrown out of work. By midsummer 1893, fully ninety percent of the work force was idle in Leadville. The American National Bank closed its doors on July 3. A number of smelters closed. Labor took the blow in a variety of ways. Some went fishing or hunting, apparently out of frustration and also in hopes of providing some food. Others left the Magic City in hope of finding work someplace else. Still others engaged in leasing or placer mining. Begging, crime, especially burglary, increased. Children helped supplement meager funds by gathering coal along the railroad tracks. The county provided some food for the destitute.

Fortunately the camp had a great resilience and recovery began almost at the moment of greatest depression. The American National Bank reopened its doors on August 19, 1893, after a seven-week closure (the Carbonate National Bank was not forced to close), and the panic withdrawals that were predicted never materialized. Two days later the Bimetallic Smelter reopened. On September 14, 1893, miners agreed to a wage drop from three to two and one-half dollars a day in all months in which the price of silver was under eighty-three and one-half cents per ounce.

Leadville in the 1890s. Photo Source: *Colorado Historical Society.*

Almost all of the downtown mines were in full production by the end of the year, pumping water at the usual phenomenal rate. "The pumping plants at the Maid [Maid of Erin] and Penrose had set records by pumping over 1,000 gallons of water per minute." It was reported that the downtown mines pumped 15,000,000 gallons of water every day, which amounted to 28.6 tons of water for every ton of ore produced.

On December 23, 1893, the *Herald Democrat*, the result of mergers by C. C. Davis of the *Leadville Daily Herald*, the *Leadville Weekly Democrat* and the *Evening Chronicle*, stated that the miners might be thankful that Christmas for the presence, not of silver, gold, or lead, but the "much humbler" iron ore in the district. "If the testimony of leading mining men of the camp is to be believed it is the salvation of Leadville." Manganese, copper, and gold were also major factors in the recovery. And especially one famous mine, the Little Jonny.

The discovery of the Little Jonny seems lost in a maze of conflicting stories, deals, and trades that see the trail leading in one case to the famous Rose Tree Inn Museum in Tombstone, Arizona, where the heirs of Samuel Christy Robertson claim that he discovered the Little Jonny. Others

claim it was located by three Irishmen, who sold it for a pittance. One of the sons of Erin, learning of the mine's wealth, is said to have taken his own life. Hollywood insisted that Leadville Johnny Brown located it for his wife, Molly.

The Little Jonny is located in the middle of an ill-defined area called the Gold Belt, which stretches from Iowa Gulch on the south to Little Ellen Hill on the north. It is bordered east and west by Ball Mountain and Adelaide Park. It was reported in 1895 that the combined production of the mines from the Gold Belt was "not less than six hundred ounces of gold daily." Exploration in the Gold Belt was extensive and made more accurate by the newly developed diamond drill. It was estimated that some sixty shafts and drill holes were being sunk in 1895, and if they were laid end to end the total would exceed four miles. "Think of it! Four miles of holes! And each one will continue to descend untill gold, hot lemonade or a Chinaman is struck."

Still, it was the Little Jonny that captured the country's imagination. In its early years the Little Jonny was a major producer of silver and lead. The mine became the property of the John Campion interests and was, along with a number of other rich properties in the area, incorporated

175

The Ibex Mining Company, built around the Little Jonny. *Photo Source: CMHC Lake County Public Library.*

as the Ibex Mining Company, destined to become one of the West's most famous producers, not of silver, but of gold.

The man who, Hollywood notwithstanding, was the real "Leadville Johnny" was John F. Campion, organizer, promoter, and general manager of the Ibex Mining Company. John Campion was a native of Prince Edward Island. According to an interview with Campion after the turn of the century, he stated he came to Leadville in 1879. He bought and sold claims, usually doing quite well for himself. His wealth increased, and he was able to amass enough capital to enable him to begin working his properties instead of simply acting the part of a trader. His first major property was the Elk Consolidated Mining Company. Shortly after the successful development of the Elk property, which incidentally introduced Campion's practice of naming his properties after cloven-hooved animals, he and associates were able to purchase the Little Jonny and a number of adjacent claims, which became the Ibex holdings. In 1893 James Joseph Brown became superintendent of the Ibex properties. The owners, Eben Smith, A. V. Hunter, Charles Cavender, and John F. Campion, put Brown to work deepening the Little Jonny in search of a second ore contact.

Brown's major problem was a dolomite sand

John Campion, bearded and on the front seat, his top hatted coachman at the controls, and a group of merry makers spilling over the sides. *Photo Source: Author's Collection.*

176

that continued to cave, in spite of all efforts to timber it. The owners knew they had the right man for the job when Brown devised a method of using baled hay to hold the sand, then "driving timbers endways so as to prevent caving." Once through the sand, the Little Jonny treasure vault was opened. Vast quantities of high grade gold and copper were discovered. So rich were the deposits that in 1894 the company paid a million dollars in dividends. James J. Brown got his share of those dividends since the grateful owners rewarded his efforts with 12,500 shares of Ibex stock.

Today James J. Brown is best remembered as the husband of Molly Brown, whose heroism during the sinking of the *Titanic* made her an international celebrity. Her life story, as portrayed on Broadway and in the movies as Meredith Willson's heroine in *The Unsinkable Molly Brown*, has kept the Brown story of rags to riches alive, if not well. Mrs. Brown, known to Leadville friends as Maggie, did much to color and perpetuate her own legend with such stories as being rescued from a cyclone while adrift on the Mississippi by none other than Hannibal's most famous citizen, Samuel Clemens. Facts seem to indicate that her only meeting with the famed writer was while a waitress in Hannibal's Park Hotel. Another of Maggie's tales had its origin in her cabin at the Louisville Mine near Leadville. She is said to have burned some $10,000 to $300,000 accidentally in the cookstove. The amount continues to rise, but a conservative estimate by Caroline Bancroft, Mrs. Brown's only biographer, suggests it was around seventy-five dollars, all in coin, and recovered from the coals when the fire cooled. She hobnobbed with the rich and famous, thought about entering politics, and tried the stage. When she died in 1932 the *Daily News* of Newport, Rhode Island, stated she was the daughter of an Irish peer. It was quite an honor, and Mrs. Brown, whose roots were Shanty Irish from Hannibal, Missouri, would have loved it.

James J. Brown and John F. Campion were two of that new breed of mining men who took the reins of the Cloud City's metals industry in the late eighties and early nineties. The hit and miss, devil-take-the-hindmost, methods were gone, and educated, hard-driving professionals took over. Men like Tingley S. Wood, who had come to Leadville in 1879, and through careful management and hard, shrewd work found himself one of the leading figures in the industry; Eben Smith, hard and abrupt, a Pennsylvanian who came west with the first of the boomers, landing first in California in 1852 and moving with the tide until he arrived

Margaret Tobin Brown. *Photo Source: Denver Public Library Western History Collection.*

in Leadville in 1883, where he made a name for himself as manager of the Maid of Erin properties; and Major A. V. Bohn, energetic and often inspired, a Civil War veteran of some distinction, who arrived in Leadville with the early tide of pilgrims in 1878 and carefully worked his way up the ranks, managing, among others, the Matchless, Lucy B. Hussey, and by 1895 his own, Bohn Mining Company. Henry W. Smith, Robert O'Neil, Charles North, James A. Shinn, Max Boehmer, and James T. Briggs all made their mark in Leadville mining, but not with the same colorful nonchalance of an August Rische or the happy happenstance used and abused by the brothers Long and Gallagher.

The year 1895 was a banner one for the Leadville mines. It was clear that the Panic of 1893 was over when the Leadville mines posted an annual total production of over nine million dollars. It was the best year since 1889, and out of that production came an amazing figure. Lake County had produced more silver than in any other year in her history, except the boom year of

The Leadville Ice Palace, 1896. The smoke is from the smelters in California Gulch. *Photo Source: Colorado Historical Society.*

1880, almost nine and one-half million fine ounces.

It was time to celebrate, and celebrate they did. The people of Leadville with one dollar subscriptions and several lump sum contributions built the largest ice structure in the history of such architectural nonsense. And it was grand.

It was a great frost-covered Norman castle and covered over three acres. The entrance was flanked by a pair of ninety-foot towers, while the walls, made of ice blocks three to five feet thick, were topped with ice parapets, and the corners dignified by smaller, sixty foot towers. Inside of all that ice was a sturdy frame building with a roof of ice crystals and steel. In the center was a large clay-based ice rink, flanked on either side by heated, well-lighted dining rooms, though one generally served as a dance hall.

During the reign of what was called the Leadville Crystal Carnival, hundreds of clubs, military organizations, fraternal groups, and civic bodies, as well as thousands of individuals from around the country, visited the palace. They saw skating exhibitions, rock drilling contests, ice sculpture, merchant displays, costume contests, and they skated, danced, ate, and rode the toboggan. Beginning January 1, 1896, it was one long celebration until March 28, 1896, when the palace closed. And, like Christmas, few people remembered the

reasons for celebrating, but all remembered the celebration.

The ice palace had been discussed in Leadville for a number of years, and cities such as St. Paul and Montreal had built several, but the time had not been right. Then, suddenly, coming off of the economic collapse of 1893 the people of Leadville decided to tell the world that the Magic City was still alive and well and the Leadville Ice Palace was born. It was also considered a good investment, since it was assumed large numbers of "low landers" would come to Leadville, visit the palace, stay in the hotels, eat in the restaurants, and generally spend money and have a good time.

Considerable time was spent in organization, design, and size. It was the town's enthusiastic consensus that the West's greatest mining camp could support nothing less than the world's greatest ice palace. And in Leadville greatest meant biggest. Tons of ice were cut from local ponds and lakes. Additional ice was shipped in by rail. An unexpected problem developed when mother nature decided to take a holiday. In December, just when construction was in full swing, the weather turned balmy. It started December 2 when the temperature was thirty-five degrees. By the twelfth it was up to a daytime high of sixty-five degrees, which was unheard of. The *Herald Democrat* summed it up, "When a fellow wants a

One of the many bands
to visit the Ice Palace.
*Photo Source: Denver
Public Library Western
History Collection.*

Hundreds of societies, lodges, and
fraternal groups, like the Elks, visited
the Ice Palace between January 1 and
March 28, 1896. *Photo Source:
Author's Collection.*

Incorporated Under the Laws of Colorado, 1895.

Nº 355   The Leadville Crystal Carnival Associat'n   10 Shares

CAPITAL STOCK,
$20,000.00.

20,000 SHARES.
$1.00 EACH.

This is to Certify, That _L. S. Tober_
is the owner of _Ten_
Shares, of the denomination of ONE DOLLAR EACH, of full-paid,
non-assessable Capital Stock of The Leadville Crystal Carnival Association,
transferable only on the books of the Association on the surrender of this
certificate properly endorsed.

Witness, The seal of said Association and the signatures of its President and
Secretary, at Leadville, Colorado, this _Tenth_ day of _December_
A. D. 1895.

_____ Secretary.   _____ President.

STOCK NON-ASSESSABLE.

Photo Source: Author's Collection.

The toboggan slide from the Ice Palace end on West Seventh Street. The tall
building near the center of the photo is the courthouse. *Photo Source: Denver
Public Library Western History Collection.*

180

One of several dozen ice sculptures. *Photo Source: Denver Public Library Western History Collection.*

Tingley S. Wood. *Photo Source: Author's Collection.*

linen duster and a palm leaf fan to visit the Ice Palace . . ., and a fur-lined ulster and toboggan suit to attend a Fourth of July picnic, the less I hear about the weather the better.''

Economically the Ice Palace was a dismal failure. The "low landers" did come, but they did not stay and they did not spend. They came in on the morning train, sack lunch in hand, visited the palace, ate their lunch, and caught the evening train home. By mid-February Leadville people had had their fill of parties, fetes, fireworks, and festivities. It was almost with a sign of relief that the local papers announced the closing, March 28, 1896. Still, it was a grand celebration, and in retrospect, even better. As years slipped by, the Leadville Ice Palace took on a magical quality and for brief moments from that day to this Leadvillites have paused, reflected, and smiled as they recalled their fabulous palace of ice.

XIII

Strike

Loud-mouthed agitators are already talking about the possibility of a strike in Leadville, and viewing the election of Newman to the position of Sheriff as a possible harbinger of such an event. What nonsense! Such rot is unworthy the consideration of intelligent beings. No strike is eminent, nor has the feasibility of such a thing been entertained by the miners of the camp.
Leadville *Free Lance,* November, 1895.

Gradually miners realized that unionism was not their reason for failure in 1880, and they slowly began to drift back into the ranks of the Knights of Labor. By the end of the decade of the eighties the Knights had solved a number of minor issues through a host of Leadville locals. The Lake County Miners' Union, organized in 1884 or '85, became an assembly of the Knights in 1889.

The Knights first real Leadville test since the devastating strike of 1880 came in 1893 as a result of the financial panic of that year. A number of mines closed and more were talking of closing because operating costs were so high and the price of metals so low that it was a losing proposition. On September 14, 1893, the mine managers and the Knights of Labor agreed to lowering miners' wages from three to two and one-half dollars a day in those months when the price of silver dropped below eighty-three and one-half cents per ounce. "Miners working shafts or wet places to be paid 50 cents per day additional." At the time of the agreement, the price of silver was seventy-three and one-half cents per ounce. It would be years before the price rose that high again.

It is unknown what percentage of the miners were members of the Knights in 1893, but the absence of any noticeable protest to the arrangement would indicate that even if the miners were

not enrolled in the union, they were not in disagreement. Other features of the agreement did cause trouble eventually. First, there was no term on the agreement. It froze the wages of miners forever if the price of silver failed to reach eighty-three and one-half cents, and even if silver did climb above eighty-three and one-half cents, it was fixed at three dollars per day. Another unforeseen factor was the development of new areas and new marketable minerals, especially gold and copper. Was the price of silver going to fix the wages in those mines as well?

In Butte, Montana, in 1893, out of the same economic situation that created the $2.50 per day wage scale in Leadville, a new union was born that changed the whole structure of mining in the West. The Western Federation of Miners' first Colorado activity was organizing the workers of the Cripple Creek mines, where, in 1894, they scored a "partial victory" for striking miners. Leadville was, in 1895, the state's largest ore producer. The new union, if it was going to be successful, had to take a stand in Leadville. After all, some Leadville mine owners were paying $2.50 for nine- and ten-hour days, which were worse conditions than had existed in Cripple Creek before the strike.

In May 1895, the Western Federation of Miners was successful in getting a local, called the Cloud City Miners' Union, Local number 33, established. By May of 1896 the local had 800 members and was beginning to rival the old, somewhat tired, Knights of Labor. The next month and a half saw the Cloud City Miners' Union jump from that 800 figure to 2,600. Of those 2,600 on the rolls, over two thousand were in good standing. In six weeks the newly organized rival to the Knights became the only viable miners' union in the Magic City. Some claimed their numbers accounted for ninety-five percent of all the miners in the community.

How in the space of six weeks were they able to manage such phenomenal growth? A look at Leadville in the spring and early summer of 1896 may not give us the reasons, but it may eliminate some quick, but inaccurate, assumptions.

The town seems to have been fully employed. There was not, as is often the case, a large segment of idle workers, a core of discontent. While the $2.50 a day wage agreement was still in existence, seventy percent of "the miners and trammers of Leadville were receiving $3 per day or more." One assumption often made is that the cost of living had priced the earlier wage out of the market. In our own era it is easy to understand that belief, but Leadville's cost of living in 1896 was less than during the years 1880 to 1893. Much of that drop was the result of the Panic of 1893, but the competition among railroads and the growth of western agriculture had a lot to do with the gradual lowering of prices. The fact still remains, though, that three dollars per day was a subsistence wage and thirty percent of the miners were still below that figure. Those drawing the lower wage contended that to make ends meet they must work every day including Sundays.

Most of the men in the mines were married. By working every day of the week they could earn $75.00 to $77.50 per month. "It will cost them $65 a month to exist; that is, $30 for groceries, $10 for rents, $10 on the average for clothing, $6 for fuel, $4 for water, $3 for milk, and $2 for insurance; total $65." Most men worked between twenty-four and twenty-eight shifts a month, off three to seven days "through sickness or something." If any misfortune befell them, such as serious illness or injury, they would be forced into debt and possibly never be able to recover. J. D. Thomas, who, with his son, ran a modest wallpaper store on East Fourth Street, asked in a letter to *Harper's Weekly,* "Is it possible to pay men too much wages who daily and hourly face the probability of a sudden and violent death." Whatever the salary, was it enough for the hazards of mining, the uncertainties, the rigors?

Certainly the Cloud City Miners' Union exploited the danger and working conditions in its membership drive, but it also must have made good use of the Cripple Creek success. Leadville miners, then and now, are a proud group, and it is unlikely that success in Cripple Creek would be viewed as the result of Cripple Creek superiority. Leadville miners surely looked at that situation and noted the ironic twist that Leadville was the

Typical time book of the period. *Photo Source: Author's Collection.*

greatest mining camp in the world in every aspect but pay. The surprising thing is that the union seems never to have thrown Cripple Creek's wages up to the Leadville mine owners, who were also unwilling to be second to anyone, especially upstart, Johnny-come-lately, Cripple Creek.

The union, using fear rather than pride to increase its membership, resorted to spreading the story that those managers who were paying the higher three dollar scale were going to drop fifty cents to the lower rate. The story persisted throughout the strike, but the manager who was supposedly responsible for the opinion steadfastly denied it when later questioned by a state legislative committee. The union occasionally might have initiated some workers with threats of physical violence, but that seems to have been an uncommon threat. More often the threat was in the form of a "suggestion that unless the miner joined the Federation, he would be unable to find work in Leadville or in any other camp in the Rockies."

The Cloud City Miners' Union's phenomenal growth was not the result of outside agitators, or foreigners who did not appreciate the American system or their opportunities as Americans, as most mine owners and managers asserted. Rather, the new local and the Western Federation of Miners set the torch to the angry fuel that had long been available in Leadville as in other western mining camps. All suffered in the resultant conflagration.

During the frantic campaign to sign up members, the Western Federation of Miners held their annual meeting on May 11, 1896, in Denver. The Leadville situation was discussed at length, and on May 23, 1896, President Edward Boyce of the Western Federation of Miners; J. R. Amburn and E. J. Dewar, president and secretary of the local union; and John Ahern of the dying Knights of Labor, met with S. W. Mudd, Eben Smith, and F. Robbins, powerful members of the Leadville mine owner and manager fraternity, to discuss a uniform three dollar wage. The request was turned down, with one owner saying, "You [came to] the wrong fellow, as we are losing money in Leadville as it is."

The situation remained outwardly quiet with Local number 33 continuing its membership drive until June 10. A second committee was appointed to visit all the mines paying the two and one-half dollar wage and report back to the assembly. This committee of four appears derelict in its duty, and at the meeting on June 17 reported that it had not yet carried out its charge. It was given an additional two days to complete its work.

On or about June 12 the mine managers held a secret meeting at which a written agreement was proposed. The results of that meeting remain unknown and the document was never made public. Little action seems to have been generated at the meeting, possibly the result of the refusal of one mine manager to join. Still, it does indicate the early resolve of most of the managers to act in concert in dealing with the labor situation.

On June 19 the union's investigation committee, led by president J. R. Amburn, visited most of the managers paying the lower wage. They informed the managers that they were requested by the union to ask for a fifty cent a day increase for those receiving the lower, $2.50 per day, wage. A few of the managers agreed, but most refused. Several wanted to know if their refusal meant a strike. The committee replied that they could not answer the question. That evening the Cloud City Miners' Union met. About twelve hundred men were present, and after hearing the committee's report, a strike vote was called. "By substantially a unanimous vote those present decided to call out all employees receiving less than $3 per day." The strike was called for that night at 11:30 P.M. "when the men would come up from the mines for supper." Thirteen mines were affected, and 968 men were on strike Saturday, June 20.

Governor Albert W. McIntire, upon hearing the strike news, met with his deputy commissioner of labor, William H. Klett. It was decided that Klett should leave for Leadville immediately. He arrived in Leadville on Sunday, June 21, but was unable to "secure a conference" with anyone in authority until the following day.

Klett was out early Monday morning, first visiting the Union's headquarters at 506 Harrison Avenue. Next he called at the offices of John Campion, "who was generally recognized as the spokesman for the mine owners and operators." At Campion's office at 401 Harrison, Klett found not only Campion, but K. L. Fahnstock, Campion's right hand man, S. W. Mudd and C. T. Carnahan of the Small Hopes and Resurrection, and a number of other important gentlemen. Klett had probably wandered into a secret mine managers meeting, but was unaware of it, or its consequences for the community and miners.

Klett stated his mission and asked the managers their point of view. He was told that, with one exception,* all paying the $2.50 wages were

*That exception was Campion's Little Jonny. He had 18 men earning less than $3.00 per day out of a couple hundred miners.

The Ibex, Leadville's most famous producer in the 1890s. *Photo Source: Colorado Historical Society.*

depressed silver mines. The total cost to the thirteen mines affected would have been less than $500 per day. Mines like the Coronado would have been forced to increase their operational costs $20 a day. Klett suggested arbitration to the owners and managers, and they quickly agreed. The miners turned the suggestion down when Klett proposed it to them. They felt there was nothing to arbitrate. They had one request and that was their stand.

The mine owners and managers, in response to the union stand, concluded a second secret agreement, unknown until it came out after the first of the year as a result of a legislative investigation. In that agreement the owner-manager clique agreed:

First. That we will decline to submit to such, or any, illegal and inequitable interference from whatever source it may emanate.

Second. That we will immediately close down all mines now operated by us in said Leadville district, and keep such mines, and also the mines heretofore closed down by us, closed until such a period of time as the majority of the signers hereof shall agree to open the same.

Third. To aid each other at any and all times

that it may become necessary, in the furnishing of men for the protection of property, and also in the furnishing of pumpmen and engineers when the pumpmen and engineers employed shall be or may be induced to desist from working.

Fourth. To not make any terms or agreement of any sort with the miners except by the consent and agreement of a majority of the signers hereto.

Fifth. To not recognize or treat in any manner or at any time with any labor organization.

This agreement to continue in force until such a time as the same shall be dissolved by a majority of the signers.

The first response for someone reading the above agreement must be the realization of how sorely the editorial advice of Carlyle Channing Davis, editor of the *Daily Chronicle* and important figure in the strike of 1880, were missed. The second response might be mixed, but surely it was clear to any who saw the document that by not recognizing the union the managers made effective negotiation impossible. It is also clear that they wanted to break the strike and discredit the union, and not resolve the problems that caused the disturbance. The union position was equally intransigent. Two groups, both unwilling to give an inch, both convinced their cause was just — the result, a long and bitter fight.

The mine owners closed the mines to all but pumpmen, firemen, and engineers three days after the strike began, putting another thirteen hundred men out of work. Almost twenty-three hundred miners were idle in Leadville by the twenty-third of June.

On the night of the strike the president of the union had appointed an executive committee of twenty, generally called the Committee of Twenty, for the purpose of organizing and running the strike. "From the evidence it would appear that no records were kept of the proceedings of this committee." The lack of records was no doubt a decision by design, since much of their activity was illegal, and even if it was not, management would surely seek reprisals.

One of the first acts of the Committee of Twenty was to order a shipment of Marlin rifles and "ten or fifteen revolvers." Some sources claim the rifle order was for five hundred, but the legislative committee claimed they purchased one hundred rifles for $1,700. The alleged purpose for buying the rifles was the protection of life and property. The rifle shipment arrived July 12 and was delivered to Cornelius McHugh (Charles McHugh), a local sporting goods dealer on East Fourth Street. From there, they found their way into the hands of local strikers.

The Committee of Twenty quickly followed their rifle order with the organization of a relief committee. Striking married men could get "money-order cards" for groceries in the amount of ten dollars. They also opened two soup kitchens that doubled as lodging houses for single men. Funds for these activities came largely from the Western Federation of Miners' treasury. The two soup kitchens, one located on East Seventh Street and one located on Toledo Avenue near the Bon Air and Bohn shafts, served not only soup, but were the focal points, or front line command posts, for union activity. Many of the rifles purchased by the union were stored there. Much of the union strategy was hatched in the soup kitchens, and since they housed single men who had neither wife nor family to consider, they provided the leadership with a hard core of radical followers.

On July 6, 1896, John Campion, sitting out the strike at his home at 901 Logan in Denver, received a letter from A. V. Hunter in Leadville. Hunter had word that the union intended to call the remaining union men out of work. Those men were the pumpmen, firemen, and engineers, who

were keeping the mines in operating condition. If the pumps were stopped, the mines would fill with water and it would be months, possibly years, before they could be reopened. Hunter asked Campion to come to Leadville so they could "take whatever precautions that we can to prevent our property from being drowned out." He also suggested Campion try to hire four or five engineers and pumpmen in Denver, and keep them ready to board the first train to Leadville if it became necessary. He then voiced his fears: "It is a sure thing with me that we are going to have trouble with these fellows, and plenty of it before we get through with them." In closing he noted that he would have called Campion, but felt sure that the union was tapping the wires.

As news from Leadville continued bad through July, the governor became increasingly concerned. On July 21 he sent a telegram to Michael H. Newman, newly elected sheriff of Lake County, and asked him if the reports of violence, near-violence, and intimidation were true. Newman replied that if persons were molested, no complaints were made to him. He went further to explain that even though there was a strike, "the laboring men are perfectly quiet and orderly." On the following day, July 22, 1896, Newman sent another telegram and claimed he had located the source of one of the problems. People, hoping to avoid trouble and "acting through the best motives, thinking to protect life and property, have stopped suspicious-looking men and prevented their entering town."

The governor did not wish to interfere unless absolutely necessary for fear of being accused, as was Pitkin in 1880, of acting precipitously. He chose to believe the sheriff of Lake County, who was by all accounts a union sympathizer, if not in cahoots. In addition, Newman was, during this period, under indictment for taking bribes from gamblers. "He was tried in Fairplay on July 31 and was found guilty as charged." Through a variety of legal maneuvers he was not ousted from his office until after the first of the year.

"So strong was the union's hold on its members, and its ability to intimidate strike breakers, that none of the major mines managed to resume production during June and July." The situation began to change in August. Several of the mine owners determined to open even if it was with skeletal crews, assuming, and with reason, that as soon as the mines were open and running, miners in twos and threes would begin to desert the union and come back to work, hat in hand, ready to go back at the old hours and wages. On or about the tenth of August the Coronado began making preparations to reopen, and did so with a staff of seventeen local men on August 17. The Emmet, near Finntown, announced its plans to reopen, and the Bohn, one of the downtown mines, opened again at the old scale and hours on September 5, 1896.

On August 18 the mine owners issued an ultimatum that informed miners that August 22 was the deadline. The mine owners intended opening all the three dollar mines after the lower wage scale mines were open. If the miners failed to make application for work on or before August 22, the "companies represented will consider this proposition rejected and no longer binding upon them in any particular." The mine owners were determined to open their mines. The first step was to offer to take local miners back at the old wage; if that failed, and they no doubt assumed it would, they were prepared to import "scabs" from other areas. Most of the miners rejected the offer to go back to work, and the first door closed.

By forcing the miners' hand and threatening the one sure way to break the strike, that of opening the mines with "foreign labor," the mine owners precipitated an increase in tension that eventually led to a show of force by both parties. It was not altogether necessary to import labor from out of the state, since there were many men in Colorado who were willing to volunteer. Phil Harrington's letter to John Campion late in July was typical of many.

Dear Sir

In view of the Labor troubles in Leadville I thought there might be some changes in your staff at the mines under your management. and therefore I would ask for a position as Foreman. I was Foreman of the Iron-mine in 1884 & 85 and also in that capacity on several smaller mines about that camp I was the discoverer of the ore body in the mcKeon shaft under F. G. White to whom I would refer you. also to Trimble & Hunter

Respectfully yours
Phil Harrington

Harrison Avenue looking north on the eve of the miners' strike. *Photo Source: Colorado Historical Society.*

The letter was mailed from Ward, Colorado, a mining camp in Boulder County. There is no way of knowing Campion's specific response to the letter, but we can assume that miners who could get by the union guards along the routes into the city were welcomed by Campion and other mine owners. Another miner from the Cripple Creek district, Dan Hanley, notified Campion "I am satisfied that in this district I can get you at the least 75 miners." The miners, Hanley assured Campion, were good workers and nonunion, and they all agreed with him; "pay a man what he is worth hire and Dischage whoume you place," and he went on to claim, "that has alwas been my stile. . . ." One cannot help but wonder if there was a greater psychological motive than grammatical behind Hanley's capital letter on "*Dis-chage*" and lower case on "*h*ire."

With the constant flow of offers, it is little wonder that owners and managers assumed there were many men willing to work and that their cause was just; that the Leadville miners were blocking the wheels of progress and preventing good honest men from working. Some blamed foreign-born elements, mainly the Irish, and insisted good American men wanted to work.

It became increasingly clear, though, despite outward appearances to the contrary, that the mine owners were not in agreement. While some talked of reopening mines, and in fact did so, the owners of the Penrose and Bon Air announced on August 30 that they had pulled their pumps because of the cost of keeping them running. The pumping operation of those two mines unwatered dozens of other mines in the area. The threat was real. But it was the Leadville businessmen who responded, not the union. On September 2 they pledged $3,000 to start the pumps again. They sent representatives to both management and union hoping to find a ground that could lead to a settlement. There appeared no common ground. As mentioned, the Bohn reopened on September 5. The union called all topmen, engineers, and firemen out on the seventh because the mine was not paying the three dollar wage. Most men left. Also on the seventh, the Bimetallic Smelter closed, leaving the Arkansas Valley to process what little ore was shipped from the area.

Edward Boyce, president of the Western Federation of Miners, came to town and the union met on September 9. Nothing is known of the meeting's results, but it was clear that the miners were not going to give up without a fight. In the days immediately following the meeting, miners working at the Coronado were "assaulted and rumors spread the Emmet would be blown up."

Sometime before the strike, the Coronado management had caused an eight-foot fence to be built around their property. As the situation worsened, they decided to add an additional six-foot enclosure inside the original structure. They also fortified the interior. "On the 11th, the building of a fence and watchtower" was started at the Emmet, which eventually included the fortification of the ore pass over the road up Stray Horse Gulch. East of town a number of other mines built guard towers. One near the Fortune consisted of double thick wooden walls with stone in between. Steel gun ports faced in all directions from the top of the structure.*

On September 14, the union came up with the most farsighted and easily the most revolutionary proposal of the strike, or of the period for that matter. It was a dream of the old Knights of Labor that someday the laborers would operate the factories and industries and split the profits. It was also the dream of Marx and Engels. It was not a dream usually associated with the Leadville miners, though, and whether a dream or nightmare no one can say, since the mine owners apparently did not even dignify the request with a reply. But, in a published statement, the union offered to "lease all of the down town mines, paying to the owners thereof 25 per cent royalty. The union will drain these mines, operate them and pay the standard scale of $3. For the faithful performance of this, the union agrees to sign a bond in the sum of $100,000. . . ." The union seemed serious about the proposal, and the mine owners' refusal to reply gives us little to determine their attitude on the subject, other than it was unacceptable. But why? Surely it smacked of a precedent that they were unwilling to establish, but it also suggests that those mine owners who were crying about hard times, were at the same time unwilling to accept twenty-five percent of the gross product. In other words, they were doing a lot better than they wanted anyone to know.

On the seventeenth of September the miners held their regular meeting. The men officially reacted to the accusations of violence on the part of the union in stating that they "denounced such occurrences in the severest terms possible, and especially assaults and interference with personal liberty, as cowardly and unmanly." They then requested the secretary and president "demand that the mayor and board of aldermen enforce the

---

*The structure was still standing a few years ago, and still is, unless some mindless scoundrel has dismantled it and carted it off to decorate his basement.

The Coronado protected by a board fence. *Photo Source: CMHC, Lake County Public Library.*

Guard tower on Little Ellen Hill. *Photo Source: Author's Collection.*

Samuel Danforth Nicholson. *Photo Source: Author's Collection.*

law by closing all saloons at 12 o'clock midnight, and keep them closed."

The following day, September 18, the mayor, Samuel D. Nicholson, complied with the union's request. He issued his own statement about law and order and the respect for property; then, to see that the request had the necessary teeth, he increased the city police force. Many businessmen, remembering how quickly the strike of 1880 was ended when troops arrived, kept a steady flow of letters, calls, and telegrams headed toward the governor's office. The local officials, well aware of the power of the union vote, steadfastly stood against the use of state troops.

There were two things the union could not abide. The first were strike breakers, or "scabs," brought in from outside the district to run the mines, and the other was the state militia. They were forced to tread a narrow path of successful but acceptable levels of intimidation; enough violence or threats of violence to scare off the strike breakers, but not enough to induce the governor to send troops. Bands of "regulators" were

formed shortly after the strike began and they met all incoming traffic and suggested that men looking for work either head back where they came from, or join the union in its fight for higher wages. They were generally successful and actually picked up a number of new union members. With the management's ultimatum of late August, it became clear that the mine owners had decided to force the issue, which meant large numbers of "foreign labor." The die was cast. A confrontation was inevitable.

The night of September 20 was clear, "the moon was shining brightly," and it did not seem the proper setting for desperate deeds. Shortly after midnight, residents on upper Seventh and Eighth streets were roused from their beds and told to get their families out. All questions received the same harsh reply, "There's trouble coming."

The Coronado workings spilled over the 600 block between East Seventh and Eighth streets and stood dark against the moonlit sky. A stick of giant powder exploded inside the defense compound of the Coronado, and another, and another. With the first explosion, one hundred to one hundred and fifty strikers began to pour an unrelenting rain of lead into the Coronado buildings and fortifications. The shots were fired "from Eighth street and from the alley running east and west between Seventh and Eighth streets." Fire was immediately returned by the seventeen men and a boy inside the fortifications. The attackers' first objective was to blow up the massive fuel oil tank. A relatively small party of attackers stationed themselves outside the fortifications near the tank, which stood in the northeast corner of the property, and "hurled not less than half a dozen sticks" of dynamite at the tank. Finally, one of the explosions ruptured the feeder line, and fuel oil began to run out of the tank. It was soon ablaze and rapidly spread flames to the stacked timbers and from there to the end of the building housing the boilers. The men inside the compound escaped the burning engine room and made their stand in the shaft house. They got set for the attack they expected to come at any moment, but the strikers were content to let the flames do their job.

Downtown the shooting and explosions had aroused the whole town, and the flames alerted the fire department. There seems to be no reason to assume that Mayor Nicholson delayed the fire companies or even wanted to, but it was later said that A. V. Hunter, seeing Mayor Nicholson in the

The Coronado after the attack and fire. *Photo Source: Colorado Historical Society.*

Vendome Hotel, ordered him, "Get the fire company out, or I'll blow your head right off." Nicholson ordered the entire fire department out, and they rushed to the scene. Meanwhile, the battle continued to rage, but the end was coming as the flames enveloped the shaft house. Fenced out is fenced in, and suddenly the fortifications that were built to protect the defenders trapped them inside the burning inferno. Some of the defenders made a dash for the Seventh Street fence, pushed and shoved, and scrambled over. The greater number climbed up in the shaft house and raced across the trestle that crossed Orange Street to a mine dump on the west side of the property, and down the Eighth Street side to safety. As they raced they were easy targets running along the skyline. Some accounts claim one defender was hit in the toe, but that appears to have been Martin Martinson, who was not shot, but broke an ankle jumping to safety.

As soon as the fire companies arrived, they began laying hose and preparing to fight the fire. It has been reported that they were warned not to hook up a hose, but contemporary news accounts make no mention of this. Jerry O'Keefe,* foreman of Hose Company Number 2, "seized the nozzle" and prepared to turn the full force of the water on the fire when a shot from behind "sent O'Keefe to the earth, bleeding from a mortal wound." Armed men, hidden in the vicinity of the mine, prevented the firemen from doing their duty and the fire raged. A group of about five men, led by Fire Marshal Goodfriend, pulled the hose cart along Orange Street to a place somewhere near the point at which the Coronado trestle crossed over the street, and began to unravel hose. Suddenly three men leaped from behind a house on the east side of Orange Street and ordered, "Drop that hose." The firemen complied, one of them complaining, "I'd stay, by God, but I do not want to be shot down in cold blood." Other firemen did

*If a warning was given, it fell toneless, soundless, on Jerry O'Keefe, whose hearing was extremely poor, and under the circumstances could not have heard a shouted warning not to hook up the hoses.

not even get to the fire. The Hook and Ladder Company was stopped at the corner of Orange and Sixth streets, a block from the fire, and informed that if they attempted to move, their horses would be "shot down."

The fire at the mine had begun to burn out, but it was fast spreading to the houses in the vicinity, especially those in East Eighth. The people of Leadville began to arrive in large numbers, armed to the teeth. The strikers, seeing the numbers, quickly retired and regrouped. Local merchants teamed up with the fire companies to halt the spread of the fire and save as much as possible. Most of the houses that were lost belonged to striking miners and few had insurance enough to cover their losses. By six o'clock in the morning of September twenty-first, the flames were under control.

The Maid of Erin and the Emmet were also slated for destruction and possibly the R.A.M. A fire was started at the Maid of Erin, but it was spotted and extinguished by William Conley. Later, examining the shaft house, which was the building set afire, enough giant powder was discovered beneath the floor "to have blown the building to atoms." After the attack on the Coronado, the bulk of the attacking force moved east up Stray Horse Gulch to the Emmet. The force in the Emmet was lead by Joseph P. Gazzam, a Missourian, and superintendent of the Small Hopes Mining Company. He may well have been responsible for the whole confrontation, but more of that later.

Gazzam heard the explosions at the Coronado and also received phone calls from town telling him the situation, so he was ready when the strikers arrived. The strikers made no attempt to conceal themselves and seemed to wander onto the scene with little or no discipline. Earlier in the evening, Gazzam had sent a couple of men, Shriver and D. F. McComb, to the R.A.M. He gave them three rifles, an extra in case something happened to one of them, "more than their share of ammunition," and the instructions that they were not to fire unless they were fired upon, but in that case to fire fast and furious, giving the impression they were a group of defenders instead of just two. They were further instructed to hold the property as long as they could, and "get out as best they could."

Around three in the morning the mob attacked the Emmet, opening their assault in much the same fashion as they had against the Coronado. A dynamite bomb ripped a large hole in the fence surrounding the property and a hail of lead

followed the explosion. Several other bombs were thrown, but not all of them exploded. Also, fire bombs were thrown, all aimed at igniting the fuel tank. The strikers were not successful and, due to the rifle fire from within, no one was able to breech the fence, if indeed anyone wanted to. The attack, according to Gazzam, lasted about forty-five minutes. Then the attackers withdrew and silence returned.

Gazzam went up top to see if he could see anything, but all seemed quiet. He returned to his post in the yard and suddenly three shots were fired from within the enclosure, in the southeastern section. Gazzam shouted to the defenders and told them to hold their fire and not waste ammunition. Immediately a voice called out, "For God's sake, cut out the shooting!" Gazzam called to know who it was, and Sheriff Newman shouted back, "I am the sheriff of Lake County." The men in the enclosure hooted and catcalled, and one, Joe Henault, asked, "Are you that blankety-blank, red headed, blankety-blank of a sheriff?" Newman answered that he was one and the same. "The men had to laugh at a hardboiled western sheriff of that day owning up to all the allegations." He was then asked his business by Gazzam, and Newman told him he wanted to go around the fence and search for his deputies, who were supposedly on duty protecting the mine. Gazzam, knowing Newman's sympathies lay with the strikers, said no. That satisfied Newman, and he left.

Sometime later a Doctor Galloway, in the company of the sheriff and about a dozen deputies, arrived and requested passage up the road past Gazzam's fortified trestle to treat a wounded striker. The group, carefully watched, passed without incident. After daylight, it was clear that the attack was over, and the crew in the Emmet began to venture forth and examine the damage. The smoke stacks on the top of the buildings were riddled with bullet holes. The fuel tank, the major objective of the attack, was undamaged. Near the assay office, they found an improvised cannon and a length of chain. Later they found another length of chain "imbedded in the wall of the boiler room." It appeared the strikers had only fired the cannon once, possibly because it was ineffective, or more likely, defective. The outside of the east fence had been soaked with coal oil, but never ignited.

The two men in the R.A.M. were never attacked and thankfully missed the whole show. One man was officially noted as killed in the attack on the Emmet, while three men lost their lives according to the police count in the attack on the Coronado. Added to Jerry O'Keefe and another striker, who died later of his wounds, the official death toll was six. But it was claimed by many that the death toll was as high as forty. Steve Philbrick, recalling the event many years later, claimed many unidentified men were "buried secretly by the railroad tracks."

The damage to the Emmet and Maid of Erin were negligible, but the Coronado was almost completely destroyed above ground. Some of the equipment was salvagable, but the total damage was put at $25,000, which in today's terms would be someplace in the vicinity of one-quarter of a million dollars.

Earlier it was noted that Joseph P. Gazzam might have been the cause of the whole confrontation. Gazzam later explained that during the strike it became necessary to either start the mines or pull the pumps. He was, at the time, in the employ of S. W. Mudd, general manager of the Small Hopes Consolidated Mining Company, as superintendent, and as such was responsible for a number of properties. When Gazzam was in-

formed of the situation, he suggested importing miners from the lead mines of Joplin, Missouri. These miners, Gazzam claimed, "were native born Americans and could not be intimidated by gunmen." Mudd liked the idea and plans were laid to import enough Missourians to staff the Coronado, Emmet, and R.A.M., which explains why they were hit and why the miners attempted to destroy the plants. The strike leaders reasoned that if the Small Hopes Consolidated Mining Company imported large numbers of "scabs," only to find, when they arrived, that the mines were inoperable, the owners would have had a considerable expense on their hands and would be financially pushed to the wall. With the miners' rationale clear, it becomes equally clear that they intended no loss of life, and probably the death of Jerry O'Keefe, while not accidental, was surely not premeditated. It was not that the miners were such poor shots as Gazzam claimed, nor the angle they were firing from, but the fact that they were not trying to hit anyone. It seems unlikely, for instance, that several men could run along the raised trestle at the Coronado with fifty or more

Colorado State Militia on duty at the Emmet. *Photo Source: Colorado Historical Society.*

rifles firing on them with no one hit. But the miners' cause could not be served by shooting the mine defenders, their fight was with the owners. The guards, on the other hand, first could not have realized that the lead flying around them was not meant for them, and second, that they had law on their side. They were protecting property, a sacred trust. They shot to kill, and kill they did.

The miners lost much more than they gained with their desperate gamble. At almost the first shot Sheriff Newman telegraphed the governor for the militia. "The situation here is beyond my control." In another telegram signed by Judge Owers and Newman, they pleaded, "Send militia as soon as possible." Others in the community cried wolf, and the governor immediately complied. While the town awaited word on the militia, the citizens, who had armed themselves for the fight at the Coronado, seized control. On the afternoon of the twenty-first, a large citizens' meeting was held in Weston's Opera House (Tabor Opera House). The following day Mayor Nicholson, supported by a large body of community leaders, asked the governor to declare martial law.

The governor was wasting no time. On the afternoon of September 21 the first companies of Colorado Militia arrived by train. The town quieted. The miners waited; most seemed determined to see the strike through to the end. While military forces were called in on the twenty-first and more arrived in the days following, Governor McIntire did not invoke martial law.

On September 25 the first trainload of Missourians arrived. General Brooks, commander of Camp McIntire, the newly formed military compound located on the baseball field just north of the city limits, ordered troops to Malta to ride with the workers into town and sent others to the Denver and Rio Grande depot on North Poplar, between Fourteenth and Fifteenth streets to maintain order. The sixty-five Missouri miners were completely encircled by troops, while a mounted cavalry brought up the rear. Company G from Cripple Creek led the way with a pair of Gatling guns. Any attacker would surely have thought twice before continuing with his plan.

The miners' destination was the Emmet, but they were marched west down Thirteenth Street toward Harrison Avenue. About half way through the one hundred block of Thirteenth Street a group of men and boys numbering around seventy-five began hurling "epithets," but nothing heavier than angry words landed on the procession. They turned south onto Harrison

Avenue and headed right down the main thoroughfare. Their route and the number of troops involved suggest that the commander of Camp McIntire decided on an immediate show of strength.

In crossing Capitol Hill, the mob of men and boys that had gathered to taunt the procession began to press close, and one officer brandished a saber at the nearest lad. The crowd immediately fell back to a safe distance. A silent, somber crowd lined the sides of Harrison Avenue, and the quietest parade in the Magic City's history marched by. No flags were waving, no shouts or cheers, just the cold stare of pent-up emotion and suppressed hatred greeted the marchers. At Fifth Street they turned east. In the four hundred block of East Fifth Street, the very heart of the Irish miners' homes, the crowd began to thicken and hostility was everywhere. The troops were halted and the situation grew tense. Captain Grove, commander of the procession, ordered the crowd back. Sullen and unwilling, the crowd milled, and when one man, more aggressive than the rest, confronted the captain, his saber flashed and the man received a stunning blow on the side of the face. The soldiers then drove the crowd back with the butts of their guns. Shouts of "Shoot them down!" echoed from the crowd, and several men ran into nearby houses. The troops readied for action, but nothing happened, and the march was resumed. The trip to the Emmet was completed without further incident. Gazzam's Missouri miners had arrived not much worse for wear.

Gazzam explained, "The Missourians were interspersed with the old miners, who were told that the Missourians did not understand our system of mining, and would have to be shown." It has been said that it was from that need that the expression "He's a Missourian and will have to be shown" was born, hence the "Show Me" nickname for Missouri.*

The attack on the Coronado and Emmet mines put the initiative in the hands of the mine owners, and they never gave it up. G. W. Steevens, writing in 1897, recalled, "If you approach a mine you will be fired on; briefly, Leadville is in a state of siege, not to say civil war.

---

*Like most folk expressions, there appears to be a number of other stories of the origin of the saying, but none are any more reliable or probable than Gazzam's. Gazzam's version is substantiated by William Ledbetter of the *Kansas City Star*, who claimed to have heard the tale in Denver in 1897. Mattie Stuthman, writing in *Colorado Magazine* in 1952, claims to have read the story years before in the Denver papers.

Martial law required certain restrictions. *Photo Source: Colorado Historical Society.*

Several hundred stand of arms have been confiscated, but signals have been seen flashing from mountain to mountain at night, and little caches of dynamite have been found near the mines.'' The threat of violence continued, but it was becoming clear that the militia had killed the ability of the strikers to intimidate or effectively fight back.

For a few days after the attack the town waited anxiously to see what might happen next. The banks closed their doors as a precautionary measure, and a few other businesses did likewise. Warrants were issued for the arrest of known participants. Those in custody were released on September 23 after posting $500 bonds. According to the *Evening Chronicle* of September 22, both President Amburn and Secretary Dewar had disappeared. Amburn's wife said she had not seen him since the night of the twenty-first. Out-of-town miners, who were not imported to work the mines, were suspected of being troublemakers and were labeled ''Vags,'' and the council determined to do all it could to enforce vagrant laws and sent a committee of businessmen and council members to local attorneys to find out what they could do about vagrants.

The city council and community, by unanimous, though not official, consent, determined to

give Jerry O'Keefe a hero's burial. His death in St. Vincent's Hospital, his family and friends around him gathered, was faithfully reported in the local papers. The Excelsior Lodge of the United Workmen, in which O'Keefe was a member, handled the details of the funeral. The city council agreed unanimously to pay all costs and asked that as many of the militia companies as could be spared participate in the funeral ceremony.

The tide was running with the mine owners. The attack, and especially the murder of the innocent Jerry O'Keefe, had decisively turned public opinion against the strikers. The militia's presence negated the pro-union attitude of the sheriff. The successful arrival of out-of-district miners made the operation of the mines possible and totally nullified the economic effects of the strike on the mine owners. On October 2 a special grand jury was empanelled to investigate the attacks on the Emmet and Coronado and the killing of Jerry O'Keefe.

Between the miners and the owners stood the militia, a group of unseasoned veterans who had been rolled out of bed in the wee hours of a Monday morning, September 21, 1896, to provide law and order for lawless Leadville. ''Many of them had no opportunity to properly clothe themselves for such an experience." Most were from lower elevations where September is considered the last part of summer, rather than the first part of winter. "They arrived in camp with thin shoes and linen or cotton underclothing." Leadville was rainy and cold and near freezing when they arrived. That quickly changed to below freezing and snow. The army was unable to feed the first contingents to arrive, so they were fed in the Vendome Hotel, where the facilities and personnel were totally unequal to the task. "The food was poor and imperfectly cooked." Tents were available in the newly designated Camp McIntire, but there was no bedding for the tents. "Straw and hay could not be procured, so the only protection they had were their blankets on the cold, muddy ground." In addition to the main camp on the baseball field, the militia established outposts at the Ibex, the Maid of Erin, the Emmet, and the Resurrection mines, where for varying periods of time, troops were housed to protect men and property.

The army quickly provided their own quartermaster unit and fed their troops and also provided winter clothing, though adequate clothing was longer in coming than the food. Sleeping conditions were improved, and life in camp generally became much more pleasant. On November 10, the camp awoke to find itself buried in snow. "When reveille was sounded at six o'clock in the morning, the entire camp awoke to find itself snowed in to the depth of two feet." It was a wet, early winter snow, and lay heavy on the tents. The stoves in the tents began to melt the snow and rather than run off the tents it ran in, "and pools of water formed in every tent" making home for the soldier more uncomfortable than usual.

Breakfast was a damp, dismal affair that consisted of standing or sitting in the melting, slushy snow, while trying to eat. After the soggy meal, regular military routine was suspended, and the men began clearing the snow from the thoroughfares. The work warmed the men and before long a vigorous snowball fight that included both officers and men was in progress. The battle lasted for over half an hour, and the list of casualties included a large number of black eyes.

Generally, the militia was treated well by the Leadville people; even the strikers appeared not

Camp McIntyre as the troops prepare to depart. *Photo Source: Colorado Historical Society.*

to bear them any ill will. John Campion, no doubt very happy about the militia's presence, sent the men a barrel of apples. In thanking Campion, Lieutenant Wheeler asked that he might return the favor and invited Campion to Sunday dinner. No record of the dinner has survived.

For the miners, the coming winter did not promise much in the way of Sunday dinners, of even apples for that matter. G. W. Steevens was writing about the same time Mr. Campion was a guest of the militia, "In this grim deadlock Leadville waits for the cruel winter. With uncalculated treasures beneath her feet, and the clammy, cold clouds pressing down on her head, she waits for aching frost and hunger to settle the matter one way, or cold steel and hot lead and dynamite to settle it the other. No surrender; No compromise; No pity."

John Campion had a number of hired detectives working for him; possibly for all the mine owners. They successfully infiltrated the union, though there seems no evidence that they worked their way into the confidence of the union's leaders. According to one "operative," the majority of the men wanted, by December 1896, to go back to work, "but are afraid of the Union." Campion's operatives continued to give him information throughout the strike and were active the following year in giving information on local political candidates that proved useful to Campion and other mine owners in their support of anti-union political candidates in city and county elections. Another item found in Campion's papers was a list of approximately three hundred names. The purpose of the list is not evident, but in checking the names, all the known leaders of the strike were on it and those names that were unknown to historians checked out as miners. It would appear that around three hundred miners were identified by Campion's operatives and possibly were blacklisted, although a blacklist has never been mentioned in the papers, or by strikers, and might well have been another of those well-kept secrets having to do with the strike of 1896. Several typed copies of the list were in Campion's papers, and one list had a number of penciled additions.

December saw President Amburn return with the excuse that he had gone home to Tennessee to see his father, hence his departure the night of the burning of the Coronado. Union officials denounced those union men who had given up and were going back to work, but the future seemed obvious to many. The last battle had been fought; the war was lost. Sheriff Newman got his walking papers on Christmas Eve when he lost

his last court appeal. The day after Christmas he started serving a six-month sentence.

Christmas 1896 stood out in stark contrast to Christmas 1895. The expectations of a gala winter carnival in the Ice Palace warmed every heart in 1895, but the expectations of a cold, grueling winter of increased privation faced most of the working people in 1896. Christmas was filled with fights and arrests. "Both the county and city jails were well filled before midnight" on Christmas Eve. The town seemed filled, not with the Christmas programs and social gatherings, as in years past, but with general drunkenness and a chip on every shoulder.

As the new year dawned, the town had a new sheriff; the state a new governor. Both provided listeners with the usual rhetoric, but nothing changed. The grim confrontation between miners and owners continued. In a show of strength, the Cloud City's labor unions paraded, honoring Eugene V. Debs, five-time socialist political candidate for president, who was in town to help encourage the miners to hang on, to keep fighting. The parade was described by a local reporter as a "funeral procession." The determination might have been there, the courage, too, but the reporter noted that it was not anger, but anxiety that filled most faces.

On January 31, 1897, the Colorado Legislature appointed a special commission to investigate the Leadville strike. The commission consisted of five Colorado legislators, Oscar Reuter, Theodore Annear, E. L. Sechrist, James F. Gardner, and Joseph Gallagher. They compiled an impressive amount of information of value to the historian, but contributed nothing to the solution of the immediate problem.

February was quiet. Resignation and defeat were in the air. Two Leadville strikes, one in 1880 and one in 1896, appeared to have been defeated. The sacrifices of the miners had been for nothing. The privation of families, the hunger of children, had simply proven that capital was stronger than labor in Leadville.

Debs and Edward Boyce, president of the Western Federation of Miners, returned to Leadville during the first week of March and on the ninth the union held a meeting. "Over 1,200 men crowded into City Hall" to determine the course of the strike. It was reported that the union's funds were almost exhausted and that to maintain the strike would put a terrible burden on the members who were working. The Cloud City Miners' Union had a new president, Peter Turnbull, a foreman from the Weldon Shaft, and he called the meeting to order. Debs addressed the

Those left to police the district after the main body of troops had returned home. *Photo Source: Colorado Historical Society.*

men, saying it was a fight between labor and money and in the end money must win. Others wanted to continue the fight, but finally a big Swede made the motion to end the strike, saying, "I'd rather declare this strike off than go scabbing."

President Turnbull called for the vote. Roughly 900 voted to end the strike. Two hundred voted to continue. Peter Turnbull mounted the platform, tears welled in his tired eyes and coursed down his cheeks. With a tremor in his voice he announced the result of the vote. The great Leadville miner's strike ended on March 9, 1897. It has lasted eight months and twenty days. The cost in lives, property, and human suffering has never been measured. Quietly the men filed out of the meeting.

The following day the militia loaded up their belongings and headed for home. The campaign had lasted 172 days and had cost the taxpayers of Colorado, by mid-February, 1897, $194,010.43. The largest number of militia in camp at one time was 827. After the first of the year the numbers were continually reduced until only 57 men remained. The average was 422 men. One man died

of pneumonia, several came down with a variety of colds and fevers; three were shot, accidentally; and one fell on his bayonet. All recovered.

The flooding of the downtown mines created more havoc than anyone could have foretold. It was assumed that the downtown mines would begin hiring within a week or so. They were two years reopening. The unwatering was an expense that many mining men were unwilling to take on. The mines had not only filled with water, but also with a fine sand that had to be mucked out before work could be resumed. The bitterness sowed by the strike outlasted all the physical evidence of the confrontation. It affected management-labor relations well into the twentieth century.

The economic stress of the strike closed one of three banks, reduced the smelting industry to little more than a subsistence level, closed a number of shops, and put a number of local white collar men out of work. The gamblers and saloon owners, emboldened by the situation, began to aggressively ply their wares. The gambling fraternity, in spite of local laws against it, began opening their closed gambling halls, openly defying the law. While Newman was in office, nothing was done and, until the strike ended, nothing much was said. But as soon as the camp began to return to normal, the hammer came down hard on vice of all descriptions, and evil days descended on gamblers, prostitutes, and their compatriots, and many left the town never to return. As one reporter remarked concerning the shutdown of gambling, "The Goddess of Chance stood around in the chilly atmosphere between the court house and county jail . . . and wept bitter, briny, scalding tears. . . ."

All of the various investigative bodies completed their reports and filed them. Many were published. The courts finished their investigations of the Coronado and the Emmet attacks and the death of Jerry O'Keefe, and "in due time all of the indictments were dismissed."

The Magic City began to look forward to the coming spring. The miners had lost, but there still were mines to be worked and ore to be hauled, and maybe a spare bit of change now and then for an outing. The strike had taken its toll, though. Many men were forced to leave for want of work; the owners were stronger than ever and seemed intent on proving that labor worked at their behest. Shortly after the turn of the century, Leadville was the only camp in Colorado that had not gone to the eight-hour day.

XIV

End of an Era

In the years immediately before 1900 it became increasingly clear to the people of Leadville that a colorful past was rapidly slipping away. Newspaper pioneer, C. C. Davis, had lost his health and in 1895 moved to California. Dr. D. H. Dougan retired and moved to Denver, leaving his banking enterprises for other men to manage. Mrs. A. A. Blow, the last of Leadville's darling Goodell girls, moved to the Capital. S. W. Mudd, the James J. Browns, John Campion and family, and Charles Boettcher had all left Leadville. David May, probably the town's most popular

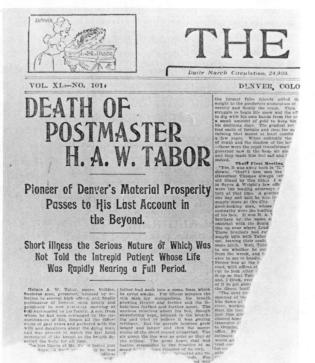

Photo Source: Author's Collection.

merchant, followed the exodus of money and success to Denver.

In March of 1897, A. S. Weston died. He had come to the valley in 1860 and was a prominent figure in county politics and business for almost forty years. Old man Derry, father of the discoverer of the J. D. Dana, and locator of one of the earliest ranches in the county, died in his home near Twin Lakes in 1899, the result of burns suffered in a household accident.

The death of Horace Tabor probably made people aware of the passing of an era more than anything else. On the morning of April 10, 1899, the man who was, more than anyone else, Mr. Leadville, died of appendicitis. His wife, Baby Doe, was afraid to let them operate. Leadville, nay, all of Colorado, was afraid to praise him too highly in light of his private life, and could not refrain from mentioning how beloved of Leadville people his first wife had been. But, as the years went by and the Tabor legend and tragedy grew, the impact of the man was lost. He became, over the years, "the old fool and his money"; Augusta became the straight-laced New England prude; and Baby Doe became the strange, tragic figure in everyone's story of rags to riches.

Is it possible to separate the man and the legend? And do we want to? The Magic City would lose a lot of its magic without Tabor; without those who strode the streets with him. To understand a flower you must pick it; to apprecciate a flower all you must do is look at it. Be content to look at Tabor as his contemporaries recalled him.

When word was received of Tabor's death, Major A. V. Bohn, longtime resident and successful mining man, recalled the first time he met Mr.

Tabor. He had arrived in Denver in February 1878, and heard that Leadville was in dire need of butter and eggs. He secured three wagons and loaded them to overflowing with butter and eggs and set out for Leadville. It was early March when he arrived, and the sun was just setting. He housed the wagons in a livery stable and set out to sell his goods. Since the town only had two general stores, owned by Charles Mater and Horace Tabor, it would not take him long to survey the market. He talked first with Mater, who told him to come around in the morning. Dissatisfied with that, he located Tabor's store and went in. "It was a little place, dingy and filled with tobacco smoke. A dozen or so miners were sitting around on cracker boxes squirting tobacco juice into a sawdust heap. A man in his shirt sleeves was sitting on the counter talking."

The major, after looking the place over, asked to see Mr. Tabor.

The man on the counter replied, "I'm the man."

Bohn told about his cargo and Tabor exclaimed, "You're the man I'm looking for," and he immediately volunteered to go down to the livery stable and see the goods.

It was around nine o'clock when they reached the livery stable, and cold. Tabor immediately set about examining the goods. He was satisfied with the quality of the merchandise and offered sixty cents a pound, which was three times what Bohn had in the cargo. Bohn immediately accepted, and set out to find himself a hotel.

The next morning, early, he walked by Tabor's store. The eggs and butter were prominently advertised in the window at sixty cents a dozen and sixty cents a pound. He had to find out the reason for selling at the buying price, so he went in. "But where do you come in?" asked the major in surprise. "You paid me sixty cents."

"Oh, that's all right," said Tabor cheerfully. "The boys haven't tasted butter and eggs for so long that I wouldn't ask them a cent more. They can have 'em for just what I paid."

The year before Tabor died, in April, the United States went to war against Spain, which made it the biggest news story of 1898, and probably the most popular war in the country's history. It was called "a splendid little war," did not cost much, was short, and was a monumental success for manifest destiny and Teddy Roosevelt. In Leadville, as throughout the country, men flocked to the recruiting offices to serve their country and get in on some of the glory before it was over.

In Leadville people were amazed with the speed with which Governor Alva Adams got the Colorado National Guard mobilized. War was declared on April 25, and they were ordered to report April 29. Leadville's infantry companies E and F, and their cavalry company, Troop A, were wined and dined. The cavalry was given a silk flag, courtesy of the ladies of Beggs Dry Goods Company, to carry into battle with them. A gay, but tearful, parade led by Major A. V. Bohn and members of the Grand Army of the Republic escorted the infantry companies to the Denver and Rio Grande depot; then most hurried back to the armory. A new parade was formed and everyone, laughing and crying, escorted the cavalry to the Midland depot, where midst handshakes and tears and shouts of encouragement, Leadville's brave boys in blue went off to war. The infantry saw action in the battle of Manila, but the cavalry got to Florida too late and missed the boat. The war in Cuba was soon over. Teddy and the Rough Riders had already become national heroes, and Leadville's Rough Riders had nothing to do but relax in the Florida sunshine.

In 1896 and 1897 the Leadville Blues had been state baseball champs and everyone agreed that Leadville's semi-pro team was one of the best in the West. With that in mind it comes as something of a surprise to find that they were discontinued in 1899. Reasons given were the trouble with maintaining the field and the cost of running a professional club.

The fall of 1898 had been very dry, only one-half inch of snow fell the whole month of September, and only one day was cloudy. The balmy weather of Indian summer continued well into

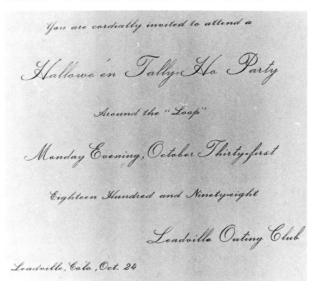

You are cordially invited to attend a

Hallowe'en Tally-Ho Party

Around the "Loop"

Monday Evening, October Thirty-first

Eighteen Hundred and Ninety-eight

Leadville Outing Club

Leadville, Colo., Oct. 24

Photo Source: Author's Collection.

October and occasioned a number of forest fires around the state. Toward the middle of the month some snow did fall, the fire danger abated, but the weather continued pleasant and nothing, not the way the squirrels held their tails nor the amount of pollen spread by the evergreens, gave any warning of what was to come. October's total snowfall consisted of fourteen inches, which is not at all above normal and certainly nothing to grow alarmed about. November was pleasant through Thanksgiving, and there was no reason to feel that this winter would be any different than the ones in the immediate past.

The previous winter the Colorado Midland had "surrendered possession of the Busk Tunnel Railway" that had provided them a longer, lower tunnel over the continental divide. They felt the rates were too high, so they repaired the tracks and trestles up to the old Hagerman Tunnel. The Midland found the winter maintenance on the old route was none too difficult and, to the surprise of the Busk Tunnel Railway, planned to use the old route again during the winter of 1898-1999.

On November 26 it began to snow. By the thirtieth of the month, twenty-six and one-half inches of snow had fallen. It was the first major storm, and a big one at that, but not overwhelming. The snowfall in December only amounted to a little over fourteen inches and the November storm was quickly forgotten. The weather in December, while dry, was cold and most of November's snow remained after the first of the year.

The November storm officially ushered winter in. The Magic City abandoned wheeled vehicles for sleighs, the prospectors who spent winter in the city came down from the hills, and a round of winter parties began with sleighing and ice skating and the usual winter balls and socials. Christmas was gayer than it had been for years, owing to the somewhat recovered state of the community's economy after the devastating effects of the strike of 1896. The downtown mines still were silent, but most men who wanted work were able to find it. The storm king even condescended, not on Christmas Eve, but on the twenty-first, to drop eight inches of new snow on the Cloud City, just to see that the magic of a clean, white Christmas was not destroyed.

The new year was born amid much gaiety and good cheer. During the first two weeks of January two light snows settled on the city. Then, on the fifteenth of the month it began to snow. An inch fell. On the sixteenth it snowed all day and, when night fell, fourteen inches of new snow lay on the ground. The second major storm. Nothing out of the ordinary. After all, Leadville lay over 10,000 feet high in the middle of the Colorado Rockies. One could expect a little winter. On the twenty-second, three more inches fell. On the twenty-fifth a storm moved in. Five days later the storm was over. Forty-one and one-fourth inches of new snow lay on top of the previous week's seventeen inches of snow. Suddenly everything came to a standstill. Almost five feet of snow had fallen during the last two weeks of January. The railroads were stranded, and roads drifted and impassable. Three Denver and Rio Grande engines hooked in tandem set out on the twenty-eighth of January to clear the Blue River Branch over Fremont Pass. Not far out of Leadville they heard, over the roar of the engines, a deafening rumble and saw a swirling white cloud. The squealing of brakes was muffled by the roar of the avalanche. The outer edge of the slide struck the lead engine and rolled it over. The second engine was thrown on its side; the third miraculously remained on the track, even though the caboose behind it was swept off the rails and buried in the snow. The crew was unhurt, but the Blue River Branch had to wait while the crew walked back to town for help.

The Midland had fared even worse. The approach to the Hagerman Tunnel was blocked near Busk, the entrance to the new, lower tunnel that the Midland had refused to use. The rotary snowplow was sent out and blasted its way through the drifts and finally made it to, then through, the Hagerman Tunnel. On the west side they encountered a trainload of livestock, which immediately set out along the newly cleared track. The three engines that were used in the climb up Hagerman Pass remained with the train as an added precaution, and they began the downhill trip into Leadville. They were approaching the second snow shed above Busk, when the engineer whistled down the brakes. The weight of the snow had collapsed the shed. The driving wind blew in the track behind them. They were trapped in the middle of a driving blizzard at over 11,000 feet. There was nothing to do but wait for help. Meanwhile, "the cattle slowly froze to death."

Out of Leadville came the regular passenger train. When it reached Busk it stopped to wait for the stock train. After it failed to arrive, the passenger train began to cautiously inch its way up the pass. When they reached the first snow shed above Busk they found it collapsed. Working their way on up to the second snow shed on foot, the crew found the stranded stock train. There was nothing to do but go back to their passengers, tell them they were snowbound and would have to sit it out until help arrived. The

South Park* was tied up between Leadville and Como; Alpine Pass was closed.

In town, the shutdown of transportation had serious effects on the coal supply. Not only was it difficult to deliver — every contrivance imaginable was used — but the supply quickly began to get dangerously low. Sixty-five carloads of domestic coal sat snowbound at Malta. Finally the tracks west to Malta were cleared, mostly by hand, and the fuel reached the city. Of even graver consequence was the shutdown of most of the mines simply because they could not be reached by either men or supplies. Approximately two thousand men were thrown out of work after they had just begun to recover from the miners' strike.

The weather cleared on the thirtieth of January and for a week or so remained pleasant, and most services were resumed, somewhat impaired by passes that remained closed, but alternate routes and shared routes made it possible for the railroads to supply the Cloud City. Then on February 8 it began to snow again. In three days it snowed twenty-nine inches. If the January storm had been a freak storm, then it was beginning to look like a freak winter. Again the railroads ground to a halt.

The night of February 7, when the storm moved in, Midland and Rio Grande passenger trains were stranded near Snowden, some ten miles south of Leadville in Hayden Flats. There they sat on parallel tracks, while the wind herded the snow in and around the cars. Inside the situation was nothing less than delightful. The cars were well heated and, as one passenger on the Rio Grande later explained, lunch baskets were opened and shared, salesmen opened their samples, and a foraging party set out to explore the rest of the train. Their success was pronounced with the serving of hard boiled eggs, courtesy of the engineer's fire box and some unknown grocer in some unknown city. After the eggs came fried slices of beef, cooked in the fire box on a coal shovel. Soon sleighs arrived to take the passengers to town and while welcomed by the passengers, there was none of the screaming, shouting, and shoving associated with desperate people. Rather they welcomed their rescuers with the grace, charm, and dignity of the well fed. Little wonder!

*The Denver, South Park and Pacific in 1898 was no more. It was the Denver, Leadville and Gunnison Railway, but went into receivership in 1899 and became the Colorado and Southern; most people in '98 and '99 were still calling it the South Park.

Hundreds of miners found work as "snowbirds," a name given to men who had helped clear snowbound tracks in the winter of 1884-1885. George W. Cook, longtime railroad man and president of the Keno Mining and Leasing Company, prevailed upon "mine and smelter managers and the businessmen to put up the money" and offer $1.75 per day to any man who wanted to shoulder a pick or shovel to clear snow from the impassable rails. On February 10, 874 men set out. Their first task was to reopen the Rio Grande's track from Malta to Leadville. Armed with picks and shovels, their lunch baskets, and dressed in several layers of clothing, they set out at seven in the morning. By nightfall trains were hauling long needed and awaited coal, coke, timber, and foodstuffs into the city.

For those whose business took them out of the city, or for that matter required that they journey to Leadville, the weather was an almost impossible burden. Pat Ryan recalled staging between Leadville and Twin Lakes in what was remembered as the "hard winter." On one occasion he was heading home to Twin Lakes after a particularly difficult trip into town. He did reasonably well until he reached the vicinity of Snowden. There were no roads to follow; all he could do was try to follow the packed base beneath the new snow. "Every little way the horses would get off the road into the drifts; then I would have to unhitch them and take all the load out of the sleigh and carry it up unto the road." Back in the sleigh he would go "maybe a quarter of a mile" and then it would happen all over again. When he reached the Derry ranch at about nine in the evening, he and his horses were exhausted. The Derrys insisted he stay, but he was equally insistent. The folks at home would be worried about him, so he pushed on, asking for a lantern to light the way. Before he was out of sight of the house one of his horses was down. Charles Derry, locator of the J. D. Dana, had been watching him, and when he saw Ryan was in trouble he set out to help him. By the time Derry reached him there was no question in Ryan's mind. He would have to avail himself of the Derry's hospitality and spend the night.

The next morning he set out. Old Sam, the sick member of his team, was led, and Ryan and the other horse pulled the sleigh to the top of the hill. Shortly he encountered searchers who were setting out to find him. The whole party returned home, grateful that nothing serious had happened to him.

After the first February storm, Denver and

January 1899 in front of the C. N. Priddy residence at 220 West Eighth. *Photo Source: Author's Collection.*

Rio Grande officials met in Denver and guaranteed the people of Leadville that the city would have coal and food even if no one else got served. It boosted the town's morale.

No major storms hit the city during the remainder of the month of February, but the sun seldom shone, and it snowed on fifteen of the month's twenty-eight days. When the month ended, an additional five feet of snow had fallen on top of the previous month's five feet.

During the middle days of February the people of Robinson, just north of the summit of Fremont Pass, began to grow uneasy. It had been weeks since the railroad had made it in to them. A group of Robinson men and Mr. and Mrs. Phillip Baker set out for Pando and the Rio Grande. Mr. Baker was fifty and his wife forty-seven, and the twelve-mile trip would have been something of an ordeal even in the summer, but with ten feet of snow on the level it was foolhardy. They set out, ten miners and the Bakers, two sleighs and fourteen horses, plus enough food for three or four days.

At the end of the first day they had struggled a little over a mile, the second and third days were not much better. On the fourth day it was clear that they were not going to make it with the horses and provisions they had, so the Bakers donned the party's two pair of Norwegian snowshoes and, with enough food for a lunch, set out on foot for Pando, some nine miles away. The miners went back to Robinson to get more help and supplies. Eight hours later, in a blinding snowstorm, the Bakers arrived at Pando, "where they found friends and shelter until morning." They then boarded the train for Leadville.

A couple of days later the miners in Robinson managed to open a road from the mining camp of Robinson and the twin villages of Kokomo and Recen, to Pando. Supplies began to move to their rescue. Also, a number of women and children were taken to Leadville for the remainder of the winter.

Edward Fitzsimmons and Lou Finnegan had the unenvied task of repairing the telephone line between Twin Lakes and Aspen. Their job was the repair of the Leadville side of the mountain, while an Aspen team worked on the other side. The pair set out from Twin Lakes with a toboggan loaded with food, wire, and tools. In the fourteen miles that they covered, they reported seeing thirty-six snow slides, many of which had ripped through their telephone line, burying the remains under tons of snow and debris. Most of the slides were of moderate size, but some ranged a quarter of a mile across. On one occasion they had just finished the repair of a line and were a short distance above the site, when they heard behind them a "terrific roar and deep rumbling." They turned and "the air seemed filled with snow, stones and trees." The wind along the course of the avalanche was so great that "boughs and branches snapped like pipe stems."

That slide took out twelve telephone poles and required a considerable amount of time to repair. When finished, they continued their trip up the valley. It took them fourteen days to finish the trip and on their return they reported that the cabins along the way were virtually buried in the snow, "but the inhabitants have plenty of food to last till spring."

When they reached Twin Lakes, they reported the snow to be about nine feet on the level, and "all the gulches and ravines are obliterated, so that the country presents a level appearance." The people of Twin Lakes were pleased to see the pair safely returned from their trip. It was the twenty-second of February and everyone in Twin Lakes, including Fitzsimmons and Finnegan, converged on the Patrick J. Ryan residence for George Washington's birthday party. It was a party the like of which neither visitor had seen before. "The 'hop' will long remain in the mind of Fitzsimmons as a pleasing end of what, as he says, was 'the worst trip he ever made.'"

The *Herald Democrat* of February 25 complained of the "croakers" who, on seeing it snow some the previous day, claimed the storm was not over. They pushed for the "bright side" and claimed the "optomists are willing to make bets that Leadville's climate will be most salubrious until St. Patrick's day. . . ."

The clouds began to move in by the end of the month and on the last day of February it began to snow again. March 1 came in like a lion and so did the second, third, fourth, and fifth. When the sun did come out on March 6, the city lay buried under forty-four inches of new snow. No one bothered to report on the salubrious predictions of the optimists. They were too busy digging out.

The fierceness of the storm made even old-timers take notice. The wind whipped the new snow into a frenzy in near zero temperatures, packing and freezing the white stuff into any available cranny or crevice. As soon as the shock of the storm was over, dozens of men around town were saying the oft' repeated debunker, "if you think this is bad you should have been in the San Juans, Black Hills, Nome, or the Sierra Nevadas." Robert Berry, one of the first men in the area, recalled the winter of 1871-1872 when sixty days of snow piled so high in Oro City that only the eaves and roof above Tabor's store were visible. The winter of 1884 was said to have been worse. The storm did not last as long, but there was more snow, according to Berry.

Most residents seemed satisfied with the quality of Mother Nature's work, and had no reason to want to risk her wrath further by questioning the quality or quantity of the present winter's snow. Many, in looking around at their world of white, observed the humor of it all, and signs such as the following began to crop up. "Keep off the grass." "Don't pick the flowers." Or, how about, "This lawn reserved for tennis grounds." One person made the mistake of saying he expected the storm to continue on until the twentieth of March at least. He was immediately set upon by listeners in the vicinity and was forced to flee "to escape their wrath."

Nature and man combined to rid the city of some of the snow before spring removed it officially. Warm water from the mines flowed down a number of ditches in the city, and people shoveled snow into them, letting the warm water do its job. On other occasions snow was hauled out of town in wagons and dumped. Hackmen, for instance, decided that there was too much winter piled up in front of the Hotel Vendome (Tabor Grand renamed) and took it upon themselves to remove the excess. Ten wagonloads later the front of the hotel was once more visible from Harrison Avenue. Homeowners who had no crew willing to haul the snow out of town did the best they could. Many were forced to tunnel out to the street. Others cut deep trenches to the streets and to the "necessary" out back.

Skiing had never been anything more than a method of getting around in winter for the people of the high mountains and proved to be nothing more than that in 1899, but it was a popular method.

The storm of the first week of March further confounded the efforts of the railroads to dig out. Hagerman Tunnel had not been reached by a railroad train since the first big January storm.

Throughout the month of March work with plows and snowbirds continued, but progress was very slow, every foot having to be cleared by hand.

The weather had been so bad late in February and in the first week of March that the *Herald Democrat* felt compelled to note on March 7, "Leadville saw a sunset last night for the first time in many weeks." The sunset seemed to herald the end of winter. The weather turned warmer, and while the snow did not begin to melt, it at least settled. Temperatures ranged in the high thirties and forties. As the end of March approached and sunny April was just around the corner, people began to seriously think of digging their way out.

28. Piled on top of all the previous snow was a very wet blanket of new snow thirty-one inches deep. It seemed that snow was going to be the new order of things. Every last storm was followed by another last storm. No one knew it on March 28, but in the next month only nine inches of snow would fall. March 28, 1899, saw the end of the great snow falls of 1899.

Between the fifteenth of January and the twenty-eighth of March, ten weeks, 187 inches of snow fell on Leadville, over fifteen and one-half feet. More fell in the mountains around the city. The Colorado Midland's Hagerman route was closed for seventy-eight days straight; "the mines were shut down by the most prolonged

Snow breaking in early winter with a rotary. Later the snow broke the rotary. *Photo Source: CMHC, Lake County Public Library.*

On March 18 the Rio Grande's rotary broke down at the bottom of Breece Hill, a couple of miles from the Ibex, its goal. Clearing the line would have allowed the owners to reopen the mine and put a lot of men back to work. The situation seemed hopeless, when the miners stepped forward and volunteered to dig out the rest of the track. After all, as they explained, they were tired of being idle and wanted to get back to work.

On the morning of March 20 the volunteers assembled at the Rio Grande depot at 7:00 A.M. and set out for Jonny Hill. The following morning it started to snow. The storm lasted until March

snow storm in the history of the district." Many did not open until summer. And through it all the Leadville Public Schools continued to operate.

Shortly after the last storm a few prospectors from the vicinity began waking up, apparently like the spring-roused bear, and came to town. One, Martin Goring, from Sugar Loaf, told how snow had completely covered his cabin and he had simply hollowed out around it and formed corrals and outbuildings under the snow that were capable of housing a couple of jacks and the hay necessary for their support. He also tunneled to the portal of his mine and had continued to work the claim all winter long. He was quite pleased with his arrangement and expected that it would last well into spring.

Another visitor, Peter Fitzgerald, slipped away from his diggings in Iowa Gulch for a short sojourn in the Magic City. While there he told of his hunting exploits. His cabin was not far from a well-used game trail. The trail in summer went through a low spot, but the snow had simply filled in the low, and Fitzgerald, who had been in India in his younger days, "decided to dig a pit under the crusted snow." The plan, of course, worked. Animals crossing the crust, when they got to the pit, broke through. When Peter came to town he was caring for a pair of mountain sheep and a mountain lion. His immediate problem was what to do with them come spring. There are no stories about a mountain lion who held a grudge and ate his benefactor, so it appears that Peter came up with a satisfactory solution.

In town, the last big storm had brought with it a considerable amount of moisture. When it abated, the snow froze and provided a solid crust atop all the previous snow. The summit of West Eighth Street hill was called Klondike Hill. "The snow is packed in a solid mass in the road, and when going over it with a team the drive is about on a level with the second stories of the residences."

One of the most extraordinary stories of the snow depth concerns George Burkhardt and a sleigh full of lumber. Burkhardt was working as a teamster for the S. L. Smith Lumber Company. He was called upon to haul a load to the upper end of Big Evans Gulch. He set out, walking some of the time, riding some of the time. Periodically he would stop and let the horses blow a bit and check his directions, since almost all the familiar landmarks were under the snow, making the road difficult to follow. He stopped near the greying remains of the old town of Evansville, and rested the horses. When he urged them on with a click of his tongue and a flick of the reins, they were unable to move the sleigh. He backed them a foot or two. It was not frozen down, but when they went forward they stopped again at the same point. Something was clearly wrong, so George walked around the sleigh, and on the other side of the load he saw something sticking up through the snow in front of the runner. He brushed the snow

A loaded sleigh in front of the S. L. Smith Lumber Company. *Photo Source: Colorado Historical Society.*

Leadville High School shortly after its completion in 1900. *Photo Source: Colorado Historical Society.*

away and suddenly it dawned on him what it was. It was the steeple of the old Evansville School!

Spring was not long in coming. A little over two inches of snow fell in May, but most days ranged in the fifties and sixties. The problems of winter now became the problems of spring. All that snow, when it melted, had to go somewhere.

Harrison Avenue was back to the days of the "annual regata" when the camp was just founded and the street was a notorious quagmire. The streets of town were crisscrossed with rivulets of water that, once they established themselves, cut streets into impassable jigsaw puzzle pieces. The roads to the mines were covered with ice and mud, making it almost impossible to ship ore or haul supplies. The railroads were busy trying to open the passes into the area. Hagerman was finally opened just before the last storm in March, but closed then for a short time while it was recleared. The High Line, the South Park's route north out of town, was finally opened on May 25.

The most important boost to the local economy was the opening of the local mines, and most important of those was the reopening of the downtown mines, closed since the strike of 1896. The process began in earnest in the fall of 1898, but, because of winter and funds, it was the following year before the mines could be worked. The unwatering process required massive pumping operations, not only to get the water out, but to keep it out. Franklin Emmons reported that the downtown mines pumped, in April 1899, fifteen million gallons of water per day!

The economy of the camp was shaky as the snow melted and with it the memory of the winter of 1898 and 1899, but the Magic City was looking forward to the twentieth century with considerable optimism. A number of modern homes were constructed during the last summer of the nineteenth century. Modern in the sense that they had central heat, indoor plumbing, and were going away from the ornate style of the Victorian period to a more conservative, less conspicuous look. A new federal building was being planned that would house all federal offices including the Post Office. It was not completed until 1905, but the assurances that it would be built made it clear to the populace that at least the government had confidence in the future of the camp. In March of 1899 the Leadville School Board voted to approve the building of a new high school, to be located in the one hundred block on West Ninth. The plan called for a three-story building, the third floor being little more than a finished attic, sixty-by-ninety feet on a side, with a basement. The estimated cost was $32,875. The building was completed the following year, and students and teachers occupied the building in April of 1900. Also in the planning stages was a city library, partially supported by Andrew Carnegie, and opened for business after the turn of the century.

The awareness that the past was rapidly becoming irretrievable and that it was a lot of fun and worthy of reliving, at least in part, motivated a number of early settlers to form the Society of Leadville Pioneers. They met regularly to enjoy each other's company and to "collect and preserve" information dealing with the Magic City's early history.

Had the old camp finally became civilized? Well, the trappings were there, but the deep-seated refinement that comes of generations of smug security was absent. It was still possible to get some fight out of Leadville people, and for little or no cause.

The Colorado and Southern, the remake of the old Denver, South Park and Pacific, laid track in the southern end of Graham Park. Coming around Iron Hill the Denver and Rio Grande prepared to cross the newly laid C & S track with their own new line. "The Rio Grande had their teams, horses and plows on the ground when the South Park engine and fifty men rushed in." Mr. Irving of the C & S ordered his men to pick up the nearly fifteen yards of track that had been laid on the opposite side of the C & S line, and using it as a battering ram, they charged "into the midst of the horses, carts, plows and men on the other side." Dust and curses filled the air as "men and horses scattered in all directions." The ram was then dropped neatly "at the point where the other side sought to effect a crossing."

It looked as if open war would break out. The C & S planted a pair of ore cars on the spot where the Rio Grande wanted to cross their right-of-way and armed seven men with shotguns to stand guard. Calmer minds prevailed, though, and an agreement was worked out by officials in Denver, and the Denver and Rio Grande built an overhead crossing. Had it been left up to the Leadville contingent, a settlement might have been reached, but a few heads would have been cracked in the process.

Not only was it possible to get a bit of fight out of Leadville in 1899, but it was not too late to start a legend. The Moyer Mine had a reputation for mysterious deeds almost from its inception. Early in the mine's history, there was a terrible mine disaster in which twelve miners were trapped and killed in a cave-in. Their bodies were never recovered and it's said they continue to haunt the mine in protest. Much of the time they rendered various services to the miners, such as frightening them away from potential hazards. One such case concerned a young trammer named Johnny Cumfrey. John was pushing his car through a drift moments before shift change one night, when it was halted by some unseen power. He pushed harder and looked up into a face, white and cold, "intense with woe and agony." That was enough for John. He dashed out of the mine and called for his time. The other miners talked him out of quitting, and he went back down. When he got there he found his tram buried by rock. The ghost had saved his life. That convinced Cumfrey. He quit and vowed not to return. Time and friends got the better of him and sometime later he returned. He worked part of a shift, fell down a stope and broke his leg. After his accident all the talking in the world could not change his mind. He was finished with the Moyer.

Senator Gallagher and his haunting of the Moyer is one of the most misunderstood and misquoted stories in all of Leadville lore. It concerns a Senator Gallagher, who was not related to the Gallagher brothers, nor was he a Leadville man, nor did he work in the Gallagher Mine.* Usually the senator is depicted as an ex-senator from Leadville in the 1880s. Actually he was a state senator from Clear Creek County, Silver Plume to be exact, and a member of the joint legislative committee that investigated the miners' strike in 1897. He was feeling a pinch in his economic affairs and came to Leadville in January of 1900. He found a job in the Moyer and was only on the hill a couple weeks when he was caught by a short fuse and killed. The story tellers have waxed eloquent ever since. One story suggests that the senator was a disbeliever and had come up to the mine to disprove the stories of ghosts. He was confronted by one of the twelve ghost miners at the mouth of the shaft. Gallagher, in an attempt to prove to the massed miners that there was nothing there, walked through the ghost and fell

*In all the directories of Leadville mines, there is no listing of a Gallagher Mine, but those who knew the three Gallagher brothers referred to their holdings (Camp Bird, Pine, Charlestown, Keystone, and Young America) as the Gallagher Mines, and they entered Leadville folklore as the Gallagher Mine.

to the bottom of the shaft. His ghost later roamed the mine property, chasing and frightening people away from the mine.

Another story, usually linked with Gallagher and the Moyer, is constantly repeated to frighten small boys and overly brave little girls. It concerns two miners working alone in an isolated drift late one dark night. They were the only two in the mine and the bucket was down. The next morning when the day shift arrived, they hoisted the bucket and found one of the miners' heads in it. Chilled by what they saw, they went down and found the other worker with a pick in his back. The body of the other miner was never found. The men were convinced it was the work of ghosts, or tommyknockers, as they were called. For some reason the major factor in their thinking was the absence of a body and the fact that the bucket was down. They reasoned that anyone going into the mine to do murder would have to either be in the mine, and there was no one, or he would have had to come up in the bucket, and the bucket would be up.

The facts of the story, if there are any, seem lost in the fiction of the telling, and the story's source is now lost. Still, it is indicative of those tales that seemed to sprout in the damp, dark passages of Leadville's mines and have since grown and matured with successive tellings.

Europeans gave Leadville mining a great boost when the Belgians developed a cheap and efficient method of smelting zinc ore. Another Leadville boom was on its way, and 1900 gave promises of good times in the twentieth century. Untold mineral wealth was yet to be discovered. In 1900 Leadville miners had given little or no thought to zinc, bismuth, manganese, tungsten, tin, or molybdenum.

Leadville as it looked in the early years of the twentieth century. *Photo Source: CMHC, Lake County Public Library.*

XV

Triumph and Tragedy

Leadville at the turn of the century had a pair of banks, the American National Bank, housed in a magnificent stone and brick building on the southeast corner of Fifth and Harrison Avenue, and Hunter and Trimble's Carbonate National Bank at 311 Harrison Avenue. The same three railroads continued to serve the community. Postal Telegraph-Cable Company and Western Union Telegraph competed with Colorado Telephone for the communication business. Seven schools educated the children of Leadville. Of those seven, one was Saint Mary's, a Catholic parochial school. Eleven houses of worship filled the needs of Leadville people, as did a hundred plus saloons. The town boasted a brick manufacturer, two bicycle shops, and three book stores. Charles Boettcher had long since left for Denver and greater fame, and his hardware store had become the Leadville Hardware Company. David May was also gone, as was May Company. Daniels, Fisher and Smith had become, simply, J. W. Smith Dry Goods Company. Daniels and Fisher, like so many others, saw the growth potential of the Mile High City and took their money and experience and invested it in Denver.

Two large hotels, the Tabor Grand, renamed Vendome, and across the street, the Delaware, handled most of the traveling trade, while a number of smaller hotels and several boarding houses took care of the semi-permanent traffic. The Leadville Illuminating Gas Company was fighting a losing battle with the Leadville Light Company. Gaslights cast their final romantic glow in 1901, when the two combined their efforts, converted the city lights to electricity and became the Leadville Gas and Electric Company. An indication of how settled the town had become was

the drop in lawyers — 120 in 1880 to 21 in 1900.

Five smelters served the needs of the Leadville District. The old Elgin plant north of town had become the Boston Gold-Copper Smelting Company and was the only one of four Big Evans smelters still in operation. The Union Smelter was erected south of the old Leadville Blues baseball field, and the Leadville Public Sampling works was housed in the ruins of Governor Grant's famous plant on Front Street. The Arkansas Valley Smelting Plant and the Bi-Metallic Smelter, erected on the site of the old La Plata Smelter in 1892, were part of the newly organized American Smelting and Refining Company.

Over four thousand miners worked in the Leadville mines on the first day of January 1900, producing over three thousand tons of ore each day. The ore averaged between ten and twenty dollars per ton. Thomas Tonge, writing in *Engineering Magazine* in 1900, proclaimed, "The permanency of Leadville is absolutely assured, and all present indications are that there will be profitable mining in the Leadville district a hundred years hence." As the twenty-first century draws nigh, it appears that Tonge was correct, but the almost three generations that separate the Tonge prediction from current soothsayers were difficult, heart-breaking years of regression and change, of hope and hopelessness, of courage and despair. And, if there is a Leadville character, it was molded more by this experience than by the boom and bust, chicken today-feathers tomorrow, attitude of the silver era.

After 1900 the Leadville mines produced a more balanced variety of minerals. Looking back through the previous two decades a number of factors contributed to the successful development of what was called the Composite Era. First, smelter costs had been reduced considerably. Second, cost of coal had dropped seventy-five percent since 1880 and fifty percent since 1890. Third, cost of pumping had been cut in half with much, but not all, of that reduction the result of reduced coal prices. Fourth, freight rates had gone down fifty percent. Fifth, local teamsters had been replaced at all but a few out of the way mines by railway spurs. The above reduction in major expenses, plus the stability of wages, made it possible to work a number of low grade ore bodies that earlier showed no economic promise.

Zinc became the most important single metal of the period when early in 1899 zinc ore from the Moyer mine was shipped to Belgium, via Galveston, Texas. Its impact and the difficulties of making such a shipment were similar to August R. Meyer's shipment of silver ore to St. Louis almost one-quarter of a century earlier. In 1901 two zinc processing plants were erected in Colorado, and zinc production in Leadville shot up from a little over one-half million dollars in 1899 to over two million dollars in 1902. Silver and lead production remained relatively steady on a year to year basis, but over the period, slid downward. Gold production for the Leadville district hit its peak in 1900 when it accounted for roughly one-fifth of the district's total annual production. Copper production usually complemented gold production, since the two were often found together. Two newcomers to Leadville production history were manganese and bismuth. Few statistics were recorded for them or for old standards like iron and nickel. The best estimates

indicate production of all four were under one million dollars per year, not so much because of a shortage of ore, but rather difficulties in smelting and especially in marketing. "Leadville," exclaimed the *Herald Democrat* in exasperation, "can supply the world's demand for bismuth, but the syndicate that controls this metal will not allow it to be marketed."

During the miner's strike of 1896 the downtown mines were allowed to flood, and it was not until the eve of the twentieth century that they were pumped dry again and were in full production. The unwatering of the downtown district provided a tremendous boost to the local economy. Several hometown leasing companies were formed around the turn of the century. These new enterprises took leases on a number of mines, giving them control of a specific area. They then set about developing large scale operations that included purchasing the newest machinery and using the latest technology, which in turn made the working of low grade ores quite lucrative.

Late in 1907 the economic recovery of the Leadville district was halted, as it had been halted so many times before, by events outside of the district, outside of the state, and often outside of the nation.

The Panic of 1907 was brought about by the tight money policies of the government, extensive growth based on credit and poor banking policies. The money crisis dried up the metals' market, and for a short time Leadville teetered on the brink of disaster. The downtown district was once again allowed to flood, closing the whole area. Gold continued unabated, but the silver-lead market plummeted, and zinc died. The ef-

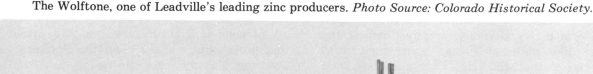

The Wolftone, one of Leadville's leading zinc producers. *Photo Source: Colorado Historical Society.*

The serving crew in the "banquet stope" of the Wolftone. *Photo Source: CMHC, Lake County Public Library.*

fects were not seen in the production figures of 1907, but the following year the Magic City's output went from over ten million dollars in 1907 to one-half that in 1908. Zinc income dropped over seventy percent.

Fortunately, the panic was of short duration and recovery began almost immediately, aided by the discovery in 1910 of zinc carbonates in a number of important mines. Recovery was also aided by a few farsighted mining men who realized Leadville would come back strong if owners did not panic. One such leader was Samuel Danford Nicholson, president and general manager of the A.M.W. Company, a combination of the Adams, Maid of Erin, Wolftone and several lesser properties. Nicholson, two-time Leadville mayor, practical, hard-headed, and devoted to Leadville, continued to run the pumps in his mines, worked his men, stockpiled his ore, and in so doing kept a number of other Carbonate Hill mines, dependent on the A.M.W.'s pumps, open. When the panic was over Nicholson had 20,000 tons of ore stockpiled and was not burdened with the heavy start-up costs that faced other, more cautious, producers.

Early in 1911 Nicholson decided to celebrate the rebirth of Leadville mining, and especially the tremendous zinc carbonate potential of the A.M.W. Company, with a great underground banquet in the Wolftone. The idea was not new; the Yak Tunnel had hosted underground events, but it is the "Bobby" Burns Day banquet, January 25, 1911, that everyone remembers. The great body of zinc ore in the Wolftone was so immense that it was "Measured, not in feet, but in 'acres.'" The mayor of Leadville, Henry C. Rose, proclaimed January 25, 1911, a legal holiday. The festivities were city wide, celebrating not only the discovery of vast quantities of ore in the Wolf-

Mrs H.H.Norton

Mr. S. D. Nicholson requests the pleasure

of your company at

Lunch at the Wolftone Mine

January twenty-fifth, nineteen hundred and eleven

Sleighs will leave the Vendome hotel

ten-thirty a. m. sharp

Photo Source: Author's Collection.

tone, as well as in other mines in the district, but that Leadville had again survived the vicissitudes of the mining industry.

The guest list included 250 well-known Coloradoans and residents of the Cloud City. A seven-piece orchestra played in the flag and bunting bedecked "banquet stope," while John E. Miller's staff from the Star Bakery served the luncheon. It was a grand day for Leadville and was topped off with the announcement that a new discovery had been made. Nicholson had sent an unidentified sample of zinc ore to the Colorado School of Mines, only to find that it was indeed unidentified. The new mineral was named nicholsonite in honor of Leadvile's man of the hour.

Water, as mentioned several times, was the Leadville nemesis. The ultimate solution was generally agreed upon; tunnel deep beneath the mining area and drain the mines from below. What was not agreed upon was where to tunnel from and how to finance the undertaking. The problem the Leadville mines presented was their depth. It was impossible to enter the district any place short of the Arkansas Valley without coming in above the deeper working, and the cost of what was called the Malta Tunnel scared most away. Discussion of such a project had been carried on since the 1880s, and work actually was started in 1892, but was halted because of the silver crisis in 1893. In 1908, Max Boehmer, highly respected mining engineer, reopened the topic with an open letter to the *Herald Democrat.* Good men and arguments supported the project. The success of the Yak Tunnel in California Gulch was constantly pointed out. If it was successful at its depth, then how much more successful would be the Malta Tunnel some six hundred feet deeper.

The arguments for the project were sound, but three overwhelming objections killed it. The one million dollar plus price tag, expensive dead work through three miles of wash, and the barrenness of the mineral area at the tunnel's great depth. The hope of striking pay ore was limited since, at its depth, the tunnel, once east of the downtown and Fryer Hill area, would be in barren granite — fine for drainage but void of metal values.

The Yak, in spite of the discussions, was quite another matter. In 1889 Professor A. A. Blow, manager of the Silver Cord Combination, began developing a tunnel from California Gulch under his property on Iron Hill. The Blow Tunnel, as it was called, was about four thousand feet long in 1894 when it was purchased by the Yak Mining, Milling and Tunnel Company, headed by August R. Meyer. Meyer and his associates, among whom were ex-mayor William H. James and ex-governor James B. Grant, decided that the recent gold discoveries on Breece Hill, and more specifically in the Ibex properties, could be unwatered and worked more effectively through a tunnel. In addition, they would no doubt expose a number of exciting prospects along the tunnel's route.

In 1904, during the last week of April, the Yak Tunnel made contact with Ibex No. 4, two miles from the tunnel's mouth. Mules were used

Yak Tunnel at the base of Iron Hill. *Photo Source: CMHC, Lake County Public Library.*

up to that time for transportation and haulage, but in October the whole Yak operation was converted to electricity with the completion of the Yak Power Plant. Additional electricity was sold to many of the mines in the region, and a contract was entered into by the Yak and the Leadville Gas and Electric Company on November 15, 1906, to supply power to the city.

It was decided to develop the tunnel past the Ibex property on Breece Hill, the original Yak incorporators' goal, and tap the mines in the upper end of Evans Gulch. Shortly after World War I the Yak reached Resurrection No. 2, about three and one-half miles from the mouth of the tunnel. Mines all along its route were unwatered, a benefit for which they paid the Yak Mining, Milling and Tunnel Company. Many of the mines along the route were worked through the tunnel and for that privilege they also paid. The company owned a considerable number of claims outright, others they leased and paid royalty on, still others were held in "perpetual contract," which gave the Yak an easement through the property and allowed the owner to work his own mine if he desired. He was expected to pay for transportation and unwatering services, plus a ten percent royalty on all ore he shipped.

The Yak Tunnel provided its owners with a steady income for almost half a century, and it is still a part of local mining operations. It enabled several marginal properties to operate in the black by lowering their overhead. It cost, for instance, an estimated $4.42 per ton in 1911 to mine ore through shafts. The average cost per ton of ore through the Yak Tunnel for the period 1908 to 1913 was about $1.97, or a net savings of $2.45 per ton.

Social life in the early years of the twentieth century, when good women did not drink, and good men did, saw an evening division of the sexes. The men went to their favorite haunts, the Topic, Otto Thurns, the Elks' Club Bar, or "Billy" Markley's, and the women played bridge. As one woman recalled, it had "its good points, namely, we wives got rid of our pestiferous Lords and Masters being under foot." All of the teas and socials of the nineties seem to have evolved after the turn of the century into cutthroat bridge for married ladies. The hostess always gave a booby prize and a first prize, many of which were quite expensive and well worth a special effort to win. "Honestly, I wouldn't have been surprised to see the lady of the winning score march home with a diamond ring on her finger." And the food, before national physical fitness caught on, was

fattening, delicious, and plentiful.

After talking about the violence, noise, footpads, and vigilantes of Leadville's youth, it might be hard to imagine those same bridge playing matrons striking out for home, long after dark and unafraid, returning to unlocked homes. But when Leadville became respectable it also became honest. Mean dogs and bad sidewalks were the most frightening things confronting these ladies.

One of the most popular social activities was the Sunday drive, no longer with old Dobbin, but in the new car. Several clubs organized, and great honor was bestowed upon the driver who, each spring, was the first to negotiate Tennessee Pass. In concert with the advent of the automobile was the cry for better roads. As early as July of 1915 the telephone company was providing a free road bulletin service.

The Weston Opera House, nee Tabor Opera House, became the Elks Opera House late in 1901. About $20,000 was spent on remodeling before it reopened on December 11, 1902. It became the social center of Leadville for the next fifty years.

As the effect of the Panic of 1907 was not really felt until the following year, the same was true of World War I. It was not until 1915 that the impact of the increased demands of the combatants was felt in the mining industry of the West. Several developments were the direct result of that increased demand.

Plans were made to begin unwatering the downtown district in 1914. Production from those important mines, closed by water since the Panic of 1907, began in 1915, and they were in full production by 1916. Also, the mines on Fryer Hill were brought back into production as a result of

Leadville Saloon at the turn of the century. *Photo Source: Author's Collection.*

Automobile outing on Tennessee Pass in 1913. *Photo Source: Colorado Historical Society.*

Derry Gold Dredge. *Photo Source: CMHC, Lake County Public Library.*

an unwatering project started in 1915 through the Harvard shaft. South of town on the old Derry Ranch near Twin Lakes, a gold dredge began operation, working the ancient gravels of "old man" Derry's hay ranch. In the first year of operation the 50,000-pound "digging spud" hauled up "about 90,000 cubic yards of gold-bearing-placer dirt a month, at a profit of 10 cents per cubic yard." The dredge continued to operate throughout the war and sporadically into the mid-twenties.

With all the zinc that Leadville produced from 1900 to the beginning of the Great War, it never possessed a zinc smelter. Several mills produced concentrates, but it was not until April of 1915 that Western Zinc Oxide Company, Leadville's first zinc smelter, shipped the district's first refined product.

By far the most important and lasting of the wartime additions to the Leadville mining scene was the opening of the vast molybdenum reserves on Bartlett Mountain. Bartlett Mountain sits almost astride the continental divide and looks westerly toward what old-timers called Arkansas Pass, later named Fremont Pass in honor of the Pathfinder, John Charles Fremont. The pass

separates the headwaters of the Arkansas River from Ten Mile River, an eventual tributary of the Pacific-bound Colorado. The general area atop the pass was called Climax, after the Colorado and Southern's station at the 11,320-foot summit.

In 1879 Charles J. Senter, Civil War veteran and graduate of the Indian wars in South Dakota, arrived in Leadville with Juanita Crowfoot, his Indian bride. After a short time in the Magic City he set out for the Ten Mile District, built himself a cabin in or near the shortlived boom town of Carbonateville, and began placer mining. On August 17, 1879, he staked a pair of claims (not recorded until 1895), the Gold Reef and Gold Reef No. 2, high on the southwest side of Bartlett Mountain. The years passed, gold alluded him, but he continued to work the area and puzzle, not about the gold, but the heavy, grey, black-lined rock that he found in abundance. In 1890 he sent samples to Colorado School of Mines and was told it was a commercially worthless "composite ore carrying antimony, graphite and sulphur." In 1896 he met, by chance, a Mr. Britton, tin manufacturer from Cleveland, who became interested in the ore, thinking it might contain tin. Britton took samples with him to Swansea, Wales, where

Molybdenum mine at Climax. *Photo Source: AMAX*

he was going on business, and there the material was correctly identified as molybdenum.

In Iowa young Otis Archie King, five-foot-five, one hundred and forty pounds soaking wet, and full of ambition and "the darndest little fighter" in the Climax story, was just finishing college. He went into banking in Wayne, Nebraska, where he came to the attention of one of the directors, Wilson H. Pingrey, who owned a mine near Kokomo, a mile or so downstream from Senter's cabin. The mine suffered from mismanagement, and Pingrey, sensing King's aggressive ability, offered him the manager's job. King immediately accepted.

Not long after King arrived in Kokomo he was visited by "an old man with long gray hair and kindly blue eyes" named Charlie Senter. It was 1912 and Senter was still trying to peddle his molybdenum. King visited Senter's claims on Bartlett Mountain, and after looking the site over, asked how much Senter would take for the pair. Forty thousand was the reply. King took a two-year option on the Gold Reef claims for five

hundred dollars plus fifty dollars a month, and started digging.

In the meantime, Pingrey's Kokomo property was showing signs of being played out, and he instructed King to find him another mine. King was successful and located a lead-zinc producer near Silverton, Colorado. Unfortunately, the ore was extremely complex. King leased the Leadville District Mill in California Gulch, hired a mining engineer named George Backus, and the pair set about solving the problem of the sulphide ores from Silverton. They employed a British flotation process that was not only successful with their Silverton ores and Leadville's own lead-zinc ores, but also with the ores from Bartlett Mountain. Having found a way to produce molybdenum concentrates, King was ready to market his product. He shipped almost six thousand pounds of molybdenum sulphide to the York Metal Alloy Company in York, Pennsylvania, in 1915. They paid a reported $2,525 per ton. Giddy with success, he received a letter from the company explaining that his was the largest shipment of

Digging for molybdenum under Bartlett Mountain. *Photo Source: AMAX.*

molybdenum ever made by any company and would satisfy the world's need for two years. What to do with a mountain of the stuff? Disillusioned, King let the Pingrey Mines and Ore Reduction Company's option on the Senter claims lapse in July of 1916.

In the years before World War I Germany pioneered the use of molybdenum in armament steel. It was not until late in 1916, two years after war broke out in Europe, that America began to experiment with molybdenum on a large scale. Three months after King allowed the Senter option to lapse, the nation suddenly began to express a demand for molybdenum. He quickly renewed the options and began producing molysulphide.

In 1881 in Frankfurt, Germany, a merchant family of German Jews incorporated the old family business of Philipp Abraham Cohen as *Metallgesellschaft* (metal company). Several years before, a daughter of Cohen, Sarah Amalie, married Raphael Moses of London, England. Moses, by court decree, changed his name to Ralph Merton. A son, Henry Ralph Merton, established Henry R. Merton and Company of London. A second Merton son, Wilhelm, became a leading figure in the *Metallgesellschaft* in Frankfurt. The family, by the early 1880s was firmly established in Germany and Britain as ore, mineral, and metal traders.

The Ladenburg family, prominent members of Frankfurt's monied upper crust, married a daughter to Wilhelm Merton. In 1880 the Ladenburg family established a private banking firm in New York City called Ladenburg, Thalman and Company. The stage was set.

It was Christmas Eve, 1886. Wilhelm Merton, the family's recognized leader, sat visiting with Jacob Langeloth, deputy member of the executive board of *Metallgesellschaft*. Langeloth told Merton about his recent visit to London and the wonderful things he had heard about the potential of America, and he recommended the establishment of a company there. "Within half an hour, Wilhelm Merton had authorized the venture."

By June of 1887, at Wilhelm Merton's insistence, the London, Frankfurt, and New York companies created a fourth American corporation called American Metal Company, Limited (Amco). They engaged in trade and reduction, but excluded mining as too risky. Shortly after the company was organized, the Ladenburg/Thalman interests pulled out and their stock was picked up by members of the London/Frankfurt interests. From 1887 to 1914 the company prospered as the

American part of an international metals triumvirate. On the eve of the First World War, the *Metallgesellschaft* owned forty-nine percent of the American Metal Company's stock. The remaining half was held by London associates, family members, and a few minor American directors. On the eve of the Great War, less than forty stockholders controlled the American Metal Company, and none of them had ever heard of Bartlett Mountain, but they would.

Over the years, Charles Senter was not the only one groping around Bartlett Mountain. Sam and John Webber and E. G. Heckendorf of Denver had staked a number of claims on Bartlett Mountain in 1890. They had their find assayed and were told it was graphite, so they dropped the claims. In 1895, a Professor Linderman correctly identified their ore as molybdenite. Between 1889 and 1902, Senter became active again and located four more claims lying parallel to and adjoining his earlier patents, the New Discovery, Mountain Chief, Mountain Maid, and New Discovery No. 2. Shortly after locating the four he sold them to a pair of Nebraskans, Hugh Leal and D. P. Turney. In 1902 Leal discovered molybdenum while looking for a "gold bearing fissure" on the south slope of Bartlett Mountain. King picked up a $100,000 option on the Leal property with terms similar to those he gave Senter, but later allowed the option to lapse.

Heckendorf and the Webber brothers were discouraged, but they, too, had not given up. They located a number of claims in the area between 1911 and 1914. Then, according to his own account, Heckendorf secured options on the Leal claims, a pair of Senter claims (the Gold Reef claims King had dropped options on), and two located by a local rancher named Buffehr. In October 1916, he presented Max Schott, the American Metal Company's representative in Denver, with a proposal to develop the properties. Schott sent a couple of representatives of Amco to investigate the site. The report was favorable, and the American Metal Company took options on the property on November 16, 1916.

It was the policy of the metals' triumverate to create a subsidiary in risky ventures such as the one on Bartlett Mountain, so they began organizing the Climax Molybdenum Company. Heckendorf and Associates were to get twenty-five percent of the stock and the remaining three-quarters was to be divided up among various individuals, "chiefly officers and directors of Amco" with the company retaining a scant, low risk, seven and one-half percent. In the meantime, the work in Colorado was carried on through the

American Metal Company. Also, to muddy an already muddy stream, in 1904 or 1905 a G. A. Gillaspey staked the Denver claim in the midst of others. When Heckendorf was picking up options he attempted to get one on Gillaspey's property, but was unable to do so. The developers of the Denver claim, in the midst of the Heckendorf options, organized the Molybdenum Products Company, built a mill and began producing molysulphide.

Finally in January of 1918 the legal work was done and Climax Molybdenum Company was born. As finally organized, Heckendorf, the two Webber brothers, and an unknown investor named Dr. Harris each received stock in the company equal to five percent for a total of twenty percent. What happened to Senter and Buffehr? Heckendorf had options on both properties in the summer of 1916. Later, when King decided to get back in business, Senter and Buffehr apparently bought up their options or had escape clauses in the option, and rejoined King. With the withdrawal of Senter and Buffehr, Heckendorf's one-quarter interest in the company was apparently reduced to twenty percent.

The situation, then, in 1918 on Bartlett Mountain saw the Denver claim being worked by the Climax Molybdenum Products Company; the Senter claims being worked by the Pingrey Mines and Ore Reduction Company, Otis Archie King at the helm; and the Heckendorf-Webber property in the hands of Climax Molybdenum Company, easily the most vigorous and best financed of the trio. In mid-August 1917, before Amco's subsidiary corporation (Climax Molybdenum Company) was ready to take over, the syndicate approved the spending of $300,000 for development. In February 1918, when the newly incorporated subsidiary finally took control, ore bins, a crusher, mill, bunkhouses, an 800-foot jib back tramway, and a mile long aerial tramway had been completed, and some three hundred men were at work.

The Climax Molybdenum Company had no love for Otis Archie King, nor his Pingrey operation. They first tried intimidation, but he would not be intimidated. They took him to court, and in thirteen tries were unsuccessful, but the hearings were expensive and the resources of the Pingrey interests were not near those of the opposition.

Climax Molybdenum Company during the lean years immediately following World War I. *Photo Source: AMAX.*

Finally, late in 1918, a compromise was reached. Climax Molybdenum Company purchased the Ella N (King's own claim) and the Pingrey water rights necessary for milling operations, for $40,000. Shortly after King sold out, Gillaspey's Molybdenum Products Company threw in the towel. Then in 1926 King capitulated completely and sold the remaining Pingrey holdings for $300,000.

When the United States entered the war in April 1917, the government froze all foreign assets. The Merton Company, because of its German association, was already in trouble with the British government and was forced to liquidate. In 1920, two years after the war, the U.S. government sold the American Metal Company stock held by the *Metallgesellschaft*. The shares were bought by members of American Metal Company and the rest went to interested American investors. American Metal Company, which started as an American branch of a European family enterprise, became wholly American in 1920. The Climax subsidiary of the company was almost dead at the time. The demand for molybdenum in England and Russia during the war prompted the Climax development. Then Russia signed a separate peace at Brest-Litovsk in March 1918, and the Russian market was dead. Eight months later the war ended. It left the mines on Bartlett Mountain producing more molybdenum than the world could use. Climax Molybdenum Company was forced to close in March of 1919. The shutdown looked permanent, and the investors would have sold, if anyone would have bought.

Science, in the person of Brainerd Phillipson, a 1913 Columbia graduate, oresman, and honor student, sold industry, especially the automobile makers, on moly steel. In 1924 Climax Molybdenum went back into production. Looking at the Leadville record at the time, one could hardly believe that the mines on Bartlett Mountain would ultimately out produce the Leadville District.

When Europe went to war in August of 1914 the concern in Leadville was for the price of metals, and what effect the war might have on production. As the war progressed, however, and the Belgian atrocity stories began to work their way across the Atlantic via Britain, Leadville began to take sides, and since there were large numbers of Northern Europeans in the Magic City, a certain amount of unpleasantness, name calling for the most part, tended to cool the American melting pot.

As the war progressed and industry across the country expanded because of the increased demand for goods in Europe, labor was in great demand. Between 1915 and 1917 large numbers of Mexican Americans began to arrive and work in Leadville's smelters. Most came from northern New Mexico and the San Luis Valley of Colorado, but a considerable number were Mexican nationals escaping the upheavals convulsing that country during World War I.

War news was important, but on January 1, 1916, domestic affairs predominated. On that day, Leadville suffered the most severe social blow of its history. Prohibition was enacted in Colorado. Voting on the amendment to the state constitution was held on November 3, 1915. The state approved the amendment. Lake County disapproved it two to one. Sixty-six saloons closed in Lake County. Fifty served the Leadville area. Seven wholesalers folded. Leadville's venerable Columbine Brewery planned to convert to "some temperance drink." They failed to make the change. The amendment also closed three drugstore liquor departments. The City of Leadville lost over $27,000 in annual revenue and approximately 210 men were thrown out of work. For a workingman's town like Leadville, it was a setback equal to a smelter strike or a serious drop in the price of metals.

It might be worth noting that the first arrest in the new, dry year of 1916, made on February 14, was for drunkenness. The effects of the new order were quickly felt as the citizens' cache of stockpiled booze was consumed. It was rumored on the eve of prohibition that a complete still was hidden above Sugar Loaf, and it was rhetorically asked, "Will the new law tempt the venturesome. . . ?" It was assumed not. In fact, the New Year's edition of the *Herald Democrat* saw one soothsayer proclaiming, "It does not seem probable that 'bootlegging' will become common in Lake County." By the end of the year, local courts would hear eighty-two cases concerning liquor violations.

Late in the summer of 1916 raids on speakeasies and arrests of bootleggers were making headlines. The following year twenty-six "soft drink parlors" opened up in old saloons. Most did not limit themselves to soft drinks. When a drunk was apprehended, and several were, they were usually fined three dollars and costs, and then asked where they got the booze. The standard response was, from "a little old man." It was possible to purchase alcohol for medicinal purposes provided a permit was secured from the courthouse. Lake County had the distinction of being

Leadville, a cold winter day, on the eve of World War I. *Photo Source: H. B. Leith.*

the sickest county in Colorado based on comparative populations.

April 6, 1917, the United States declared war on Germany and her allies. Leadville went to war with the usual mustering of bands, an abundance of flags and bunting, and speech making, all of which generated a marked eagerness on the part of a large number of innocent young men to find the nearest recruiting office. As the war progressed, that "unpleasantness" toward natives of the Central Powers, characterizing the period before America became involved, suddenly grew cruel and often vicious. "Draft slacker" became a bad word, and several young immigrants, many of whom could not even read the draft notices, were corraled and told to join or else. Many were faced with fighting against their own countrymen, but in Leadville, as in other communities around the nation, that excuse did not wash. The city herded all of the town's vagrants together in June of 1918 and issued a "work or fight order." Eight were jailed. When the war ended, the bitterness lasted for years. It took another World War to wipe it out altogether.

The great influenza pandemic that began its sweep of the globe during the closing moments of the war, struck Leadville in early autumn. The first Leadville death from the flu epidemic was recorded on October 1, 1918. By the end of the month the death toll was averaging ten a day. Mines closed, schools closed, public meetings were forbidden, strict quarantines were enforced, and grocery deliveries halted. Burial of the dead had to be accomplished within twenty-four hours, and funerals had to be held in mortuaries rather than in private homes with no more than four relatives permitted to attend. By Christmas, the worst was over, but 223 new graves attested to the fury of the three-month scourge. Worldwide the death toll climbed to thirty million.

The weeks and months that followed the war were not good to Leadville. The Midland Railroad went into receivership and was dismantled. Her yards were turned over to the city for recreational purposes. Metal prices dropped, and many of the mines were forced to close, Climax among them. Food prices skyrocketed during the war, but wages failed to keep pace. Prices did decline momentarily after the war, but by March of 1919 butter was selling for seventy-five cents a pound and flour was up to $6.25 per hundred, double what they had been before the war. Locally the mines were posting one dollar a day wage cuts, which would put most miners at $3.50 a day, virtually wiping out the modest gains they had made during the war years.

On April 20, 1919, the miners walked out. Three days later, they accepted a fifty-cent an hour compromise cut in pay, and went back to work. Several mines failed to reopen because of the falling metal prices. Statistics dramatically tell the story. In 1916, the district's banner year, production stood at over sixteen million dollars; three years later in 1919, it had dropped to less than five million. Leadville's population in 1900 was over twelve thousand. In 1920 it stood at forty-five hundred; a sixty percent population loss in twenty years. And the worst was yet to come.

The Greenback, a major producer during the twenties. *Photo Source: Author's Collection.*

XVI

Hard Times

Mining, like agriculture, never really recovered from the recession following World War I. There was a slight upward surge in metal prices in the late twenties, but the surge was too short-lived and, coupled with the increased cost of operation, was unimportant in the long run. Nineteen twenty-nine saw the stock market collapse, and with it the financial well-being of the nation. The Leadville district's production bottomed out in 1932 when a scant $143,142 worth of ore was produced. It was a struggle back up the ladder, and it was not until 1942 that the Magic City began to exhibit some of that old metal magic.

During the period between the wars, several attempts were made to increase production; the most famous and serious attempt was the Canterbury Tunnel. In October of 1920, a reorganized and revitalized Leadville Chamber of Commerce held a meeting of important mining men and discussed possible programs for stimulating the local economy. A survey was taken and the consensus indicated they preferred a locally supported mining effort in the Prospect Mountain region. Planning began immediately, and the Leadville Mining Development Company was incorporated on January 1, 1921. The company was organized for $150,000 at $1.00 per share, and its purpose was the construction of a tunnel running from the northwestern slope of Prospect Mountain, an area known as Canterbury Hill, southeast

This group of Leadville miners never saw the boom of the eighties or the flush years before World War I. They lived through the hard times between the World Wars. *Photo Source: Rose Green.*

John Cortellini, the most prominent figure in the Leadville mining and political scene from 1920 to 1945. *Photo Source: Rose Green.*

stockholders. The corporation was headed by some of the leading metallurgical minds of the district, with ex-governor Jesse F. MacDonald at the top of the list as president. John Cortellini, president of the Chamber of Commerce, was vice president, while William Harvey, Ezra D. Dickerman, and Joseph W. Clarke served as treasurer, consulting engineer, and secretary, respectively.

Stock sold well and work began on March 8, 1921. The project was a model of barebones operation. Nothing was wasted, much was donated and, as Mr. Cortellini explained, no one, not even the directors, received "a cent of the money invested except the men who use the 'pick and shovel' in the mine." Over the years the tunnel consumed thousands of local dollars, unwatered a number of marginal mines, and failed to discover any major bodies of good ore. After tunneling almost four thousand feet, the project was abandoned in the late twenties.

A more successful project, the Leadville Deep Mines Company, was initiated by Stevens and Leiter's old Iron Silver Mining Company in 1922. Unwatering of a large area of the northern end of Graham Park and Stray Horse Gulch near Finntown with massive, steam-driven pumps began in May of 1923. Such important producers as the Mikado, Greenback, Wolftone, R.A.M., Robert Emmet, Pyrenees, Adams, and Mahala were leased by the company and began producing in 1925. The area was active and quite productive until 1931 when known ore bodies were exhausted and prices did not justify further exploration. Nothing significant has been done in that area since their closing. The following year the parent company, the venerable old Iron Silver Mining Company, founded fifty years earlier in 1878, closed down, with no hope of reopening. Her

beneath the Evans Gulch, Fryer Hill, and Stray Horse Gulch area. The company's first objective was to unwater the mines on Fryer Hill as well as those in the northern sections of Iron and Carbonate Hills. Their second objective was to discover enough pay ore along their route to pay expenses and hopefully provide a handsome profit to the

John Cortellini at the mouth of the Canterbury Tunnel watching the unwatering operation. *Photo Source: Heritage Museum and Gallery.*

mines were exhausted and prices had fallen so low that development work was out of the question.

In 1931 the price of metal was so low that gold was the only product worthy of mining. Leadville's one hundred plus working mines in 1900 had shrunk to twenty-six by 1931. By 1933 silver had dropped to twenty-three and one-half cents an ounce, the lowest ever recorded.

In 1933 America had a new president. He promised a New Deal for the American people. A part of that New Deal was a gold purchase plan. The U.S. treasury bid the price of gold up from twenty dollars an ounce to thirty-five dollars an ounce, where it was "pegged." The action had an immediate effect on Leadville's gold producers. The Ibex spent $30,000 upgrading and by 1937 was the largest single shipper to the Arkansas Valley Smelter. After years of inactivity, placer operations started again in California Gulch, and more talk of drainage tunnels, a sure sign of hope springing eternal, spread through the Magic City. Drainage projects designed to get federal support were continuously submitted during the thirties, as were requests for a lead-zinc subsidy. Neither bore fruit.

Climax continued to grow throughout the decade before World War II, and in the mid-thirties Climax built a town for its employees that included the finest in recreational facilities, an excellent school, and a well-equipped, well-staffed hospital. Even so, many miners, as roads and maintenance improved, chose to live in Leadville and drive the twelve miles to work.

During the years before the stock market crash, Leadville sensed the demise of the Leadville district and tried unsuccessfully to develop alternate industries. David M. Hartford Productions, late of Hollywood, claimed they were going to move, lock, stock, and silent film sets, to Leadville in 1920. They actually began building west of the city in October of 1920. Another company, Art-o-Graf, announced in November of 1920 that they were going to build "temporary studios" in the Magic City. In December the *Herald Democrat* reported that Art-o-Graf plans were taking "definite form in connection with the production of a motion picture in Lake County." They all went away and nothing ever came of Leadville's chance to be the Hollywood of the Hills.

Mine crew at the Garbutt in the early 1930s. *Photo Source: Rose Green.*

229

Climax mine in 1930s, atop Fremont Pass. *Photo Source: Author's Collection.*

Ice, cut from nearby lakes, an activity that had been around for years, was thought for a time to have some commercial value for the community, as was the growing of lettuce. Several crops were grown, but only in the best years did the project pay. South of Leadville, at Buena Vista, the same project prospered and added sustenance to that community, but Leadville's chances of agriculture on a paying scale were fleeting.

The twenties were fitful times for Leadville; times of great hopes and false starts, disillusionment, and great fun. For a while in 1920 it looked as if the Colorado Midland would get back on its feet. A summer was exhausted getting the tracks in shape and repairing the Busk-Ivanhoe tunnel, then, with the line ready to go into operation, word was received on October 22, to "start junking the Aspen branch of the road." The Midland went into receivership for the last time a few months later. The old Midland grade to Aspen was converted into an automobile route and was used continuously until 1943, when the Busk-Ivanhoe Tunnel (renamed Carlton Tunnel) became too dangerous to keep open. It is now used solely for water diversion.

When the Midland folded, its property on the west side of town was given to the city for recreational purposes. Leadville built a baseball diamond, which is still in use, named Carlton Field, in honor of the Midland's last president. Another portion of the area was converted into a tourist campground called Schraeder Park. The city chipped in $250 to help with the project and the rest was donated by local citizens. Tourism was an alternative to mining that appeared to have some real merit, and the park was filled with summer campers even before it was completed.

In the twenties the second largest business in Leadville, other than mining and smelting, was bootlegging. There is no way to determine the number of people who directly or indirectly owed their livelihood to the production, transportation, or sale of illegal hooch, but it was considerable. It has been said that the local stills not only supplied Leadville, but much of the state as well. The town, of course, paid a price. Its 1880s reputation for villainy and transgression was not enhanced by being central Colorado's liquor capital in the 1920s. Stills were located and raided in all the abandoned mining areas around the city, and in many of the boarded-up buildings in town, including Tabor's old bank. Several fires and explosions were attributed to the bootlegging industry, while a number of people were hospitalized and a few died of "Alcoholic poisoning." The most important direct result of prohibition in Leadville was, like the rest of the country, the lawlessness it fostered and encouraged. As one news reporter put it after a recap of the murders, holdups, burglaries, and vandalism in 1923, "As it was in the beginning, is now and ever shall be, Leadville without law, Amen."

The struggle to keep Leadville alive and well in the early twenties, and to present a bright, hopeful face to the world was difficult. A Denver paper noted that Leadville's 1920 census was unkind, and explained the population had dropped forty percent in ten years. "Experts say Leadville has been pretty well worked out. Don't tell that to a genuine Leadvilleite." Frank Vaughn, editor of the *Herald Democrat* and part-time poet, was a full-time Leadville booster. In 1922 he penned a poem called, "We're Going to Keep the Old Town on the Map," and in it he admitted, "Times have been a bit distressing/And troubles came in crowds," but with a burst of local chauvinism,

finished, "We will give to friend and brother/A message of good cheer,/And, you bet, we'll keep the old town on the map." Saying it was one thing. Doing it was another.

The late twenties looked promising compared to the early twenties. The city began paving Harrison Avenue. By 1930 the job was done, and fifty years of mud disappeared. The hope for the new fledgling tourist industry was high, and the mines were doing well. Then the bottom fell out. The cutting edge of the depression sliced into Leadville in 1931, and the only good thing that could be said for '31-'32 was that the area had a mild winter. By 1932 the Arkansas Valley Smelter could not even operate one of its three furnaces on a regular basis. In July 1932 the thermometer reached an all-time high of eighty-six degrees and the city an all-time low when it was announced that the city treasury was empty, and until taxes were collected in August, the city of Leadville would not be able to pay its bills. A number of suicides were recorded in 1932, not the suicides of the destitute or wealthy, but workingmen for whom there were no jobs. The saddest of these was a Twin Lakes gentleman, Captain

Kids and burros—all was not grim. *Photo Source: Author's Collection.*

Harrison Avenue during the waning moments of the depression. *Photo Source: Library of Congress.*

Thomas J. Blue. Captain Blue, seventy-seven years old, had lost his wife, Hattie, two years before. In a note for his friends he explained,

> Reason for this act is I am financially broke, not a dollar income and no prospects of any, and the probabilities are I will in a short time become helpless and a burden to my friends — tired of life so why prolong the worry. Goodbye, Friends.

He wrapped a towel around his head so that he would not bleed on himself and present his neighbors with a distasteful picture, spread a quilt on the floor of the woodshed to sit upon, and shot himself with a .22 caliber pistol. After a life of hard, productive work, he, like so many others, could not face the realities of loneliness, uselessness, and complete destitution. He took, in his mind, the only honorable alternative.

To all but those who lived there, Leadville seemed doomed. In 1932 United Press wrote "to the effect" that Leadville had become a ghost town: the Little Jonny was full of water, "Harrison Avenue, once the scene of bustle and business, was now deserted," and the railroads had

abandoned the town. As far as railroads were concerned, United Press was almost correct. By the end of the depression, Leadville's three railroads had been reduced to one, the Rio Grande, and it discontinued "through passenger service" late in 1939. As for desertion, by 1930 the population of the Magic City had shrunk to 3,771 people. Judging from school population figures, it continued to shrink until 1932, when an estimated 3,400 people lived in Leadville. And the Little Jonny? It managed to operate, almost alone, throughout the depression.

It seems remarkable, on the face of it, that only one business folded in Leadville in 1932, but that is no doubt the result of the difficult times before '32. Only sound, well-established businesses had managed to survive to that point, and apparently it would require more than a market crash, rock bottom prices for metals, and a jobless decade to make them fold. Gradually some light began to appear. The smelter was running regularly again in 1933. Chain stores like Safeway, J. C. Penney's, and Gambles opened outlets in Leadville, expressing their belief in the future of the town. A number of CWA (later FERA) and WPA projects put men to work. Later the CCC camps provided a number of jobs for young men. In 1935 the *Herald Democrat,* always boosting local spirits, claimed under the headline, *Past Year Showed Marked Progress In Local Mining,* that "The obituary of the Leadville district has been written so many times that it has become rather stock material." It seemed Leadville, all commentary to the contrary notwithstanding, had made it through another crisis.

While the future looked much brighter in 1935, a vital link with the past was lost. Elizabeth Bonduel McCourt Tabor, the second Mrs. H. A. W. Tabor, was found dead in her cabin at the Matchless Mine on March 7, 1935. Baby Doe, as she came to be called, was already a legend — during the thirties the Tabors were the subject of two biographies and a movie. The lives of Baby Doe and Horace — their love affair, their riches to rags marriage, Horace's death, and Baby Doe's self-imposed penance of thirty odd years at the Matchless Mine had been fantasied and fictionalized to the degree that even those who knew the facts forgot them.

In the years that followed, the Matchless Mine became a shrine of sorts. People from all over the country came to see the cabin where she lived and the mine she alternately worked, leased, and brooded over. Lessees after her death had to fence the property to keep the curious from getting in their way. So much interest was generated in Leadville as a result of the death of Mrs. Tabor that it "led to the formation of an historical society for Leadville." The new society, the Leadville Historical Association, picked up where the original pioneer group left off and successfully preserved a number of important books, documents, furnishings, the Nellie Healy home, and James V. Dexter's cabin.

Leadville in the thirties was quiet. The town and the nation had recovered from the social madness of the twenties, and it was once again safe to walk the streets of Leadville after dark. You might get stopped by a stranger, but he was not carrying a gun, rather he was a representative of the "hobo jungle" north of town, and all he wanted was a handout. In 1933 prohibition was repealed and Leadville held a mock funeral for "Mr. Eighteenth Amendment." He was buried by

Matchless Mine shortly after Baby Doe's death. *Photo Source: Author's Collection.*

a mass of mourners amidst massive bouquets of onions, weeds, and carrot tops on the northwest corner of the baseball field. The "dry" era ended with a solemn graveside ceremony and the legal popping of a cork. The Liberty Bell Theater filled many hours with movies, variety shows, and even cooking classes. The Elks Opera House did double duty as home of the Elks and civic stage for talent shows, musical programs, and school graduations. The radio was as much an institution in Leadville in the thirties as in the rest of the land. A good many miners went downtown after supper for their evening libation, but always made it home by nine to listen to "Amos 'n Andy."

Change was coming; the winds of war blew increasingly stronger throughout the late thirties. The *Herald Democrat* summed up America's feeling in January 1939 by explaining, "Hitler is merely trying to piece the map of Europe together in a new way, which is by no means the first time a paperhanger's ideas of matching the living room paper failed to coincide with those who have to live in the room." By fall the Great War had been resumed in Europe. The price of metals went up, jobs became plentiful, but the war hung over the country like a pall. Everyone hoped it would go away, realized that it would not, and knew that someday, somehow, they would become involved.

Sunday, December 7, 1941; the waiting was over. It was almost with a sigh of relief that the nation began to gear up for war. In the early stages, war came to Leadville as it did the rest of the country, in a series of good-bye parties, roaring drunks, and cold, gray dawn vigils at the local bus depot. World news pushed metal prices, dog bites, and the weather off the front page of the

Herald Democrat. The war was fought in the local paper by cartoon characters like Scorchy Smith and Dickie Dare who carried the battle to the "Japs" six days a week. And the radio, the world in the living room, brought two-mile high, mountain-surrounded Leadville every bit as close to the war as other cities in the land. But the United States Army took Leadville one step closer.

On March 31, 1942, Leadville received the official word that the United States Army would be building a multimillion dollar training camp at Pando, a Rio Grande Railroad siding about seven miles north of Tennessee Pass. Construction of the camp, designed to house over fifteen thousand troops and support personnel, began the following month. The influx of construction workers in 1942 is said to have doubled the population of Leadville. Doubled is doubtful, but their numbers were considerable and the effect on the economy was like water on a weed. The town jumped into action. Harrison Avenue was jammed with traffic, business boomed, salaries rose, and the Magic City was back in business.

The new army camp's job was to train the recently organized Tenth Mountain Division in the arts of mountain/winter warfare, an art that few in America knew anything about. Leadville's part in the project was to serve as staging point for the development of the camp and provide, as the largest community in the area, the social amenities for the troops on liberty. It was decided that usual miner amenities might not be suited for the young mountain men, and Leadville was asked to clean up its traditional vices. Gambling, illegal in Colorado, was closed down once again in Leadville. The shady ladies of State Street were told to leave town, and the red lights winked out all up and down the street only to be rekindled in other parts of town. It was agreed that if the girls were going to remain, they would have to submit to an examination every three weeks by the county physician.

The camp was dedicated on June 14, 1942, and named after General Irving Hale, a Denver graduate of West Point. Construction was completed in November of 1942 and, while the camp was ready and occupied by Christmas 1942, Leadville was not ready and was declared "out of bounds" because of the gambling and social diseases running amok among Camp Hale construction workers living in Leadville. It was not until late February of 1943 that the Colorado Board of Health and United States Army declared Leadville safe to visit. Areas of Leadville had several lapses during the Tenth Mountain's occupation, but in the end the army lost very few troops in

Leadville. In fact, many thought the Leadville experience good preparation for what they were asked to face in Europe.

Camp Hale, or Pando as most called it, was a miserable place in the winter. At 9,300 feet it had as much winter as any place of similar elevation in Colorado. The camp sat in a pleasant, mountain-ringed meadow on the headwaters of the Eagle River. It could not have been better designed for escaping the sun's rays while at the same time trapping and holding cold air and smoke. Many of the men suffered all winter from what was called the "Pando hack," a cold air and smoke induced cough that was not heard again in the region until the fireplaces in Vail began to stuff that valley in similar fashion. It was with great relief that the troops boarded buses bound for Leadville on Saturday, February 27, 1943, for

Camp Hale, north of Tennessee Pass. *Photo Source: Leroy Wingenbach.*

Tenth Mountain Division. *Photo Source: Francis Bochatey, Leadville's* Herald Democrat.

their first liberty in the Magic City. The town was impressed with the young men, and many soldiers made lasting friendships with local citizens, wrote to them throughout the remainder of the war, and several returned to Leadville at the end of hostilities. There was, of course, some suspicion at the outset, and one Tenth Mountaineer recalled that the division had a number of European members, and when they would fall to singing German and Swiss drinking songs in the Leadville bars, it was thought at first that the division was riddled with spies.

The Tenth Mountain Division spent the greater part of three winters in the region, then in July of 1944 moved to Camp Swift in Texas for final preparation. They sailed for Italy early in 1945. Their combat record, the casualties they suffered, their pride and devotion to duty and to one another is a story that all America can take pride in. The great number of them who returned to Colorado and assumed leading roles in the development of Colorado's mountain recreation industry is ample evidence that they left Camp Hale, Leadville, and Colorado with more than the

"Pando Hack."

World War Two provided Leadville its first major economic impetus in over twenty years. For most people, they were years of plenty, change, and opportunity. Leadville was even able, finally, to get government support for its pet project. A government financed drainage tunnel was begun north of town near the earlier Canterbury Tunnel. Early in November 1943, Interior Secretary Harold Ickes signed the papers that initiated the construction of a $1,400,000 tunnel three miles long, that would, it was hoped, unwater a major portion of the Leadville district. By March of 1945 the tunnel had only been driven a mile, the project was out of money, and Ickes was asking that the construction funds be paid back out of the anticipated increase in mine revenues. A request for an additional $1,600,000 by Colorado's senators, Johnson and Millikin, was turned down. The war was winding down, victory was in sight, and Leadville's potential production was no longer needed. The tunnel halted at sixty-six hundred feet and waited for the next war, which was not long in coming.

On the eve of the Korean War, the Bureau of Mines, after a thorough examination of the Leadville district, persuaded Congress to appropriate $500,000 to finish the project. The work was completed by 1952, and some 6.8 billion gallons of the 11 billion estimated in the two basins drained by the tunnel had already run by the tunnel's portal. But by then the Korean War was in its last throes, the price of metals had dropped, and Leadville mining men were saying, "We told you so." The tunnel was too high and failed to drain the deeper workings of most of the promising properties. The final result of all drainage projects, except the Yak Tunnel, has been failure. None have even paid the cost of construction, much less made any money.

Leadville, throughout World War Two, the Korean War, and the intervening years, produced over forty million dollars worth of minerals, with a major portion of that coming from the Ibex and Resurrection properties, both drained by the Yak Tunnel. The average for the period was about three and three-quarter million per year, and in one year only, 1952, did production exceed six million dollars. A far cry from World War I when the average production was over twelve million dollars a year and prices were about half that of the period 1941 to 1953. But Leadville was not supported by the Leadville district alone as it had been in World War I. Climax production just during the years 1940-1944 produced a whopping $121,575,865. A post-war recession halved those figures in the next four years, but by the mid-fifties Climax was back on track producing over forty million dollars a year.

In the fifties it gradually began to dawn on Leadvillites that theirs was an economically sound community. It was time to catch up with the rest of the nation. Leadville had done no building during the twenties and thirties, other

Harrison Avenue, 1948. Prosperity was back thanks to World War II and a deepening Cold War. *Photo Source: Denver Public Library Western History Collection.*

than revising old buildings for new uses. The Orthodox Jewish Synagogue at 119 West Fifth was torn down to make repairs on the other at Fourth and Pine, which was converted, then, into an apartment house. In 1936 Vincent P. Sullivan built a home at 714 Poplar. "It was the first house built in Leadville since 1915."

The tone for the next decade was set in the early fifties by a teenager, quoted as saying, "Who'd want to live in this crummy town — everything in it is old." Adults echoed the younger citizen's feelings, and Leadville set in motion the greatest period of change since Edwin Harrison came to town in 1877 and started his smelter.

Old-time Leadvillites initiated a successful bond issue in 1951, after failing the year before, to put in a modern sewer system. The problem was first brought to everyone's attention during World War II when the Colorado Health Department, checking on the welfare of the Tenth Mountain Division, discovered that most of Leadville was without sewer facilities and that the area served by sewer was served by the same one constructed in the 1880s. In 1952, the following year, a school bond issue passed and construction began on two new schools that would replace Ninth Street and Central schools, constructed in the 1880s. In 1953 the county hired Dick Ferguson to head the county's new recreation department and expand its somewhat meager and worn facilities. In 1954 the second St. Vincent's hospital, finished in 1901, was condemned, and a

local citizens' group began raising funds for a new hospital. They were successful. The new hospital opened in 1958.

In June of 1942, Leadville lost one of its most historic structures. The upper floors of the Lake County Courthouse were destroyed in a spectacular fire on June 29, a fire that took not only the courthouse but the Court Exchange building next door. Since the fire, the county had housed its offices in the crowded, rebuilt first floor of the original building. In 1955 a new, modern courthouse was built on the original property, but set back from Harrison Avenue. In the same year a new bank building at Fourth and Harrison opened for business. The following year a number of new homes were started on the west side of town. In the next two years, 1957 and 1958, a new convent was built for the Sisters of Charity, a medical center, adjacent to the new hospital, was completed, the Elks moved out of the old Tabor Opera House and into a modern, "up-to-date" building on West Fifth. The county's school districts consolidated, most of the town's streets were oiled, Safeway Stores built a large store with convenient parking north of town, and St. Mary's School remodeled, sporting a new coat of paint and the necessary glass brick so characteristic of the fifties, but so out of place on the gothic revival buildings of Victorian Leadville.

So extensive and so complete was the transformation that *Look Magazine*, in its February 17, 1959, issue, named Leadville one of its All America City award recipients. The *Carbonate*

Lake County's famous old courthouse on the eve of disaster. *Photo Source: Author's Collection.*

The Court Exchange fire consumed itself and Lake County's venerable old courthouse in 1942. *Photo Source: Author's Collection.*

Lake County's new courthouse. *Photo Source: Author's Collection.*

Chronicle noted the progress with unreserved pride when it exclaimed that Leadville had made the "great transition from a mining camp into a typical American community." For the first time in Leadville's history she took no pride in her uniqueness. For the first time in her history she wanted to be Anytown, U.S.A.

But in 1959 Leadville was still a mining town, a one-industry town, and open to the vicissitudes of the mining industry. There were those who sought to change all that. Large numbers of new faces filled the streets. New faces sat on the Chamber of Commerce board of directors. People from other locales, with other experience, and other ideas, came to Leadville because of its winters, not in spite of them, came to Leadville because of the mountains, not in spite of them. They were people who saw the history of Leadville not as a local heritage of pride and accomplishment, but as a saleable commodity; they were people who saw the snow and thought, not shovel, but ski.

Old-time Leadville people became caught up in the wave of commercial adventure. Suddenly all manner of projects began to catch hold. Climax started the ball rolling in 1960 with the announcement that they were going to close their company town. They planned to move the whole community into a subdivision they had started months before in an area north and west of Leadville's city limits, called West Park. A new elementary school and a new high school were called for. New enterprises sprang up. There was no room for the old. Few business leaders and local officials had need of Leadville's historic relics. The old Liberty Bell Theatre was purchased and demolished by the county and was replaced with grass. The old St. Vincent's Hospital, constructed so painfully in 1879, was torn down. Hunter and Trimble's bank was dismantled and taken to Aspen. In 1962 and 1963 fires took several lives and the Union Block, built in 1887 by Tabor and the Guggenheims, the DeMainville Block, constructed about the same time, and the historic home of William H. James, located immediately south of Healy House.

By the mid-sixties, Leadville had a different look, a different feel — even a different sound.

Gone was the lonely, melancholy whistle of Leadville's last steam engine, old 641. The bells of Ninth Street and Central schools no longer called students to class, nor did the proud, sonorous tones of Saint Mary, the bell in the tower of Annunciation Church, call Catholics to worship, nor did the whistle at the smelter call men to work. The Arkansas Valley Smelter, the longest continuing business in Lake County, closed early in 1961. Her furnaces, buildings, and equipment were sold for scrap.

Progress suggested the disincorporation of Leadville, the hiring of a city manager, and the creation of the Leadville-Lake County Planning Commission. The old Leadville City Codes were scrapped, and a firm called Banks Municipal Codes wrote a new set of laws for the Magic City.

The Chamber of Commerce, with the help of county funds, created a new image for Leadville — the "Follow Moly to Leadville" slogan, coupled with a Debbie Reynolds looking lady in gay nineties dress, adorned billboards, pamphlets, and stationary. It was asserted that "if you missed Leadville, you missed Colorado." The chamber commissioned a study of Leadville's potentials — it was suggested that the old slag heaps around the city might be used to make rock wool or tile. Public Service Company also produced promotional materials and discussed the advantages of settling in the mountains around Leadville. The federal government added their money to the motion for change when they approved the multimillion dollar Fryingpan-Arkansas project. A project that would include

Leadville in the 1970s, an uneasy blend of old and new, of elegant and tawdry, of double wides and gothic grandeur. *Photo Source: Author's Collection.*

enough tunnels for diverting water, which had they been used for mining, could have unwatered most, if not all, of the major mining areas in Colorado. Leadville greeted the news with enthusiasm and miniature frying pans.

In March of 1962 the local planning commission hired Sam Huddleston, landscape architect and planning consultant, to design a Leadville-Lake County master plan. Leadville abandoned much of the hard-won wisdom it had accumulated over the years and in the process forgot who it was. But in July of 1962 the miners at Climax reminded Leadville of its origins. Almost two thousand men walked off the job, and Leadville had to consider its loyalties. Summer business was good and the effects of the strike were endurable. Tourists by the hundreds had found Leadville, and a number of construction projects in the area provided jobs for the striking miners, but with the first snows of winter, the Magic City froze up. It was 1896 all over again. And while the strike of '96 lasted longer and was more violent and bitter, the Climax strike of 1962 was painful enough. And when it ended in January of 1963, Leadville was chastened.

The strike gave voice to conservative elements in the community. Conflicts between progressive newcomers and natives — strike wary merchants and miners, depression reared old-timers, historic preservationists, and the growing environmentalist movement — culminated in the rejection of Huddleston's three-year planning effort, his master plan, and a proposed Urban Renewal project for the City of Leadville. The city fathers, bitter in defeat, turned their collective back on other planning and zoning projects, development of building codes, and participation in the regional planning board. The city manager plan died an inglorious death at the polls, the disincorporation plan was dropped, and such dreams as the Fryingpan-Arkansas Project, sought after and applauded in the late fifties and early sixties, now came under increasingly heavy fire.

The reaction to the Anytown, U.S.A. theme of the fifties and early sixties was as powerful as the movement that made Leadville an All America City in 1959, but it was a negative movement. It provided no alternatives, no new acceptable courses of action. It was nihilistic. With one course decisively defeated it was necessary to design a new course. As Leadville approached its centennial in 1978 a solution had not been reached; a satisfactory marriage of past and present had not been concluded.

Epilogue

A group called Voice by Choice, whatever that means, led the fight against Urban Renewal. When the plan was defeated, community leadership fell to this group. They were either unwilling or unable to handle the responsibility and for a decade Leadville had no recognized consistent leadership. Those who were active in city and county government, on the board of the Chamber of Commerce, or served on the planning board during the first half of the sixties, dropped out of local affairs. A decade later not one single member of the above organizations was active in local affairs.

In the late sixties mining returned to the Leadville district in the form of Asarco, a joint venture on the part of American Smelting and Refining Company and the Resurrection Mining Company. Since then, Day Mines, Incorporated, has developed the Sherman Tunnel and is shipping ore from the Leadville district.

What is the future of mining in the district? Mining men still claim that wealth is there, but talk of drainage tunnels has been stilled. It is not unlikely that the people of Leadville will see, as the metals crisis deepens, the open pit mining of major portions of the old historic Leadville district, a move that will undoubtedly set off all manner of historic, environmental, and mining convolutions.

And what of Leadville and its search for an identity capable of seeing it through its second century? Young people, many of whom are natives of Leadville, are beginning to fill the leadership void. Some older citizens, many of whom were burned in the rejection of the sixties, are now willing to share the wisdom they gained at the expense of their peace of mind and pride. Many are again willing to accept a role in casting the future of Leadville. Reasonable people realize mining cannot support Leadville forever, and alternatives must be found, but *any* alternative, as in the early sixties, will not satisfy today's Leadville. Alternatives to mining are necessary, but they must be compatible with historic Leadville, alpine Leadville, and scenic Leadville. And they must be designed by and for the people of Leadville, or they will be unacceptable. The one thing that most of Leadville citizens seem agreed upon is that whatever they do, they must not again lose touch with their heritage. Leadville no longer wants to be Anytown, U.S.A. It wants to retain that unique character that makes the Magic City magic.

Source Notes

Chapter I

Detailed accounts of the discovery period in California Gulch are nonexistent. I relied heavily on the reporting of Lewis Dow in the weekly *Rocky Mountain News* and a number of "how it really happened" articles in the early Leadville newspapers. The reminiscences of H. A. W., Augusta, and Maxcy Tabor were useful.

The records of the California Gulch miners, their letters, and contemporary photos of the area housed in the library of the Colorado Historical Society provided many of the hard facts of discovery and organization. The scrapbooks and unorganized materials collected by the Society of Leadville Pioneers provided several leads and a lot of color.

A number of standard works were consulted throughout the book and should be mentioned before going further. Of primary importance are R. G. Dill's account of the period, 1860-1880, in his "History of Lake County," a section of O. L. Baskin's *History of the Arkansas Valley, Colorado,* 1881, and Don and Jean Griswold's *The Carbonate Camp Called Leadville,* 1951. Samuel Franklin Emmons and his associates at the U. S. Geographical Survey produced several papers on the Leadville area that are models of careful, exhaustive research. The back issues of *Colorado Magazine* and *Engineering and Mining Journal* provided a constant flow of questions and answers, of color and fact.

Chapter II

Though brief and infrequent, the articles and letters in the *Engineering and Mining Journals* of the period 1876-1878 were quite helpful. The diaries, interviews, and reminiscences of the Tabors, William H. Jackson, William H. Stevens, and Charles S. Thomas were of primary importance, as were the early accounts of mining in the region, namely: R. O. Old's *Colorado: United States, America, Its Mineral and Other Resources,* 1872, and Ovando J. Hollisters' *The Mines of Colorado,* 1867.

The Colorado Historical Society's library provided, as usual, important primary source material. Research at the Huntington Library produced an assay book, 1873-1878, which was invaluable. Boom town chronicles and mining guide books by such writers as Lewis A. Kent, George B. Dresher, and Thomas B. Corbett were consulted. Newspapers such as the *Lake County Reveille* and the *Carbonate Weekly Chronicle* from Leadville, and the *Georgetown Courier, Denver Tribune, Caribou Post,* and the *Rocky Mountain Daily News* from the neighborhood rounded out the account.

Chapter III

The how-to-do-it books on mining were important sources on the miner's needs, problems, and methods. Guides for the would-be millionaire by Stephen F. Smart, Frank Fossett, C. E. Edwords, and Bronson Keeler were used. Of greater importance were the detailed accounts contained in Frank Hall's *History of the State of Colorado*, Vol. II, 1890; Charles W. Henderson's, *Mining in Colorado: A History of Discovery, Development and Production*, 1926, and, of course, Dill's account in O. L. Baskin's *History of the Arkansas Valley, Colorado*, 1881.

A major contribution to the information available on Leadville is Don and Jean Griswold's condensation of the *Herald Democrat* files in their newspaper series called "Leadville: A City of Contrast." Two very colorful articles from the period provided much of the flavor of Leadville on the eve of greatness: A. A. Hayes' "Grub Stakes and Millions," published in February 1880, in *Harper's New Monthly Magazine*, and Ernest Ingersol's "The Camp of the Carbonates: Ups and Downs in Leadville," published in October 1879, in *Scribner's Monthly*. Illustrations in the latter publication, many by Mary Hallock Foote, were especially interesting.

Original accounts by Leadville pioneers housed at Healy House-Dexter Cabin, the files of the *Colorado Magazine*, and materials provided by Jane Norton Kintz dealing with the Giddy Betsy put flesh on the bones of several lost mine stories.

Chapter IV

For the discussion of the first merchants and the organization of the site that became Leadville, I owe much to a pair of fine dissertations: Eugene Floyd Irey, "A Social History of Leadville, Colorado, During the Boom Days 1877-1881," University of Minnesota, 1951, and James Edward Fell, Jr., "Ores to Metals: The Evolution of the Smelting Industry in Colorado, 1864-1921," University of Colorado, 1975. Newspaper accounts, as usual, were important, especially the premier Leadville paper of the period, the *Daily Chronicle*. Several books about the period were used, two of which were of primary importance: *Charles H. Dow and the Dow Theory*, by George T. Bishop, Jr., 1960, and *Horace Tabor, His Life and the Legend*, by Duane Smith, 1973.

The accounts of the founding of Leadville have, for the most part, been based on R. G. Dill's account published in 1881. It notes the founding and naming of Leadville, January 18, 1878, but the name Leadville was used publicly at least four months earlier. The answers to the founding of Leadville were found in the papers of the Society of Leadville Pioneers and in the U.S. Postal Service Records housed in the National Archives.

Of course, the Griswold's *Carbonate Camp Called Leadville* and Dill's account of early Leadville in the *History of the Arkansas Valley, Colorado* were consulted several times, as were the Colorado Historical Society's Harrison and Tabor holdings, the Lake County Public Library's Colorado Mountain History Collection, and several issues of *Colorado Magazine*, especially those dealing with transportation, and specifically with the Georgetown-Leadville stage line.

Chapter V

For the hard facts of discovery, nothing served me better than the records of the Lake County Clerk and Recorder's office. Fine color and behind the scenes dealing was revealed in several works from the period, the more important of which follow: Willis Sweet, *Carbonate Camps, Leadville and Ten Mile of Colorado,* 1879; Bronson C. Keeler, *Leadville and Its Silver Mines,* 1879; George B. Dresher, *A Description of Colorado, Leadville, and the Sovereign Consolidated Silver Mines,* 1881; Lewis A. Kent, *Leadville,* 1880, and Ernest Ingersol, "Ups and Downs in Leadville," *Scribner's Magazine,* October, 1879.

I discovered some excellent insights in an interview with H. A. W. Tabor in *The Great Divide,* January, 1892. George Hook set the story straight in a letter preserved in the Historical Archives of the Society of Leadville Pioneers. Housed in the Bancroft Library are the words and deeds of August Rische in an interview, July 27, 1886, in Ouray, Colorado. Additional information on Mr. Rische was recorded by Charles S. Thomas, "Random Colorado Memories," Colorado Historical Society. Duane Smith's fine biography, *Horace Tabor, His Life and the Legend,* 1973, documents the business side of Tabor and his associates. The story of Van Brooklyn was related by Irving Stone in *Men to Match My Mountains,* a very readable account, published in 1956.

For biographical information, I relied on the files of the Colorado Historical Society, the Western History Collection of the Denver Public Library, U.S. Census Reports, "The Passing of the Pioneers" section in *The Trail,* and Alice Polk Hill's *Colorado Pioneers in Picture and Story,* 1915.

Other authors consulted include the Griswolds, R. G. Dill, and Frank Hall, his *History of the State of Colorado,* Vol. II. Newspapers, always a good source of color, leads, and biographical tidbits, were consulted. Material was specifically used from the *Herald Democrat, Rocky Mountain Daily News,* and that compendium of clippings, "The Dawson Scrapbooks," housed at the Colorado Historical Society.

Chapter VI

Books and articles from the period provided much of the color. Willis Sweet, Bronson C. Keeler, and George W. Bishop, Jr., mentioned earlier, were used, in addition to *East by West: A Journey in the Recess,* Vol. I, by Henry W. Lucy, a critical English traveler, published in 1885. The two articles mentioned earlier, "The Camp of the Carbonates: Ups and Downs in Leadville," *Scribner's Magazine,* October 1879, and "Grub Stakes and Millions," *Harper's New Monthly Magazine,* February 1880, were especially useful in giving the tenderfoot point of view.

Reminiscences by Eddie Foy, *Clowning Through Life,* 1928; Charles McClung Leonard, "Forty Years in Colorado Mining Camps," *Colorado Magazine,* July 1960; William B. Thom, "In Pioneer Days," *The Trail,* October 1926; and Judge Furrow's recollections preserved by the Society of Leadville Pioneers were invaluable.

Information on minorities was provided by the *Daily* and *Weekly Chronicles,* an article by Patricia K. Ourada, "The Chinese in Colorado," *Colorado Magazine,* October 1952; "The Sixth Street Irish," William and Edward Kerrigan with Michael Donovan, Colorado Mountain History Collection; Eugene Irey's dissertation, and a master's thesis by Elmer Carlson, "The Role of the Swedish People in the History of Colorado," University of Northern Colorado, 1936.

The files of the Colorado Mountain History Collection in the Lake County Public Library yielded the George R. Elder letters, edited by his grandson, Robert Elder, and a letter from Frank McLister, while the files of the Colorado Historical Society provided George A. Hynes' letter, January 1, 1879. Material on Mary Hallock Foote came from two sources, her letters housed in the library at Stanford University and her biography, *A Victorian Gentlewoman in the Far West,* edited by Rodman W. Paul, 1972. The preservation of the story of fur-bearing trout, at least in print, was the work of Levette J. Davidson and Forrester Blake, editors of *Rocky Mountain Tales,* 1947.

Chapter VII

Stories, anecdotes, and color came from a number of sources, many mentioned earlier, such as Irey's dissertation, "A Social History of Leadville, Colorado, During the Boom Days, 1877-1881"; George R. Elder's letters; the Griswolds, both their "Leadville, a City of Contrast" series and *The Carbonate Camp Called Leadville;* George W. Bishop, Jr., *Charles H. Dow and the Dow Theory;* Henry W. Lucy, *East by West: A Journey in the Recess,* Vol. I; and Willis Sweet, *Carbonate Camps, Leadville and Ten Mile, of Colorado.* Other sources briefly consulted for descriptive material and anecdotal information include C. C. Davis' charming and very personal look at the Carbonate Camp, *Olden Times in Colorado,* 1916; Edward J. Hoyt's *Buckskin Joe: Being the Unique and Vivid Memories of Edward Jonathan Hoyt,* edited by Glen Shirley, 1966; Philip W. Whitely's, "Twelve Colorado Characters," *Denver Westerners Monthly Roundup,* February 1967; *Rocky Mountain Mining Camps: The Urban Frontier,* 1967, by Duane Smith; and *Ghost Towns of Colorado,* 1947, a W.P.A. Writer's Program project.

The section on the theater in Leadville owes much to Eddie Foy's biography, *Clowning Through Life,* 1928. Charles Vivian was mentioned in several works, but the two I relied upon most heavily were Imogen Holbrook Vivian's biography of her husband published in 1903, *A Biographical Sketch of the Life of Charles Algernon Sidney Vivian* and A. L. Rowse's very readable, *The Cousin Jacks: The Cornish in America,* 1969. Dorothy M. Degitz's detailed account of the "History of the Tabor Opera House at Leadville," *Colorado Magazine,* May 1936, was excellent.

Newspapers as usual provided much of the day to day information. I found the files of the *Leadville Democrat, Daily Chronicle, Carbonate Weekly Chronicle* and the *Herald Democrat* most helpful. The material on Mollie May came mainly from Kay Blair's fine little booklet, *Ladies of the Lamplight,* 1971, though I owe the poem to Leadville's poet laureate, Frank Vaughn, in his book of poems, *The Spirit of Leadville,* 1929.

Chapter VIII

I used the George R. Elder letters, housed in the Colorado Mountain History Collection, Lake County Public Library, for much of my information on the legal profession in Leadville. Other sources used include: Duane Smith's *Horace Tabor, His Life and the Legend,* 1973, and Sewell Thomas's *Silhouettes of Charles Thomas,* 1959.

For doctors and dentists, and the general health of the camp, I relied heavily on Irey's dissertation, "A Social History of Leadville, Colorado, During the Boom Days, 1877-1881," the files of the *Daily Chronicle* and *Herald Democrat,* and a delightful paper presented in 1970 by William J. Rose, long-time Leadville dentist, called "Folklore of Teeth," Colorado Mountain History Collection.

A history of Leadville's newspapers has been written by almost every newspaper editor in Leadville, not carefully, but profusely. The three newsmen I found myself using the most, but with a grain of salt, were: Carlyle Channing Davis, *Olden Times in Colorado,* 1916; R. G. Dill, "History of Lake County," in *History of the Arkansas Valley, Colorado,* 1881; and a Colorado Historical Society interview, March 7, 1923, with Edward M. Hawkins. In addition, I used the *Colorado Miner,* a Georgetown paper, and early copies of the *Daily Chronicle* and *Leadville Democrat,* plus the Lake County Clerk and Recorder's records.

Orth Stein has fascinated many writers and historians, myself included. I consulted a number of authors such as Dill, the Griswolds, Perry Eberhart's *Treasure Tales of the Rockies,* 1961, and Crofutt's *Grip-Sack Guide to Colorado,* 1885, though I relied most heavily on the following: Donald E. Bower's fine article, "The Fantastic World of Orth Stein," *American West,* May 1973; C. C. Davis, *Olden Times in Colorado,* 1916, and an excellent paper, "Orth Stein: From Riches to Rags," *Mountain Diggings,* January 1975, by Linda Kiester, a young student who uncovered the story of Stein's beating in Denver.

For Leadville business, I relied heavily on local papers, standard histories, and contemporary publications. I used the Griswold's *Carbonate Camp* and "City of Contrast" series extensively, as well as Dill and Frank Hall's *History of Colorado*, Vol. III, 1891. I also used such contemporary authors as Bronson C. Keeler, Stephen F. Smart, and W. W. Borden, plus Lewis Cass Gandy's very personal biography, *The Tabors, a Footnote of Western History*, 1934.

Geraldine Bowles Bean's dissertation, "Charles Boettcher: A Study in Pioneer Western Enterprise," 1970; Alice Polk Hill's *Colorado Pioneers in Picture and Story*, 1915; the *Leadville Democrat*, January 1, 1881; and Charles Boettcher's own reminiscence, "The Flush Times of Colorado," 1884, housed in the Colorado Historical Society Library, provided the information for the section on Charles Boettcher.

David May appeared in several Leadville works, but those I used were: Allen duPont Breck, *The Centennial History of the Jews of Colorado*, 1960; Don and Jean Griswold, "Leadville, a City of Contrast," *Herald Democrat*, October 8, 1965; and "The May Story," a 75th anniversary publication, Colorado Historical Society.

General information on merchants and business houses was found in the *Leadville City Directories*, in the holdings of the Society of Leadville Pioneers, Colorado Historical Society, and in the files of the Leadville papers.

Irey and Dill were used in the discussion of freighting, as was Ivan W. Crawford's "The Leadville Muleskinner," *Colorado Magazine*, July 1958.

The smelting industry was well documented in a dissertation by James Edward Fell, Jr., "Ores to Metals: The Evolution of the Smelting Industry in Colorado, 1864-1921," 1975. I also found a considerable amount of material in past issues of *Engineering and Mining Journal;* in Emmons, Irving, and Loughlin, *Geology and Ore Deposits of the Leadville Mining District, Colorado*, 1927; and Charles W. Henderson, *Mining in Colorado: A History of Discovery, Development and Production*, 1926. I used four period authors, Kent, Keller, Loomis, and Dill, plus the letters of John J. Vandemoer, Colorado Historical Society. For the section on August R. Meyer, I am especially indebted to George Hixon for the reminiscences of George and Hiram Weis Hixon, housed in the Colorado Historical Society Library, and Mary B. Meyer, for letters and copies of family documents. Material on James B. Grant was found in Dill, Frank Hall, Alice Polk Hill, and Quantrille D. McClung's "The Governors of Colorado — Their Ancestries and Interests," *Colorado Magazine*, May 1946.

Some of the smaller smelters and mills were discussed in William M. Thayer's *Marvels of the New West*, 1887, and Richard A. Ronzio's detailed, "Colorado Smelting and Reduction Works," *The Westerners' Brand Book*, 1966. The assaying/smelting process in Leadville was best described in Ingersols' "Ups and Downs in Leadville," and Louis D. Ricketts' dissertation, "The Ores of Leadville and Their Modes of Occurrence as Illustrated in the Morning and Evening Star Mines," 1883. Problems and prices were discussed by Fell in his dissertation and by Hall.

The Guggenheim story was developed from Bruce Chatwin's article, "The Guggenheim Saga," *London Times*, November 23, 1975; Donald Fremont Popham, "The Early Activities of the Guggenheims in Colorado," *Colorado Magazine*, October 1950; Harvey O'Connor, *The Guggenheims*, 1937; and the files of the Colorado Historical Society and the Lake County Clerk and Recorder.

For the section on the charcoal industry I am indebted to Georgina Brown, editor, "In the Charcoal Days of Leadville," *Mountain Diggings*, January 1976; the Griswolds' "City of Contrast" series, February 23, 1968; the files of the *Herald Democrat;* and C. C. Davis, *Olden Times in Colorado*, 1916.

Chapter IX

General information was drawn from a number of sources. Newspapers, especially the *Carbonate Weekly Chronicle*, the *Leadville Democrat*, and the *Denver Tribune*, provided much. Also important were such early accounts as Bronson C. Keeler's *Leadville and It's Silver Mines*, 1879, and J. L. Loomis's *Leadville, Colorado*, 1879. *Clowning Through Life*, Eddie Foy and Alvin F. Harlow, 1928, George R. Elder's letters, and "Sketches of Leadville Pioneers," collected by the Society of Leadville Pioneers, Colorado Historical Society, were of considerable interest. Eugene Floyd Irey's dissertation, "A Social History of Leadville, Colorado, During the Boom Days, 1877-1881," 1951, was an important source of local statistics.

Throughout this chapter, Don and Jean Griswold's "Leadville, a City of Contrast," condensation of the Leadville papers (*Herald Democrat*), and the Colorado Historical Society's Sam Howe Scrapbooks were invaluable sources of anecdotes, trivia, and fact.

The tragic story of Leadville's vigilante action is best described in Patty Wiese's "The Man Whose Death Brought Law and Order to Leadville," *Mountain Diggings*, January 1975. Other sources used include the *Leadville Democrat* and *Colorado Graphic;* George R. Elder's letters; Archives of the Society of Leadville Pioneers; R. G. Dill, "History of Lake County," in the *History of the Arkansas Valley, Colorado*, 1881; the Griswold's *Carbonate Camp Called Leadville*, 1951; and the Lake County Sheriff's Jail Record, May 1879-December 1881.

The tale of John D. Morrisey was drawn from Agnus Wright Spring's "Midas of the Mountains," *Frontier Times*, February-March 1969, and Charles S. Thomas's "Random Colorado Memories — John D. Morrisey," Colorado Historical Society. The anecdote about the gondolas, often related "let 'em breed," was corrected for me by Dorothy Shelton, heiress to Leadville's Alderson family. The war at the O'Donovan-Rossa was described in the Griswolds' "City of Contrast" series, February 25, 1966, and in the *Carbonate Weekly Chronicle*, February 28, 1880.

The story of the lady of fortune is from the *Carbonate Weekly Chronicle*, September 11, 1880. The *Denver Tribune*, in a pair of articles, July 13, 1881 and October 17, 1881, told the story of Kate Armstead. Doc Holliday's tenure is described in E. Richard Churchill's neat little book, *Doc Holliday, Bat Masterson, and Wyatt Earp: Their Colorado Careers*, 1974.

The saga of Martin Duggan was compiled from several sources. Of considerable importance was the "Dictation taken from Martin Duggan, Leadville, Colo., September 4, 1885," Bancroft Library. I relied somewhat on a previous work, Edward Blair, "Leadville's Marshall Who Knew No Fear," *Empire Magazine*, May 16, 1971. The account of the shooting of officer O'Connor was developed from the *Colorado Miner*, May 4, 1878, the *Georgetown Courier*, May 2, 1878, and Lewis A. Kent's *Leadville*, 1880.

The *Evening Chronicle*, the *Daily Chronicle*, the *Rocky Mountain News* and Duggan's "dictation" were sources for the Elkins-Hines affair. The shooting of Louis Lamb was drawn from my "Leadville's Marshall Who Knew No Fear," the *Rocky Mountain News*, and the Griswolds' "City of Contrast" series. The story of Duggan and the "Hebrew" was found in the Archives of the Society of Leadville Pioneers. The death of Marshall Duggan was condensed from "Leadville's Marshall Who Knew No Fear." Details were checked in the Griswolds' "City of Contrast" series and the articles in the Sam Howe Scrapbooks. The final note on Martin Duggan's murderer was found in the *Rocky Mountain News*, May 27, 1904.

Chapter X

This chapter owes much to Don and Jean Griswold and their detailed condensation of Leadville's newspapers in a series published in the *Herald Democrat*, "Leadville, A City of Contrast." The material on Father Robinson and the early history of the Catholics in Leadville was condensed from Henry W. Lucy's *East by West: A Journey in the Recess*, Vol. I, 1885; Sister Mary Buckner's *History of the Sisters of Charity of Leavenworth, Kansas*, 1898; and the Griswolds' "City of Contrast" series. Thomas Uzzell's Leadville experiences and background were drawn from the *Leadville Democrat*, January 3, 1880; R. G. Dill's "History of Lake County," in *History of the Arkansas Valley, Colorado*, 1881; and Mary Uzzell Plattner's affectionate, "Thomas A. Uzzell, 1848-1910," a reminiscence housed at the Colorado Historical Society.

Joseph C. Weber's dissertation, "The History of the Public Schools, Leadville, Colorado, From 1877-1957," 1957, was invaluable. The *Carbonate Weekly Chronicle*, January 3, 1880, and the *Leadville Democrat*, January 1, 1880, provided considerable insight. Specialty items such as the "Revised Course of Instruction and Regulations of the Public Schools," June 5, 1883, and the "By-Laws and Rules and Regulations of the

Public Schools of the City of Leadville, Colorado," July 1899, from the files of the Colorado Mountain History Collection, Lake County Public Library, were delightful and informative. The Griswolds' "City of Contrast" series was again used, as was Sister Mary Buckner's *History of the Sisters of Charity of Leavenworth, Kansas,* and Dill's "History of Lake County." Also consulted was Don and Jean Griswold's history, *The Carbonate Camp Called Leadville,* 1951.

Various aspects dealing with the social life were drawn from the Griswolds' "City of Contrast" series; period papers, especially the *Carbonate Weekly Chronicle* and the *Leadville Democrat;* Eugene Floyd Irey's dissertation, "A Social History of Leadville, Colorado, During the Boom Days, 1877-1881," 1951; the Historical Archives of the Society of Leadville Pioneers; the Griswolds' *The Carbonate Camp Called Leadville;* Frank Hall's *History of the State of Colorado,* Vol. III, 1891; and the letters of George R. Elder, Colorado Mountain History Collection, Lake County Public Library.

Matters of Victorian deportment were refined with the help of the *Little Flirt,* 1871; the *Manual of Social Forms* by Maude Cooke, 1896; and John H. Young's *Our Deportment,* 1882.

The section on the Goodell family owes much to Helen Cannon's fine article, "First Ladies of Colorado: Mary Goodell Grant," *Colorado Magazine,* Winter 1964. Excerpts of Frank Vaugh's "Christmas in the Clouds," are from his delightful little volume of verse, *The Spirit of Leadville,* 1929. The Leadville version of "Home on the Range" is from Kenneth S. Clark's "The Story of Colorado Home, the Original 'Home on the Range,'" an insert included with the sheet music, "Colorado Home," published by Paull-Pioneer Music, Inc., 1933; and John I. White's ". . . And the Skies Are Not Cloudy All Day," *American West,* September 1975. Mary Hallock Foote's autobiography, *A Victorian Gentlewoman in the Far West,* edited by Rodman W. Paul, was a delight, and very useful, as was Mary Lou Benn's, "Mary Hallock Foote, Early Leadville Writer," *Colorado Magazine,* April 1956.

Chapter XI

The National Archives' Postal Records yielded up a number of heretofore unpublished facts. George W. Bishop, Jr., *Charles H. Dow and the Dow Theory,* 1960; Bronson C. Keeler, *Leadville and Its Silver Mines,* 1879; Lewis Cass Gandy, *The Tabors, a Footnote of Western History,* 1934; W. W. Borden, *Borden's Leadville, A Treatise on Leadville, Colorado,* n.d., all provided insights, facts, and color. Also used was the *Daily Chronicle,* January 1, 1879, and a George R. Elder letter, February 7, 1879, Colorado Mountain History Collection, Lake County Public Library.

The origins of the Leadville Fire Department were gleaned from Eugene Floyd Irey's dissertation, "A Social History of Leadville, Colorado, During the Boom Days, 1877-1881," 1951; Duane Smith's *Horace Tabor, His Life and the Legend,* 1973; Jim Cole's "We Strive to Save," *Mountain Diggings,* January 1974; and Don L. and Jean Harvey Griswold's "Leadville, a City of Contrast," *Herald Democrat,* January 14, 1966. Additional information was found in Georgina Brown's interesting "Horses . . . Sport of the Carbonate Kings," *Mountain Diggings,* April 1973; George R. Elder's letters; the files of the Society of Leadville Pioneers; and in the *Denver Tribune,* May 25, 1879. The accounts of the Grant Smelter and Chestnut Street fires were reconstructed from the files of the *Daily Herald;* the Griswolds' "Leadville, a City of Contrast" series; and Irey's dissertation.

Street improvements, local transportation, and runaways depended in large measure on the work of Eugene Floyd Irey in his 1951 doctoral dissertation, and the Griswolds' twin successes, *The Carbonate Camp Called Leadville,* 1951, and the "Leadville, a City of Contrast" series. Additional material on streets was found in Helen Vivian Wurz' thesis, "The Leadville Camp: A Colorado Mining Community, 1876-1883," 1941. Additional information on the street railway and the Herdic coaches was supplied by R. G. Dill's "History of Lake County," in the *History of the Arkansas Valley, Colorado,* 1881, and the *General and Specific Ordinances of the City of Leadville,* housed in the Colorado Historical Society Library.

While accounts of railroading in Colorado proliferate, accurate accounts of railroads in and around Leadville are difficult to come by. Of most importance to me were the *Pictorial Supplement to Denver South Park and Pacific,* by R. H. Kindig, E. J. Haley, and M. C. Poor, 1959; Carlyle Channing Davis's *Olden Times in Colorado,* 1916; John J. Lipsey's *The Lives of James John Hagerman,* 1968; Morris Cafky's *The Colorado Midland,* 1965; and the Griswolds' *Carbonate Camp Called Leadville* and "Leadville, a City of Contrast," *Herald Democrat.* Supplemental information was found in Virginia McConnell's fine account, *Bayou Salado,* 1966; in Terry Fitzsimmons' "Railroads to Leadville," an unpublished paper in the Colorado Mountain History Collection, Lake County Public Library; William Willard Howard's "The Modern Leadville," *Harper's Weekly* (supplement), December 1, 1888; Helen M. Flemings' thesis, "Mining in Leadville, Colorado, Since 1860," 1924; and the files of the Colorado Historical Society's library.

Dill, Irey, Keeler, and Charles S. Thomas in his "Random Colorado Memories," a reminiscence housed in the Colorado Historical Society Library, provided the materials on the telegraph. The *Daily Herald, Carbonate Weekly Chronicle,* Eugene Floyd Irey, and the records in the County Clerk and Recorder's office did the same for the telephone, with a special assist from Wilbur Fisk Stone's *History of Colorado,* Vol. I, 1918. Cold weather problems were found in the files of the Society of Leadville Pioneers. The problems of a long distance line over Mosquito Pass were carefully presented by Howard T. Vaille in "Early Years of Telephone in Colorado," *Colorado Magazine,* August 1928.

Kent, Borden, Dill, Wurz, and Irey all came to my assistance when I dealt with the Leadville water system. The *Colorado Miner* (Georgetown), November 23, 1878, and Ernest Ingersol's "Ups and Downs in Leadville," *Scribner's Magazine,* October 1879, were also valuable.

Problems of sanitation were seldom mentioned in contemporary accounts, except for an occasional diatribe in the *Leadville Democrat* and the *Daily Chronicle.* Also used were Irey and the "Leadville, a City of Contrast" series.

Lighting, gas and electric, was researched in Dill and Gandy. The *General and Specific Ordinances of the City of Leadville* provided hard facts, as did the records of the County Clerk and Recorder's office. The Griswolds' "Leadville, a City of Contrast" was used as well as a fine paper by William Heldman, "Electric Power in Leadville," which Mr. Heldman prepared for Public Service Company.

Chapter XII

The failure of the Little Pittsburg is best described by Duane Smith in *Horace Tabor, His Life and the Legend,* 1973. Other sources used include Frank Hall's *History of the State of Colorado,* Vol. II, 1890; R. G. Dill's "History of Lake County" in the *History of the Arkansas Valley, Colorado,* 1881; the John J. Vandemoer letters, Colorado Historical Society, and the *Leadville Daily Chronicle,* June 3, 1879.

The miners' strike of 1880 has never been fully investigated. Some studies are excellent, as far as they go. The best is an article by Paul T. Bechtol, Jr., "The 1880 Labor Dispute in Leadville," *Colorado Magazine,* Fall 1970. It, like most studies, is slanted toward the miners' point of view. The one management sided work is Carlyle Channing Davis's account in *Olden Times in Colorado,* 1916, which suffers from Davis's own biases and his lack of information on all but those areas in which he participated. In order to write a more balanced account, I consulted, in addition to the two above: Joseph R. Buchanan, *The Story of a Labor Agitator,* 1903; Mary Hallock Foote, *A Victorian Gentlewoman in the Far West,* 1972; Walter L. Church, *Some Facts Regarding Leadville,* 1881; Merrill Hough, "Leadville and the Western Federation of Miners," *Colorado Magazine,* Winter 1972; Mr. Hough's thesis, University of Colorado, 1958, "Leadville, Colorado, 1878 to 1898: A Study in Unionism"; Eugene Floyd Irey's dissertation, "A Social History of Leadville, Colorado, During the Boom Days, 1877-1881," 1951; Carroll D. Wright, Commissioner of Labor, *A Report on Labor Disturbances in the State of Colorado from 1880 to 1904 Inclusive,* 1905; and a number of newspapers from the period, most notably the *Leadville Democrat,* plus Don and Jean Griswolds' "Leadville, a City of Contrast," *Herald Democrat,* April 16 and 30, 1965. Additional material was consulted in the files of the Colorado Historical Society in Denver and the Historical Archives of the Society of Leadville Pioneers, Healy House-Dexter Cabin.

The section on Mr. Tabor and his wives was developed from Duane Smith's biography of H. A. W. Tabor; the *Tabor Family Album* by Edward Blair and Edward Cattrell; U.S. Census records, 1860 and 1870; and two Tabor articles in the Griswolds' "City of Contrast" series, September 16, 1966 and January 20, 1967.

The quick survey of mining between the early eighties and early nineties was digested from three Griswold "Leadville, a City of Contrast" articles, June 20, 27, and July 11, 1969; the *Herald Democrat*, January 1, 1888; and two impossible to be without works: Emmons, Irving and Loughlin's *Geology and Ore Deposits of the Leadville Mining District, Colorado*, 1927, and Charles W. Henderson's *Mining in Colorado: A History of Discovery, Development and Production*, 1926.

The economic panic of 1893 and the gradual recovery of the Leadville camp has been omitted from all major works. I relied heavily on newspaper accounts, especially the files of the *Herald Democrat;* a trio of "City of Contrast" articles, November 7, 14, and 21, 1969; and Manning, O'Keefe and DeLashmutt's *Leadville, Lake County and the Gold Belt,* a Chamber of Commerce type publication filled with a lot of good information and optimism, published in 1895. I used Harold Underwood Faulkner's *American Economic History,* 1960, for general background on the national and international economic situation.

John Campion deserves more attention than I could give him in this work. For information on Campion, the Browns, and the Little Jonny/Ibex complex, I used the files of the Colorado Mountain History Collection, Lake County Public Library; the Historical Archives of the Society of Leadville Pioneers; Alice Polk Hill's *Colorado Pioneers in Picture and Story,* 1915; Manning, O'Keefe, and DeLashmutt's *Leadville, Lake County and the Gold Belt,* 1895; the Griswolds' "Leadville, a City of Contrast" article, January 15, 1971; and Charles W. Henderson's *Mining in Colorado,* 1926.

The material on the Ice Palace was digested from my *Palace of Ice,* Timberline Books, Ltd., 1974.

Chapter XIII

Several studies commissioned by public agencies were of considerable help. Used were: Carroll D. Wright, Commissioner of Labor, *A Report on Labor Disturbances in the State of Colorado from 1880 to 1904 Inclusive,* 1905; and Oscar Reuter, et al., "Report of the Joint Special Legislative Committee of the Eleventh General Assembly on the Leadville Strike," Colorado Historical Society. I found useful information in a pair of books published shortly after the strike, G. W. Steevens' strongly prounion, *The Land of the Dollar,* 1897; and Clayton Parkhill and L. H. Kemble's account of the militia in *The Leadville Campaign,* 1897.

Charles Merrill Hough's thesis, "Leadville, Colorado, 1878 to 1898: A Study in Unionism," 1957; and his article, "Leadville and the Western Federation of Miners," *Colorado Magazine,* Winter 1972, were invaluable. Don and Jean Griswolds' "Leadville, a City of Contrast," a series published in the *Herald Democrat,* was used to good advantage. Specific issues consulted: March 6, 1970 through May 15, 1970. Newspapers of the period, the *Free Lance, Herald Democrat,* and the *Evening Chronicle* provided much of the day to day detail of the strike. A pair of contemporary articles in *Harper's Weekly,* "A Leadville View of the Wages Question in Colorado," October 21, 1893; and "Leadville's Determined Strike," December 12, 1896, were useful.

I was fortunate in discovering two sources that had not been fully explored. First, Joseph P. Gazzam's immodest, "The Leadville Strike of 1896," *Missouri Historical Society Bulletin,* October 1950; and the Campion Papers in the Ibex Collection, Colorado Mountain History Collection, Lake County Public Library. The files of the Colorado Historical Society in Denver and especially the Historical Archives of the Society of Leadville Pioneers, Colorado Historical Society at Healy House-Dexter Cabin, round out my sources on the strike of 1896.

Chapter XIV

I am especially indebted to the files of the *Herald Democrat*, 1898-1900, and to Don and Jean Griswold's "Leadville, a City of Contrast" series, published in the *Herald Democrat*. Specific issues consulted: May 22, 1970 through September 4, 1970, and May 10 and 16, 1970.

The winter of 1898-1899 came to life in the old issues of the *Herald Democrat*, but the hard facts of weather were provided by the U.S. Department of Commerce, National Oceanic and Atmospheric Administration, *Voluntary Observers' Meteorological Record, Station Leadville; County, Lake; State, Colo.*, September 1898 through May 1899. Excellent information on the railroads' problems in 1899 was found in Morris Cafky's *The Colorado Midland*, 1965. Additional winter material was found in *Patrick J. Ryan Remembers*, edited by his daughters, Ethel Ryan and Sue Nicholson, 1943; the Historical Archives of the Society of Leadville Pioneers, Colorado Historical Society at Healy House-Dexter Cabin; and in conversation with Wilbur Smith, heir to Leadville's S. L. Smith family, to whom I am indebted for the story of George Burkhardt's encounter with the Evansville school.

Mining problems and solutions were researched in Samuel Franklin Emmons, J. Duer Irving, and G. F. Loughlin's *Geology and Ore Deposits of the Leadville Mining District, Colorado*, 1927. The story of Johnny Cumfrey, the Moyer, and the Gallagher ghost was digested from stories my mother told me as a boy, from the "Leadville, a City of Contrast" series, and the Griswolds' *The Carbonate Camp Called Leadville*, 1951.

Chapter XV

For a look at Leadville in 1900, I consulted the *Herald Democrat*, January 1, 1901, which contained several summary sections, as did all New Year's editions until recent years. I also used the *Leadville Directory*, 1900. For mining in the same period, I used a very good master's thesis by Helen M. Fleming, "Mining in Leadville, Colorado, Since 1860," University of Northern Colorado, 1924; Thomas Tonge's article in the September, 1900, edition of *Engineering Magazine*, called "The Fourth Era of the Leadville Mining District," pp. 809-824; Charles Henderson's *Mining in Colorado*, 1926; and Samuel Franklin Emmons and associate's famous professional paper 148, or more commonly known by libraries as *Geology and Ore Deposits of the Leadville Mining District, Colorado*, 1927. All of my district production figures are from Henderson, unless otherwise noted.

Material on S. D. Nicholson is from Fleming and two Colorado biographical sources: Wilbur Fisk Stone's *History of Colorado*, Vol. III, 1918; and *Portrait and Biographical Record of the State of Colorado*, 1899. The abbreviated account of the Wolftone banquet is from the *Carbonate Chronicle*, January 30, 1911; the *Herald Democrat*, January 26, 1911; and my own account of the event published in *Westworld*, supplement, *Grand Junction Daily Sentinel*, March 26, 1978.

Water problems and tunnels were researched in Emmons, Fleming, and Henderson. I also used the July 14, 1908, edition of the *Herald Democrat*. For the Yak Tunnel, I consulted a number of works, but of specific use to me were Emmons; an unpublished paper by Rusty Stout, a local mining engineer, Colorado Mountain History Collection, Lake County Public Library; and "'The Yak' — 1894 to 1923," Colorado Historical Society in Denver.

Social doings in Leadville were brought to life in a *Herald Democrat* series in September and October 1957, by a lady with the unlikely name of Clyde Robertson. I was fortunate to be able to use a copy of her original manuscript, "Intimate Glimpses of Leadville." I also used the New Year's editions of the *Herald Democrat;* a rather shaky master's thesis done in 1930 at the University of Northern Colorado by Elizabeth Moriarity called, "The History of Lake County, Colorado"; and Don and Jean Griswold's series in the *Herald Democrat*, "Leadville, a City of Contrast," February 9, 1971.

Mining was brought up to the American entry in World War I with Emmons, Henderson, and Fleming. The story of Climax would have been much more difficult to research were it not for a timely assist and an armload of books and papers loaned to me by John Richards, Climax mining engineer and treasured friend. I used a number of sources to follow Charles Senter, Otis Archie King, and E. G. Heckendorf's tracks on Bartlett Mountain. Primary among these were: *Gray Gold*, by Otis Archie King, 1959; a two-part series in *Empire Magazine*, supplement, *Denver Post*, July 26 and August 2, 1953, by Robert W. Fenwick and Edith Eudora Kohl, called "King of Moly"; Charles W. Henderson's article, "History and Production" in B. S. Butler and J. W. Vanderwelt's *The Climax Molybdenum Deposit, Colorado*, USGS, 1933; and "Interesting Bits," *Colorado Magazine*, March 1944. For the background of Amco, I used a short but extremely detailed account published by American Metal Climax, Inc., as a preface to a gift atlas titled, "A Short History of American Metal Climax, Inc.," by Seymour S. Berfeld and Harold K. Hochschild, 1962. For the Amco development of Climax, I used all of the above plus the annual recaps in the *Herald Democrat*, and the Griswolds' "City of Contrast" series, December 18 and 24, 1970.

Prohibition in Leadville was researched in the *Herald Democrat*, especially the New Year's editions of 1916 and 1917. Also used were the "City of Contrast" articles, May 7, 14, and 21, 1971. World War I and its impact on Leadville was documented in the *Herald Democrat's* New Year's issues of 1918 and 1919. The *Herald Democrat*, January 1, 1919, and January 1, 1920, along with Rene Coquoz's booklet, *The History of Medicine in Leadville and Lake County, Colorado*, 1967, and the files of the Society of Leadville Pioneers provided the information on the great flu epidemic. The demise of the Colorado Midland Railroad was first researched generally in Morris Cafky's *The Colorado Midland*, 1965, then specific information was gleaned in the *Carbonate Chronicle*, July 8 and August 5, 1918. The cost of living, general economic condition of the camp, and strike of 1919 were digested from the *Herald Democrat*, January 1, 1920.

Chapter XVI

For metal prices after 1923, I had to substitute for Henderson, Henry C. Meeves and Richard P. Darnell, *Silver Potential and Economic Aspects of the Leadville District, Lake County, Colo.*, a Bureau of Mines publication, circular 8464, published in 1970. I also used it in the discussion of the Canterbury Tunnel and other proposed and initiated drainage projects. I consulted the files of the *Herald Democrat* for additional information on the Canterbury Tunnel, plus a paper by Carvel "Lefty" Stout, "Local Environment, Geology and Mining," Colorado Mountain History Collection, Lake County Public Library. Information on the Leadville Deep Mines and Iron-Silver Mining Company is from the *Herald Democrat*. Metal prices and number of mines is from "Leadville, a City of Contrast," *Herald Democrat*, July 16, 1971; C. W. Henderson's "Gold, Silver, Copper, Lead, and Zinc in Colorado in 1931," in *Mineral Resources of the United States, 1931*, Washington, D. C., Bureau of Mines, 1933, pp. 527-528.

Life in depression Leadville was researched in the files of the *Herald Democrat*; "City of Contrast" series, July 16, 1971 and July 23, 1971; Dennis Reece's "The History of Banking in Leadville," special project in history, Colorado Mountain College, 1976; J. D. Wilder's "Building City Street 10,000 Feet Above Sea-Level," *The American City*, January 1930; and in the archives of the Society of Leadville Pioneers.

Material on the Tabors, Matchless Mine, and the development of the Leadville Historical Association came from, again, the *Herald Democrat* and the pioneer society. The final gasp of prohibition is from the Griswolds' "City of Contrast" series, July 16, 1971. World War II was researched in the *Herald Democrat* holdings of the Colorado Historical Society, as were Camp Hale and the Tenth Mountain Division. Additional material on the above was found in "The Invisible Men on Skis," by Rene Coquoz, Boulder, Colo., Johnson Publishing Company, 1970; a nice reunion publication by Leroy Wingenbach, called "Tenth Mountain Division; A Remembrance," c. 1965; and Cal Queal's "The Men of the Magnificent Tenth," *Empire Magazine* of the *Denver Post*, December 4, 1966. The story of the drainage tunnel was condensed from *Time*, November 8, 1945; *Business Week*, March 15, 1945, December 17, 1949, and March 22,

1952; and, as mentioned earlier, the Bureau of Mines publication, *Silver Potential and Economic Aspects of the Leadville District, Lake County, Colo.,* by Meeves and Darnell.

The files of the *Herald Democrat; Look,* February 17, 1959; "Leadville and Lake County, Colorado; The Master Plan," by Sam L. Huddleston for the Leadville-Lake County Regional Planning Commission, August 1963; and Rene Coquoz's "The Leadville Story," published by the author in 1959, provided the material on the fifties and sixties.

Index